FOOD CHOICE AND SUSTAINABILITY

FOOD CHOICE AND SUSTAINABILITY

Why Buying Local, Eating Less Meat, and Taking Baby Steps Won't Work

DR. RICHARD OPPENLANDER

LANGDON STREET PRESS

Langdon Street Press
322 First Avenue N, 5th floor
Minneapolis, MN 55401
612.455.2293
www.langdonstreetpress.com

ISBN-13: 978-1-62652-435-4
LCCN: 2013951468

Distributed by Itasca Books

Book Design by Kristeen Ott

Printed in the United States of America

Food Choice and Sustainability was printed with post-consumer recycled nonchlorinated paper and soy ink.

To all those who strive for a healthier,
more just, and peaceful planet

AUTHOR'S NOTE

A number of statistics used throughout this book will undoubtedly change, in one direction or the other, by the time—and after—this book is published. Facts and figures related to this important topic will be continually updated on my various websites, www.ComfortablyUnaware.com, www. InspireAwarenessNow.org, and through my blogs, Comfortably Unaware Facebook and Twitter presence, lectures, and any other communication medium that makes its way into mainstream general public use.

CONTENTS

ACKNOWLEDGMENTS

Many times in life there needs to be a final piece to complete the puzzle—a single connection, nucleus, component, or concept to complete the whole. With my research, understanding, and conveying reality-driven perspectives about food choices, that puzzle piece was given to me by my devoted wife, Jill. Without her bringing such an enormous intuition and love of other living beings into my life—particularly with her care of and for animals—and subsequent rigid support of my work, the complete story could never be told. I don't know if it is possible to relate an accurate view of the health of our planet without looking very closely at the other living entities with which we share our earth and how we treat them.

Our decision to raise and eat animals creates a triad of negative impacts—to our planet and other living things, to our own human health, and to the animals that we raise and slaughter to eat. Two of these three categories are covered so aptly by various educators that it has allowed me to research, write, and lecture about the area with the least amount of proper attention—our planet's resources.

Although the topic of what we eat is typically absent from discussions about sustainability, the negative impact of certain foods on human health is becoming common knowledge. Many researchers, authors, and educators have blazed the trail of truth regarding the human health benefits of eating a purely plant-based diet. For them and their tireless work, I am humbly grateful. Although there are many, I would like to particularly thank Drs. John McDougall, Neal Barnard, Dean Ornish, and Caldwell Esselstyn, and encourage everyone to become familiar with the work of these pioneering practitioners and their programs. I want to thank Drs. T. Colin Campbell and Michael Greger for their research and then relentless dissemination of the truth about our food choices. Special recognition must be made to Brian Wendel, creator and executive producer of the documentary *Forks Over Knives,* and all those associated with the production and distribution of this extraordinary film.

I suppose the single disconnect that may define our civilization more than any other is how we treat the animals around us. This aspect is addressed so very well by a number of compassionate animal rights/welfare leaders and advocates that I will provide only new or understated insights and perspectives regarding the animals we slaughter or biodiversity loss. Particular thanks for their continued efforts in this regard go to Dr. Jane Goodall, Dr. Melanie Joy, Dr. Karen Davis, Colleen Patrick-Goodreau, Dr. Will Tuttle, and Dr. James McWilliams.

Consumers now can find an array of wonderful cookbooks with incredible, easy-to-prepare vegan recipes. Authors such as Lindsay Nixon, Chloe Coscarelli, and Julieanna Hever present to us remarkably delicious purely plant-based meals. They open the door to the world of truly healthy, compassionate, great-tasting food. There are, of course, so many others, all doing their part to further the important message and encouraging change.

PREFACE

Food Choice and Sustainability is not a typical nonfiction book, and it's not about what to eat. It is about accurately defining "sustainability" as it relates to food choices and making a fundamental change in our lives to better achieve it. It provides both hard facts and unique insights as to why this change is necessary and then sets forth a clear path to follow. *Food Choice and Sustainability* builds on my first book, *Comfortably Unaware*—filling in blanks, connecting dots, and most important, providing a prescription of food choice sustainability for individuals, academic institutions, NGOs, and other organizations, business leaders, communities, developing nations, all other countries, and policymakers. It may appear that this book was written for two distinctly different audiences: those wanting to become more aware and those who want to effect positive change who may need more detailed information and scripting on how to do so. It was, indeed, written for both.

  Food Choice and Sustainability is a book about sustainability—of our planet, our resources, and ourselves. For most people, the word sustainable means "lasting a while" or "enduring" and unfortunately it's usually customized or molded to fit a momentary need or want—all fairly subjective. For me, sustainability must account for the realities of time, space, relativity, and optimization. The concept of being sustainable must project beyond self to include society and future societies, human and non-human life—both domesticated and wild life. The thought of achieving sustainability must extend through many layers—economic, social, ethical—not just ecological—and ultimately be carried by our choice of foods.

While *Food Choice and Sustainability* is indeed a book about sustainability, at the same time, it is a book about food choice and responsibility, which are intertwined inextricably with the concept of achieving sustainability.

Global depletion is a term I have used over the years to describe the loss of our primary resources on earth, as well as the loss of our own health due to our choice of a certain type of food. Therefore, global depletion essentially is about sustainability, but we need to hear it from a different direction and with a more accurate view, through an unfiltered lens. Most of us have heard about the atrocities of factory farms, the issues with high-fructose corn syrup, and the industrialization or processing of foods and their contribution to obesity—all important topics. But these simply are small fragments of the picture.

The largest contributing factor to all areas of global depletion is the raising and eating of more than 70 billion animals each year and the extracting of 1–2 trillion fish from our oceans annually. It's simply not sustainable whether factory farms are in the equation or not. Because the word "sustainable" is often misused, I advocate the term "relative" or "optimal" sustainability.

Even as we deplete our natural resources, we add 230,000 new human mouths to feed each day. It's predicted that in just eighteen years, there will be a 40 percent global water shortage (over 1 billion people already are without adequate drinking water; 2 billion are without running water for cleaning and hygiene). Nearly 1 billion people are affected by hunger; 6 million children will starve to death in 2013.

Nevertheless, of the 2.5 billion tons of grain harvested in 2011, half was fed to animals in the meat and dairy industries; 77 percent of all coarse grain went to livestock. Many of our planet's issues—dwindling resources, food security concerns, increased climate change, hunger and poverty, loss of biodiversity, pollution, declining human health and escalating health care costs, and the ravaging of oceanic ecosystems—can be eliminated or at least significantly minimized by a simple, collective change to a healthier, more peaceful, plant-based food choice and thereby more efficient, more compassionate food-production systems.

Almost every decision we make every day is based on our culture—what we've learned; what someone has told us is acceptable or necessary. This does not necessarily mean it's a good idea. For example, the practice of bloodletting was used for more than 3,000 years before we realized at the end of the nineteenth century that it wasn't so healthy for us after all. Yet today we accept culturally driven practices, especially with food choices involving animal products, that are much more unhealthy—for our planet and for us—than bloodletting. And by all accounts, we don't have 3,000 years to get it right.

INTRODUCTION TO
AWARENESS AND
FOOD CHOICE

economic collapse ⬆
environmental collapse ⬇
social disorder ⬇

Earth's resources are not infinite. Many researchers feel it is not a question of *if* our planet will reach a point of no return but *when* it will happen—because we are already on our way. We already are witnessing signs of irreversible effects on our environment, effects that could result in the end of civilization as we currently know it. Is this sensationalism? Not at all. Many scientists and futurists cite the three most critical issues as economic collapse, environmental collapse, and then, eventually, social disorder. They feel the most imminent concerns—the two that will begin the snowball effect—are irreversible global warming caused by greenhouse gas emissions (by way of fossil fuel use) and reaching peak oil (the point in time when the global production of oil reaches its maximum rate, followed by decline until we run out). Experts feel irreversible global warming and peak oil will both occur very soon because we seem to be unable to lessen our dependence on gas, oil, or any of the other fossil fuels, and we do not have a suitable energy alternative in place. But it is not peak greenhouse gases or peak oil that should most concern us; it's peak *everything* … and lack of awareness as to why it is happening or an appropriate plan to solve it.

For instance, what researchers fail to address is that those three critical issues are precipitated by a common denominator—food choice. What we eat affects all areas of global depletion (the collapse of our health and that of our environment, as discussed in my first book, *Comfortably Unaware,* 2011) and once that process begins, it sets into motion economic instability, which in many cases will be followed by social unrest. We have seen this sequence of events occur throughout history, most recently due to water shortages and food-price increases across North Africa and the Middle East in 2010 and 2011 and with increased effects of climate change.

After all, it really won't matter how economically viable or stable a country is if it runs out of water or land, or if greenhouse gases and subsequent climate change reach irreversible proportions, catalyzing the melting of ice caps, the rising of sea levels, and the loss of buildings, land, crops, and lives.

We eventually will experience a redefining of the word "wealth." Instead of viewing parameters such as economic, political, or military power, very soon a nation's strength will be measured by its natural resources—the environmental support systems and how they are managed.

Some are concerned with how we will feed the 9 billion people expected to be in the world by the year 2050, with an estimated 2 billion of them affected by hunger. As Juergen Voegele, director of the Agriculture and Rural Development of the World Bank, stated, "We will be able to feed 9 billion people by the year 2050, but it will require very significant investments in agriculture [research and development] and in overall productivity increases." Parts of this statement are true, in that we do have the ability to feed 9 billion people and we will need substantial increases in productivity, but neither can be easily accomplished without changing the *type* of food we consume.

Instead of significant research and development expenditures, there first should be investment in education of which food types and agricultural production systems are the most resource-efficient, providing us with the healthiest food to eat—food products that have the very smallest global resource footprint. The primary reason we fail to make the progress necessary for balancing food needs, supplies, and ecological and human health is that we continue to include an unnecessary factor in the equation—eating animals.

Estimates from the Global Footprint Network (an international think tank working to advance sustainability) show that we are—and have been—in an "overshoot" mode, essentially using our planet's resources at a rate of 1.6 times of what it can provide. By the year 2030, it is predicted that we will need two full Earths to sustain what we are taking from and doing to our planet at our current rate of consumption. Although prior to 1960, we used only a fraction of Earth's natural resource capacity, between 1975 and 1980 we reached a 1:1 use-to-capacity relationship. The overshoot mode and subsequent cause for alarm began in the early 1980s and has increased steadily every year since, reaching the point where we are today. As with many problems we face as a society, the solution becomes embedded in layers of suppressed information, apathy, lack of clarity, and inability to act decisively and in a cooperative fashion on a national or international level.

Organizations such as the World Wildlife Fund (WWF), the Swiss Agency for Development and Cooperation, Global Footprint Network, Worldwatch Institute, United Nations, and others have established a number of initiatives to assist governments in understanding the dire state of our planet, regarding resource depletion. All have related the urgency and have presented a generalized road map to resolution. Suggestions made by these organizations, such as "moving energy systems away from dependency on fossil fuels, preserving bioproductive areas, and restoring unproductive areas" would help reduce demand of certain resources, but they do not properly define causative factors, nor do they outline specific steps for resolution. While these organizations may recognize that the well-being of human society is ultimately linked to the ecological capital on which it depends, not one of them properly relates the predominant impetus behind the loss of Earth's resources, and none provides candid dialogue as to the proper solution.

The Blue Planet Prize (recognizing outstanding efforts that contribute to solving environmental problems) in 2012 was awarded to Drs. Rees and Wackernagel, the originators of the Ecological Footprint (a resource accounting tool that measures how much nature we use), an indication of the appreciation for their important work. However, even though their organization, the Global Footprint Network, has quantified the general conclusions of others—that "climate change, deforestation, overgrazing, fisheries collapse, food insecurity and the rapid extinction of species are all part of a single, over-arching problem"—our global demand to eat animals, which is the primary instigator of that over-arching problem, has yet to be addressed.

Our collective choice of foods as they involve animals—raising and eating livestock and harvesting fish—is the single largest contributing sector for global depletion. Our combined demand for and consumption of animals are more responsible than any other factor for:

- inefficient agricultural land use
- depletion of our oceans
- climate change
- pollution
- increased risk of the four most common diseases and five most common cancers found in the Western world
- increased health care costs and loss of productivity
- depletion and use of freshwater
- loss of biodiversity, and
- the prevalence of world hunger

We are pumping massive and unsustainable amounts of resources into a machine that then involves the slaughtering of 1 to 3 trillion animals each year, to spew out unhealthy products that some call "food." The relationship between our food choices and true sustainability is well established, and our very survival will ultimately depend on bringing this precept to the forefront.

Worldwide, there is a significant concern for becoming "sustainable" ("truly" or "fully" sustainable), yet at the same time, there is a clear lack of accuracy in both defining and quantifying that term, particularly as it is applied to food choice. It is time we introduce the concept of optimal "relative sustainability"—providing a semblance of real comparison related to facts, rather than unsubstantiated perception. Universal use of the term *relative sustainability* would allow individuals, organizations, and governments to make informed—and therefore, better—decisions regarding a specific food choice and understand the true impact it has on our health and that of our planet.

Many institutions and communities are rallying around concepts such as "locally grown," grass- or pasture-fed, free-range, cage-free, sustainable seafood, real food, slow food, "cool food," farm-to-table, farm-to-campus, organic, biodynamic, traceable, small family farms, CSAs (community supported) and urban agriculture, and humane—all of which are fueled by the desire to move away from factory farms and industrialized food-production systems. However, none of these will be successful in the long term if they include raising, slaughtering, and eating animals or harvesting fish from our oceans or by way of aquaculture.

How do these organizations define "healthy"? How do they define "sustainable"? How do they define "humane"? Who is defining these terms for them? If their definition is wrong, then their entire movement will be wrong.

Food Choice and Sustainability explores our current and future direction of food choice, carefully examining the word "sustainable" as it is applied, particularly the grass-fed livestock and aquaculture (fish farm) movements. As a society, our food choice opinions and decisions are shaped by a number of influences—cultural, social, political—but many seem to be coerced by individuals or organizations that are driven by economic motives, without full understanding of global depletion (sustainability). One would have to ask, then, how is this happening, and why are we being ill advised? This book will help answer these questions and what *you* can do about it.

We all tend to live within our own microcosm, unaware of what might be happening elsewhere in the world. This is particularly true with our direct or indirect use of resources. Awareness of the choices we make on a daily basis and adopting proper decisions will ultimately facilitate movement in the right direction.

We must come to grips with the magnitude and urgency of the problem. The logic of eating "less meat" and taking "baby steps" needs to be thrown out the window with the animal products it supports. This book will suggest that we are not babies and are quite capable of creating positive change in the world.

Food Choice and Sustainability examines the issue of world hunger, revealing unique perspectives and solutions, suggesting that the best approach would be to create a framework that simplifies a complex situation—a road map of sorts that guides us to the one factor that connects all geographic regions of the world—food choice.

The overriding reason there has been little improvement in the number affected by hunger and poverty in countries in Africa, for instance, is because food supply has always been separated from the multitude of layered factors. In order to create sustainability for these people, there first needs to be a more precise defining of the term "sustainable," and then there needs to be a stratified approach in its application. Hunger and poverty form a cycle, each affecting the other and involving education and resource use. In many sub-Saharan countries, hunger and illiteracy affect 66 percent of their population. More than 75 percent are engaged in agriculture, but it is on topsoil that has become eroded; what's left is infertile after years of trampling and overgrazing of livestock.

With over 100 million cattle, goats, and sheep, Ethiopia has one of the largest animal herds in the world. These animals require water, land, soil, feed, energy, time—little of which Ethiopia has. And in the end, livestock-driven agriculture produces animal products that their people can ill afford to consume, as plant-based foods provide the most sustainable nutritional and environmental foundation.

The effects of increased global warming and climate change will be felt most by those in developing countries where drought and heat waves exacerbate existing water scarcity and food security issues. The relationship of food choice and production systems must become properly positioned. *Food Choice and Sustainability* opens the door to understanding this reality.

There was a period when all that humans chose to eat was derived directly from the earth—it was already available. That time is no longer with us. We now must actively produce food, and we must not be myopic in our decisions. We also can no longer suppress or mismanage information about this topic. It's time that avenues of information open, appropriate platforms are established, and everyone hears the message of *Food Choice and Sustainability*. If we are to survive as a society or species, we must recognize our role as stewards of this planet, recognize those forces that imperil us, and then act responsibly and quickly to create change.

We must make the correct choices—for our own well-being, for other living things with whom we share this planet, and for all those who will come after us. It's also time to realize our role in asking for so many sentient beings to be killed every minute of every day. We need to seek a higher level of conscious eating. This is the ethos with which we need to live and by which we will be remembered when future inhabitants of Earth judge how we preserved—or ruined—their planet.

Food Choice and Sustainability discusses how we must work together to increase awareness and then act from this platform of knowledge to implement positive change. The time is *now*.

1

Climate Change and
the Easiest Way to Mitigate It

WHILE ALL ASPECTS of global depletion are significant and mandate appropriate and urgent action, climate change is the common thread woven between them—with a timeline much shorter than that predicted by those with a voice (policy makers, other visible organizations and authors, and the media) and certainly shorter than any of us would want to witness. While eating animals creates loss of resources and unsustainable food production systems, it is the effect on climate change that links and exacerbates every other category of global depletion, and our very survival may depend on it. If this seems a dramatic statement to you, it is only because the reality of the effects our food choices have on climate change and the severity of the problem have been suppressed, if not mismanaged. It's time to change that.

Although we can most certainly still find deniers amongst us, global warming and climate change is real and on the increase—and we will see it expressed as exaggerated changes in weather, which is then often translated into hardships or disasters affecting global economics, food production, water availability, and human health. In 2012, there were record heat waves throughout the United States, with more than 4,500 record high temperatures set across the country just in a thirty-day period from early June to early July (National Climatic Data Center). The preceding six-month and twelve-month periods from June 30 were the warmest ever recorded. During the last two weeks in June 2012, all-time high temperatures were recorded in 170 cities across the United States.

As expected, the extended periods of increased temperatures exacerbated drought conditions throughout the country, straining electricity and water usage and challenging food production and businesses. There are extremes in the other direction as well, with the Northwest—in particular, the state of Washington—recording its seventh coolest month ever in June. The National Oceanic and Atmospheric Administration (NOAA) predicts La Niña–related heat waves are now twenty times more likely to occur than fifty years ago. By 2080, heat waves that usually occur once every twenty years are expected to occur once every year, and the extremes in weather that were seen in 2012 will only worsen every year after. The NOAA points out that nine of the top ten warmest years ever recorded globally occurred from 2000 to 2011.

In a study published in the *Bulletin of the American Meteorological Society*, scientists wrote, "Currently, attribution of single extreme events to anthropogenic climate change remains challenging." They feel that attribution is possible for single disastrous events, but it would need to be framed in terms of probability rather than certainty.

There is a definite connection between climate change and dramatic, imposing weather, although it is often not direct or simple. Most researchers feel that climate change itself most likely does not cause a single drastic weather-related event, such as a killer tornado or monsoon (although I feel this is a conservative view). However, there is consensus that climate change does take a naturally occurring weather event, such as rain, wind, heat, cold, etc., and makes it that much worse—climate change exaggerates the effect, an intensification of water and heating/cooling cycles. Heat waves become longer and hotter. Cold fronts become colder; rain becomes downpours, perhaps leading to flooding. This, in turn, leads to many difficulties, if not disasters. One of many examples can be found in Texas, where in 2011, climate change added to the impact of an already existing La Niña, so that a heat wave was twenty times more likely to occur than it would have fifty years ago—and Texas did have its warmest, driest year on record. Another example can be found in Britain, where November 2011 was the second warmest ever recorded (dating back to 1659), and researchers concluded that climate change made that extreme high temperature average sixty times more likely than it would have been in 1960.[1]

Meteorologists feel there are four classes of extremes related to weather: high heat, heavy precipitation and flooding, duration and intensity of droughts, and extremes related to higher sea levels—which have all intensified in the last thirty years. The World Meteorological Association released its report in 2011, *Weather Extremes in a Changing Climate*, summarizing the previous decade of dramatic weather events seen worldwide. Between 2001 and 2003, Canada and Alaska saw their warmest winter on record, with Europe witnessing the hottest summer since 1540. In 2004 and 2005, there were a record number of cyclones seen in Japan, twenty-seven named tropical storms, and fourteen hurricanes in 2005 across the Caribbean, Central America, and the United States, including Hurricane Katrina, which killed over 1,300 people. In 2006, Africa saw its worst flooding in fifty years, while the U.S. saw its worst season for wildfires, and tropical cyclones ran across the Pacific and Asia, with one storm killing over 1,200 people in the Philippines. Brush fires and heat waves wreaked havoc throughout most of Australia in 2009. And even though 2010 was another warmest year on record, it saw cold-temperature extremes in Asia, Europe, and parts of North America, with Pakistan experiencing its worst flooding in history, destroying more than 1.8 million homes and killing more than 1,700 people.[2]

Where that report left off at the end of 2010, new and much worse weather changes picked up. In 2011, there were record droughts and wildfires in Texas, with entire communities running out of water, yet a record amount of ice storms, snow, and tornadoes occurred across the rest of the country. The month of April 2011 alone saw 875 tornadoes. While there were record-setting high temperatures and droughts occurring in some parts of the U.S., many states were struck with record lows, such as Oklahoma, which saw its temperature plummet to 31 degrees below zero and the most recorded amount of snowfall in a twenty-four-hour period. The National Oceanic and Atmospheric Administration reported in December 2011 that the U.S. had seen either an excessively wet or excessively dry year for 60 percent of the country, noting damages caused by flooding along the Mississippi River, higher numbers of tornadoes, drought and wildfires in the West, and Hurricane Irene that killed more than fifty people and caused, at minimum, $10 billion in damages. The NOAA reported that in the thirty-year period from 1980 to 2010, there were an average of 3.3 serious weather events per year, causing at least $1 billion each in damages, while just in 2011, there were twelve—a 400 percent increase from the prevailing annual average.

Climate change and associated weather extremes affect us by damaging property and lives, negatively impacting businesses, and imposing economic stress. In 2011, insurance companies paid more than $100 billion in claims for disasters in the U.S. that were related to weather.

While record-setting flooding was occurring in Pakistan in 2010, Russia found itself with a heat wave contributing to forest fires, the deaths of 56,000 people, and major agricultural concerns, such as loss of its wheat crop. In all, there were, at minimum, twenty countries in 2010 that set records for heat extremes, while at the same time more rainfall than ever before, collectively, over all countries on earth. In 2011, many countries suffered record weather-related disasters, including swings from drought in the Horn of Africa to heavy rainfall over much of Asia. Thailand suffered from flooding, costing $45 billion in damages. In 2011, Brazil saw heavy rains and landslides, while in Europe there were heat waves and drought conditions. In Australia, 2010 through 2011 was the wettest two-year period on record, following a decade-long dry spell.

The 22nd annual NOAA *State of the Climate* report found that the Arctic was warming about twice as fast as the rest of the planet, on average, with Arctic sea ice shrinking to its second-smallest recorded size. And at the other end, Antarctica recorded its highest temperature in history, 9.9 degrees F, on December 25, 2011.

The NOAA states its mission is "to understand and predict changes in the Earth's environment, from the depths of the ocean to the surface of the sun, and to conserve and manage our coastal and marine resources." As with many research-based organizations, the NOAA is well equipped to provide us with a better understanding of the state of our planet, so it is fulfilling part of its stated mission. But what about "to conserve and manage our coastal and marine resources"? Similar to other organizations, it is time they and we translate that information into action. If our species is contributing to climate change or to the demise of other innocent species because of our definable actions, then it is time we stop those actions, especially if there is an easy solution.[3]

Many agricultural experts are concerned about the effect that heat waves, intensified by climate change, have on crops. The Corn Belt in the U.S., for instance, and as an example of other grain-producing areas of the world, is always heavily affected by extremes in heat and drought. But with the potential for diminished crop production and drought conditions, we need to remember where all those crops and water are going. Seventy-seven percent of all coarse grains grown in the world and over 23 percent of all agricultural water used globally are being pumped into livestock, not to us. Weather extremes that are molded by climate change may be the wakening call the world needs to realize that our resources should not be used for animal food production for two compelling reasons:

1. It is not efficient or sustainable on many levels, with or without the challenges of climate change and extremes of weather.
2. It is one of the two largest contributors to the very problem of climate change.

With his book *An Inconvenient Truth*, Al Gore began a campaign to educate the world about global warming and our carbon footprint, for which he was awarded the Nobel Peace Prize in 2007. This furthered the process of creating a collective understanding regarding what we are doing to our planet in terms of affecting climate change. That was a good thing. With what could be considered an ideal platform from which information can be delivered to the largest audiences possible, Mr. Gore focused on carbon dioxide, global warming, and reduction methods, such as using less electricity and driving hybrid cars. That was a bad thing.

Although he began a wave of consciousness about curbing our carbon footprint and changing out light bulbs, Mr. Gore essentially created a larger gap of misunderstanding and suppression about the vastly more comprehensive issue of changing out food choices—beginning with the effect on climate change. It must be clearly understood that climate change, caused by greenhouse gas emissions (GHG) and global warming, is but one component of the much larger and more insidious problem of global depletion—and that one of the two primary sources of human-induced (anthropogenic) GHG emissions is from raising livestock to eat. Then, it also must be understood that the most important single thing that we should do about global depletion or climate change is to take a good look at what's on our plate.

Was Mr. Gore's information important? Yes.

Was it the most important piece of the puzzle of sustainability and what we should focus on? No.

As a society, we have shown a tendency to make behavioral changes only when that change is easy to make or when it's socially acceptable, and Mr. Gore's principles became fairly easy to accept—conceptually and functionally. But the issues expressed in *An Inconvenient Truth* essentially obscured the reality of a much larger issue that was already in existence but moving under the surface of awareness. This larger issue of global depletion due to eating animals wasn't discussed at all by Mr. Gore because the topic is far too controversial; he would have lost his audience. Also, Mr. Gore himself raises and eats animals and has ties to the meat and dairy industries—it would have been far too "inconvenient" for him to bring it to the forefront. Nevertheless, it's not just carbon produced from our energy industries that needs to be addressed; it's what we are eating that needs to change.

Deforestation and burning of fossil fuels account for most of the CO_2 production. Because CO_2 forms the largest fraction of GHG and since burning fossil fuels accounts for a significant portion of CO_2 emissions, it is easy for many individuals and organizations to focus on this when trying to solve our emissions problems. Industries such as those producing electricity and sectors such as transportation have become easy targets for Mr. Gore. Inanimate objects like cars and planes and buildings that produce CO_2 emissions became his primary targets as the GHG emissions/climate change case was built. But what about the other types of greenhouse gases and other emitters? What about emitters that are also the major contributors to other areas of global depletion, not only affecting climate change but also loss of land, fresh water, and biodiversity on earth? It seems obvious that the world needs to cast attention on that problem first, although discussing the need for factories to reduce CO_2 is a bit more "convenient."

In the U.S., what began as a "cap and trade" CO_2 reduction plan in response to Mr. Gore's campaign, evolved, with promotion by Sen. Kerry in 2009, into talks of a cap on GHG emissions only for utilities, initially, with other industries phased in years later. This plan included a modest tax on gasoline, diesel, and aviation fuel, incentives for oil and gas drilling, nuclear power plant construction, carbon capture and storage, and renewable energy source such as wind and solar. Food choice and production related to animals was nowhere in the discussions, and the plan faded with no legislation. It is clear that the U.S. is unwilling and incapable of any meaningful movement forward—the meat, dairy, and fishing industries are too powerful and influential; our policy makers are indifferent and lack adequate awareness levels; and the public is generally apathetic and misguided.

Four categories of information related to climate change issues are not properly recognized and thus are mismanaged:

1. Climate change is very real; it's occurring now and worsening, and the situation is urgent.
2. Human activities producing GHG emissions significantly affect climate change.
3. Raising animals is one of the largest contributors to anthropogenic GHG emissions and, therefore, human-induced climate change.
4. Any food movement away from "factory farms" to grass-fed or pastured systems will not solve the problem.

"We must not delude ourselves. Even if implemented fully, existing commitments for emission reductions by 2020 are collectively not enough to put the world on a path that would give us even a 50-50 chance of avoiding a warming of 2 degrees C above 19th-century temperatures."—Fatih Birol, chief economist, IEA, 2011

The scope of the problem—the realities of climate change

As I have mentioned, the climate change (and associated weather extremes) we see today is caused by global warming, which, in turn, is caused by an increase in GHG emissions. GHGs are emitted by both natural means and by humans. GHGs (which also include water vapor and ozone) are those that absorb and emit infrared radiation.

Three of the five greenhouse gases found in our atmosphere— carbon dioxide, methane, and nitrous oxide—are produced in large amounts by human activities.

It is thought that of all human-produced GHG, 72 percent is in the form of CO_2, 8 percent methane, and 13 percent nitrous oxide. According to the NOAA, these three GHGs continued to rise in 2011, and the global average atmospheric concentration for carbon dioxide exceeded 390 parts per million for the first time, an increase of 2.1 ppm in 2010.

The concentrations of CO_2 and methane have increased by 36 percent and 148 percent, respectively, since 1750. These levels are much higher than at any time during the last 800,000 years, the period for which reliable data has been extracted from ice cores. Less direct geological evidence indicates that CO_2 values higher than this were last seen about 20 million years ago.

But both nitrous oxide and methane are much more powerful greenhouse gases than carbon dioxide. Expressed as a factor of CO_2, methane has a Global Warming Potential (GWP) of 72 for twenty years, meaning it is seventy-two times more powerful (or will trap seventy-two times as much heat in our atmosphere) as CO_2. Nitrous oxide has a GWP of 298 for 100 years, indicating that it is 298 times as powerful as CO_2, or will trap 298 times as much heat as CO_2 over a hundred-year period of time. [4-14]

Since 1850, the use of coal, gas, and oil (fossil fuels) has increased as the dominant source for global energy use. This has led to a dramatic growth in CO_2 emissions. Agriculture, specifically animal agriculture, has led to increased production and emissions of methane and nitrous oxide gases in addition to increased CO_2 emissions by burning fossil fuels and deforestation. Together, energy and agriculture are the largest contributing sectors to anthropogenic greenhouse gas emissions—61 percent and 37 percent. Some feel this ratio may be on the order of 47 percent and 51 percent. Although there are other naturally emitting sources of greenhouse gases found on earth, what we produce by burning fossil fuels and raising animals to eat is what causes climate changes. We have little control over natural-emitting sources, but we have great control over the sources of GHG that we create.

According to the 2006 United Nations report, livestock accounts for 9 percent of anthropogenic CO_2, 65 percent of anthropogenic nitrous oxide, and 37 percent of anthropogenic methane, although many researchers now feel livestock's contribution is much higher than this.

Many organizations today conduct research on climate change. One of the more respected entities is the Intergovernmental Panel on Climate Change (IPCC), considered the leading international body for the assessment of climate change.

The fourth Assessment Report by the IPCC (AR4) concluded, "Most of the observed increase in the global average temperature since the mid 20th century is very likely due to the observed increase in anthropogenic greenhouse gas concentrations."

A Special Report by the IPCC in June 2012 divulged findings similar to others already discussed. In a calculated and conservative fashion, IPCC expressed that although it is difficult to attribute single extreme events such as tropical cyclones to anthropogenic climate change, there is strong evidence of other effects. According to the IPCC, anthropogenic greenhouse gas emissions have led to the following, on a global scale:

1. warming of extreme daily minimum and maximum temperatures
2. intensification of extreme precipitation
3. increasing sea levels and coastal high water

In other words, there will be, perhaps, more devastating weather extremes than what we have already experienced in store for the world, as greenhouse gases increase.[15]

A Synthesis Report (AR5) by three working groups of the IPCC will be released and available in October 2014.

In November 2011, the International Energy Agency (IEA) and its chief economist, Fatih Birol, warned in its annual World Energy Outlook that *the world will see irreversible climate change and lose the ability to limit warming if very strong action is not taken in the next five years.* Researchers with all organizations generally agree that global temperature increases must be capped at 2 degrees Celsius (3.6 degrees Fahrenheit) above preindustrial levels seen prior to 1850, or "catastrophic changes" will likely be triggered. In the Outlook, the IEA was quite clear that the window of opportunity to limit temperature increases to 2 degrees C will close beyond the year 2017. Mr. Birol voiced the concern that many others have—that leaders and policy makers are not addressing the problem adequately; therefore, "we are going in the wrong direction in terms of climate change." The IEA report stated that even if current commitments by various countries to reduce emissions were fulfilled, it will still most likely result in an increase of more than 3.5 degrees Celsius, and without fulfillment of commitments, an increase of 6 degrees Celsius or more is predicted. Many other researchers feel there is little to no chance of maintaining that global mean surface temperature increase at or below 2 degrees Celsius, and the impacts are now predicted to be much worse than previously thought—projected to trigger "extremely dangerous climate change" (Anderson and Bows).

So what does "catastrophic changes" in climate and weather mean to you? It means this: that the extremes in weather that we've seen globally in the past twelve years are a very mild version of what is in store for us as we continue to pump greenhouse gases into our atmosphere and our planet's core temperature rises further. Even though new disastrous weather events may be caused, the most significant and readily seen changes will be the worsening of heat waves and droughts. The episodes will be more severe and more frequent, with higher temperatures extending over a longer period; storms will be stronger and more frequent; and the resultant damages will be greater. Our planet has warmed 0.8 degrees Celsius (1.4 degrees Fahrenheit), since the Industrial Revolution (1750 to 1850), but nearly all of that warming has occurred just in the last forty years. And although it doesn't sound like much, 0.8 degrees C represents an enormous amount of heat over the entire earth. It has already caused ice caps to melt and oceans to rise (as well as to become 30 percent more acidic) and generally much more damage than originally predicted by scientists. Another reason for concern: computer models calculate that even if we stopped all greenhouse gas emissions today, Earth's temperature would still most likely rise another 0.8 degrees due to the heat absorption effect of previously released greenhouse gases.

By 2050, GHGs are expected to have doubled compared to what prevailed before the mid-1800s. As the core temperature rises further toward the 2 degrees Celsius mark (the low end of projections), many predict rising sea levels that will cause billions of dollars worth of damages and displace over 600 million people living along world coastlines. Extremes in heat, storms, and fires will cause water shortages that will devastate agriculture and further world hunger and the effects of famine. Food shortages will be common. With temperatures above 4 degrees Celsius, it is predicted that global production of crops will fall by 40 percent. Combined with water shortages, this would generate riots and violence over food and water, which would stress and eventually destabilize governments. Countries will likely battle, even go to war, over the diminished water and food supplies.

What the world's leaders are doing about climate change

The 2011 United Nations Climate Change Conference concluded on December 11, in Durban, South Africa. Although there was the usual drama that accompanies these conferences, ministers finally reached an agreement on a new text, referred to as the Durban Platform for Enhanced Action, which will see the Kyoto Protocol extended into a second commitment period by a number of countries. While this may seem promising, it marked the seventeenth time that a global climate change summit displayed the continued and blatant omission of addressing food choice, specifically raising animals to eat, as a significant factor.

In order to appreciate why this is so important, we should first review what the event is all about. In 1997, 194 nations drafted and adopted the Kyoto Protocol—an international treaty developed from the United Nations Framework Convention on Climate Change to identify and mitigate human influencing factors on climate change. Nations now gather annually as part of the Conference of the Parties (COP).

The intent of COP, then, is to essentially find methods of reducing the production of greenhouse gas emissions (GHG) into our atmosphere by the three principal component gases—carbon dioxide, methane, and nitrous oxide. The Protocol, as a legally binding agreement, was entered into force in 2005 with the objective to reach a target reduction of 5.2 percent GHG emissions from the 1992 levels by the year 2012. Commitments in the Kyoto Protocol were based on "joint implementation," "clean development mechanism," and "international emissions trading." Emissions trading was established to allow nations that can easily meet their targets to sell credits to those that cannot.

Although some strides have been made since 1997, with the Bali Action Plan in 2007 (COP 13) and the Cancun Agreements reached at COP 16 in 2010, the conferences have been characterized as seeing minimal progress in their first fourteen years due to differences in opinion between developed countries. Additionally, the treaty applied to only industrialized nations—"37 Annex I countries," as referred to in the Protocol—but imposed no mandate on developing countries, which includes emerging economic powers and significant GHG emitters like China, India, Brazil, Mexico, and Korea. As of December 2011, the U.S. has not and will not agree to an extension of Kyoto beyond 2012 or sign the treaty unless there is a balancing of requirements between developed and undeveloped countries. The Cancun Agreements realized the need to commit both economically strong as well as developing countries by proposing a Green Climate Fund (GCF) to help deliver financial aid to poorer nations. The GCF was proposed to mobilize $100 billion annually from private and public funds but has yet to see implementation.

As of early 2011, many scientists felt the existing Kyoto pledges were far less than what was needed to reach the UN's goal of keeping a temperature rise to less than 2 degrees Celsius—again, the calculated maximum amount, above which we will likely see truly catastrophic effects. China, India, and the U.S. are waiting until a mandatory review of new science findings scheduled for 2015. This caused postponing the redrafting of internationally binding GHG emission commitments and involvement of unsigned countries until then. With this delay, it is predicted that global warming will reach 3.5 degrees Celsius or worse in coming years, as expressed by IEA (Climate Action Tracker, 12-6-11).

The negotiations in Durban revolved around extending the Kyoto Protocol, inclusion of all nations into a binding contract, and adoption of the GCF. In the last few and extended hours of Durban, amid heated debate, an agreement was made by more than 190 nations to do just that—to continue toward a treaty that will include all emitters, define and enforce goals, and implement the GCF by 2015, which will be fully in force by 2020. Nations also agreed to create measures that would involve preserving tropical forests and the development of clean-energy technology.

The World Resources Institute described the results at Durban as a "major climate deal" that would lead to better negotiations. While on its surface, the results at Durban could be construed as purposeful, even successful, the conference did little more than simply keep future talks viable—an agreement to agree. Major emitters such as China, India, and the U.S. are still not bound, and so the outcome at Durban should be viewed as unsatisfying to anyone striving for real change in GHG emission policy. Alden Meyer, director of policy at the Union of Concerned Scientists responded by saying, "The decisions adopted here fell well short of what was needed." He added, "While governments avoided disaster in Durban, they by no means responded adequately to the mounting threat of climate change."

In December 2012, COP 18 was held in Doha and once again, the specific topic of eating animals was omitted from discussions. The two largest GHG emitters in the world, China and the U.S., didn't participate, and the 200 countries in attendance continued their lack of agreement and failure to address or resolve key issues. The critical subject of raising and eating animals (which comprises minimally one-third of our GHG/climate change issue) was skirted—buried somewhere in the topic of agriculture, which was postponed for a future COP meeting. The attention of global leaders and scientists has now turned to a presumption of the inevitability of climate change and adaptation—how we can all best adapt to worsening weather patterns, rather than putting forth the effort to mitigate it. *Adaptation* and *resilience* are becoming the key operable terms for those we rely on to solve our climate change issues.

The U.S. chief American climate negotiator, Todd D. Stern, stated that he was "hopeful that negotiations in coming years would produce a more equitable arrangement." Since the primary goal of these COP meetings is to reduce the impact that human activities have on climate change, one would have to view them as unsuccessful, since GHGs are in fact on the increase, and major contributing sectors, such as the meat, dairy, and fishing industries, have not been properly addressed.

Regarding climate change, most researchers now agree on the following:

1. Global warming is occurring.
2. Climate change is worsening.
3. Major destructive and catastrophic events—flooding, droughts, rise in sea levels, melting of polar ice caps, etc.—will occur and are directly proportional to rises in Earth's temperature.
4. Climate changes are related to increases in greenhouse gases.
5. Anthropogenic (human-induced) GHG emissions are large enough, beyond natural emissions, to be a significant contributing factor to global warming and climate change.

6. The largest sectors for anthropogenic emissions are energy and agriculture, together comprising more than 95 percent of these human-induced GHG emissions.

7. The single largest component of agricultural emissions are those from raising livestock, which contributes, at minimum, between *18 percent and 51 percent of all total GHG emissions globally.*

Although wider acceptance of a Protocol extension and inclusion of all nations into a binding international contract now seem a delayed but future possibility, there remains an obvious omission from any COP discussions and implementation strategies. What is clearly missing from this list above is a #8, which would connect the final dot—that since raising livestock is one of the single largest contributors to human-induced GHG emissions, and since the objective of all annual COP meetings is to mitigate human-induced GHG emissions, we simply need to stop raising livestock. However, this would necessitate definitive and legally binding universal language, stipulating that all countries "stop raising and eating animals"— with strict, time-activated, and enforceable measures in effect. To date, policy makers have been unwilling to do this, and there has been no such statement or regulation in the mix. With or without annual international climate change summits, with or without signed agreements, proper progress will not be made with reducing GHG emissions, until the issue of food choice is on center stage, and raising livestock is eliminated by all nations.

The role of eating animals in climate change

In 2006, much of the world was shocked by news that the burgers and steaks everyone was eating were somehow contributing to greenhouse gases and climate change. In that report by the United Nations' Food and Agriculture Organization LEAD committee, *Livestock's Long Shadow*, authors Henning Steinfeld et al. made it known that livestock's contribution to greenhouse gas emissions is 18 percent—more than that produced by the entire transportation sector (all the cars, planes, trains, buses, and trucks that we drive and fly every day in the world) at 13 percent.

Most of us are aware of this finding now and, by itself, this should have marked the beginning of the end for the livestock industry. However, although the 18 percent figure and report have been frequently cited, and therefore readily seen by the general public, minimal change in eating patterns has taken place in the years that have elapsed since that report first surfaced. While the annual U.S. consumption of beef has dropped slightly, from an average of 65 pounds per person in 2006, to 57.4 pounds in 2011, the amount of pork, chicken, turkey, fish, eggs, and dairy consumed worldwide has all increased. At 71 million tons of meat consumed per year, China's demand to produce and eat animals is double that of the U.S. Although total red meat plus poultry consumption per capita in the U.S. dropped to 200 pounds in 2011 and 2012, from 221 pounds in 2006 (total meat consumption including fish is 216 pounds per person in 2012), it is expected to rise again slowly through 2021, to 213 pounds per person (to 245 pounds total meat consumption).

Elsewhere in the world, the consumption of beef has generally increased in both developed and developing countries—thus, the net contribution to climate change by raising and consuming animals worldwide is, unfortunately, clearly increasing.[16]

Projections in demand indicate global meat consumption increasing by 68 percent and global milk consumption increasing by 57 percent from 2000 to 2030.[17]

The FAO predicts that in order to meet this demand, the number of farm animals raised each year will nearly double, from 70 billion today to 120 billion by 2050.

There are many reasons for these dismal findings and projections, but all are grounded in three primary problems. First, there remains a general lack of awareness, globally, of the connection between eating animals and climate change. Second, for those who have been introduced to the connection, there still remains disbelief or indifference. And third, those leaders and policy makers in the U.S., as well as other countries, who are in

[handwritten margin note: Worldwide consumption has increased]

touch with this problem and are in a position to make change (or impose it) simply don't have the wherewithal to step forward and do the right thing on a national or international level. It remains something they just don't want to deal with, most likely because it cuts deeply into their own cultural and social influences, belief system, and acquired taste preferences—combined with placing their concern for continued economic viability of the meat, dairy, and fishing industries above a concern for viability of our planet.[18]

Of major importance is that the 18 percent figure now associated with livestock's contribution to climate change, in all likelihood, was vastly understated—and a more accurate higher percentage very well may have been suppressed. In 2005, British physicist Alan Calverd estimated that just the carbon dioxide alone that livestock produced was responsible for 21 percent of all anthropogenic GHG worldwide. And since the UN–FAO report was made public in 2006, other respected researchers have found that livestock produce up to 51 percent of all anthropogenic greenhouse gas emissions found in our atmosphere.

51%

Researchers Jeff Anhang and Robert Goodland, environmental specialists with the IFC (part of the World Bank Group), have found the contribution to GHG emissions by livestock to be much greater than the 18 percent stated—more in the neighborhood of 51 percent (a figure they feel is "conservative"). This noticeably higher figure is primarily because data in the 2006 UN report either was underestimated, overlooked, or counted but placed into the wrong sector (assigned improperly to a category not associated with livestock). In the report *Livestock and Climate Change*, 2009, Anhang and Goodland point out specific flaws in the UN–FAO report, such as using outdated data (from the year 2000 or older), understating of land use, underreporting of methane production, and complete omission of the production of respiratory CO_2 by the billions of livestock. Instead of 7,516 million metric tons per year of CO_2 equivalents, Anhang and Goodland have found livestock's contribution to be 32,564 million metric tons, or 32.564 gigatons, per year (51 percent of anthropogenic GHG), accounted for in the following manner and measured in million tons of carbon dioxide equivalents ($mtCO_2e$):

7,516   mtCO$_2$e as in the 2006 UN/FAO report

8,769   overlooked CO$_2$ from animal respiration (breathing)

2,671   overlooked land use

5,047   undercounted methane

8,560   other categories

The Food and Agriculture Organization (FAO), which was responsible for much of the data and calculations found in the 2006 UN report, admits that CO$_2$ production by livestock is not listed as a recognized source of GHG by the original Kyoto Protocol and therefore was not accounted for at all in their report. This is interesting, because as Anhang and Goodland point out, the exhaling of CO$_2$ by livestock is really no different than if it were produced by the tailpipe of an automobile, and therefore it should be accounted for in the same fashion. And exhaled CO$_2$ production from livestock should foster the same concern that we have about CO$_2$ that is generated from cars, planes, trucks, or any other mode of transportation or industries that burn fossil fuels. As the authors Anhang and Goodland pointed out, "By keeping GHG emissions from livestock off the GHG balance sheets, it is predictable that they will not be managed and their amount will increase—as in fact is happening." Anhang and Goodland are, indeed, correct on both counts: that the omission of GHG emissions by livestock from the CO$_2$ balance sheets is translated to a lack of proper management (i.e., unwilling to halt the eating of animals) and therefore the amount of GHG produced is increasing globally.

The European Environment Agency (EEA) reported that greenhouse gas emissions in Europe increased 2.4 percent from 2009 to 2010[19], further indication to the EEA that "European demand and consumption is highly unsustainable, despite gains in efficiency," identifying "eating" as a large contributor to this finding.

According to the EPA, GHG emissions in the U.S. rose from 2009 to 2010 by 3.2 percent "across all sectors," even though since 1990 there has been an average yearly increase of only 0.5 percent. One of the reasons cited by the EPA for this significant jump in emissions is an increase in electricity use for air conditioners by the combusting of coal and natural gas, due to elevated temperatures in the summer months seen nationwide. We must keep in mind that the reason for the increased maximum and minimum temperatures is climate change, in part related to the effect of raising livestock for us to consume. It's a reality and connection that no consumer of meat wants to make, but the connection exists, nevertheless.[20]

An example of how data can be assigned to a different sector than livestock (and therefore the perceived impact softened) can be found in the EPA's U.S. Greenhouse Gas Inventory Report, April 2012. Here, the EPA designates seven primary drivers of GHG emissions, in order of decreasing emissions—energy, agriculture, industrial processes, waste, land use, solvent, and other product use. It's easy to see how GHG emissions related to the raising, slaughtering, processing and packaging, transporting, storage, and cooking of all animals and animal products can be allocated to sectors, intentionally or not. This would then artificially deflate the true values and significance of our continued demand to eat these products, without proper awareness levels or policies in place to facilitate prudent management from a climate-change perspective. For instance, aside from methane and nitrous oxide production produced by the animals and directly related to farm-specific operations, many of the emissions triggered by the raising of animals are grouped in other sectors, such as energy, industrial, land use, and even waste—thus devaluing the actual impact that eating animals has on climate change. The same is true with EPA's method of dividing emissions into "end use economic sectors"—industry, transportation, commercial, residential, and agriculture.

In 2006, the FAO and UN reported that 37 percent of all anthropogenic methane produced globally is from livestock. The half-life of methane is only eight years, whereas that of CO_2 is 100 years, so eliminating livestock would reduce our effect on climate change much quicker than even our shift to renewable energy. Anhang and Goodland also point out that the discrepancy in methane calculations from the 2006 report was created in three primary ways:

1. The GWP used by the FAO was 23, instead of the now widely accepted figure of 25, by using a 100-year time frame.

2. Instead of using a 100-year time frame, the Intergovernmental Panel on Climate Change (IPCC) now supports the use of a 20-year time frame for methane, which would put its GWP at 72, not 23 or even 25.

3. There was underreporting of methane figures.

Anhang and Goodland documented frequent undercounting in official statistics of both industrial and pastoral livestock that was not accounted for in *Livestock's Long Shadow*. In some instances, *Long Shadow* uses lower numbers than are found in related documents, such as 33 million tons of poultry produced worldwide in 2002, while FAO's Food Outlook of 2003 reported 72.9 million tons of poultry that were produced in 2002 worldwide. Another discrepancy cited by Anhang/Goodland is that the 2006 report, *Long Shadow*, states (and therefore used in their calculations) that 21.7 billion head of livestock were raised globally in 2003, yet many organizations report that 50 billion livestock were actually raised in 2002. This, in itself, according to Anhang, would result in a 10 percent increase in the percentage of GHGs worldwide attributable to livestock (28 percent instead of 18 percent). Also, many references the FAO cited for various aspects of GHGs attributed to livestock dated as far back as 1964, leaving much room for undercounting. The 2006 report also failed to count GHGs produced from the entire life cycle and supply chain, such as processing, packaging, cooking, cooling (and the fluorocarbons produced), and liquid wastes of livestock.

Major investigations about global warming and used by the FAO, UN, and others have come from a series of reports from the IPCC, involving a number of climate experts who rely on measurements of GHGs as they exist in the atmosphere—after they may have mixed with other gases. Researcher Drew Shindell and colleagues, however, found the total effects of methane emissions are substantially larger than measuring GWP in this fashion because of the need to include the effect methane has on air pollution. In other words, in addition to the direct radiative global warming effect methane has, it also has a large indirect radiative effect. Shindell et al. found that a major component of air pollution is tropospheric ozone (near-surface-level), which is not directly emitted but is formed from methane, nitrogen oxides, and carbon monoxide. The IPCC reports that are heavily cited and used by researchers and organizations globally include the effects of tropospheric ozone increases on climate but do not specify or account for the particular source. Shindell and colleagues found that the effects of methane are significantly higher because some of the warming that is attributed to smog is actually due to methane that leads to further increases in smog. According to Shindell, the effect methane has on climate change may be as much as double what is currently thought. Since livestock are responsible for a minimum of 37 percent of all anthropogenic methane production, there is great significance in Shindell's findings related to demand to raise and eat animals.

Shindell states, "If we control methane, which is viable, then we are likely to soften global warming more than one would have thought."[21]

Other researchers have similar concerns

In 2009, researchers from the UK, using detailed life-cycle analysis of a wide range of foods and processes, reported their conclusion that in order for the UK to meet its target of reducing its overall GHG emissions by 80 percent by 2050, "policy makers will need to put in place a combination of measures that change not only how we produce and consume food, but also what it is we consume." In this report, the authors related four key findings of their research, with land use being the "most striking and disturbing." They linked changes in land use overseas to food consumption patterns in their country, finding that food consumption-induced land use change increased food's footprint by 50 percent, which translates into 30 percent of all anthropogenic GHG emitted by the UK—instead of 20 percent, as was originally thought. Livestock are responsible for more than 75 percent of land-use change emissions, in addition to nearly 60 percent of all other agricultural emissions, which added more emphasis to their conclusion that meat and dairy products have a much larger overall impact on climate change than once thought.[22]

The authors reported that a vegetarian diet (with dairy and eggs), a 66 percent reduction in livestock product consumption, would reduce direct supply-chain emissions by 20 percent, which is not enough, so "a broad-based switch to plant-based products is more sustainable." They stated this would create "game-changing" opportunities but warned that policy strategies must be developed as the livestock sector collapses in the UK, alluding to the need for regulation of consumption (instead of simply halting production) in order to eliminate UK demand, which would continue livestock production and land-use change in other countries, and thereby perpetuate GHG emissions elsewhere but triggered by UK food choice decisions. Projecting the obvious difficulty with public acceptance and necessity for policy development, the authors ask the question "Now that this report has been published, what next?"[23]

It is interesting to note that whenever there is a significant study or finding exposing another detrimental effect of raising and eating animals, there appears to be a clear subversive attempt to suppress, mismanage, or disregard the information. Examples abound. In 2009, Carnegie Mellon and the WWF–UK Food Climate Research Network produced studies demonstrating that transportation (eating non-local foods) was an insignificant component of all greenhouse gases emitted in the entire food production process. Nearly all ensuing articles written by other organizations that cited this work failed to make the final connection—the elimination of all animal products (meat, dairy, and fish) from production and consumption. For instance, Sarah DeWeerdt, with Worldwatch Institute, writes (as she was quoting the Weber/Matthews' Carnegie Mellon study), "Replacing red meat and dairy with vegetables *one day* a week would be like driving 1,120 miles less per year" (May/June, Volume 22, No. 3)—thus perpetuating the Meatless Monday ("one day a week") campaign. However, Ms. DeWeerdt failed to mention anything about the very next sentence in that original Carnegie Mellon article, where the authors go one step further by stating that if every household ate a vegan but non-local diet *every* day of the year, it would be like driving over **8,000** miles less per year.

Tara Garnett, one of the contributors to the WWF–UK/Food Climate Research Network report, argues, "Broadly speaking, eating fewer meat and dairy products and consuming more plant foods in their place is probably the single most helpful behavioral shift one can make to reduce food-related greenhouse gas emissions"—which then furthers support for the "eating less meat" movement.[24]

Let's rephrase Dr. Garnett's argument to be more accurate: "Broadly or specifically speaking, eating *no* meat and dairy products and consuming *only* plant foods in their place is undeniably the single most helpful behavioral shift one can make" to reduce food-related greenhouse gas emissions. Another significant behavioral change is to address the issues in a proper manner by authors, researchers, the media, and anyone disseminating information. If it is established that a fire is burning a vital structure to the ground, room by room, let's think about putting the entire fire out—now—not simply "reducing" it.

A senior UN official and coauthor of the report, Henning Steinfeld, said, "Livestock are one of the most significant contributors to today's most serious environmental problems." In what could only be seen as buckling to the pressures of the meat and dairy industries, Steinfeld has since retracted the livestock-transportation comparison, and in 2010 published an article where he advocated eating more meat, not less, and to "produce better." Instead of suggesting the obvious dietary change to fully plant-based diets, he and coauthor Pierre Gerber argue that environmental impacts of livestock should be managed on the production side because it carries "important benefits." Their primary suggestion is a shift to monogastric animals, such as pigs and poultry, as well "continued efficiency gains in the production of feed and livestock." This all makes sense, in that these authors are livestock specialists employed by the Animal Production and Health Division of the FAO.

Anhang and Goodland, on the other hand, are environmental specialists employed by two other UN agencies—the IFC and the World Bank. Since their climate change analysis and conclusions had broadcast a more dramatic effect by livestock, it should have reached at least the same range and number of audience and created the same media buzz, if not more, as the FAO's report of 2006.

Instead, the analysis by Anhang/Goodland has been minimized, beginning with a critique of their work that was orchestrated by Steinfeld and the ILRI, which was published in *Animal Feed Science and Technology Journal*—a cattle industry-biased journal.

Others have recognized the severity of the environmental effects of raising livestock and therefore the need for stronger management of the problem. Cees DeHaan, a World Bank specialist, published a report in 2001 that called for a strategy recommending that banks should "avoid funding large-scale commercial, grain-fed feedlot systems and industrial milk, pork, and poultry production."

Livestock account for 80 percent of all emissions from the agricultural sector. A 2011 report by the Environmental Working Group found out that lamb, beef, and cheese had the highest GHG emissions out of all meat products. Ruminant animals generate more methane, require significantly more energy-intensive feed made from soybeans and corn, and produce more manure than other livestock. In some countries such as Uruguay, methane production from livestock, by itself, accounts for 50 percent of the country's total greenhouse gas emissions from all sources.[25] Estimates by Herrero et al. (2008) indicate that methane emissions from African cattle, goats, and sheep will likely increase to 11.1 million tons per year by 2030, a 50 percent jump. And these animals, as they are in most developing countries, are grazing. Factory farms are not the problem, which brings to light a critical point—climate change is not caused by industrial factory farming only. The primary reason we are seeing climate change is due to rising concentrations of greenhouse gases, a preponderance of them emitted by raising livestock. The largest contributing greenhouse gases are from methane and carbon dioxide; both are present whether the cow is in a CAFO (concentrated or confined animal feed operations) or on a pasture. In fact, it is generally felt by most researchers that methane production is conservatively 50 to 60 percent higher in grass-fed or pastured cattle than

[handwritten margin note: Livestock / all Agriculture]

in those fed grain, although that figure could very easily be much higher (Nathan Pelletier of Dalhousie University in Halifax, Nova Scotia), because much of the research in this area is arguably biased, being funded by stakeholders in the meat and dairy industry and the USDA, or the lead investigator frequently has affiliations with the meat and dairy industry. Even so, some studies still show methane production from pastured livestock to be as high as four times that of grain fed.[26]

Once one sees the connection between climate change and livestock, the next step is to clearly understand that any food movement overly focused on the evils of factory farms, while at the same time promoting "local, small farm, grass-fed" animal products, is simply ill informed.

Our collective efforts should be funneled into eliminating the raising of all animals, from a climate change as well as global depletion ("relative" sustainability) perspective. There should be no confusion.

Agricultural experts confined by conventional thought and cultural influences recognize that grass-fed cattle produce more methane than grain-fed cattle, but instead of moving away from raising more GHG-emitting animals, the conventional thought in 2012 was to ignore food choice change as an option. Heavily funded researchers are quickly at task, spending money and time, finding ways to continue raising livestock but implementing methods of reducing methane production by changing feed types, use of probiotics, and even methane vaccines, rather than focusing on the obvious and immediate climate change-limiting benefits of eliminating all livestock from food production systems.

Oceans play a major role in carbon sequestration. Approximately one-quarter of the carbon dioxide in the earth's atmosphere goes into the oceans, where it forms carbonic acid. Because of increases in atmospheric carbon dioxide, oceans have become 30 percent more acidic (with pH levels dropping from 8.25 to 8.14).[27]

In addition to our oceans becoming acidified, overfishing due to our demand to eat seafood has caused significant damage to numerous species and ecosystems. This, in turn, has an effect on climate change, yet it was not accounted for in the 2006 FAO *Long Shadow* report. Regarding this, I feel there are at least five areas that need to be recognized, accounted for, and then managed:

1. Fossil fuel used and GHGs emitted in the fishing process, handling, refrigeration, processing, packaging, transportation, cooking of all seafood taken from the oceans and then used for livestock and pet feed, which is nearing 30 percent of all fish extracted from the oceans per year

2. Fossil fuel used and GHGs emitted in all processes, similar to #1 above, for seafood taken from our oceans for human consumption

3. Fossil fuel used and GHGs emitted for fish produced from aquaculture, now at 50 percent of all fish consumed in the world

4. Effect of destructive fishing methods on coral reef loss and subsequent oxygen-carbon imbalance

5. Effect of overfishing of pelagic species on phytoplankton and algae imbalance and its subsequent effect on solar heat absorption and imbalances in normal oxygen-carbon-nitrogen gaseous exchanges

Our oceans generate more than half of all the earth's atmospheric oxygen, and phytoplankton are responsible for most of this. Herring and other pelagic fish form a balancing point for how much phytoplankton is present. Researchers at the Scripps Institution of Oceanography suggest that an increase in phytoplankton (such as what occurs by deleting those species that feed on it) would cause the earth to grow warmer due to increased solar absorption. Their simulations have shown that by increasing the phytoplankton mass in the upper oceanic layer, "sea surface temperature is increased as well as air temperature." Additionally, most of the carbon dioxide gathered by phytoplankton is derived from deep in the ocean, so any imbalance in phytoplankton will create an imbalance in the gaseous composition of our oceans themselves.

With great concern for our effect on climate change, it was the goal of Climate Healers and their executive director, Dr. Sailesh Rao, to "facilitate reforestation around the world so that carbon cycle imbalances due to human activities can be reversed." Their primary method to accomplish this was to change how people cooked—providing solar cookstoves to replace burning wood, which causes deforestation as well as emitting GHGs. This was a noble undertaking but in 2012, following five years of field work and research, Dr. Sailesh Rao realized that the positive impact of cookstove intervention is overshadowed by the enormous detrimental effects of the consumption of animals and animal products, which is on the rise worldwide. Regarding where efforts should be focused to reduce GHG emissions and climate change, Dr. Rao et al. came to the conclusion that it is much more important to address *what* we eat, instead of *how* we cook it. As stated by Climate Healers in a report from Dr. Rao, "Reorienting the human diet away from animal foods constitutes the largest opportunity for reforestation efforts to heal the climate and the planet."

In a NOAA statement about the 2011 *Climate Report,* their deputy administrator Kathryn Sullivan said, "This annual report provides scientists and citizens alike with an analysis of what has happened so we can all prepare for what is to come." My thought regarding climate change is that instead of preparing for "what is to come," we should all take steps to *guide* what is to come by eliminating entirely one of the largest two contributors to climate change—raising livestock and harvesting fish. It remains the easiest, simplest economically effective method to reduce climate change by way of reducing our anthropogenic GHG emissions. And it can be accomplished today. That's my plan, but I need some help. With a collective and immediate global effort, irreversible climate change and destructive weather patterns can be averted.

While scientists continue making the connection of climate change to extreme weather, the joint NOAA/UK Met Office study cautions, "Attribution of single extreme events to anthropogenic climate change remains challenging." That may be true for the time being or even long term, but what should not be "challenging" is the overt and significant connection of our demand to eat animals and climate change.

Some math to think about

The prevailing thought by most climate researchers is that our planet's atmosphere will only be able to accommodate another 565 gigatons (Gt) of CO_2-equivalent GHG by the year 2050, with a chance for the increase to stay below 2 degrees C. They argue that fossil fuel use is the single largest problem facing us. This is similar to the views expressed by environmentalist Bill McKibben in his *Rolling Stone* magazine article in July 2012, "Global Warming's Terrifying New Math," where he failed to discuss the significance of food choice. Despite Mr. McKibben's conspicuous oversight, raising and eating livestock has a rather significant role in our impact on climate change. If 51 percent of all GHG is, indeed, caused by livestock, this would equate to 32 Gt/year (Anhang, Goodland), which would mean that it would take only 17.6 years to reach the 565 Gt atmospheric limit. Our planet would reach this no-turning-back climate change figure by the year 2030, *even if we were to eliminate all use of fossil fuels by the "energy/industry" sector, starting today.*

Or alternatively, one might feel the 51 percent GHG emission estimate by Goodland and Anhang is excessive; that livestock's contribution to total GHG emissions is more like 31 percent. This 31 percent figure is calculated by taking 16 percent (it's generally agreed that livestock comprise 80 percent of agriculture GHG, multiplied by 20 percent, which is the generally agreed upon food or agriculture contribution to all anthropogenic GHG), added to the 15 percent generally agreed upon amount due to deforestation caused by livestock grazing and feed crop production. At 31 percent (or roughly 20 Gt emissions per year) produced by livestock, a realistic projection is that it would still only take approximately twenty-eight years to reach 565 Gt, irrespective of any fossil fuel use by the energy sector.

This is also without factoring in any of the large amounts (yet to be calculated by researchers) of GHG emitted because of our demand to eat fish—the more than 150 million tons raised each year in aquaculture and wild caught out of our oceans. For wild-caught alone, there would be GHG emissions caused by fuel usage of the fishing vessels, transport, refrigeration/cooling, processing, packaging, and cooling/transport to retail markets.

Educating the educated

And so we are now able to see the enormous depth of the problem. If all the brilliant minds—the scientists and researchers, the policy makers, the writers, educators, the advocates, business leaders, parents, friends, all those who influence—were able to cast off their own bias, shirk the cultural and social influences that bind them related to continued support of eating animal products, perhaps real progress would then be seen. After all, if these types of individuals are unable to accept the realities of the detrimental effects of our food choices and make the appropriate change to a fully plant-based diet, then how can we expect anyone else to do so?

Nearly all researchers have focused their attention and concern regarding our dire predicament with climate change on the effects of fossil fuel, blatantly omitting or underplaying any involvement by food choice, specifically the raising and eating of livestock and fish, as well as harvesting fish out of our oceans.

The disconnect can be seen with a comment from a scientist considered by many to be our most prominent climatologist, who voiced his concern about "overstatements about the role of what we eat in causing global warming." He found my statement—"the single most devastating factor that affects global warming and the environment is caused by what we eat"—to be "disagreeable."

He and other scientists may find this concept disagreeable, only to the extent that they have a general lack of awareness of the true effect that raising and eating animals has on global depletion. Everyone seems to be well aware that our energy sector, by way of fossil fuel consumption, may be the primary contributor to climate change via anthropogenic GHG emissions, not food choice. However, raising and eating animals *is* the primary contributor to all other areas of global depletion, and at 31 percent to 51 percent of total human-induced GHG emissions by all sectors, it is certainly a serious force in climate change, and it should not be swept under the rug by those who would rather look the other way (toward fossil fuels).

Most climate researchers and other environmental scientists, who are in an influential position and able to create change, admit to livestock's role in contributing to GHG emissions, acknowledging a minimal 31 percent component. But they simply cannot get past their own cultural hurdles to advocate the change needed. This 31 percent GHG contribution can be reduced to 0 percent—and we can begin today.

Fossil fuel reductions, on the other hand, are more complex and woven into the fabric of nearly all of our daily functions: how we conduct business, manage the ambient temperatures in our living spaces, and how we transport ourselves. Although eventually necessary, it would be difficult on many levels to entirely stop using fossil fuels today, but we can quite easily stop eating animals. Sufficient alternative renewable energy solutions and infrastructure are projected to cost more than $18 trillion and not be available until at least the year 2035. The cost of eating purely plant-based foods is zero, and they are available today.

When the United Nations/FAO report in 2006 stated that livestock produce 18 percent of all the greenhouse gas emissions found in our atmosphere—more than the entire transportation sector; more than all the cars, trucks, planes, trains that we drive and fly every day—this should have shaken us. It's time we advocate a much shorter timeline for action. It's time we do away with "baby steps."

News from the rainforests

In addition to respiratory CO_2 being produced by 70 billion animals raised annually in the world, excessive CO_2 in our atmosphere is also largely a problem, due to deforestation, primarily in the tropics, which accounts for one-third of all anthropogenic production of CO_2. Deforestation causes the following with regard to GHGs and climate change:

1. loss of oxygen-producing capacity of the forest plants
2. loss of ability to extract excessive carbon from our atmosphere
3. loss of longer term carbon sequestration into forest soil
4. production of carbon, emitted during the cutting and burning process

5. fossil fuel use for roads, clearing trees, and transporting
6. creation of localized climate change by disruption of water and heat cycles normally found in the forest

This is in addition to the significant impact deforestation in the Amazon and other rainforests has on all other aspects of global depletion.

The Amazon rainforest has been in existence for 55 million years and covers 5.5 million square kilometers (1.4 billion acres), extending into nine countries. Over 60 percent of the Amazon rainforest is in Brazil, followed by Peru with 13 percent, and Colombia at 10 percent of the forest. One in five of all fish species in the world and one in five of all bird species in the world live in the Amazon waters and rainforest.[28,29]

Just one square kilometer (247 acres) of Amazon rainforest can contain more than 1,100 different tree species and 108,000 tons of living plants. Many species of plants and animals have yet to be discovered.[30]

Scientists at Met Office's Hadley Centre in the UK predict that a 2 degree C rise above pre-industrial levels, widely considered the best-case global warming scenario and the target for international plans to curb emissions, would still see 20–40 percent of the Amazon die off within 100 years. A 3 degree C rise would see 75 percent of the rainforest destroyed by drought, and a 4 degree C rise would kill 85 percent of the entire Amazon forest over the next century. This is predicted to occur due to higher worldwide temperatures reducing rainfall in the Amazon region, which will then cause drought and major tropical forest dieback.

In just the past forty years, 232,000 square miles (20 percent of all the Amazon rainforest) has been cut down—more than the previous 450 years since colonization by the Europeans. This figure only accounts for clear-cutting of the forest and not degrading or selective cutting, which is more difficult to measure. According to Mongabay, 70 percent of all deforested land in the Amazon is attributed to the creation of land to raise cattle. Since 2004, Brazil has become the world's largest exporter of beef and the second largest exporter of soybeans. Before 2003, the U.S. was the largest beef exporter in the world. Ninety-one percent of all rainforest land deforested since 1970 is now used for grazing livestock. Figures released by Greenpeace in 2009 estimated that the total area of rainforest destroyed and now occupied by cattle ranches in just the Brazilian Amazon is 214,000 square miles, an area larger than France. Rates of rainforest destruction vary from region to region—all of it unacceptable. Nigeria's and Vietnam's rate of primary forest loss has doubled since the 1990s, while Peru's rate has tripled.[31]

While the mean annual rate of Amazon deforestation was 8 million acres (8,700 square miles) each year from 2000 through 2005, in 2010 it had decreased to 2 million acres, the lowest in twenty-two years but still unacceptable (World Bank, 2011). Actually, I would consider 1 acre of rainforest loss unacceptable. Nevertheless, reports of the first six months of 2011 indicate rainforest destruction is on the rise again, at 30 percent more than the same period of time one year earlier.[32] This is likely due to rising demand for beef and soy as a feed crop for livestock.

Agents from Brazil's vastly understaffed environmental agency, IBAMA, attempt to patrol and raid land grabbers, who are illegally clearing forests. But many are ill equipped and corrupt. Whether in Africa or the Amazon, rainforest destruction and loss of habitat seems to all begin with a road. Aside from only a few state and federal highways, including the controversial "soy highway," which slices 1,100 miles through the center of the Amazon from southern Mato Grosso north to Santarem in Para and the Trans-Amazon (east-west) Highway, nearly every other road is unauthorized. In all, there are an estimated 105,000 miles of these roads that were made illegally by loggers and then cattle operators.[33]

Whereas indigenous people of the Amazon understand intuitively the importance of their rainforest, the rest of the world continues to remain indifferent, if not ignorant, of the immeasurable worth of the Amazon:

- the immense amount of life it harbors (half of all the species on earth inhabit rainforests, with an unknown amount yet to be discovered)
- carbon sequestering by retaining 140 billion tons of carbon and mitigating of global warming
- production of oxygen (20 percent of the total amount in our atmosphere)

- water cycling by producing half of its own rainfall and much of the rain south of the Amazon and east of the Andes

Most researchers agree that there are nearly 80,000 acres *per day* of rainforests worldwide being destroyed, with another 60,000 to 80,000 acres per day that are being degraded ("degraded" being defined by the FAO as those rainforest areas where destruction has occurred due to logging, although cattle ranching can and does shortly follow). This equates to nearly 29 million acres of our planet's rainforests being destroyed each year.[34,35]

Deforestation in the Amazon is an example of our failure to recognize the value of this area and then to properly manage it, placing immediate economic gain ahead of true ecological/environmental costs and perpetuating grossly inefficient and destructive practices to support the global demand to eat animals.

Brazil's Forest Code and politics

Since 1965, Brazil approached protection of their large portion of the Amazon rainforest with a law called the Forest Code. Although it was not fully enforced, at least it appeared to restrict rainforest destruction. Spearheaded by Brazil's Communist Party, the Code will see major revisions, including easing of restrictions on clearing forests along rivers and hilltops, as well as providing amnesty for small-scale landowners who illegally cleared rainforests prior to July 2008. The thought is to provide economic help to smaller farmers.[36]

Controversial revisions also include a reduction in mandatory reserve requirements by landowners from 80 percent to 50 percent, and allowing the landowners to plant exotic species to restore once-cleared rainforest land.

In November 2011, the Brazilian Senate passed legislation, the revised Forest Code, reducing the amount of forest cover landowners are required to maintain and granting amnesty for farmers and ranchers who illegally cleared forest prior to July 2008. In addition to what has been destroyed within some legal framework, nearly 159 million acres of protected Amazon rainforest have been illegally cleared that were slated for reforestation under previous law. Now, for less than 988 acres, landowners won't be required to replant forest to bring their land up to the legal requirement. Required margins of forest along waterways were cut in half. Environmentalists decried the passing of this revision. WWF international director Jim Leape stated, "It will be a tragedy for Brazil and for the world if it now turns its back on more than a decade of achievement to return to the dark days of catastrophic deforestation." WWF estimates that the revised Forest Code will reduce forest cover in Brazil by 295,000 square miles, an area larger than Texas. It is estimated that more than 90 percent of the landowners in Brazil are operating illegally by selective forest clearing.[37]

In a study by Brazil's Institute of Applied Economic Research, it was reported that with these new Forest Code revisions, Brazil's emissions and deforestation targets will go unmet. Approximately 75 percent of Brazil's GHG emissions come from rainforest clearing, which releases 400 million tons of CO_2 in the atmosphere each year. If Brazil were to replant the 159 million acres destroyed illegally, it is estimated that 18.6 billion tons of carbon dioxide would be sequestered, allowing Brazil to meet its Copenhagen commitments for the next eighteen years. Large tracts of Amazon rainforest land are cleared by landowners for cattle pastureland and planted with African savanna grasses. The Brazilian government lacks sufficient funds to properly enforce rainforest-clearing laws to prevent illegal destruction, and they have created tax incentives and subsidies that favor raising cattle, the development of pastureland, and production of feed crops. Reclaiming and then reforesting land from cattle and feed operations and establishing organic, plant-based food production systems on them has yet to become a priority. This, combined with the immediate cessation of eating animals, very likely could be the most important act for us to employ as we seek measures to mitigate GHG emissions—perhaps more than half of all anthropogenic greenhouse gases.

It would make sense, then, that there should be a significant economic and moral value fostered by our global community for sustainably produced plant-based foods grown in rainforests or reclaimed rainforest land. And the same should hold true in the other direction—we should hold Brazil, and all other countries with rainforest land, economically and morally accountable for destruction of rainforest. Similarly, we should hold accountable those countries throughout the world that are demanding to eat animals raised in rainforest-cleared land or with fed crops grown on rainforest-cleared land. With tax rates and subsidies that favor cattle and pasture over rainforests, our demand for consumption of animals is encouraging loss of the Amazon. The practice of government and international support for the destruction of rainforests in order for us to eat meat has to stop.[38]

Inefficient use of land, deforestation, and climate change

The reason climate change is so strongly related to meat consumption is twofold. The first reason is that all the massive amount of animals raised on the earth to slaughter each year are producing greenhouse gases themselves—methane, carbon dioxide, and nitrous oxide. The second reason is that these animals take up space, and so forests are cut down and plants are destroyed to make room for them. The most devastating losses of forests are in our rainforests, which then contributes to climate change, because carbon is emitted in the process. Additionally, there is loss of the oxygen-generating capacity of that forest, as well as localized climate change and imbalance of the water recycling process.

When you choose to eat livestock, it is one of the most inefficient uses of our land on earth. There are 70 billion animals raised each year on our planet, up to 1.7 trillion chickens. This takes a tremendous amount of our resources, land being one of them.

Picture, for a moment, most of our planet covered with natural plant growth at one time and most of this being forests. Now picture 45 percent of all the land on earth being used by livestock—that 45 percent was originally mostly forests. All this land used to raise animals has caused great imbalances, where forests and wildlife are destroyed, and our atmosphere is changing.

This tragic deforestation is seen most vividly in our rainforests. Because we are running out of land in developed countries, we have cut down forests. Land is economically inexpensive in the rainforests, sometimes as low as $43 an acre, and it is less in the public eye and remote geographically, so these forests are destroyed without much notice—primarily by large international companies such as Cargill, Georgia Pacific, JBS, and Texaco. Pristine rainforests that have taken ten thousand to a million years to evolve are cut down in minutes in order to raise livestock. Also, over 93 percent of all the soy grown worldwide is fed to livestock, and most of this soy is now grown on rainforest-cleared land.

So you might ask, "What do rainforests have to do with me?" The answer is, "A lot." Even if the meat you are eating doesn't directly come from the rainforest area, it still has an impact, because with every bite of meat you eat, you essentially create demand. You are asking the meat-producing industry to raise more cattle, chickens, and pigs—more livestock—so more land will be used and more forests will be cut down, globally.

Many call rainforests the lungs of our planet because they breathe, taking carbon dioxide out of our atmosphere and sequestering it long term into the soil—how perfect. So when we cut down rainforests to raise cattle or other livestock or to produce feed for livestock, we release millions of tons of carbon into the atmosphere, losing trees that have the ability to produce oxygen. We also are killing millions and millions of living things— plants, animals, insects, and even tribes of people. We have already lost over ninety ancient tribes in the Amazon area. Every second, another 1.5 acres of rainforest is destroyed—and all the living things with it.

Over one-quarter of all the world's medicines originated in rainforests—drugs such as quinine to treat malaria; vincristine, a very powerful anti-cancer drug used to treat childhood leukemia; and medicines to treat glaucoma, Parkinson's disease, and many, many more have been developed from plants found in the rainforests. The National Cancer Institute has found nearly three thousand plants thus far in the rainforests that have strong anti-cancer properties.

In the past forty years, 25 percent of all the Amazon rainforest has been cut down, with many experts predicting this rainforest will be completely gone within the next forty years.

In 2010, Russia was the largest importer of beef from the Amazon area, with over $1 billion in purchases from Brazil. In 2011, Iran became the largest buyer of beef from cattle grown on rainforest-cleared land.

Since the 1970s, the U.S. has been a leading importer of beef from Central and South American cattle that were raised in rainforest-cleared land. In 2010, the U.S. did place a ban on imported beef from Brazil, but it was not because of our concern for the rainforest or for climate change—it was because meat inspectors found large residues of the antihelmetic (antiwormer) Ivermectin in beef from Brazil. Also, this ban only affected beef sold in grocery stores—that means beef in restaurants can still be from Brazil and rainforest-cleared land.

Deforestation in the Amazon is an example of our failure to recognize the effect it has on climate change and our failure to appreciate the value of this area. As a society, we place immediate economic gain ahead of ecological or environmental concerns and costs. Until we are able to completely arrest rainforest destruction, such natural resources should have an "eco tax"—a tax paid by all producers and consumers of animal products. Remember, this is not a matter of factory farming. Rainforest destruction in the Amazon is mostly because of *grass-fed cattle*—they are all grazing.

"The threat from climate change is serious, it is urgent, and it is growing." —Barack Obama

With minimally 30 to 51 percent of all human-created greenhouse gas emissions caused by the animals that we raise and eat each year, where is the connection from climate change to livestock being made? I wish President Obama's statement had been this:

> The threat from climate change is serious, it is urgent, and it is growing. Although there is much work to do in many areas, one of the largest single contributors

to global greenhouse gas emissions from human activities is from livestock, as a result of our demand to consume animals. Therefore, in order to properly address climate change, we must stop eating meat—today.

That type of statement is what we need to see from the leaders of all nations.

Despite the obvious increase in occurrence of weather extremes and associated damages, you may still be a climate-change skeptic. After all, you may not live near a rainforest, a coastline, or in an area of the world that has been seriously impacted by weather extremes or forest destruction in the past ten years, so it hasn't affected you directly—yet. But it will. And by the time our mounting influence on rising greenhouse gases, climate change, and weather becomes apparent to everyone, it most likely will be too late.

Human-induced GHG emissions are measurably contributing to climate change; it is time we strongly address the issue. It is time we do something about it in the form of a massive and concerted global educational effort, as well as creating an economic correlation—creating monetary incentives for those who comply and imposing taxation for those who do not. These initiatives should be developed, implemented, and supported by all local, regional, and national governments, and they should be directed at all individuals and businesses with international implications in place—without exception. The steps we employ to mitigate climate change will only be as effective as the collective effort and conscience of our global community. It begins with the easiest solution—change your food to all plant-based choices.

2

Depletion of Land and Fresh Water

WE ARE RUNNING out of land. A simple reason we seem to accept is that there are too many people—overpopulation—but the more complex reason is that our planet and its resources are shrinking in alarming fashion. And that's not because of the number of people on earth; it's because of what we are eating.

Forty-five percent of the entire landmass on earth is used by and for livestock. Less than 2 percent of all the animals raised in the U.S. and 9 percent of those raised worldwide are grazing, so as patterns shift toward "sustainable" grass-fed systems, land occupation by livestock and aquaculture (seafood farming) will simply worsen. One-third of the world's topsoil already has been lost, and we are losing the rest faster than it can be replaced. The structure and functioning of the world's ecosystems changed more rapidly in the second half of the twentieth century than at any time in human history.[39],[40]

Most of this is due to the effect of grazing livestock. In fact, eating *less* meat will actually mean we are using *more* land and contributing *more* to climate change, because we will be eating mostly grass-fed livestock. This seems to paint a gloomy picture—one where we actually run out of land on which to live or conduct necessary functions. The catch is, though, that we don't need to use that much land for producing food, because there is no valid reason to eat animals—not one.

Yet there are numerous valid reasons why we should stop eating animals altogether. Land use is typically viewed with a concern for producing the three F's—food, feed, and fiber. With global population expected to reach 9 billion by the year 2050, the understandable worry is that the demand for food, feed, and fiber will not be easily met, which places additional stress on already stretched and abused natural resources. It would appear we would need significant increases in agricultural productivity and must adopt new technology and production practices for achieving sustainability. Any new technologies employed, however, should pertain only to two components of the three F's—food and fiber—as the feed component should be omitted from any type of future land use to attain a more relative sustainable status.[41]

Global depletion of land regarding livestock involves the raw land used (total acreage used by grazing livestock and to grow crops to feed them), deforestation, and soil depletion by way of topsoil loss (erosion), diminishing fertility, and desertification. Wherever land has been depleted by way of grazing livestock, there is associated greenhouse gas emissions/ contribution to climate change interlaced with other aspects of global depletion such as misuse of fresh water, and loss of habitat with ensuing threatened or extinction of species.

Crop monoculture (the practice of growing a single crop or plant species over a wide area for several consecutive years) is often associated with factory farming and has been the source of frequent discussion. This agricultural practice reduces soil fertility to the point where chemicals are needed each year in order to bring up nitrogen and mineral levels. Of equal or greater importance, though, is how those monocultured crops are used. The United Nations Food and Agricultural Organization (FAO) stated, "Problems of food security and environmental degradation will need to be addressed. ... [T]he production task facing world agriculture is massive. By 2030, an extra billion tons of cereals will be needed each year."[42]

In 2011, there was a record worldwide grain harvest of 2.6 billion tons (2.5 billion tons were produced in 2010). It's been estimated that this amount is enough to feed *twice as many people* as we currently have on earth. But 43 percent of all grain produced for food purposes in 2011 went to livestock (865 million tons to feed livestock and fish and 1,175 million tons for human food; the rest of the grain was used for "other" uses, such as alternative fuels). Over 90 percent of the world's soybean harvest is used for animal feed.[43] This has been the case for many years.

Regarding "coarse grains" (corn/maize, barley, sorghum, rye, oats, millet, and some regionally important grains such as teff in Ethiopia or quinoa in Bolivia and Ecuador), 60 percent of the total world production of 1.3 billion tons is used to feed livestock—increasing by 6 percent each year. If you exclude "other uses" (for ethanol and industrial purposes), an inexcusable 77 percent of all coarse grain produced in the world is consumed by animals in the meat, dairy, and fishing industries—not by humans.

The "extra billion tons of cereals" the FAO is concerned about producing by 2030 to feed the rising population can be found today— we're feeding it to livestock.[44]

Despite this reality and oblivious to its implications, the FAO predicts that in order to meet the demand for food by the rising future population, the number of farm-raised animals will nearly double to over 120 billion by 2050 (for the expected 200 million tons of meat needed in addition to what is produced currently). This has obvious ramifications for the ensuing impact on global warming, global depletion, and global health care costs, and it will create more pressure on the production of grain that is already misused.

Conventional thought is that since an "extra billion tons of cereals" will need to be produced in the next seventeen years, because of the demand for extra food, we will either have to produce more food on the same amount of available land (agricultural intensification requiring more soil inputs and increased technology) or use more land. Neither, however, would be necessary if we simply change food choice to the most efficiently grown options—purely plant-based.[45]

Severe weather patterns invoking heat waves, drought, and storms heavily impacted global agriculture in 2012. The USDA called it the worst drought conditions in twenty-five years, designating more than half of all U.S. counties as disaster zones. Resultant low crop production will continue triggering higher food prices, causing concern for food security. Increased use of irrigation in many areas of the world will lead to aquifer draws that exceed replenishing rates. In the U.S., 77 percent of the 2012 soybean crop was affected, and with half of the crop rated as very poor, corn supply is predicted to be the lowest in sixteen years. Other countries are having similar difficulties. Wheat production from Russia, Ukraine, and Kazakhstan dropped 30 percent from 2011 due to drought in those countries. Combined, they normally supply a quarter of the world's wheat export volume. When drought occurred in 2010, Russia imposed export restrictions, further constricting global supply and causing wheat shortages and sharp increases in food prices. Russia bases most of its agricultural efforts on livestock, with a strong poultry, pig, and dairy dependence, so a large concern for their country in 2012, as it was in 2010, was feeding its livestock. Russia has more than 25 million head of cattle, so when faced with hay and pasture loss, grains such as wheat are used. Even though meat production is affected by having less grain, Russia increased its beef imports from the U.S. in the first six months of 2010 by more than 600 percent and 450 percent from Canada, compared to the previous year. With wheat crops shrinking to near 2010 levels in Russia, export restrictions may be imposed once again. Even without wheat restrictions, global grain prices increased sharply in June and July 2012.

All of this simply is more evidence of how dependent a country—and our world—can become on archaic and inefficient agricultural systems that use the preponderance of resources to raise animals for slaughter, rather than using a fraction of those resources on plant-based foods that can be used directly for human consumption. Russia has delivered the clear message that if a country cannot provide enough meat to satisfy the demand of their citizens, it will just import it from another country. The wheat crisis in Russia or grain crises in any other country is often simply a matter of inappropriate use of that particular grain and land.

There are two interesting perspectives regarding the connection between global grain production, land use, and climate change. First, regardless of severe weather patterns, deficiencies in grain production relative to demand needs to be correlated with how that grain is used. Say your family eats 50 pounds of tomatoes each year but grows 100 pounds of tomatoes in one season, typically throwing away 50 pounds. A drought-affected season that cuts your production to 50 pounds is not a problem, because you still have the 50 pounds you need. It really is an issue of how the food product is used, more than of external weather factors limiting yields. So it is with global production of grain, where nearly three-fourths of all coarse grain produced in the world is fed to livestock instead of our directly eating it ourselves.

Second, the more land we use for grazing or factory-farmed livestock and feed crops, the higher contribution we make to greenhouse gas emissions and climate change. The more climate change we experience, the more severe weather patterns we will encounter that will negatively impact crops and which will affect everyone on earth. In other words, the very crops (and the livestock they are designated for) we lose due to drought are causing the climate change that is affecting this loss.

Understanding the effect depletion of land has on other areas of sustainability can be best accomplished by examining the two principle components of land-use inefficiencies.

First, it takes far too much land to raise all livestock, particularly cattle, either in grazing scenarios or concentrated animal feeding operations (CAFOs). Second, it takes too much land to grow feed for all those factory-farmed animals and to "finish" grass-fed animals (giving the animals grain daily at the end of their lives, just before slaughtering). It is a simple matter of realizing how much feed per animal per day is required, and then how much land is needed to produce that feed, and then comparing it to plants grown for our consumption, which are much more efficient to produce and provide us with infinitely greater health benefits.

When viewing the outrageous land requirements to pasture or grow crops to feed livestock, it helps to be familiar with what the meat, dairy, and aquaculture industries call the feed conversion ratio (FCR) or the feed conversion efficiency (FCE), which are measurements of an animal's efficiency in converting feed into body mass. This is where the

Food Conversion Ratio

illogicality begins—feeding plants to animals instead of to ourselves, and then obsessing over methods to reduce this FCR ratio.

Generally, it is felt that the FCR is 8:1 for cows, 5:1 for pigs, and 2:1 for broiler chickens—meaning that it requires 8 pounds of dry weight feed to produce a 1-pound gain in weight of the cow.[46]

Feed conversion ratios will near 30:1 with grass-fed cattle operations.[47]

FCRs are routinely used by researchers and the USDA in evaluating livestock feeding patterns, but while these ratios point out blatant food use inefficiencies, the calculation method is still flawed. A greater appreciation of misuse could be garnered if both sides of the FCR equation were more accurate. For instance, instead of simply measuring how much feed is given to an animal prior to slaughter, there should be an accounting of all other energy inputs required in the farming process for raising, harvesting, and processing the particular feed. And on the other side of the equation, the number relates to live weight gain, not accounting for inedible parts of the animal's carcass, which would then increase the FCR substantially.

Researchers Asgard and Austreng found that only between 2 percent and 18 percent of a feed's macronutrients (protein, fat, carbohydrates) is actually retained in the edible parts of livestock. In the U.S., cattle usually do not enter the feedlot until they are seven to twenty months of age. As a steer reaches 800 pounds, it may gain 3 pounds of weight per day and be fed between 20 and 30 pounds of feed (dry weight) in a twenty-four-hour period.[48,49]

A great emphasis is placed on FCR, as solutions are sought for the expected global food crises as we near mid-century. The European Union Agenda 2020 flagship initiative on resource efficiency indicates that since demand for meat will increase substantially, feed is the most important single factor for the sustainable development of livestock and aquaculture production.

Therein is another problem with the FCR issue: the optimal FCR is precisely zero—no feed, no animals raised, no excessive land use, no global depletion.

It has been estimated that more than 260 million acres of U.S. forest have been cleared just to create cropland to grow grain to feed farmed animals. Scientists at the Smithsonian Institution indicate that the equivalent of seven football fields of land is bulldozed worldwide *every minute* to create more room for livestock.

A closer look at land use, grain production, and where it's all going

A tremendous amount of land is used to produce a tremendous amount of grain to feed a tremendous amount of livestock animals.

In 2011, the U.S. produced a slightly smaller amount of corn, but other areas of the world carried it to a record 900 million tons. Farmers in Argentina, Brazil, and South America are planting more corn yearly, due to expected increase in demand for animal feed use and increased competition from wheat now used as a feed crop. It is expected that worldwide demand for grain will continue to be more than output because of the heavy dependence on grain to feed livestock. Production of coarse grains in developing countries is rising fast and expected to outpace that of rice or wheat because of the increased use as animal feed and keeping in line with the growth of the livestock sector.

In the U.S., feed-grain use was expected to increase by 30.9 million tons, to 416 million tons in 2012/13 due to higher feed demand and exports to feed animals in other countries. Beef consumption in the U.S. has tapered recently, so this feed crop demand is driven by higher poultry and pig production, which is expected to continue climbing.[50, 51]

Depletion of land is related to production of livestock, which is driven by demand. Although beef production (and therefore raising of cattle) was less in the U.S. in 2011 (still, at over 25 billion pounds), production of pork, poultry, eggs, and milk are all on the increase, and beef demand and consumption is on the increase worldwide in addition to these other animal products.

Putting meat production and land-use inefficiency into perspective

Since 1950, global meat production has increased more than fivefold. Consumption of animals and animal products worldwide in terms of total tonnage has increased by more than 50 percent in the last fifteen years. Between 1960 and 2000, total global beef consumption doubled, milk tripled, eggs quadrupled, and chicken consumption went up 800 percent.[52]

Globally, beef production and raising cattle is predicted to increase by 5 percent annually (Dec. 2011, USDA), while poultry production and the number of chickens and turkeys raised each year is expected to double by the year 2020. These trends are influenced by predicted increases in consumption and imports, driven by income and population increases, particularly in Southeast Asia and Mexico where pork, poultry, and beef are all expected to rise substantially to meet demand. U.S. exports of beef were 25 percent higher in 2011 than they were in 2010 and will most likely continue increasing to meet demand from countries such as Japan, South Korea, and Russia.

While 45 percent of the land on earth is used to raise animals and food to feed them, it is estimated that only 5 percent is used to grow plant-based foods consumed directly by humans. This 5 percent, though, supplies 80 percent of the calories consumed by humans.[53]

An interesting thing happened in 2012—India became the world's leading beef exporter, due to an expanding dairy herd and increased slaughter and price-competitiveness in the international market. This is interesting because their federal law prohibits the slaughter of all cattle as well as milk cows. Enter carabeef (buffalo meat), which is included in USDA's global estimates of beef (bovine) meat production. India's exports are exclusively deboned frozen buffalo meat, somehow bypassing their long-invoked religious standards and using more land at the expense of their burgeoning human population.[54]

In Brazil, 200 million cattle roam over 500 million acres, 90 percent of which is cleared rainforest.[55]

One-fourth of all the meat produced in the world is eaten in China. In 1978, China consumed 8 million tons, as compared to 24 million tons in the U.S., but in 2012, China doubled the U.S. in meat consumption, at 71 million tons per year. There are more than 476 million pigs raised in China each year—more than half of the world's pigs—because three-fourths of their meat consumption is pork. Annually, the Chinese eat 84 pounds of pork per person. Chicken consumption in China, at more than 13 million tons per year, also exceeded the U.S. for the first time in 2012. With the increase in meat consumption, China also became the largest grain user in 2011, with one-third of their harvest feeding animals. This has affected the manner in which agricultural land is managed elsewhere in the world. For instance, more than 60 percent of world soybean exports (mostly from the U.S., Brazil, and Argentina) go to China, resulting in the clearing of rainforests and savannahs to support crop plantings (2012 Earth Policy Institute).[56]

In 2012, the average amount of meat eaten by every single person in the U.S. was as follows: 57 pounds of beef, 47 pounds of pork, 81 pounds of chicken, 16 pounds of turkey, 246 eggs, 1 pound of lamb, 16 pounds of fish, 41 pounds of cheese, 604 pounds dairy (all dairy combined, including 22 gallons of milk).

For the year 2011, the U.S. production figures for meat were as follows: 93,000 million pounds of red meat and poultry; 6,590 million dozen eggs; and 200 billion pounds milk.[57]

The first step in resolution of global depletion of our land is to use our arable land to grow plants that we can consume directly, not for animals that we raise to eat or for crops to feed these animals.

A better understanding of land use for food production begins with comparing how much land is really needed to grow food. Variation can certainly be seen with calculating yields for different items we eat, which is dependent upon factors such as geographical location, climate, and soil type. Typically, if it requires more acreage to raise livestock in one area of the world than another, then it generally will require slightly more land to grow plant foods, *but* the land needed to raise livestock is drastically more than that is needed for plants in any one given location. For instance, in some areas of the U.S., I have found grass-fed livestock farms that can raise one cow on as little as 1.5 acres of land, which equates to 300 pounds of meat (or "food") per acre. But in that same county (sometimes right next door to the cattle operation), I have seen vegetable farmers growing beans instead of cows, producing over 3,000 pounds of beans, or 16,000 pounds of spinach, or 39,000 pounds of potatoes ("food") per acre. Often these vegetables can be grown without any irrigation, which can't be said of the livestock example, where the farmer provides 15 to 45 gallons of drinking water per day to each cow and frequently irrigates the pasture or crops given to the cow to eat.

Also important is to grow plants that are highly nutritious.

In 2011, planted area for feed grain (corn, sorghum, oats, and barley used to feed livestock) in the U.S. increased by 4 million acres (Economic Research Service, USDA, May 2011). The land used just for corn in the U.S. was 96 million acres, with 50 percent of the harvest corn given to livestock, 37 percent to biofuels, and less than 3 percent directly for human food and high-fructose corn syrup. Another 56 million acres of land in the U.S. was used to grow alfalfa in 2011—all of which was destined for livestock. Buckwheat is an example of many plants that are highly nutritious that could be grown efficiently and used for direct human consumption. While containing other important nutrients, buckwheat has the highest amount of rutin (a powerful antioxidant) of any plant in the world. Yet less than 50,000 acres of buckwheat were planted in 2011 in the U.S. Until very recently, 75 percent of buckwheat production had been fed to livestock and poultry, as our culture had little idea about the many human health benefits of this nutritious plant.[58] An acre of land will produce 1,000 to 2,000 pounds of buckwheat, depending on the level of soil fertility.

Plants that provide numerous and extremely healthy benefits, such as kale and collard greens, can be harvested year round, as the leaves grow back and have the ability to survive temperature ranges from 0 degrees to 105 degrees Fahrenheit. Yields of collard greens have been seen as high as 40,000 pounds per acre per year.[59]

Meanwhile, in the summer of 2012, U.S. farmers, facing the worst drought since the 1950s, began using environmentally fragile land for livestock feed.

Instead of pursuing policy to reduce the inefficient use of cropland for feed and pasturing livestock, the USDA opened up haying and grazing on

Conservation Reserve and Wetlands Reserve land in counties affected by heat and drought. Approximately 32 million acres are enrolled in the conservation programs, which were originally established to protect land from erosion and further damage by conventional farming and raising livestock.

Depleted land and soils in developing countries

We can see global depletion of land most vividly in African countries, where issues such as land- and resource-use inefficiencies cycle back to poverty and hunger. More than two-thirds of the agricultural land in sub-Saharan Africa is considered severely degraded, and it is equally alarming in South Asia. Grazing cattle are responsible for most of this decimation, where topsoil has been lost due to overgrazing and ensuing deforestation, erosion, and desertification.[60]

All efforts for global assistance, whether from a humanitarian or agricultural perspective, should be first directed at creating the most efficient food production systems, which should build and conserve topsoil and soil fertility, while at the same time use the least amount of land, water, and other resources, and with end products that are the healthiest possible to consume. This can best be accomplished by devoting all agricultural efforts toward purely plant-based systems—no livestock, no dairy, and no chickens. To date, this has not been accomplished, because influential organizations continue to promote the raising of animals to eat as part of the affected country's culture. If anything, most organizations design their projects to enhance livestock production, attempting to remedy feed issues, cure or prevent diseases with vaccinations for livestock, and train villagers or farmers to use animal husbandry techniques that are thought to improve food security.

True food security and sustainability, especially for drought-ridden developing countries with severe topsoil loss, will be difficult to achieve without long-term soil rebuilding and the very most efficient use of their resources, time, money, and energy. In all regards, plant-based agricultural systems are most beneficial, leaving simply no room or tolerance for livestock production. All the research and project funding in the world and the very best of chicken or cattle vaccinations will not materialize topsoil or restore topsoil fertility for impoverished farmers in developing countries— only growing plants will accomplish this. Of course, this all begins with education—of the rural farmers, villagers, governmental officials and leaders, and global funding institutions and welfare organizations or NGOs (non-governmental organizations) involved. It is crucial that these entities become aware of the undermining effect of livestock on poverty and hunger, so that the appropriate steps are taken to alleviate it.

Success of organic soil-rebuilding techniques for growing all plant-based food systems in African countries will likely depend on adoption by their rural women who, by custom, produce the food crops in many African societies (while men produce the export crops).[61] This presents its own set of challenges, though, because although food security analysts argue that development strategies must reach African smallholders to be effective, women are not given the same opportunities as men, despite the fact that women farmers are responsible for the majority of food production in African countries.

Organic soil building without livestock

One-third of all topsoil on earth has been lost, most of it primarily from grazing livestock, which then leads to loss of productivity, erosion, desertification, and localized climate change. Although the preponderance of livestock on the earth (those not confined to CAFOs; 9 percent of all animals raised for food) continue to graze in a destructive manner, a movement is under way in the U.S., UK, and other countries to employ "sustainable" pasturing practices for their grass-fed operations.

Three arguments usually arise from anyone who supports the grass-fed livestock movement: (1) that raising grass-fed livestock is sustainable, which it is not; (2) that it is "humane," which by including the entire life-and-death cycle of any grass-fed animal, it is not; and (3) that grazing livestock are "good for the soil," which the following discussion explores.

Typically, animal husbandry proponents argue that livestock, especially cattle, are necessary for soil fertility, compaction, sequestration, and general healthy, balanced ecosystems. Unfortunately, the opposite has been shown to be the case. Two-thirds of the topsoil loss over the past fifty years is primarily due to grazing livestock, and there are now numerous examples of soil rebuilding, with techniques such as using cover crops and green manure rather than animal manure. Strict use of plants, however, will increase water retention, carbon sequestration, nutrient replenishing with a more complete and more adequate nutrient ratio (carbon-to-nitrogen ratio, for instance), and reduced propensity for erosion. Even if animal manure helped rebuild soil in some manner, the overall effect of this product's origin (livestock) on global depletion precludes its use, and the end product still carries human health risks. There is a widely held and gross misconception that livestock are needed for maintenance of a natural viable ecosystem or the health of a pasture. In its simplest form, this is easily refuted, because there are many examples of lush, unspoiled ecosystems existing in the complete absence of livestock or even wild grazing animals. One such example is the island country of Dominica, where there are no grazing land mammals, and no commercial livestock have been introduced, yet the island enjoys one of the healthiest, unchanged ecosystems found anywhere on our planet.[62]

One acre of land planted with cover crops for one year will have the same nitrogen contribution as 12 tons of poultry manure. The majority of raw animal and bird manures have an analysis ranging from 0.5 percent to 4.5 percent nitrogen, 0.2 to 2.0 percent phosphorus, and 0.4 to 2.0 percent potassium but have a narrow carbon-to-nitrogen ratio and are much less adequate than plants for building humus. The benefits of cover crops without the use of manure from livestock are numerous and include:

1. Prevention of erosion by reducing the impact of wind and water
2. Adding organic matter
3. Suppressing weed growth
4. Leguminous cover crops adding symbiotically fixed nitrogen
5. Capturing and recycling soluble nutrients that otherwise would be lost

6. Cover crop systems creating habitats for beneficial insects[63,64]

Organic methods of growing plants are the very best way to build topsoil and keep it fertile, long term. Even so, proponents of meat and dairy products argue that somewhere in the mix, livestock also is needed. Farmers, using the best soil nutrient-management practices, grow legumes in crop rotations to supply biologically fixed, atmospheric nitrogen instead of inorganic nitrogen fertilizer or that from animal manure. Most legume cover crops contribute up to 200 pounds of nitrogen per acre, which is mineralized over an extended period of time, so there is no runoff into streams or aquifers, as is the case with conventional chemical fertilizers or livestock manure.

Other plants such as small grains ("trap crops") can be used to capture nitrogen after harvesting crops, and they have extensive root systems that store soil nitrogen, also preventing leaching or runoff. Crop rotations also vary in terms of depth of roots—some deep, some shallow— so that efficient use of soil nutrients and water used and then replenished at many levels can be accomplished. Scientists at the Rodale Institute and many other researchers have shown clear advantages to organic soil-building techniques, where water percolation is 30 percent greater than conventional agricultural methods, so in dry years, organic farms will produce significantly higher yields of crops than those of conventional farms. An analysis of 133 scientific papers showed that organic agriculture was particularly competitive when employed in lower-yield environments, commonly found in developing countries. Water capture and retention was shown to be twice as high in organic plots, as compared to conventional plots, during torrential rains.[65] Biodynamic systems in India and elsewhere revealed decreased irrigation yields of 30 to 50 percent.[66]

Studies have concluded that organic plant-production systems are responsible for better soil aeration and drainage, lower bulk density, higher organic matter content, soil respiration (related to soil microbial activity), more earthworms, and deeper topsoil layer and are found to have less need for irrigation.[67]

Some argue that cattle are needed for carbon sequestration, but it has been found that complete cessation of grazing cattle results in a 40 percent increase in carbon storage in the soil.[68] Replacing cattle with a combination of food-producing trees and other plants results in the sequestering of 1 ton of carbon out of the atmosphere into the soil per acre in just one year.

There is general consensus that in heat- and water-challenged developing countries, organic farming builds more fertile soil than conventional methods and with higher yields. Please note that these organic methods and the numerous research findings that support them build soil with plants, not animals. The only reason animals or livestock use is mentioned in any literature is because the authors believe that animals are needed somewhere in the process, and so their manure must be accounted for. Therefore, it is used in compost or recycled back as fertilizer, which is a step better than inorganic chemical fertilizers but in no way takes the place of or improves the soil-building ability of plants. The argument for use of livestock appears to originate from an academic point of reference, but in truth, it is embedded in the cultural aspect of the world's population wanting to continue eating meat and is searching for justification for doing so.

With population increases and available land decreases, *how* we use land will be a key question to our survival on a planet with finite terrestrial acreage and resources. It makes no sense to use what little land we have on earth to create pasture for cattle to graze or for crops to feed them—this is one of the most inefficient ways to produce food. Raising animals for our use as food is indirect (plant food given to animals that are killed, then becoming meat to us, instead of plants given directly to us to eat) and resource-intensive and with an end product that is known to be detrimental to our health. The ill effects of factory farming (CAFOs) and the many reasons to move away from that been well documented, but the question is, what are we moving to? Livestock grazing has caused severe damage in the U.S. and many other countries. The Center for Biological Diversity, as part of a review of grazing, referenced over 150 scientific, peer-reviewed articles that detail the detrimental environmental impacts of livestock grazing on soil fertility, wildlife, water systems, topsoil loss, and damage to ecosystems.

A comprehensive Survey of Livestock Influences on Stream and Riparian Ecosystems in the Western United States covered more than 140 peer-reviewed studies on the negative biological and physical effects of livestock on rivers, streams, and riparian areas. In a systematic literature review, Belsky et al. found there was not a single-peer reviewed study demonstrating any positive environmental impact of cattle grazing. In the other direction, it has been widely shown that cattle grazing negatively impacts nearby water quality, seasonal quantity, stream morphology, hydrology riparian zone soils, and stream and streambank vegetation, as well as aquatic and riparian wildlife. General impacts of cattle grazing have been found to include the following, as related to nearby streams and water systems:

- Increased nutrient concentrations, bacteria, and protozoa levels
- Increased sediment load caused by erosion
- Decreased water depth
- Flow from runoff increased
- Streambank stability is reduced
  And the effects of raising livestock on riparian soils are:
- Erosion, soil compaction increases
- Water infiltration rates decrease
- Biomass, productivity, and native plant diversity are altered and decline
- Natural plant species and plant succession is impeded
- Loss of wildlife

The conventional thought is to improve grazing techniques to minimize the detrimental effects of cattle. Much time, money, and energy has been spent and is still being spent on research and development on livestock operations—trying to find ways to continue raising animals for us to eat but with less environmental damage. This effort has two major targets: (1) for developed countries such as the U.S., where it is standard practice to eat meat but that now has begun to realize that grazing cattle take up space, cause extensive environmental damage, and contribute heavily to GHG emissions and climate change; and (2) for developing countries, many of which have more land available to extend livestock operations beyond the scrutinizing eye of environmentalists. Instead of simply eliminating livestock from the food production equation in both developed and developing countries, we have embarked on a time- and money-consuming mission to accomplish the improbable—find a way to create a healthy food that somehow involves the raising of livestock without depleting resources. This is impossible, because (1) growing feed crops or pasture for grazing animals, which we then kill and eat, will never be as resource-efficient or have fewer GHG emissions, under any circumstances, as simply growing the plants for us to eat directly; and (2) as an end product, eating animals is simply not as beneficial to human health as eating plants.

In developing countries, immense effort is spent in attempting to find ways to reduce poverty and hunger. One of the components of this is, of course, the type of food the people in these countries produce and consume. It has been standard policy for all projects and assistance by organizations, whose efforts are directed at improving food security, to keep livestock in the center of agricultural considerations. Researchers and welfare organizations generally feel that grazing, pastoral cattle, sheep, and goats, as well as chickens and animal products such as milk and eggs, must be kept in alignment with existing cultural practices and improved upon in order to make progress regarding poverty and hunger. Additionally, these support groups are still under the false assumption that meat, dairy, and eggs are highly nutritious and provide health benefits to those who are malnourished, often asking, "Where would they get their protein?" This is especially true as it applies to many African countries. I feel there are two reasons for this: (1) culture in many countries is complex and interwoven into many aspects of their life, so it becomes something more easily left alone than improved upon or evolved from; and (2) eating meat is part of the culture and belief system of the researchers and organizations themselves. *How could researchers and advisors conceive of another approach to solving hunger and poverty if their own food choices include eating animals?*

In the past decade, the largest increases in livestock production have been in developing countries. This is expected to continue and is driven by demand for animal-source foods, rising affluence, and shifting livestock land use from developed to developing countries. Demand for livestock products will likely double in sub-Saharan Africa and South Asia by 2050 (FAO). Globally, livestock production has responded to increased demand by changing from extensive, small-scale, subsistence livestock production to more intensive, large-scale, commercially oriented production. Whether with industrialized production or simply increased units of smallholder farmers raising livestock, this will eventually translate into more land use, more climate change, more hunger, more poverty, and more global depletion.

Organic trends

The most optimal manner in which to approach agriculture with our planet's finite and diminishing resources is to produce as much of the healthiest food possible, using the least amount of space, water, and energy, while emitting the very fewest amount of GHGs and waste. The only food items that fit this description are plants. Animal products have been shown to be some of the most unhealthy food products, using the highest amount of land, water, and energy to produce, while emitting the highest amount of GHGs and waste.

While organic farming methods related to crop production have been proven to build soil and are much more beneficial to long-term yields and soil health than conventional farming techniques, this is not the case with organic methods related to grazing pasture, which mandates a much greater burden on land area use and inefficient food production.

Time for permaculture?

Permaculture is a term derived from the words "permanent" and "agriculture." While the word implies good intent, recent use of it has been inaccurately associated with sustainability. This is primarily because those who employ permaculture methods of food production (called "permaculturists") are doing so in an attempt to achieve sustainability, but the majority still incorporate animal husbandry into their operations, which then casts them into a state of being less sustainable than those culturing only plants.

By their own definition, permaculture is an approach to agricultural systems that replaces industrial methods with small farms that renew natural resources and work within healthy ecosystems. Introduction of pigs, cattle, chickens or any other domesticated animals into this model contradicts their own fundamental objective, but it is nevertheless adopted by way of rigidly cemented pre-existing taste preferences and cultural tendencies.

The practice of modern-day permaculture most likely began with Sepp Holzer, who, in 1962, developed a more natural approach to agriculture and pioneered the use of ecological farming at high altitudes in Austria. He was termed the "rebel farmer" because of his unconventional practices of not pruning his fruit trees (he understood that unpruned fruit trees in the Alps withstand snow loads without breaking branches), use of ponds as reflectors to increase solar gain for passive solar heating, and creating microclimates by rock outcrops to effectively change the hardiness zone for plants nearby. Although there are some variations on permaculture models, my perspective is formed by comparing the many small farms I visited in Switzerland and Austria, using the techniques established by Holzer, with those found elsewhere in the world that purport to ascribe to the same principles. Holzer's Krameterhof Farm comprises 45 hectares of forest gardens, 70 ponds, and intercropping of plants (multiple seed types) in a manner that most efficiently uses the land, resources, and restrictive growing conditions present. Based on my discussions with Holzer, I think he has the right idea, in that he centers his farming techniques around the following objectives:

1. All food should be unprocessed and ultimately be derived from the soil, water, and sun.

2. Modify the growing conditions in as natural a manner as possible to optimize those factors that are essential, such as the use of ponds for solar gain by reflection, development of microclimates by the use of outcropping of rocks, and terracing.

3. Give attention to plants as the primary food source with layered

or stacked agroforestry, competing polyculture of plantings (seeds planted together that have variations in pH, moisture, sunlight requirements), use of perennials instead of annuals, and increased culturing of wildlife and renaturalization areas.

4. Focus on animals for the work they do—such as horses or pigs to help till and/or cultivate crops, chickens to assist with insect control—not on their ultimate slaughter and use for food.

This model works well for him but it would need adaptation to other areas of the world; for instance, in arid locations or in western states of the U.S., where there is less water available.

One primary misconception in permaculture theory occurs with the inclusion of animals—that idea that manure from domesticated animals is needed for soil fertility and then that these same animals should be killed and eaten. If one's goal as a proprietor of a small farm or permaculture site were to be a steward of our planet (on a daily basis, essentially farming with the most sound ecological techniques), then raising animals would not fit at all—even raising just one cow—because of excessive land use.

Permaculture, in this sense, applies to small-scale, perhaps single-owner farm operations that produce food mostly for their own use, but it also can apply to small-scale commercial operations—the type that grows food for other consumers. Whether in a cooperative setting, direct sales, or through brokerage systems to larger distribution outlets, this will be the method that should eventually replace our current industrial agriculture systems.

A more modern version of permaculture, with some variability, can be seen with Polyface Farms in Virginia's Shenandoah Valley, where owner Joel Salatin raises numerous small and large animals for food purposes, under the guise of sustainability. Polyface has recently been highly publicized as the way farming should be accomplished in the U.S., but instead of adopting Sepp Holzer's approach of optimizing use of the land with primarily plant-based growing solutions, Salatin promotes animals and animal products. Their marketing efforts proudly emphasize the production of "Salad Bar Beef, Pigaerator Pork, Pastured Poultry (eggs, broilers, turkeys), and Forage-

Based Rabbits." Polyface Farms has had a great deal of publicity, beginning with Michael Pollan's endorsement, subsequent media coverage, and self-promotion. It is a shame to see the wrong message being sent by Salatin and his Polyface model—that their products are sustainable and healthy.

Salatin's concept of an Americanized version of permaculture as being the route we must take as we move away from impersonal, industrialized farming is appealing. Looking very closely at his operations, though, one can see that as of 2011, instead of 100 acres declared in use, Polyface is actually using 450 acres for the farm's immediate operations. When this is taken properly into account, knowing that much of the wooded areas are used for transitional penning of pigs, the annual land efficiency use is still at around one cow produced per acre, or 480 pounds of "edible" parts. This is despite his claims that he can manage "a hundred cows on an acre of pasture," which is in reality employs techniques such as mob grazing (turning his entire herd into a 1- to 2-acre area for a short time to eat) or juvenile crop rotation.

Another statement heard frequently from Mr. Salatin is "the average acre-cow-day for Polyface is 400, while the average in this area is 80." This means that, although the "400" figure is unsubstantiated, if true, 1 acre of pasture would be required to feed one cow for a period of 400 days, or about one year.

But when everything else is considered, the ratios are still quite clear. There is no doubt that Mr. Salatin believes he is making the very best use of his land with raising an assortment of livestock. Also, there is no doubt that if he chose to modify operations to use his land *without* raising livestock, concentrating only on plant-based foods and with proper organic techniques, he could produce per acre between 5,000 and 30,000 pounds of plant foods that are much more nutritious than the 480 pounds he is currently realizing with animal products. And there would be no greenhouse gas emissions, unnecessary water usage (22,000 gallons per cow over a two-year period of time), and needless slaughtering. Many people now use or support Mr. Salatin's concepts in an attempt to convey what they feel is the most appropriate, "fully sustainable" method of producing food—but it is not.

There are only three primary reasons that permaculturists and Polyface Farms proponents feel it is necessary to incorporate raising animals into a permaculture setting. They think that:

- animal products eaten for food are healthy for us to consume.
- animals are needed for their manure to be assured of proper soil fertility.
- animals are essentially an organic method of controlling weeds and insects.

My reasons for not including animals in small farm/permaculture settings are as follows:

1. Animal products are not healthy for us to consume. This conclusion is now convincingly supported by literature, science, and epidemiological studies.
2. Plant products are the healthiest foods for us to consume. This is also heavily supported by numerous studies.
3. Producing plant foods creates a much more efficient use of land at 10 to 100 times more food per acre than animal products (15 times more protein).
4. Soil fertility can actually be better achieved through the proper use of plants, not animals.
5. Any fresh water used should be for our direct and conservative use, not given to animals.
6. There is no need to add greenhouse gases to our atmosphere.
7. There is wasted energy, time, water, and lives in the slaughtering process of any animal.

Polyface Farms may appear to be "sustainable" because it is sustaining the Salatin family and a circle of customers from an economic and food volume standpoint. With the focus on raising animals to produce meat, however, Salatin is promoting unsustainable food production systems and a philosophy wrought with lack of awareness and misleading virtues as evidenced by their statement of purpose:

"We are in the redemption business: healing the land, healing the food, healing the economy, and healing the culture. Writing, speaking, and farm tours offer various message venues. Experience the satisfaction of knowing your food and your farmer, building community. We are your clean meat connection."

Raising livestock on marginal land

I often hear the argument that livestock can be raised by letting them graze on otherwise marginal or unusable land, eating foliage where nothing else can grow.

This is a curious thought because edible plants for humans can be grown in the most challenging climates and soils—basically, anywhere. Certainly, wherever cattle can comfortably live and where plants for them can grow, we can grow plants for us to eat.

For centuries, American Indian tribes have collected and eaten wild plants native to what would seem to be inhospitable desert areas in southern Arizona. These include leaves, fruit, flowers, and roots. In what would appear to be non-fertile sand throughout the desert and dry areas of the Southwest, we can find edible plants, such as the saguaro and cacti apple, sunflowers, velvet mesquite, green amaranth, chuparosa, desert lily, desert lavender, and even scrubby shrubs like the soaptree yucca and roots such as wild carrot. If the American Indian tribes of our Southwest had decided to allow cattle to graze, they most likely would have exhausted any plant food source for themselves.[69]

Plants such as buckwheat are quite hardy, thriving in very poor soil conditions and living through freezing temperatures, droughts, and excess rain. Buckwheat is gluten-free and contains high amounts of lysine and all eight essential amino acids. It is highly nutritious and provides one of the highest amounts of rutin (a powerful phytonutrient) of any source. Rye and barley are capable of growing in harsh conditions, and quinoa (technically a fruit) has been grown by the Incas for more than 5,000 years in and around the Andes, at altitudes as high as 12,000 feet. Quinoa is quite a rugged plant and has been known to grow in extremely dry, hostile conditions, even where grass will not grow.

There are a number of grains, leguminous plants, and food-producing shrubs and trees that can be grown in extremes of temperatures and water conditions, displaying overall more hardiness, pest resistance, and soil-building characteristics than conventional plants. Growing these types of plants would serve "unusable" land much better than subjecting it to grazing cattle.

Harsh agricultural conditions and a complexity of overlapping social and economic challenges in many regions have made them more vulnerable to the effects of climate change. More than two-thirds of the land in many developing countries in Africa has become highly eroded and desertified. The solution to many of these problems lies in a concerted effort to restore lands, which now seem harsh and inhospitable, with forests, wildlife, and indigenous plants such as cassava, pomme du sahel, shea nut, soursop, okra, and other leguminous plants—all of which can be grown on land made "unusable" by trampling livestock.[70]

Saving the world with livestock—the Savory approach

A number of hurdles obstruct the path of evolution toward more sustainable, peaceful food production systems. One such hurdle is the perpetuation of belief that sustainability can be achieved if we simply modify our current animal production systems. Many authors, scientists, and organizations are happy to spread this message and have ample perceived public platform to do so. This invariably leads to distortion of reality, suppression of facts, and an appeased global audience still clinging to some form of justification for eating meat.

With two annual conferences and worldwide acclaim, the TED talks have brought audiences "Ideas Worth Spreading" since 1984. During one of these talks in February 2013, which garnered a standing ovation, Allan Savory—a Zimbabwean biologist, farmer, and environmentalist—argued that grazing livestock is the answer to our global population explosion, climate change, and restoring the many lands that are turning to desert. In his twenty-two-minute talk, he dramatically built the case that two-thirds of the world is desertifying (becoming desert-like with the loss of all topsoil and fertility) and that the only option we have to solve this "perfect storm" is to "do the unthinkable—to use livestock bunched and moving as a proxy for former herds and predators to mimic nature. There is no other alternative for mankind."

Mr. Savory uses these profound remarks to introduce us to his work with the Savory Institute and their attempts to restore desertified grasslands with what he calls "holistic management and planned grazing"— essentially a form of short-term grassland management or intensified rotational pasturing techniques, now employed by many grass-fed operations and permaculturists. According to Savory, using large herds of cattle "addresses all of nature's complexity and our social, environmental, economic concerns."

Savory's TED talk was compelling and certainly provided what all carnivores wanted to hear (hence, the standing ovation). Nevertheless, it was riddled with inconsistencies and unsupported claims, and it suppressed key information in a calculated manner.

Two distinct misrepresentations characterized his talk: (1) that desertification is an isolated problem by itself; and (2) that increasing livestock production in affected areas of habitat loss will solve the problem of desertification. Perhaps the more significant of the two is the very precept from which he built his case—that desertification is a stand-alone concern, impacting food security and our future survival. It is actually a manifestation or side effect of something else—deforestation, which is a by-product of our choice of foods.

Aside from naturally occurring deserts, which are healthy components of our earth's varied ecosystems and habitats, there are two forms of man-made deserts—those that were once primary ancient grasslands/savannas and those that were once forests. Grasslands are being lost at an alarming rate. However, of much larger concern is that most grasslands were once forests, and we are cutting down forests at a rate of 30 million acres per year, globally. Another 20 to 30 million acres of forests are being degraded (destroyed by thinning and creating roads and disruptive corridors). These deforested areas are eventually converted to grasslands for cattle or for cultivating crops to feed livestock. Savory focused the audience's attention to a NASA aerial photograph of the world, and he highlighted regions that are most affected by desertification—the Amazon basin, numerous countries in Africa, and temperate regions in Asia—but he failed to mention that nearly all of those areas were once forests, now turned into pastures for cattle. Nearly 90 percent of the deforested areas of the Amazon are the result of the meat and dairy industries. These deforested areas then become eroded and eventually desertified, losing valuable topsoil along the way.

The problem at hand is that we eat meat. Eating meat causes demand to raise more livestock, which is a miserably inefficient use of land as well as other natural resources, requiring from 2 to 20 acres to support just one cow. Therefore, in the pursuit for more land, raising livestock causes deforestation. Deforestation then causes erosion and topsoil loss, which then causes desertification. If we stopped deforestation, we would stop desertification. If we stopped eating meat, we would stop deforestation as well as loss of ancient grasslands.

Savory provided the audience with examples of restored land using his livestock and grazing techniques in Africa, Argentina, and Mexico. Argentina, though, has lost over 66 percent of all its forests over the past seventy-five years, with current deforestation rates at 210,000 acres per year. Over 40 percent of all plant and animal species are negatively impacted in that country. Zimbabwe, where most of Savory's studies have been conducted, is destroying their forests at a rate of 1 percent per year, which doesn't sound impressive, but they have already lost more than 85 percent of their original forests, primarily due to raising livestock. Desertification is occurring as a by-product of this deforestation as well as combined with subsequent pastoral herding. Savory states the cause of desertification is somewhat a "mystery." But the primary cause is due to grazing livestock. It is no mystery.

Closer examination of Savory's techniques of holistic management reveals they do not work as well as he states. His idea of "mimicking nature" is to place up to 400 percent higher cattle density in small, desertified areas of grasslands and rotate them in an attempt to replicate the movement and soil compaction by hooves of massive ancient herds of grazing animals. Numerous authors have studied the effect of Savory's and similar methods in Africa and North America and have demonstrated that, in most cases, short-duration grazing "reduced individual cattle productivity due to stress from heavy stocking and movement of cattle" and that these methods "do not provide a unique means to favorably modify rangeland composition." [71,72,73] When compared to rotational grazing, studies have shown that conventional continuous grazing methods displayed greater plant health and production in 87 percent of the cases.[74]

Although Savory proclaims worldwide success of his methods, it is the consensus of many researchers that intensive rotation grazing (such as the Savory technique) as a means to increase vegetation and animal production "has been subjected to as rigorous a testing regime as any hypothesis in the rangeland profession, and it has been found to convey few, if any, consistent benefits over continuous grazing." Drawing that conclusion in 2008 after comprehensive review of a number of studies, Dr. David Briske from Texas A&M and other researchers added in their synthesis paper, "It is unlikely that researcher oversight or bias has contributed to this conclusion, given the large number of grazing experiments, investigators, and geographic locations involved over a span of six decades."[75]

Studies by the chief of field and pasture extension in Zimbabwe (Gammon 1984) and others (Vaughan-Evans, 1978) compared the Savory Grazing Method (SGM) to less intensive management and showed that Savory's methods were "not superior to less intensively managed areas." One study pointed out that during an eight-year period of time, where SGM showed some degree of success, there happened to be an unusual amount of rainfall (50 percent above normal for that area), which likely boosted any positive results Savory had recorded. Within two subsequent years of normal rainfall, continued use of SGM produced an observed progressive deterioration in pastures and animal performance.[76]

Savory argues that many desertified areas of the world can only be used to grow animals, not plants, to feed people, suggesting that there are no alternatives to eating meat for people living in these areas. One of these areas Savory uses as an example is the Greater Horn of Africa (GHA), which comprises eight countries and covers 6 million square kilometers. The entire region has experienced severe conflict and disturbances in some form in the past decade, and it is one of the most highly desertified regions in the world, having lost more than two-thirds of its topsoil. Here, Savory argues that providing them with livestock is the only hope they have of saving their families because, as he states, "95 percent of the land in the GHA can only feed people from animals." Savory's approach for this region would be to raise livestock in massive numbers to help restore pastures and then slaughter them to help feed people. Typically, these areas are drought-ridden and the people plagued by poverty, hunger, and illiteracy. It would make more sense to optimize sustainability by producing a type of food that is the most efficient to grow—least water usage, no GHG emissions, least land needed, and healthiest for humans to consume. When compared to plants, raising livestock seems illogical. Wherever pasture can grow or be restored to feed livestock, other plants could be grown as well to be eaten directly by humans. It's interesting to note that livestock already occupy 44 percent of the total land surface of the eight GHA countries and are directly responsible for use of the sparse natural resources available for their human population. The country of Eritrea, for instance, has a human population of 5 million people yet is using their sparse resources to support 6 million cattle, sheep, and goats. Ethiopia is cutting down 25,000 acres of their forests each year in order to make more room for their growing herd of livestock, now the largest in Africa, while their human population suffers from lack of food. It's quite clear that use of sparse and dwindling natural resources for livestock in the GHA is essentially choking the struggling human population. Yet Savory's plan would be to add more livestock to the region.

And then there is the problem with loss of biodiversity. Savory has not addressed how he plans to restore loss of the ecosystems and plants, animals, and insects that were originally present *before* livestock ruined the landscape. When he places cattle and livestock into an area that has been deforested and now desertified, what is the plan to bring back the natural, indigenous flora and fauna?

Many desertified areas, including those in semi-arid regions, would be much healthier and more productive if restored in a resource-efficient manner with indigenous drought-resistant plants, agroforestry, implementing terracing and other organic methods, or plant-generated microbiological measures, rather than with livestock. One of these measures is the reintroduction in desertified land of arbuscular mycorrhizal fungus (AMF) and various plants, such as legumes, which then form a highly evolved mutualistic relationship. This is one of many complex symbiotic interactions lost when cattle are introduced to an area.

Forests and reforestation provide the following categories of health to the environment with the absence of cattle or other livestock:

- Diverse non-timber forest products, including herbs
- Edible plants
- Fruit
- Coffee
- Tea
- Gums
- Resins

It also provides ecosystem services such as:

- Watershed protection (natural control of water, reduction of erosion)
- Maintenance of biodiversity and conservation (species of plants, animals, and insects)
- Carbon sequestration
- Balance of atmospheric oxygen

There is another way, then, to mimic nature—by truly mimicking nature. Adding domesticated cattle to desertified landscape as a measure to compensate for our mistakes of decimating the normal flora and fauna over the decades creates many issues. Savory's methods may indeed restore some desertified grasslands but so would plant-based food production systems or simply reintroducing the original natural blend of species (plants, animals, insects, microbes).

Wherever Savory speaks, he conveniently fails to mention that deforestation and degradation of tropical forests and subsequent transformation to pasture are the primary global reasons for initializing erosion, decreasing soil fertility, and eventual desertification and heavy contribution to climate change. Prevention, therefore, is key, not acting in a retrospective manner with concepts that confuse industries, agriculturalists, and consumers.

If "mimicking nature" is what he desires, then Savory should consider reintroducing the 10 million acres of forests lost each year in Africa (part of the 4.5 billion total acres lost globally over the past few hundred years), primarily due to the introduction of livestock. He should add the correct number and density of wildebeests and other grazing mammals that were lost due to deforestation—add the 140,000 lions, leopards, and other predators back into the equation and all other wildlife and biodiversity that has been destroyed over the years by human activities—*that* would "mimic nature." [77]

From 1955, when he served as game ranger/officer in Northern and Luapula provinces of Rhodesia (now Zambia), through 1969, Savory supervised the killing of game animals and advocated the mass culling of elephants and hippos, convinced that they were destroying the habitat. Savory was also a farmer, game rancher, consultant, officer in the Game Department, and politician based in Southern Rhodesia (now Zimbabwe). As such, he called for a project to slaughter more than 40,000 elephants— until it came under heavy criticism when officials realized that these gentle, innocent giants were not the problem. [78] While Savory was arguing for a calculated slaughtering of animals, others, such as Lawton and Gough, were suggesting that elephants were not the problem at all. Rather, it was the repeated burning or human-induced fires in the dry season (from slash-and-burn/swidden agricultural methods) that might be the real reason for desertification. At the time, R. M. Lawton was an ecologist with the Land

Resources Division of the British Directorate of Overseas Surveys, and Mrs. Gough was a skilled observer of animal behavior in Zambia.[79]

There is the question of motives behind Savory's advocacy for increasing cattle and livestock production. He states that he loves elephants, yet slaughters them. He loves wildlife yet kills them. He refers to the indigenous people of Zimbabwe as "drum beaters" and offers us his own bias of the human scale of intelligence in the statement "Everyone knows this, from Nobel Prize laureates to golf caddies."

Savory's holistic management or "mimicking nature" philosophy appears to be merely a facade of many sorts, since his operation and overriding objectives are in full support of increasing the meat and dairy industries. This is evidenced by his stated philosophy, which is supported by every program with which he's been involved in the U.S. and developing countries over the years. His leading team members (director of research and all co-founders of the Savory Institute) are derived entirely from the meat and dairy industry. Most of them own and continue to operate very large cattle and other livestock ranches for the purpose of slaughtering, selling, and eating meat, not necessarily to improve their own grasslands.

According to Savory:

"If we just do it on half the world's grasslands I've shown you we can take us back to pre-industrial levels [of GHG] while feeding people. I can think of almost nothing that offers more hope for our planet, for your children and their children and all of humanity."

Restoration in this sense is complex and insidious. It is true that mob/rotational grazing by livestock could help selected, previously desertified areas in certain developing countries. But it comes with a price undisclosed by Savory or other permaculturists—misdirected resource use. The same land used for grazing could be used for producing plant foods for humans to eat directly. Water is being used for livestock, rather than directly by humans. There is an increase in GHG emissions, disposition (slaughtering) at the end of the animals' tenure, and production of a food product that is much less healthy to eat than any of a number of plants that could have been grown. On its surface, Savory's process may look attractive, but it obscures the Savory Institute's objective of feeding a certain portion of the world with increased meat and dairy products by way of herd management of desertification.

It is difficult for Savory or any "expert" to see beyond his own limiting factors of cultural influences—if he eats meat and promotes its production, it will be difficult for him to accept concepts that call for its elimination. Yet this is a perfect example of the type of argument to which we will be continually subjected, wrongly influencing the masses, as we journey toward a healthier planet. It's time the TED talks consider *not* spreading at least one of their "Ideas Worth Spreading."

A view of some of the many small, local, organic farms considered "sustainable"

As I traveled and visited numerous fish or livestock farms in the world, an interesting phenomenon was readily seen. Whether farming conventionally or in a grass-fed/pasture manner, each farm operator typically believes he is doing exactly the right thing regarding food—for our planet and for the customers who ultimately consume these animal products. I found a vivid example of this in the United Kingdom, where two farming neighbors both believed quite strongly that they were "sustainable." One was a grass-fed operation, Vowley Farm, the owner of which stood adamantly by this contention; and the other, living immediately next door, was a conventional family-owned dairy farm operation, where the cows never saw daylight and lived in congested, dingy confinement—both owners felt exactly the same way!

UK author Rick Stein wrote about Vowley Farm and owner Mark Stanton in his book *Local Food Heroes of Great Britain*, proclaiming the virtues of this grass-fed paradise, referring to Mr. Stanton as a "Food Superhero" because of Vowley's commitment to raising animals in a pastured "natural" setting. Mr. Stein was most impressed by Vowley Farm's entire operation but "especially that we care for the animals from birth, right through to sale, doing much of the butchery as well, and everyone raves about the taste of the meat."

Vowley Farm, near Swindon in southwest England, is small, comprising 110 acres—all used for the raising of pastured animals, including British White cows, Gloucester Old Spots pigs, Norfolk Black turkeys, and Ixworth chickens. The cows are rotated between four fields, 3 to 10 acres each, every two to six weeks until the winter months of November through February, when they are then kept indoors in small quarters. These cows are kept for thirty-four months before being slaughtered. Pigs are bought from another farm at two months and raised in 30x50-foot outdoor pasture areas, surrounded electrified fence. These Gloucester pigs are kept there and fed a mix of soybeans, barley, and goat whey until they are eight months old, at which time they are slaughtered. Turkeys are purchased elsewhere and then brought to the farm as six-week-old chicks in May, raised for six months, and then slaughtered just before Christmas as part of the cultural ritual. All chickens are similarly kept for about nine months to one year prior to slaughtering them for meat. Regarding his thoughts on sustainability, he is "aspiring to be biodynamic not organic and is using homeopathy instead of conventional veterinarian medicine."

Outspoken proponents of these types of local, small, organic livestock farms feel this form of producing animals for us to eat is "sustainable," when the individual farmers, if pressed, can present quite a different view.

When asked how his operations fit with local and global sustainability as a model, Mr. Stanton replied adamantly, "*Nothing* that we do on this farm is sustainable, because it uses too much land, and there are too many people in the world. We can't possibly feed enough people with the way we are doing things."

This is even though Mr. Stanton feels his operations are as "sustainable as one can find." When discussing water use with his farm manager, Dougal, who came to Vowley in 2006 as part of the WWOOF (World Wide Opportunities on Organic Farms—a volunteer work experience) efforts, they explained, "Ninety-five percent of all the water used on the farm is for cows, and if you had to give water to them by hand some days, it's quite depressing how much water they use."

All cows are given names except for some of the males, "who are not given names because they go off to slaughter." Dougal also commented, "I'm a cow person; we talk to each other." A bit earlier in the conversation back at the house he had stated, "At time of slaughter, all of the cows and pigs are stunned with a bolt gun to the head and then their necks are slit, and they are bled to death." When I asked how he felt about this regarding the humane factor, the response was, "You can't be too sure, but they all should be unconscious with the bolt to the head." All carcasses are kept in their cold room, storing until being sold locally.

Dougal explained that all chickens and turkeys are slaughtered on site by "hitting them hard over the head with a club, then breaking their necks." Then they are bled and plucked. Dougal admits that the rendering "unconscious" state for these birds is "iffy."

Regarding their pigs, it is stated on their website: "Pigs are amazing animals. They express a deep satisfaction for life and all that it presents. When you sit with them, they will come and greet you, and you will hear a contented grunt as they root around." In conversation, both Dougal and Mark referred to their pigs as "smart," "clean," and "very social." Additionally, Dougal wanted me to know that they "pay careful attention to have the pigs sent off to be slaughtered two or three at a time with their best buddies, who they play with every day because they are so social." The paradox created becomes more pronounced when reading another statement from the Vowley Farm website: "They get big very quickly and produce sausages and bacon worth getting out of bed for!" This odd behavior of naming and petting each of these individuals and marveling at their social skills and sensitivities, while then shooting them in the head, slicing their throats, and eating them is baffling to me. Is this the manner in which our land should be used to produce food?

While the Vowley Farm considers itself "as sustainable as possible," working with organic, grass-fed, free-range/pasture methods immediately adjacent to them, I found the Mark and Ian Beven Dairy Farm works under small, conventional, CAFO methods. While operating under fundamentally opposite precepts, the Beven brothers feel they are producing "very sustainable" animal products.

Together, they own 120 acres, which are used to house their cows and primary dairy operations with another 150 acres under a lease contract, which are used for producing crops to feed the cows. This leased land is also used to pile and spread manure because they exceed the allowable amount of waste on their 120 acres. Regulatory officials dictated that the Bevens "needed somewhere else to put it."

Their father and mother started the dairy farm in 1972. Today, Mark and Ian have 140 dairy cows and 150 young stock (of which twenty-nine are male calves for beef) less than two years old. At two, they can reproduce and begin to produce milk until the age of eight, when they are less efficient (feed conversion ratio lessens) and then are "fattened quickly and slaughtered." The dairy cows produce 110 to 130 calves per year, half of which get put back into the herd as "milkers" and the other half are killed for veal at a young age.

Mark admitted to using between 60 to 90 liters of water per day per cow for drinking purposes and 10,000 liters per cow per year for cleanup. Total water use is 18 to 20 cubic meters per day for the farm, which equates to over 5,200 gallons of water each day for drinking purposes of the cows. All of this is metered water (20 cubic meters per day is the county's legal limit). With each of their dairy cows producing three to five gallons of milk per day, their farm—considered one of the more "sustainable" small, local dairy operations—still requires fifteen gallons of drinking water per one gallon of milk produced. This is in addition to the water needed for irrigation of the alfalfa and feed grain fed to each cow each day, amounting to another 250 to 300 gallons per gallon of milk produced.

This operation houses its cows all year long, feeling "it is secure this way." But 30 percent of the entire herd had to be killed due to contracting bovine viral diarrhea. The owners admitted that 50 percent of the herd has the condition in some capacity right now.

Mark and Ian feel quite strongly that their operations are "sustainable" and that they are using feed by-products and the land as ethically as possible, with "ecology in mind." The owners also feel that they are using manure to spread "for the environment." Also, they acknowledged that one cow requires 8 tons of dry food to eat per year and that 1 acre of land will produce 4 tons of grain, so it takes 2 full acres of land to feed one cow. They feel that "grass is not a complete food on its own, so these [cows] are fed protein extracts, sugar beet pulp, and wheat residues."

Klesick Farms in the Pacific Northwest raises cattle "as efficiently as anyone could," explained the directors of Cascade Fresh Harvest Coalition. A small operation but viewed by many experts as the type of farm we should promote in the U.S., Klesick raises twenty cows per 26 acres, purchases them at six to nine months old, keeps them from April through October, rotates pastures, and slaughters them on site. (He leads six to eight of them to the edge of the fence with grain to eat, Klesick related to me, and then "my hired local butcher drives right up to the fenced-in area with his butcher truck and kills them by shooting each one in the head, slices their necks to bleed, and then drives the carcasses off to cut up. It's pretty efficient." Customers can pick up the parts they pre-purchased at the butcher's cooler, such as "ribs, rear, tongue, head, etc." There is no USDA jurisdiction for the slaughtering, because the carcasses never cross state lines and the dead animals are distributed to the cooperative owners who pre-purchased them. The cattle slaughtered range in size but average carcass weight for sale of "meat" is 450 pounds, which would equate to around 346 pounds of meat per acre of land used. Water is given to the cows from city main lines. Klesick has "no idea how much water is given to the cows. They just drink it, and I give it to them." He considers himself a "steward of the land." Many vegetable farms in the area produce between 2,000 pounds and 15,000 pounds of product per acre.

Andrew Stout sits in a supervisory capacity for numerous boards for the furthering of produce in the Cascadian area and owns Full Circle, an organic vegetable operation in the state of Washington. His vegetable operations (using land near the Klesick small livestock farm) is producing over 2 million pounds of sixty different types of produce on 354 acres, spread out over three locations in the county. This equates to 6,415 pounds per acre of organic produce.

Growers of organic beans that serve as suppliers to Eden (the largest processor of organic beans in the world), across Michigan and neighboring states, generally recognize yields of 2,000 to 3,000 pounds of beans per acre (pinto, black, garbanzo, navy, adzuki, kidney) and never use irrigation—no depletion of water. Many of these farms are located in the same county, with exactly the same growing conditions as farms that are engaged in grass-fed beef or dairy operations that use land and water at the rate of 2 to 5 acres and up to 1 million gallons of water per cow per year—all while emitting 3 to 4 tons of methane and carbon dioxide per cow before slaughter.

And so it seems to be, farm after farm across the U.S. and in developed countries—factory farms predominate operations and volume, and the vast majority of small and medium operations are family owned, producing what many supporters feel is "very sustainable" food, although the operators know it may not be. But they continue raising animals and manufacturing animal products at the expense of our land and freshwater resources.

It is no longer a factory-farm issue; it's a raising-animals-to-eat issue.
Agriculture, whether land- or water-based, can no longer be viewed as simply an act to produce food. As a process, agriculture is now intertwined with many other concerns, such as national and international economics and the societal effects of gender and culture. No concerns are as crucial, however, as the effect agricultural systems have on our planet's ecosystems, natural resources, and our own health. With efforts to produce more food at less cost, concentrated animal feed operations (CAFOs), known as "factory farms," and agribusiness (industrial farming) have become the modus operandi for much of the world's food production. This is certainly true in developed countries and now over 90 percent of all animals raised globally are raised in confined settings. Initially, in the United States, chickens led the way, by being the first animals to be raised indoors in confined conditions during the early 1900s. With the use of newly discovered vitamins, antibiotics, and vaccines, growers began producing more animals in less space, while expanding operations

to include cows, pigs, and other animals by the 1960s. At the same time, chemicals developed for use during World War II began serving as synthetic pesticides and added to a mounting armamentarium of new herbicides and chemical fertilization methods to artificially increase soil nutrient needs for short-term increases in crop yields. By the turn of the twenty-first century, the entire food production system in the U.S. had been morphed into what we see today, with large agribusinesses growing most of what we eat and raising animals and also the grain to feed them—with heavy economic support in the form of government subsidizing. Seed companies such as Monsanto, Cargill, and ADM are increasingly controlling which crops are grown by way of vertically integrating research, production, and distribution within their own organizations. Monsanto produces 70 percent of all genetically engineered (GE) crops grown worldwide, while ADM and Cargill control 65 percent of the global grain market through their combined control of vast shares. On its surface, it appears that the cumulative effort of these large businesses has been able to provide, by way of efficiency of scale, more food at a lower price than small independent farmers. However, the true cost of raising this food to our environment, to displacement of smaller operations, and to our own health has been externalized, for which we all will ultimately have to pay. But it is not the method of production in raising and harvesting animals that is the essence of the problem; it is the very product itself.

Our current agricultural systems have been established and are being perpetuated by the type of food we are demanding to eat. Our food choices, in turn, have been shaped and strengthened by numerous influences—cultural, political, economic, and social. Our farmers—those who actually produce those items we eat—are then subject to molding by the massive collective influence of many factors; they are essentially chess pieces in the game of food production. The techniques employed by our farming community in order to accomplish the economic demands placed on them have caused the loss of one-third of all topsoil in the U.S. (it requires 500 years to replace one inch of topsoil), irreversible (in our lifetime) depletion of ice-age aquifers such as the Ogallala, significant contribution to climate change, the destruction of natural habitat and wildlife, an increase in many disease states, and a health care crisis. Agriculture occupies 55 percent of the land in the contiguous United States but *livestock* and the crops grown to feed them occupy 78 percent of that agricultural land. Conversion of ecosystems types into farming landscapes has significantly impacted many species, taking its toll on biodiversity. Habitat loss from land conversion is the leading cause of species endangerment and extinction in the U.S. and globally. According to USGS, 98 percent of the native prairie in the Midwest and elsewhere has been converted to livestock grazing and feed crops.

Globally, 60 percent of the total available pastureland (45 percent of all land, in general) is covered by grazing systems—animals plus pasture for them. These grazing systems supply 9 percent of the world's production of beef and about 30 percent of the production of sheep and goat meat. These startling figures make sense because of the heavy land use requirement for each animal raised and ratio of protein per acre realistically attainable as an end product.

You might ask, "But isn't the system of raising grass-fed livestock sustainable?" This question is frequently posed and may likely be one of the keys to our future on Earth. The answer we are beginning to hear most often is "Yes, grass-fed livestock is very sustainable." Popular author/activist Michael Pollan, voted as one of the world's 100 most influential people by *Time* magazine, gave this particular response and was heard by 23 million viewers when he appeared on the *The Oprah Winfrey Show* in 2010.

Eating meat from grass-fed livestock, along with fish, dairy products, and eggs, becomes a natural path for most people who want so badly to hang on to the false sense of "needing" versus simply "wanting" to eat animal products. It is the path of least resistance, replete with misinformation and layered in cultural and social influences. The concept of migrating toward grass-fed livestock is understandable, in that it is much easier for the general public to accept—much easier than the more obvious evolutionary need to move away from eating animals altogether.[80]

The local small farm and grass-fed livestock movement is quickly gaining momentum, in part due to the promotion by various and quite visible organizations, as well as by authors and lecturers such as Mark

Bittman, Joel Salatin, Michael Pollan, Jonathan Safran Foer, and many others. On its surface, this movement appears to be a remedy for much of what they assert is wrong with our current agricultural practices. They claim that if consumers demanded that meat now be raised on small family farms and on pastures, it would accomplish many things. *According to them,* it would:

- create a more "sustainable" way for food to be produced.
- result in less pollution.
- provide a "healthier" type of meat.
- break down the economic monopoly of our current large agrobusinesses in support of the local and small farmer.
- establish an entirely humane way for animals to still be used for food.

Let's look more closely, though, at this list. The *proponents* of raising grass-fed animals feel that factory farms are the entire problem—that once we move away from them, all will be solved. This belief is entirely at odds with what the individual owners/farmers of grass-fed operations are stating with regard to their awareness of the gross land-use inefficiencies of their own operations), as well as what actually will occur as our agricultural systems move away from factory farms and toward grass-fed systems. It's ironic that those who are merely advocates of the grass-fed movement—authors, lecturers, politicians, the media, the public—do not have a true grasp on the impact of the movement they are supporting. Yet, they are the ones influencing us.

In reality, this is what will happen as a move is made away from factory farms toward grass-fed livestock. There will be:

- less grain used.
- less fossil fuel used.
- less pollution that occurs in a concentrated fashion (same amount of waste but spread out over a larger area).
- less pain and suffering by the animals, but only while they are being raised.

At the same time, though, raising grass-fed cattle and other livestock will also do the following:

- Increase greenhouse gas emissions, worsening climate change.
- Vastly increase the inefficient use of the minimal land we have left on Earth.
- Increase the rate of global biodiversity loss (plants, animals, insects) due to an increase in loss of habitat and disruption of natural food chains.
- Further contribute to world hunger.
- Continue the unnecessary depletion and inefficient use of our scarce freshwater sources.
- Perpetuate our own ill health by eating these animal products.
- Add to our existing national health care crisis, insurance inequities, and lack of productivity.
- Create a false justification for the slaughtering of billions of animals annually, most of which will be killed in the very same inhumane manner as those raised in factory farms.

To be "very sustainable," as Mr. Pollan and others have stated, the practice of raising cows, pigs, turkeys, chickens, goats, and sheep on pasture would have to *not* detrimentally or irreversibly impact any of our resources, other living things, or us—which is quite clearly not the case.

With grass-fed livestock operations, there is still depletion of water and climate change. Methane production is minimally 40 to 60 percent higher in grass-fed cattle and for a longer period—raising cows for two to two and a half years instead of one year, as for grain-fed cows. There will also be a negative oxygen exchange with respiration—oxygen taken out of our atmosphere and carbon dioxide being produced—by the billions of animals. With any plant foods, on the other hand, you will actually create the much more positive effect of taking carbon dioxide out of our atmosphere and producing oxygen, with no methane created.[81]

As we've seen, raising livestock currently uses more than 45 percent of the entire landmass on Earth, with only 9 percent of all these animals being pastured. Imagine how much land it would require to pasture all of the more than 70 billion animals we now raise each year. Annually in the U.S., we raise 98 million head of cattle and 70 million pigs, with only 3 percent of them pastured (only 1 percent of *all* livestock is pastured in the U.S.), yet we still utilize 78 percent of all land used for agriculture in order to raise animals to eat.[82,83]

Many authors (John Robbins, David Pimentel, and Jeremy Rifkin, among others) have suggested that somewhere between 5 to 25 acres is needed to raise one cow completely on pasture. In order to achieve the most accurate overall assessment of land use (as well as other aspects of global depletion), including how many acres is required to support one grass-fed cow, I used an approach with two methods of research. The first was conventional interview—I contacted over sixty different educational institutions and supervisory organizations in the U.S. and other countries, such as agricultural experts at Michigan State University, Iowa State University, University of Wisconsin, and UC–Davis, as well as the USDA and California Cattleman's Association. My second method, which I feel was most beneficial and accurate, was my own field research, conducted by visiting over 150 farms since 1992 in the U.S., as well as in many other countries, such as Australia, Chile, Canada, the UK, France, Switzerland, the Netherlands, Austria, Malaysia, many island countries, and others including nearly every region of the U.S. This data was much more valuable to me, because I was able to determine unadulterated, on-site characteristics and patterns of resource use, types and care of animals, psychology of the owners, *actual* acreage used and for what purpose, water consumption, and many insights. From the combination of both methods, all observations and subsequent calculations support the fact that one cow cannot be raised on anything less than 1.5 to 30 acres, and a pig on 1 to 5 acres (although I suspect the pigs would tell you they would like more). The high end of the range (25 to 30 acres) were operations in some public-leased, government-owned rangelands in our western states and dry sparse or depressed rangelands in other countries. At the other end, there are a few grass-fed operations that have been able to produce approximately one cow per 1.5 to 2.5 acres, due to their geographically more conducive, resource-rich location. This was rare. The very highest amount of production gained by farms considered the most "sustainable" in the U.S. or in other countries is still not more than 300 pounds per 1 acre of land ("dressed-out carcass" weight of their now-slaughtered cow; 450 pounds divided by 1.5 acres). This low end should not be considered the norm. It is relative to geographics and therefore climate and resource availability. It needs to be pointed out that these figures have included models adhering to the most widely accepted and highest yielding techniques, such as rotational and juvenile growth pasturing and mob grazing.[84]

With just the cows and pigs we currently raise to eat each year, placing them all in so-called "very sustainable" pastured conditions at the appropriate acreage per animal would require 2,520,000,000 acres of land, just in the United States alone (that's 168 million pigs and cows combined, multiplied times an average of 15 acres per animal required to sustain it). To put this into clear perspective, the United States only has 2,260,994,361 total land acres in its *entire* mass.[85] And we can't omit the raising on pasture of the 250 million turkeys, 7 million sheep, and over 9 billion chickens that we consume each year in the U.S.[86]

Others are beginning to take note of our inefficient use of land related to raising livestock. Vaclav Smil, author of *Feeding the World*, has calculated that it is impossible for everyone on the planet to eat animals and animal products, such as people in the affluent world do now. According to him, it would require 67 percent more agricultural land than the earth possesses.

It is not just the quantity, however, but also the quality of land that is heavily impacted by grazing animals. With inevitable soil compaction and subsequent damage from erosion, runoff, desertification, and severe loss of biodiversity (plants, animals, insects) the effects are long lasting— and certainly not sustainable. Although the grazing impacts of grass-fed operations would be somewhat less than with conventional farming, they are still substantially more than with organic, fully plant-based systems.

From a land-use efficiency standpoint, you can produce, on average, fifteen times more protein from common food plants than you can from animals on any given area of land.[87] If growing spirulina or chlorella, you could produce nearly 2,000 times more protein than from animals.[88,89]

When considering yields, keep in mind that most grass-fed cattle require one and a half to two full years (sometimes up to three years) on pasture prior to being slaughtered, which would then produce **30 to 90 pounds** of meat per acre of land used, on average (450 pounds of carcass divided by 5 to 15 acres land). On the other hand, many fruit, grain, and vegetable combination yields will, on average, realize up to **237,000 pounds** of food over a two-year period on a 5-acre parcel of land! (This is calculated using a kale, potatoes, oats, and peaches combination; pounds per acre times 5 acres, times two years.)[90]

A brief glance at annual yield averages for some of the many plants that can be grown for food are as follows:[91]

Plant	Pounds per acre per year
Kale	20,000
Collard greens	14,000
Tomatoes	30,500
Potatoes	39,700
Wheat	6,300
Oats	3,200
Spinach	16,000
Apples	15,600
Peaches	32,200
Strawberries	68,000

Yields of plants are typically higher in areas such as California, where there is a more favorable climate for growing and in some cases for irrigation. Organic yields are typically 70 percent less than conventional growing, which is consistent with data found in other developed countries. However, in developing countries, yields of organically grown fruits, vegetables, and grain have shown to be, on average, 150 percent higher than the same crops grown conventionally.

Although the figures provided above reflect average production for the entire U.S., many plants harvested can be as much as twice the respective number. Kale yields, for instance, can be as high as 40,000 pounds per acre per year in certain areas of the country, such as Oregon.[92,93,94]

An important exercise I conduct frequently in my workshops and lectures is to conceptually give everyone in the room 1 acre of land and ask them to grow any food they choose. We compare the resources it takes to produce beef on that 1 acre versus growing a combination of plant-based foods. I use kale, quinoa, and hydroponic tomatoes, as an example, although there are thousands of other combinations. I essentially walk the audience through all areas of global depletion, remembering that in most regions of the country, it will take 2 to 30 acres to actually raise one cow. The end result is that with the plant-based food system example (using the figures displayed above), they will grow thousands more pounds of food that is infinitely healthier for our planet to grow and for us to eat—a system whereby many more people can be fed—which then affects global food pricing and availability, agricultural education in developing countries, and ultimately reduces the propensity for world hunger.

Factory farms as a necessity
There will be continued growth of factory farms despite efforts by many organizations and the media to support the grass-fed movement.

A well-known and respected farmer in Michigan, who raises only grass-fed cattle, once said, "We need factory farms." What an odd statement that seemed to be when I first heard it. He, like many other small farmers across the country, had transitioned his conventional beef operations out of concern "for the environment" and a desire to "grow healthier food." He then continued, "You have the numbers—just do the math. It takes too much land for everyone to raise cows this way. We will never get away from factory farms. We can't."

Almost every farmer running a grass-fed operation that I have interviewed over the past twenty-five years in the U.S. and other countries firmly believes that factory farms are a "necessity," because they know how inefficient their own pastured animal operations really are from a land-use standpoint. The only ones who will say otherwise are Joel Salatin and the Polyface Farms fans, who have obvious marketing motives. But their model will not work on a global basis for all the reasons discussed here.

And then there is the hidden perpetuation of inhumanity with our move *away* from factory farms. It is interesting to me that pasture or grass-fed proponents consider these operations to be "humane" simply because of the improved conditions of life afforded the animals, as compared to those found in factory farms. That is partly true, but all grass-fed operations still slaughter their animals—many in the exact same manner as do factory farms. (More on this in chapter 8.)

Growth of cattle down under

As with nearly every other developed country in the world, Australia is a major cattle producer and consumer and is expected to become one of the top beef producers and exporters in the world by the end of 2012, along with Brazil, India, and the U.S. (among other things, the United States had the distinction of holding the number one spot for beef production in the world in 2011). With the importing of over 2 million head of cattle and 800,000 tons of fresh beef and veal in 2011, the U.S. also has become the world's second largest *importer* of beef, following only Russia.[95,96]

With seemingly vast amounts of open land, Australia is considered a grass-fed wonderland because most of their 200 million sheep and cattle raised annually are pastured. Even so, Australia is seeing an increase in cattle going to feedlots and being "finished" on grain prior to slaughter, and it expects this trend to grow to 31 percent of all cattle raised by the year 2020. In the U.S., there is heavy marketing and media coverage about grass-fed/pastured livestock products, but the USDA predicts our country will see increases in cattle that will be raised, or at least finished, *on grain in feedlots* instead of being 100 percent grass fed. This is largely due to the demand for grain-fed meat by Mexico, the largest importer of U.S. grown beef, whose citizens favor the "marbled" taste of grain-fed cows and the obvious fact that grain-fed cattle in confined (concentrated) feed operations are simply more efficient to produce and with much less land usage than in grass-fed situations—which is still a few thousand times less efficient than using land to produce plant foods for us to consume.[97,98]

As you drive the roads through any cattle district in Australia, you will see many, many cattle and sheep, a few kangaroos, and an occasional wallaby, among other things. One sight that you will not see, though, is miles and miles of corn or soybean feed crops, as can be typically seen along any stretch of highway in the U.S. (especially in the Midwest). This is because cattle raised in Australia do, in fact, graze for most of their lives, but it is with heavy land use and an irreversible toll on wildlife. The loss of biodiversity is blatant and measurable and, unfortunately, it is with an apathetic view.

Among the many livestock operations I visited in Australia, there is a region in Gippsland, Victoria, that represents one of those very few areas in the world where resources such as water, land, and even their climate are considered ideal for raising livestock sustainably. Streams and spring water are abundant, and pasture can grow year-round, so it has become a prime location for grass-fed livestock operations such as cattle, pigs, sheep, and even goats. It is also Australia's premier area for grass-fed dairy operations. The trend seen in Gippsland and across Australia is to produce smaller cows and in less time by keeping them milking at their mother's side in pastures and then letting them grass-feed until ten to eleven months of age, slaughtering them at an average weight of 265 kg (583 pounds). This method is, of course, fueled by demand—in this case, by Japan *and the U.S.*—for meat from smaller, younger cattle. Interestingly, from a land-use standpoint, this method of "sustainable" agriculture occurring in the most favorable conditions in Australia and perhaps in the world *still uses minimally 2.5 acres to raise just one cow*. When it is all said and done, that one cow will provide 300 pounds of meat, which results in **120 pounds per 1 acre** of land used in one year. For reference, an organic vegetable farm, just down the road from these livestock operations in Gippsland, produces on average **5,000 to 10,000 pounds per 1 acre** of food, such as tomatoes, fast-growing greens, and herbs that are infinitely healthier for us to consume.

Although throughout Australia, the total number of farms has decreased, the size of an average farm (by "size," I am referring to the number of livestock raised as well as acreage of land) is increasing, similar to what is occurring in the U.S. However, cattle farm operations in Gippsland remain smaller, averaging 50 to 500 head of cattle per farm, and they adhere strongly to grass-fed/pastured philosophies of operational methodology and marketing protocols.

As Australia becomes one of the largest producers and exporters of beef, it is at the expense of the health of their country; loss and inefficient use of their resources, particularly land; and the declining health of their citizens.

The U.S. is the second largest importer of Australian beef in the world (following Japan). The meat you are eating may have actually come from Australia—part of the 200,000 tons ($1 billion worth) we import each year from their country, which is contributing to deforestation and loss of biodiversity in that country. Grazing livestock currently use over *1 billion acres of land* in Australia, or more than 56 percent of the entire landmass of this country.[99]

The rate of deforestation in Australia is increasing as quickly as anywhere else in the world, with 600,000 acres lost in 2011. Approximately 90 percent of this deforestation is due to cattle. The majority of this forest destruction is in areas where koalas live—or once lived (nearly 80 percent of the koala habitat has been decimated). Therefore, the world demand for beef equates to more land needed to raise cattle, which results in forest loss and turning this land into pastures, which destroys the natural habitat of species living on our planet—it's all connected.

It's time we think about other species and habitat loss from excessive land use when we eat beef or any other form of animal product that is considered food for us. Whether it comes directly from Australia or any other country, is plucked from our oceans, or even is raised in your own backyard—meat is not "food"; it is a destructive human-induced process.

Even if the beef on your plate today is not directly from the grasslands of Australia, it is one of the building blocks of the meat and dairy industry that casts its ominous shadow over our planet. With every bite of beef taken, we effectively stamp another vote of support and create the demand for more and more livestock to be raised and slaughtered throughout the world. This then perpetuates global depletion of our planet's resources and creates substantial increases in risk factors for loss of our own health.

So then, why do we want to raise grass-fed livestock? I have examined the arguments we hear for continuation of this movement, which are:

- Moving away from factory farms (anything is better than CAFOs)
- Humane
- Healthier product to consume
- Sustainable
- The way our great-grandparents farmed
- Natural part of permaculture; necessary for soil fertility
- Our government and that of other countries support it by way of education, subsidies, and other measures
- Proponents (such as Pollan, Salatin, and the media) tell us it is better

Ultimately, however, there may be only two main reasons for eating meat in a grass-fed, local, and organic fashion (or any meat, for that matter). For most, I believe it is because there is lack of awareness—being comfortably unaware. For the others who choose to consume grass-fed meat, it might be similar to cigarette smokers who grope to find logic in the illogical, who have exhausted all attempts to justify the habit—it's simply because they want to.

In the end, there is no good reason to eat animals. Massive amounts of land on earth are consumed and compromised because we choose to eat animals. Nothing truly beneficial or sustainable will come of raising and eating animals in any agricultural format.

Freshwater abuse: where is it all going?

One of the most pressing issues that we have today regarding sustaining our life and future life on earth certainly has to involve water. While many are concerned about water scarcity, the matter is really one of water management.

At the end of the twentieth century, the concern was peak oil, which is still a concern. As we move further into the twenty-first century, however, it is clear that the most precious commodity is water, not oil. From 1941 to 2011, the world's population tripled but the water consumption quadrupled, leaving 37 percent of the population facing severe water stress by 2020, despite 16x10 (to the 6th) tons of rainfalls per second around the world.[100]

Since the Second World Water Forum in 2000, a few organizations, such as the United Nations Advisory Board on Water and Sanitation, suggest that there is a rapidly expanding gap between the demand for water and our supply.

It is expected that our planet will see a 40 percent shortage of freshwater by the year 2030. Along with climate change, water security is most likely going to become one of the largest challenges we will face, and it is happening today.[101]

There are regional variations in urgency and stress—you may not even be aware that there is a problem—but water scarcity is already a reality in many parts of the world. An estimated 1 billion people in the world are without adequate freshwater supply to drink, while 2.5 billion are without running water, which presents many social, political, and economic issues. Water resources are local, but shortages become regional, national, and global concerns. One-third of the world's population lives in countries with moderate to high water stress (defined by the United Nations as where water consumption exceeds 10 percent of renewable freshwater resources). Estimates from the UN indicate that two out of three people in the world might be living in regions that are water stressed by the year 2025, as water withdrawals are expected to increase by 50 percent in developing countries and 18 percent in developed countries by then.[102,103]

A study by the Natural Resources Defense Council found that one-third of all counties in the lower United States (1,100 counties spanning fourteen states) will face water shortages by 2050, with more than 400 of them at "extremely high risk."[104]

There are, indeed, concerns voiced by many organizations that we are reaching a pivotal point regarding use of resources with our activities on earth, and this is particularly true with water. Along with reaching a point of maximum use of fossil fuels such as oil (with irreversibly declining reserves), many believe we have reached "peak water" as well. Why are we running out of water? Because we have used and continue to use freshwater as if it is a fully renewable resource and as if it is infinite in quantity. It is not.

Freshwater resources are scarce—it is just 2.5 percent of all water on earth, and 70 percent of that is locked in glaciers, snow, and the atmosphere. This leaves accessible freshwater at less than 1 percent (0.4 percent). While some water is replenished through the natural evaporation/precipitation cycle, much is gathered from underground aquifers or surface water, such as rivers and streams.

Although considered a closed, looping system (the total amount of water on earth and in our atmosphere, found cumulatively in all forms, never changes) and technically renewable, the amount of freshwater available for our use at any given time is not constant—it is not inexhaustible and is subject to being depleted faster than it can be renewed.

Many aquifers are being drawn down at rates as high as 250 times their ability to recharge. Deep groundwater aquifers that took thousands of years to form are being drained in many areas of the world, such as the North China Plain, the Ogallala in the High Plains of the U.S., and California's San Joachin Valley. California groundwater extraction exceeds recharge rates by up to 2 million acre-feet annually.[105]

The primary reason for such a shortfall of supply can be found in how we use and abuse it.

With regard to surface water sources such as rivers, streams, and lakes, there are already heated debates and arguments between those areas and countries using upstream water systems and the affects of those reliant on the very same waterways downstream. Diversion, use for industries and energy, and pollution all affect surface water sources globally.

While there is a gap between water demand and the ability to provide a truly sustainable supply, a much larger gap exists between what *needs* to be done to close that gap and what is actually being accomplished.

Where is all the water going? How is it being used?

Within the UN's projection of a 40 percent water shortage by the year 2030, it is predicted that 17 percent more water will be required for food production to meet the needs of the growing global population. Some of the world's water crisis is related to the lack of physical availability of water, but much is due to unbalanced power relations, poverty, and related inequalities. For this reason, water scarcity often is roughly divided into two categories: "apparent" scarcity, which exists when there is water availability but it is inefficiently and wastefully used; and "real" scarcity, which is caused by insufficient rainfall or large populations depending on a limited resource.

We use freshwater in many ways other than simply for drinking, including for industrial purposes. Approximately 70 percent of all water used globally is by agriculture, mostly due to irrigation of crops, with 29 percent of that being used by livestock.[106,107]

Water used in the U.S. for agriculture is estimated to be nearly 90 percent for non-hydroelectric, consumptive purposes. Of that, approximately 50 percent is used for livestock, primarily in irrigated feed crop settings.

Certain areas, such as the Colorado River and the Ogallala, San Joachin, and the Columbia River Basin in Washington State are using water at a rate closer to 72–75 percent for livestock. Yuma County, Arizona, is one of the largest vegetable production areas in the U.S. Every one of their 230,000 acres used for agriculture is irrigated with water from the Colorado River. But a significant amount of that acreage is used for feed crops and hay given to livestock grown in that area. Some of Yuma County's cattle companies have more than 120,000 head of beef cows on a single lot.[108]

While we use less than 1 percent of all water consumed for drinking purposes in the U.S.—**50 percent of all the water used in the U.S. is given to the animals we eat.**[109]

There are 70 billion animals raised and killed each year on earth. They all require water. A few billion of these animals need up to forty or more gallons per day—that's over 100 times what we, as individuals, need to consume daily. While agricultural irrigation is responsible for the majority of global water use, the problem is the irrigation of *feed* crops, alfalfa, and pastures as well as the drinking water that are given directly to livestock. Choosing to eat only plant-based foods would essentially omit the middle step in our current inefficient system that uses the vast majority of our freshwater on earth to provide sustenance for animals that we then turn around and eat. Timely correction needs to be at the very center of any global water management strategy.

We face many varied challenges with water management, and not all are related to food choice. For instance, China has and will continue to have a significant water quality issue because of the rapid growth of its use in industry. Still, China also has one of the largest rates of increase in beef and pork consumption, which will continue to implicate them, as well as all other developed countries, in water waste. India and many African countries, with over 90 percent water usage going to agriculture, can close the water demand-supply gap significantly simply by implementing water-saving measures with improved irrigation, soil preservation and fertility techniques, and reduction of inefficient use of water (that given to livestock or feed crops). However, similar to our greenhouse gas emission issues with livestock, the very best management method of our water scarcity problem is to simply eliminate the largest and most unnecessary contributor—livestock. Livestock systems depending on grain-based feeds are more water-intensive than systems relying on pasturelands. In the U.S., though, 99 percent of all livestock are raised on grain feeds. Simply changing the ratio to more grass-fed/pastured animals would not be advisable, since it would effectively increase the amount of water required per animal (as they are more active and for a longer period of time) as well as drastically increase land used.

There are basically three ways we use water to raise livestock:
1. To irrigate crops for them to eat (feed crops), pastures, and alfalfa
2. For the animals to drink

3.   To clean (equipment, areas, slaughtering, processing, etc.)

In understanding the enormous impact that eating meat has on global depletion of drinking water, it is important to have a grasp on just how much water is used in each of these areas. Crop irrigation varies with the type of feed grown, geographic region, and the amount of feed consumed by each type of livestock. Many pastures (grass-fed) operations resort to irrigation similar to those growing feed crops. According to the Water Footprint Calculator (a guide created by the Water Footprint Network, an organization whose mission is to promote the transition toward sustainable, fair, and efficient use of freshwater resources worldwide), the average amount of water needed to produce just 1 pound of meat from various sources is as follows:

> 1,799 gallons for 1 pound of beef (6.6 pounds feed, 32.6 pounds roughage, 18.6 gallons for drinking and processing)
> 731 gallons/sheep
> 127 gallons/goat
> 576 gallons/pig (4.2 pounds grain, 52.8 gallons for drinking and processing)
> 468 gallons/chicken (2 pounds grain, 2.4 gallons for drinking and processing)
> 880 gallons water for 1 gallon of milk
> 60–120 gallons water to produce one egg
> 11.6 gallons to slaughter and process one chicken

It requires a maximum of 40 gallons of water to produce a pound of pulses (crops such as lentils, chickpeas, peas, and beans) as excellent sources of protein, as compared to beef, which requires minimally 45 times as much water.[110-114]

The figures above appear to be the most sophisticated and comprehensive set of data and calculations, despite leaving a significant void in explanation of regional and national variances. For instance, other figures that have been used widely since the mid-1990s are 2,500 to 5,214 gallons of water required per pound of beef (Marcia Kreith for the Water Education Foundation), 815 gallons per pound of chicken, and 1,630 gallons per pound of pork. Organizations supporting the production of meat, such as the American Grass-Fed Association and the National Cattlemen's Beef Association, state that it only requires 441 gallons of water to produce 1 pound of beef.

The precise water footprint of any animal product depends on the production system from which the meat was derived. Grazing, mixed, or industrial methods all vary in water use within the system, the composition, and origin of the feed. *Some analysts feel that the total water footprint of beef from factory-farm systems is lower than that of beef from grazing or pastured systems.* This is due to the larger feed conversion efficiency found in beef produced by industrial farms (although this grain-fed type of beef generally has a larger blue and gray water footprint than grass-fed). Even conservative estimates place the average water footprint per calorie for beef at twenty times larger than for grains. And since livestock are raised primarily as a source of protein, it is important to know that the average water footprint per gram of protein of beef is six times larger than for grain. These ratio differences become even greater when comparing beef to legumes.

It takes over 5,000 gallons of water to produce 1 pound of meat?
In my book *Comfortably Unaware*, I mentioned that it could take over 5,000 gallons of water to produce 1 pound of meat, which has raised the question, is that number inflated? This must be viewed in a relative sense and therefore is not exaggerated at all. After conducting research in more than ten countries and in nearly every state in the U.S. regarding food production systems (in this case, grass-fed, conventional, and animal operations within academic settings), I found there were five primary categories or models of water usage pertaining to beef production:

1. True CAFOs
2. Beef produced from dairy and cattle, fed high alfalfa-content feed
3. Grass-fed/pastured
4. Pastoral
5. Combination of two or more of the above

In true confined (or "concentrated") animal feed operations (CAFOs, or factory farms), grain is the predominant feed source for cattle, although many can be raised on pasture for a few months prior to being "finished" with grain in feedlots. Nearly 100 percent of all grain used as feed for livestock is irrigated, on average, three to four months, and a number of authors, researchers, and academic institutions relate water usage to be in the range of 2,000 to 3,000 gallons per pound of meat derived, based on this knowledge. This is the source from which authors such as John Robbins derived the widely accepted figure of 2,500 gallons. Water Footprint Calculator places the estimated water requirements to produce 1 pound of beef at 1,799 gallons. However, these calculations were based on reasonable but slightly lower amounts of irrigated grains and roughage for feed as a global average but not as applicable to the preponderance of meat consumed in the U.S. Nevertheless, a range of 1,800 to 2,500 gallons could be easily argued, as it is likely a reasonable average.

Keep in mind that a significant amount of beef also enters our food supply from the raising and slaughtering of dairy cows and cattle fed high alfalfa-content hay, as part of a pasturing process or in contained areas. **As many as 9 million cows are raised and slaughtered in this fashion per year.** In California, over 900,000 acres of land are used to raise alfalfa (from 2000 to 2008, it was over 1 million acres), where 75 percent of this alfalfa is given to dairy cows. It's a terrible misuse of land and water because *every* one of those 900,000 acres in California is irrigated at an average rate of 1 million gallons of water per growing season of six months. One cow will eat, on average, 5 tons of pasture or hay per year. This requires 1 to 2 acres of properly irrigated, properly fertilized pasture, and over two years of raising the cow. So with no grain, grass-fed-only beef, my calculations (and from what I have seen on many farm operations that I have visited) are that it requires 4,167 gallons of water per pound of this type of beef produced (2 million gallons per 480 pounds of meat) for the pasture or alfalfa hay that fed the cow + 46 gallons, minimally (22,000 gallons per 480 pounds for drinking water) = 4,210 gallons, added to the 400 gallons of water required to slaughter, wash down, and process the carcass. This, then, could then be rounded to 5,000 gallons on average (especially if any amount of irrigated grain was also fed to the cow, as it is in many instances) to produce 1 pound of beef in California—or anywhere else in our country or the world with similar irrigation schedules. The number would be slightly higher with dairy cows, as they tend to drink two times the amount of water of beef cattle. I have verified these numbers with numerous sources in the USDA, California State Agriculture officials, those in the State Water Project, and my own research in the fields and on farms throughout California as well as other regions in the U.S.

If we looked only at the water that one of the billions of "sustainable" grass-fed cattle drinks (not accounting for feed or processing), it would still require 20,000–22,000 gallons over a twenty-four-month period to raise just one cow. That amount of water is the equivalent of a person taking a five-minute shower each and every day for 6.7 years.

Regardless of whether the number is 5,000, 2,500, or even 1 gallon, any water used to raise livestock or feed for them—instead of food or drink for us—should be considered unnecessary and excessive.

In the Imperial Valley, water from the Colorado River is diverted (one-fifth of all the water of the river) through the Imperial Canal, and 70 percent is used in one way or another for livestock. Alfalfa is grown in this area, using up to 2 million gallons per acre per year (UC–Davis).

Total water used just for one year of hay in California is projected to be 1.8 trillion gallons (900,000 acres, all irrigated at 50–80 acre inch per acre per year).[115]

The average yearly rainfall in the Imperial Valley is less than 3 inches and water is sparse in other areas in California where alfalfa hay is grown. Knowing this, I find it interesting that the largest importer of their hay for the past few years has been the United Arab Emirates (UAE), who is importing hay from California because they are concerned about the scarce water supply for their own citizens. Saudi Arabia will soon follow, essentially importing water from California via hay for its animals that are then consumed by their citizens. This virtual water loss will be a growing trend—certain countries depleting the natural resources of other, more unaware countries, such as the U.S., Brazil, and others, so they may "prosper" with importation of animals and animal products. These animals are produced in countries where true environmental costs of production continue to be externalized and a proper economic metric has yet to be affixed to products that are the largest contributors to global depletion— livestock and fish. These opportunistic countries will continue to take a similar approach as the UAE by utilizing their limited water supply more for human consumption than for crop or animal production, while taking advantage of countries such as the U.S., which doesn't know any better or is letting economics dictate a better state of ecologic reasoning. Subsidies for heavy aquifer water use for livestock and feed crops remain strong, as farmers pay only 5 to 10 percent of what residents pay in the Ogallala and San Joachin regions, which encourages continued growing of alfalfa and depletion of freshwater.[116]

Typically, most areas of the world will have predominant use of either surface water (lakes, streams, rivers) or groundwater (aquifers). In California, there is a combination of both, with an approximate 60/40 water usage blend of the Sacramento-San Joachin surface water systems and diversion of the Colorado River, with underground use such as from the San Joachin aquifer and others. In times of drought, California places restrictions on surface water and becomes more reliant on heavy withdrawals from aquifer systems. Visual indicators of these water withdrawals can be seen in many areas of the world, most notably, perhaps, near Mendota, California, where subsidence has caused a 28-foot drop in land elevation in some areas. Subsidence occurs when excessive amounts of groundwater have been withdrawn from an aquifer, and ground cratering results. Once water has been removed from the sediment and subsidence has taken place, it cannot be replaced.[117]

This also can be readily seen in many counties in Texas and elsewhere in the world. Subsidence is occurring in the state of Guanajuato, Mexico, where the water table is falling by 2 meters or more per year due to withdrawals, to support the growing livestock and feed crop industry there.

There are many examples of rapid groundwater depletion. In India, due to irrigating rice fields in the North China Plain, its two aquifers systems are becoming quickly depleted. In the U.S. there is depletion of aquifers in North Carolina, Arkansas, the Columbia River Basin, and others. Perhaps the two most significant examples of groundwater depletion in the U.S. and water management abuses (how water is used) can be found in the San Joachin and Ogallala aquifers.

The San Joachin Valley forms the backbone of California's agricultural industry, the nucleus of the Central Valley area, which produces 25 percent of the nation's food on less than 1 percent of the country's farmland. Land subsidence in excess of 1 foot has affected more than 5,200 square miles of irrigable land—one-half the entire San Joachin Valley. This has been called "the single largest human alteration of land" (USGS). It, along with the Ogallala, will likely be the single largest human alteration *of water*, as both aquifers (San Joachin and the Ogallala) are expected to be completely drained within sixty years (San Joachin) and twenty years (Ogallala).

At an average depth of 200 feet, the Ogallala is the most heavily depleted aquifer in the U.S. and the world's fastest disappearing freshwater source, losing 150 feet of depth in the past twenty years. The Ogallala's misuse is driven by our food choices, and it is another management issue that we have known about for at least twenty to thirty years, yet it continues today. It is a vivid example of just how powerful various influences are on our decisions about food.

The Ogallala is one of the largest aquifers on earth. It has water formed from glaciers 12 million years ago; recharge rates of less than a half inch per year; and is being drawn down at a rate of 3 to 10 feet per year. It now is predicted to be gone as soon as the year 2030. Since the 1960s, farmers have irrigated this land, receiving subsidies to use this water to grow crops to feed cattle, as almost half of all cattle raised in the U.S. comes from just four states in this area—Nebraska, Iowa, Kansas, and Texas, which accounted for 49 percent of the United States commercial red meat production in 2010.

The vast majority of the Ogallala abuse and depletion has been to support the largest cattle herds in the U.S. and the corn that feeds them.[118,119]

When confronted with the very real potential of running the Ogallala aquifer dry, a movement in the late 1980s supported creating a pipeline to Lake Michigan, one of the Great Lakes, with the thought to pump water from Lake Michigan back to all the livestock operations. This brings us front and center to the real problem—water management and perhaps changing food choice. We need to find another solution. We could, for instance, eat all plant-based foods, which are far less water-intensive. We do not need to eat cattle from the High Plains states or anywhere else to survive. We do, however, need water.

Over 70 percent of California's alfalfa is produced in the Central Valley, which constitutes the majority of land use. All of it is irrigated. Therefore, the largest single human alteration of land in the world is caused by the largest, most inefficient consumer of water—livestock.[120]

Worldwide, alfalfa is grown on approximately 79 million acres. The majority of it is irrigated, and 70 percent of it comes from the United States, Russia, and Argentina—countries suffering now from frequent periods of heat, drought, and water stress. Wherever water scarcity is found in the world, particularly with irreversibly overdrawing of aquifers, livestock typically is involved, leaving the indelible mark of our insatiable demand to eat them. Between 50 and 75 percent of all water withdrawal from the largest aquifers in the world—Ogallala, North China Plain, San Joachin, Columbia River Basin—can be attributed to livestock and the alfalfa, corn, sorghum, and other crops they eat; their drinking water and the water used to generally service them; processing and packaging animal products; and the slaughtering process.

One of the goals of the Millennium Development Goal (MDG) is to cut by half the proportion of malnourished people in the world by 2015, amounting to just under 1 billion people. This becomes not only a remarkable agricultural feat but also will be one of the world's largest water resource challenges. Instead of a green revolution, which helped lift large parts of Asia out of a hunger crisis beginning in the 1960s, any new agricultural movement with similar intent for the world's malnourished will have to be designed with a keener eye on long-term environmental sustainability, focused on freshwater management. Without adequate water, food cannot be produced. Much of this focus will need to be on how to use whatever scarce freshwater we have in the most efficient manner possible (which food types are produced and whether they are the most water-efficient), as well as improving use of various sources of water.

There are three classifications for sources of water: blue (surface and groundwater/aquifers), green (rainwater stored in the soil as moisture; that is, used in evapotranspiration), and gray (polluted water associated with production of all goods and services). Generally, the water used in agricultural systems that has been found to be most unsustainable is that from ground or aquifer sources and surface water, which falls into the blue and green water categories. Direct water consumption by human activities depletes blue water, making it less available. This includes all nonagricultural activities (industry, services, domestic), as well as agricultural activities such as crop irrigation, livestock drinking-water use, use in associated factories producing inputs (seeds, fertilizers, animal-feed processing, etc.), and those producing animal products such as the dairy industry, slaughterhouses, tanneries, and poultry operations. Although worldwide agriculture represents 70 percent of "water" usage, this refers to total blue water withdrawals, but it is responsible for 86 percent of all blue and green water use (World Water Assessment Programme, 2009). Livestock farming, however, uses 15 percent of all our water withdrawals on earth, 33 percent of water used in rain-grown crops, and 68 percent of that for permanent pastures and rangelands.[121]

Historically, conventional water resource planning and focus has been on blue water, but this represents one-third of freshwater resources, which is rainfall over the continents. Analysis of food production needs to incorporate both blue and green components—the water flow through rivers, lakes, and aquifers and vapor-water flow to and from soil back to the atmosphere.

Today's agriculture in developing countries suffers from drought and is exacerbated by climate change but also from large water losses. These losses occur in three major ways: by inefficient crop irrigation where only 30 percent of the water applied is actually used by the plants, uncaptured rain-fed agriculture where in sub-Saharan Africa as little as 10 percent of seasonal rainfall is used as productive green water flow, and by diverting most of their water resources to livestock or feed crops. Tropical grains such as maize, sorghum, and millet are grown in many developing countries where rainwater is not used productively and with the increased tendency to use as feed for animals. While strategists are calling for innovative methods to manage sudden excesses of precipitation and frequent periods of drought, it will be equally as important to shorten the path taken for providing food and water to those that are suffering and to take the unnecessary link of livestock and feed crops out of the food, water, and energy flow.[122]

Much of the freshwater crises can be solved through virtual water trading, where food will be produced in areas of the world that have ample supplies of fresh water and then exported to water-scarce regions. This is already occurring in arid countries in the Middle East. But only 5 to 10 percent of the world food production is being traded on the international market and without adequate purchasing power, communities in countries facing the largest growth in food demand will need to develop the most water and land resource-efficient production systems. Food security for countries with a high prevalence of hunger and poverty will be attained more adequately with a quick transition to the most efficient use of their land and water resources—not "more" efficient use; the "most" efficient use, which can only be with plant-based food systems. This would ultimately help the overall health of status of their citizens as well.

The difficulty I've found with examining water use percentages (as well as with research in other areas of global depletion) is that there are biases at play relative to the motives and profiles, not only of the organization itself but also of the authors. An example of this can be found between the data of the FAO, which was produced primarily by those with livestock interests or backgrounds (preferring to use 70 percent as the amount of global water used by agriculture and 23 percent as livestock's withdrawal of that), and information derived from an independent academic institution, such as that at the University of Twente in the Netherlands. This latter group found agriculture's contribution to the global water footprint to be at 93 percent, with meat and dairy combining for 29 percent of all water used by the average person in the world. Viewing it in terms of human consumption, the demand for irrigation absorbs about 74 percent of all water used by people, against 18 percent used for hydropower and other industrial uses and 8 percent for households. Most researchers examining data and water use in the U.S. will use the following definition, as taken from the USGS:

Agricultural water use can be divided between irrigation and livestock. Irrigation includes all water applied to farm or horticultural crops; livestock incorporates water used for livestock, dairies, feedlots, fish farms, and other farm needs.

According to this definition, it is quite apparent that any figures pertaining to water usage taken directly from the USDA or USGS will not necessarily accurately reflect all water involved in feed crop production specific to livestock. A more realistic number of gallons drawn (water footprint) or percentage of water use can be calculated by first ascertaining the percentage of each irrigated crop used for animal feed or the total production yield as well as total volume or percentage of water drawn. Although between 1 and 2 percent of all water use in the U.S. is given to livestock for strict drinking purposes, most U.S. governmental agencies such as the USGS stated as of 2012, "consumptive use is estimated at 67 percent for livestock"—with 60 percent of that water derived from groundwater sources and the remaining from surface water.

Much of the water used in the U.S. or worldwide—and therefore a large component of the water scarcity concern—is water used to grow feed crops. But what about the water given directly to the animals for drinking purposes? All livestock needs to consume water.

Although many factors affect these values (e.g., geographics, climate), the average amount of drinking water needed per livestock animal **per day** is estimated to be:

35–45 gallons/milking cow
20–30 gallons/dry cow
12 gallons/beef cattle
5–8 gallons/pig
4 gallons/goat
2 gallons/sheep
15 gallons per 100 turkeys
9 gallons per 100 chickens[123]

Even if we only focused on the 1–2 percent water usage by livestock for their drinking purposes and excluded all the other massive amounts of water used for irrigation, it still equates to *4–8 billion gallons of water given to livestock every day* in the U.S. alone.

I often discuss the water consumption and sustainability issue in my presentations by using the following illustration:

According to the EPA, the average household of three in our country consumes 50,000 gallons of water in one year for indoor use. That's quite a lot of water, and it is what we are focused on in times of drought—how to reduce it. However, this estimate does not include the water required to bring food to our table, which is by far the most important factor in our water consumption. Consider that the average person in the Unites States consumes 206 pounds of meat in one year— 46 pounds of pig, 58 pounds of cow, 102 pounds of chicken and turkey, in addition to 248 eggs and 616 pounds of dairy products. This equates to 405,000 gallons of water per person per year consumed just to support that animal product diet. A more accurate view—something the EPA should be aware of and concerned about—is that every household of just three people in the U.S. uses well over 1 million gallons of water each year, not 50,000 gallons. And 96 percent of that outrageous water use results directly from their choice to eat animals. Whenever there is a drought or water shortage anywhere in the country, does the government ever step up to declare a state of rationing meat or dairy? Of course not—but why not?

Many of the small vegetable and fruit farms I've visited grow their products without any irrigation. Navy, kidney, soybean, and black-bean farmers in the Midwest produce between 2,000 and 4,000 pounds of beans per year with no irrigation whatsoever. Fruit and vegetable growers in other countries have harvested up to 20,000 to 40,000 pounds of various produce, simply on existing rainwater.

Using all possible green and blue water sources, conservative global averages for the water needed to produce any meat or animal product are as follows: it requires three times more water to produce milk than vegetables, ten times more water to produce eggs, fourteen times more water to produce chicken meat, nineteen times more water to produce pork, and forty-eight times more water to produce beef than vegetables.[124] Because between 40 and 60 percent of the fruit and vegetable production in the U.S. occurs in dry areas, such as California's Central and Imperial Valleys and Arizona's Yuma area, which need large amounts of irrigation, the base figure of water used to produce 1 pound of an assortment of vegetables is high.

At one of the first dairy farms I visited a few years ago, I was told that 7,000 gallons of water are needed to keep a dairy cow alive for one day, and each cow will produce on average 20–25 gallons of milk per day. The ratios have not changed much since then, with anywhere from 300 gallons to 1,200 gallons of water needed to produce just *one* gallon of milk. How "sustainable," then, is milk from a water-use standpoint, even if it is organic, grass-fed, *and* local? The water required for milk production is drinking water for the cow as well as water needed to produce the grain and alfalfa that the cow eats in one day. Water is also needed for the sanitation process before and after each cow is milked, for washing down the stalls and corrals, and for washing and sanitizing all lines, holding and carrying tanks, and equipment. It is a very water-intensive process—all to produce a liquid that we would be far better off not drinking in the first place (75 percent of the population is lactose intolerant, and milk is implicated in numerous disease states such as diabetes, obesity, certain cancers, and cardiovascular diseases).

There are two primary types of commercial dairy operations in the world. One is the small, family-owned farm, and the other is the much larger, more industrialized operation. Although different in size, they both are quite similar in terms of the end product; the unnecessary use of resources;

the land, air, and water pollution generated; and the lack of awareness with regard to their contribution to ill health.

Food waste as it relates to water scarcity

There is now a movement to reduce global food waste, and the U.S. needs to take the lead, as Americans throw away more than an estimated 30 percent of our food via mismanagement along the entire inefficient journey of harvesting, transporting, storage, processing, and packaging. According to the Stockholm International Water Institute (SIWI), approximately 40 percent of the world's food supply comes from the 18 percent of farmland that is irrigated, so this method of farming is a cornerstone of global food security. Because of global water depletion in the past few decades, more farmers are turning from rivers to aquifers for their water supply, causing groundwater reserves to become unsustainable and even drying up. It is an issue of irrigation technologies but more an issue that the majority of irrigated crops are being used for feed instead of food.

A 30 percent loss of food due to waste is now recognized as a major issue in attaining global food security. Arjen Hoekstra, director of the Netherlands-based Water Footprint Network (a nonprofit and academic institution that developed the water footprint concept), feels that understanding the supply-chain losses is critical to solving the food-waste and subsequent water-loss problem. The SIWI sees opportunities for reducing waste by "improving water efficiency in the field" with better rainfall capture and irrigation technologies, which can be installed through more funding and technological assistance. The SIWI even advocates more awareness among the public, farmers, and businesses about water-use inefficiencies in agriculture, but to date there has been no specific discussion as to proper water-management solutions. While feed-crop irrigation is identified as a major user of global water, Hoekstra and institutions such as the SIWI have yet to offer solutions that would result in precise and immediate water-efficiency gains—such as simply eliminating livestock and feed crops from the global equation of water consumption. This, of course, would mandate addressing the single catalyst, which is our demand to eat meat, and thereby crossing lines that are difficult for these leaders, as they would confront cultural, political, and societal norms. Presenting data, proposing responses to potential crises in general formats, and outlining the need for change is easier for them to accomplish and more politically correct than spelling out the ABC's of water management (or land or any other area of global depletion).

We have a water crisis. Our very survival as a civilization may depend on the decisions we make and the actions we take now. Eliminating water-use inefficiencies is the correct approach. The most inefficient use of water in which we engage is in raising livestock, which also happens to be the largest user of water as a single food product. Eliminating the eating of meat would effectively reduce our collective global water footprint *more than any other single factor*. Soft, indirect, and passive statements, such as the pronouncement made by 2008 Stockholm Water Prize winner John Anthony Allan—"We need to eat in ways that save our health, ours and the environment"—are ineffective. Eat in *what* "ways"? Just say it.

We are all stakeholders regarding global depletion, and we all need to be involved in its solutions. Frank and relevant communication by our leaders is in order, and the cessation of the raising of all livestock is needed—now.

With its substantial gains in affluence and population, China is consuming more meat and therefore quickly becoming the largest user of water for consumptive purposes. Rice production uses 21 percent of all global agricultural crops, and while Asia accounts for 90 percent, China grows 30 percent of the global output of rice. China, however, also produces 40 percent of the corn and 27 percent of wheat globally.[125]

Rice production in Asia (90 percent is irrigated) is one of the least water-efficient crops in the world, using on average 449 gallons of water per pound of rice. In China, rice uses 50 percent of their total agricultural water consumption. But the water shortages they are facing in the north and northeast aren't entirely from the production of rice. Maize has experienced the highest growth rate of all crops, doubling production in the last sixteen years to nearly 200 million tons. The reason for this tremendous growth in China is their increased demand for meat and the subsequent growth of the livestock sector. Currently, 75 percent of the corn produced in China is used for livestock feed. Sixty years ago, over 70 percent of corn was used for direct human consumption. The most water-stressed areas in China, such as the North China Plain, grow corn—45 percent of the land in that area is used for corn—and it is being irrigated. Additionally, CAFOs in China are on the increase, and water is a key input to feedlots of 20,000 or more head of cattle per lot, barns holding more than 15,000 pigs at a time, and confined poultry operations of more than 100,000 birds per building. The majority of China's largest livestock facilities are located near densely populated cities, so there will be increased competition for water as the supply dwindles. Consumption of liquid dairy products from their expanding dairy operations is expected to reach over 100 million tons by 2030, tripling the amount seen in 2008. It is expected that China will increase its number of cows by 1 million per year to keep in line with demand. This rapid rise in consumption of dairy products is a direct result of the rapid rise in urban population and lack of awareness as to the water requirements and other detrimental environmental implications. China's rising human population is indeed responsible for the current water concern and future crisis occurring in that country. But the reason for this crisis, as it is elsewhere in the world, isn't the demand for drinking water; it's what they choose to eat. And the solution to that begins with the dissolution of all livestock operations.

The true economic value of water
There should be immediate economic policies established based on water use and its true value and cost to replace. To this point, any increase in need or demand for water has been met with problem-solving to provide more water (e.g., desalination, digging deeper wells, devising water diversion schemes, or "borrowing" from nearby surface water). Instead, we need to reduce

demand by recognizing those sectors that use the most water and establishing parameters and economic incentives to minimize consumption. This could be accomplished with an "eco-tax." If the water used unnecessarily for raising and slaughtering livestock was taxed appropriately (proportionate to total global use and value based on ability to renew the resource), a price would have to paid that consumers and producers of meat would not be able to afford, and we would be well on our way to solving the water-scarcity problem.

Why are we raising livestock in water-stressed regions?

In many areas of the world, freshwater scarcity coexists with hunger, poverty, and inefficient use of marginal natural resources available. These are the same regions that have the highest amounts of water used in inefficient ways for agriculture. Improved irrigation, soil-building techniques, and enhanced rainwater capture would all help matters but no more so than using what little water is available for drought-resistant, water-efficient crops for human consumption. It is commonly thought that livestock is an important component in the agricultural systems. Many believe that in arid and semi-arid regions, extensive grazing of livestock is the only means of producing high-value agricultural products within the given agro-climatic conditions. Pastoralism and agro-pastoralism (raising livestock in a grazing fashion from land to land, without direct ownership of the property) is seen in nearly all developing countries, particularly in Africa, where raising and eating animals and animal products have become woven into the culture, social, and religious life of the people. But livestock are not essential. Raising livestock and the feed for them creates gross imbalances in freshwater availability for direct human use, as well as creating great land-use inefficiencies. Livestock are a large impediment to lifting a region or country from the poverty/hunger/ill health cycle. Growing crops to feed livestock in developing countries requires 2 trillion cubic meters of water per year (264 gallons in one cubic meter), and the production and servicing of livestock animals takes another 536 billion cubic meters each year.[126,127]

As a region, the Middle East suffers from minimal freshwater resources and lack of rainfall. The population is expected to double in the fifty years between 2000 and 2050, yet their livestock numbers have already doubled since the mid-1960s to 412 million head, while the number of poultry found in any one year has increased ninefold. *The total amount of water needed for that many cattle alone, just to drink each day, is over 10 billion gallons.* And that does not account for any water used in irrigation of crops grown to feed the cattle each day or for water consumed by the other few billion animals raised for food in the Middle East. The demand for meat is projected to increase dramatically in response to increases in urbanization, affluence, and human population.

Approximately 92 percent of the total water withdrawal of the Middle East is directed toward agriculture. As the demand for meat increases, so will the demand to produce more livestock, which places further demands on limited water supplies. Livestock in this region includes camels, cattle, goats, buffaloes, pigs, and sheep. Cattle increases were as high as 70 percent from 2006 to 2009, with sheep increases as high as 309 percent. While there appears to be great business opportunities by expanding the domestic and export markets for livestock in this region, it will be at the expense of already critically low freshwater resources.[128]

Saudi Arabia, as an example, has withdrawn 90 percent or more of its water supply from aquifers. It produces many vegetables and fruit for human consumption, but it also grow feed crops and alfalfa for their livestock. Saudi Arabia's national agricultural development objective is to reduce the importation of livestock feed and animal products as they increase their own production, keeping up with the increase in demand for meat within their country.[129]

With limited freshwater and a looming water crisis across the region, increasing the number of livestock and feed crops grown in Saudi Arabia doesn't make much sense. Each year, Saudi Arabia feeds, waters, and then slaughters 3.2 million sheep, 1.65 million goats, 220,000 cattle, 186,000 camels, and 575 million chickens.[130]

Pakistan is one of the most water-stressed countries in the world, with 94 percent of all water withdrawals going to agriculture, one of the highest of any country. The cause for water stress is the constant cycle of drought and flooding found in Pakistan—either too little water over a long period or too much water delivered all at once. About 66 percent of their water consumption is from surface sources, but the 34 percent from groundwater is depleting the aquifer systems. As of 2008, the human population of Pakistan was 177 million, but they also had to feed and water a population of 136 million livestock (27 million buffalo, 26 million sheep, 53 million goats, and 30 million cattle). In periods of significant drought, they have to find a way to provide 600 million gallons of water each day, just for the cattle segment of that large domestic livestock herd, which is a very small fraction of the amount used to irrigate crops to feed them. While the international community has been concerned about water-management protocols in Pakistan, the number of cattle in that country increased by 50 percent in the ten-year period from 1996 to 2006. The Pakistan Water Strategy, prepared in 2001, is a national plan for water development and management, but there is no formal agricultural policy and no thought of how water could be used much more efficiently by changing food preferences and growing plant-based foods.[131]

In fact, with 4 percent growth in 2012, the government of Pakistan has identified the livestock sector as a source of great business opportunity and export revenues, so plans are being made to expand the industry. Seven major projects are under way, with heavy funding to provide veterinary services to livestock farmers, develop feedlots, and install infrastructure to help reduce waste and pollution, among other things. It is disappointing to see so much effort and money funneled into an industry that will simply erode more of Pakistan's resources and drain its supply of water.[132]

Only 13 percent of the country of Afghanistan has clean drinking water available. Increased pollution, inadequate infrastructure to supply water, and destruction from conflict are all factors for a significant water shortage. Nevertheless, water still has to be supplied to their large livestock population, last measured and easily under-reported in 2003 as consisting of 4 million cattle, 9 million sheep, 7 million goats, and more than 12 million poultry.

In Ethiopia, 42 percent of the population has access to clean water supply, but only 11 percent has access to clean sanitation. Women and children, assigned the task of obtaining water, many times walk six hours to collect water, only to collect it from unprotected, potentially contaminated water sources. Yet Ethiopia has one of the largest herds of cattle in all of Africa—over 50 million head—with each cow needing between forty to seventy times as much water to drink than a human each day. Chad, Ghana, Laos, Cambodia, Rwanda, and Bangladesh all are areas where less than 15 percent of their population has access to clean, safe water.[133]

The effects of groundwater depletion on rising seawater

An estimated 20 trillion tons of water has been removed from aquifers without being replaced. For many years, Saudi Arabia had been growing irrigated wheat and other crops in the desert, using water from deep fossil aquifers, many of which are now dry, so most wheat is imported. They reached peak water around 1998. The level of the water table in northern India is dropping by nearly two inches every year. The rate at which freshwater aquifers are withdrawn has more than doubled in the last few decades. If water were pumped from the Great Lakes in the United States at that rate, the lakes would be completely dry within eighty years—70 percent from agriculture, and 30 percent of that from the animals we raise and eat. The highest rates of groundwater depletion can be found in the world's major livestock and feed-crop centers of Northwest India, North and Northeast China, Northeast Pakistan, California's Central Valley, and the midwestern United States.

There are two distinct problems with rapid withdrawal of water from deep freshwater systems. One is that the fossil water from these deep aquifers is pumped out much faster than it can be replenished, so they will be irreversibly exhausted, many within our lifetime. Another is that this water is channeled into fields, and it eventually flows into the oceans. It is, in many ways, a one-way transfer that has caused a measurable rise in sea levels, on average, of 1 millimeter per year since 1961. Future storage of rainwater could offset this change but to date, this has not happened. Researchers found that the effect on rising sea levels by pumping of groundwater could be as much as five times larger in scale than the melting of the planet's ice caps in Greenland and Antarctica. Sea level expert Professor Robert Nicholis at the University of Southampton in England commented, "The water being taken from deep wells is geologically old, and there is no replenishment. Sea levels would rise 10 meters or more if all the world's groundwater was pumped out."[134]

So if we begin to run out of water, what do we do? Since 97.5 percent of the earth's water can be found in its oceans, the easiest solution seems to be to desalinate or dig deeper into the earth to find more water. Our civilization displays a curious instinct when confronted with a problem related to overconsumption—we simply find a way to produce more of what it is we are consuming, instead of limiting or stopping that consumption. Water is no exception.

There are over 21,000 desalination plants worldwide, producing 3.5 billion gallons of potable water per day. But desalinated ocean water is the most expensive form of freshwater, with infrastructure costs of collecting, distilling, and distributing it and amounting to, minimally, five times as much economic expense as the next highest source of harvesting freshwater. This presents an obvious hurdle for desalination efforts in developing countries.

Any attempt at widespread desalination would create a heavy toll on our already ravaged oceans and oceanic biodiversity. Marine biologist Sylvia Earle, former chief scientist at the U.S. National Oceanic and Atmospheric Administration, describes it best: "Oceanic water is filled with living creatures, and most of them are lost in the process of desalination. Many are microbial and some large organisms—a cross-section of life in the sea—part of the hidden cost of doing business."

Additionally, desalination presents issues with disposal of residues—essentially, concentrated saltwater sludge. In naturally freshwater-deprived areas such as the Caribbean, it might make sense to desalinate the ocean water, but elsewhere, many freshwater management practices should be implemented first to save costs and environmental damage, beginning with simply eating only plant-based foods, which saves both land and water.

New technologies needed? Rethinking our water-use strategies

There are as many reasons for our lack of freshwater as there are our many uses for it. As climate change worsens and the global population increases, concerns will deepen. The largest use of water—at over 70 percent—is food production, and the largest contributing single food type to this is meat.

Instead of looking to water-management technologies, we should look at choice. Confronting the reality of how much freshwater is wasted due to our choice to eat animals begins the solution process.

A new era of water scarcity has arrived, and it will require an enormous shift in strategy regarding how we view and manage water, particularly freshwater. This will be critical in the developing world. Many think that the primary effort should be in improving agricultural efficiencies by way of new irrigation systems and drought-resistant crops. The United Nations Environment Programme (UNEP) actually has called for "limiting consumption of meat and dairy products." The most critical changes—those necessary for the most effective, measurable, long-term water-management success—will be the eradication of meat from our diet. New irrigation systems and drought-resistant crops will surely be needed, as well as implementing methods to rebuild soil fertility and innovative ways to manage green water (precipitation), but all these should apply to producing plant-based foods if true progress is to be made. Developing and attaching proper pricing to reflect the true economic value of water should be mandatory, especially for food producers—despite its being a politically aggressive move, as free access to water has been viewed as an inherent right. Being unable to pay an appropriately affixed eco-tax for water would likely result in collapse of the meat and dairy industries. However, as individuals and governments remain unable or unwilling to address raising and eating animals and animal products, it will further stress resources, creating competition, especially for freshwater, which will then increase the risk of instability and government failure. Many countries at risk—such as in North Africa; the Horn; the Arabian Peninsula; and Southwest, Central, and South Asia—are already fragile politically, environmentally, and with a compromised health and economic status of their citizens. The world has 263 shared international water basins, where, for the most part, adequate shared-use agreements do not exist. This will become more of an issue when many of these basins begin to run dry. It makes sense for all countries to use water in the most efficient manner possible. Clearly, if there is only 1 gallon of water left in a basin or well, it shouldn't go to water a cow or to irrigate crops to feed it.

Jessica Yu, director of *Last Call at the Oasis*, a documentary on the global water crisis, reflected on her days growing up in northern California and the depth of our water crisis: *"I realize now that all I really knew was drought. I didn't factor in climate change, groundwater depletion, contamination, outdated water laws, the battle between industry and the environment, etc., etc."*

This not only sums up the depth of the problem but also highlights the insidiously detrimental effects of our choice to eat meat—the underlying link and major contributor to every one of those problems Yu didn't factor in.

The World Economic Forum—an independent international organization committed to improving the state of the world by engaging business, political, academic and other leaders of society to shape global, regional, and industry agendas—held its annual meeting in 2010 to create an alignment for use of the analytical water footprint toolkit (developed by the Water Resource Group) and the many stakeholders (business, civil, government). The goal was to build a demand-driven public/private platform to support government and policy making regarding the worsening water security situation worldwide. Agreement was made to accomplish this by pursuing the ACT (analysis, convening, and transformation) process, building coalitions to develop transformational policies and programs, projects, and partnerships in the water sector. The ACT model is already employed in India, Mexico, Jordan, China, and South Africa. This alignment and tool is an essential framework for water-policy reform.

In order to make real gains in strengthening water security, however, I feel we need to properly define water-use inefficiencies. In this case, the ACT model is a well-built framework, but the structure is only as solid as the components it holds. Those components need to identify and translate the major drivers of water use, the connection to food choice, and advocate change. Creating a platform and engaging businesses, the public, and governments is the path to take with such a diverse and crucial issue as water use. Precise definitions and specifics of direction need to be in place before platforms can be established and governmental policies are suggested.

There certainly is a water/food/energy/climate nexus related to water security, and the largest contributing factor to all four components is found in our demand to raise and eat animals. We will not be able to solve water- or food-security issues without first solving our inability to precisely articulate and then address this fact.

3

Our Oceans and Aquaculture

"THE OCEANS ARE in trouble. We are at a crossroads in history, and the actions we take—or fail to take—in the next decade will decisively impact the future of our seas and of our planet."

The above statement by the Save Our Seas Foundation is the belief of nearly all associated researchers and is considered an understatement by many. Our oceans hold 97.5 percent of all water found on earth and are responsible for producing over half of our planet's supply of oxygen, driving weather systems, buffering extremes of temperatures, absorbing 70 percent of CO_2 from our atmosphere, and harboring 80 percent of all the life on earth (found hidden beneath the waves), while serving quietly as the foundation for 100 percent of all life on earth. Our oceans are actually one global ocean, which is the circulatory system of our planet, pulsing with nutrients and energy, transporting water masses, and driving natural forces that maintain life on our planet. Without healthy oceans, our planet cannot be healthy. When our oceans die, we die.

We think of our oceans as having diverse ecosystems with robust habitats. Today, human activities have created direct and indirect pressures on our oceans that are felt everywhere on earth. Interdependent and fragile ecosystems are collapsing, many habitats have been destroyed, and marine species have been driven to extinction and others are on their way. The very resilience we felt our oceans represent is fading quickly.

Most organizations and the scientific community feel that the six main threats to our oceans are climate change, overfishing, predator loss, pollution, destruction of habitat, and bycatch, or what I prefer to call "bykill"—all the innocent sea life caught, killed, and discarded in the process of attempts to catch the specific targeted fish.

I feel, however, that a more accurate view is that our oceans are being destroyed in three major ways but by only *one primary reason*. The three ways are as follows:

1. Climate change (warming and acidification)
2. Fishing (which contributes to climate change and pollution and is by far the largest single reason for species and habitat loss, bykill, coral reef and other ecosystems destruction, and change in oxygen/ nitrogen/carbon balance)
3. Pollution (direct waste from ships of all types; indirect from land runoff)

Weaving its way through these factors is the *primary reason*, which is our global demand to eat seafood and livestock. Raising livestock on land negatively affects our oceans by way of increased greenhouse gas emissions and climate change, as well as by creating massive amounts of surface pollutant runoffs that eventually make their way to the ocean. Nitrogen runoff from livestock operations on land has created expansive "dead zones"—oxygen-depleted areas in oceans where there is no life. There are now over *four hundred* of these oxygen-depleted areas worldwide, affecting 95,000 square miles in our oceans.

Dead zones have grown eightfold in size since the 1960s. A dead zone in the Gulf of Mexico has doubled, just in the last twenty years, and is now the size of the state of Massachusetts. Low levels of oxygen in the Chesapeake Bay have caused dead zones in the bottom waters, and similar dead zones are apparent in the near-shore waters of Scandinavian coasts and the East China Sea. The world's largest dead zone is in the Baltic Sea, where deeper waters now lack oxygen year-round.

The number of dead zones in the world is doubling every ten years.[135]

Effect on and by climate change

When climate change is considered a major factor in the demise of our oceans, it must be remembered that 30–50 percent of all anthropogenic GHG is due to raising livestock. Therefore, any meaningful discussion pertaining to climate change's adverse impact on our oceans needs to be first translated to the tangible effect of the meat that we find on our plates.

The effect that livestock has on climate change is profound and has resulted from overgrazing and land-use change, deforestation, and the direct and indirect emissions of GHG (methane, CO_2, and nitrous oxide). This, then, negatively impacts our oceans in two major ways—warming and acidification, both of which alter marine ecosystems.

Oceans' heat capacity is 1,000 times that of the atmosphere, so they are key climate moderators, absorbing heat in the summer and releasing it in the winter in gradual fashion. Researchers have determined that 90 percent of the excess heat added to Earth's climate since the 1960s has been stored in the oceans, with 2009 recording the warmest ocean temperatures since recordkeeping began nearly 130 years ago. As oceans warm, extreme weather events will be more common and destructive, and sea levels will rise. Oceanic life thrive in specific water temperatures. They have sensitive thresholds, above which their ability to reproduce, grow, or even live is impaired. Warmer water also leads to stratification, where vital nutrients become trapped in deeper water, preventing phytoplankton from performing their function of transforming nutrients into energy. This is one of many disruptions affecting the entire oceanic food web by disruption of the base of the web. Phytoplankton absorb vast amounts of carbon dioxide, converting it into oxygen and plant biomass. Photosynthesis in marine plants fixes about 50 million tons of carbon per year.[136,137,138]

By absorbing nearly 50 percent of all human-produced GHG, oceanic water CO_2 levels have increased, and the pH is lowered because seawater becomes more acidic in the process. Oceanic pH levels have dropped by 30 percent (8.25 to 8.14) from pre-industrial levels, making it difficult for certain species to survive. At the current rate of worldwide GHG emissions, researchers feel the ocean's acidity could double by 2100.[139] The effects of this acidification can be devastating, particularly to calcifying organisms (sea snails, shellfish, and corals). Warming temperatures and acidification, in combination, stimulates the growth of algae, which inhibit and replace kelp forests, which are one of the most productive and important ecosystems on our planet. Acidification interferes with the communication of whales and dolphins and the most basic and essential life systems, such as feeding and reproduction. It is felt that even the most optimistic estimates of future GHG in our atmosphere will translate into oceanic CO_2 levels that will mean the end of all corals.

Dwindling sea life, loss of species

"While many human activities strain the marine environment, the primary factor in the oceans' decline is our demand for seafood. The science is unequivocal and for the most part the news is not good" (*Turning the Tide: the State of Seafood*, 2011).

Although many are concerned about life in our oceans becoming affected by global warming, commercial fishing is creating looming and more imminent extinction for vast amounts of sea life.

Thomas Huxley, in his 1883 inaugural address to the International Fisheries Exhibition in London, asserted that overfishing, or as he termed it "permanent exhaustion," of our oceans was scientifically impossible, and he stated that "all the great sea fisheries are inexhaustible." Unknowingly, the reality was that by 1883 when he made those remarks, marine fisheries were already in a state of collapse. New England fisheries were in recognized decline twelve years earlier, and at the time of Huxley's address, the Atlantic halibut fishery had already collapsed and has never recovered. This tells us two things: we didn't know much about what we were saying then regarding the health of our oceans, similar to what we find today; and overfishing, driven by economic incentives to meet our unnecessary demand to eat fish, has been with us for a while, although not at the extremes we are witnessing today.[140]

Unlike terrestrial devastation by way of food choice, it is difficult to accurately quantify (measure, track) the effect humans have on our oceans by way of fishing. The vast array of oceanic ecosystems present is fragile, interconnected, and poorly understood. That is why the oceans are in trouble—we are conducting actions on a living, vital earth system without understanding or caring about the results of those actions. Whether not caring or not understanding, it is a reckless manner to carry out the business of feeding ourselves.

Many believe that commercial fishing is governed by regulations that help to prevent overfishing, which has led to use of the word "sustainable" in the fishing industry. However, catch limits are imprecise, there are no enforceable rules regarding bykill, and fishing generally occurs without regulatory jurisdiction. It is estimated that, minimally, 26 million tons of unreported fishing occurs worldwide ("minimally" because that is only the amount that can be accounted for; many project a figure two to three times this much).

The demand to eat seafood requires massive extraction of life from our oceans. Today, there are over 4 million commercial fishing vessels in the world. This act of extracting sea life ("harvesting") creates two forms of destruction:

- loss of species
- damage to physical landscape and ecosystems as a result of loss of species and from fishing methods employed

Fish are taken from our oceans to feed us, to feed fish grown in factory fish farms (aquaculture), and as bycatch (bykill). In 2011, 165 million tons of fish were harvested; 98 million tons were wild caught (taken out of our oceans) and 67 million tons from aquaculture. Between 26 and 78 million tons of additional fish are killed each year incidentally as bykill and thrown overboard.[141]

A quick snapshot of the current state of our oceans reveals a dismal picture. Of the seventeen primary fishing stocks (subpopulations of a particular species of fish) worldwide, *all* are either overexploited or on the verge of collapse.[142] Examples of commercially extinct areas are the Grand Banks near Newfoundland and the Georges Banks off New England, both once considered the most productive on earth. At less than 1 percent their original numbers in these waters, now there simply are no fish. With 1,081 types of fish listed as threatened or endangered, 85 percent of the world's fisheries have been pushed to or beyond their biological limits. Ninety percent of all large predatory fish—tuna, sharks, swordfish, cod, halibut— are gone. Scientists predict world fisheries could collapse entirely by 2050, if fishing continues at current levels.[143-146]

By changing the population of one species, fishing alters the shape and composition of entire marine ecosystems by way of a cascading effect on their predators and prey. Also, fishing leads to serial depletion, where a commercially desirable species becomes depleted, and the industry simply shifts its focus to the next most economically valuable species—a form of exploitation by fishing down the food web.[147,148,149]

Fishing organizations and fishery managers currently establish catch limits, based on the maximum sustainable yield (MSY) of a particular species. The MSY guides the fishing industry to establish the total allowable catch (TAC), now used by most producers. As noted, however, catch limits are imprecise. Additionally, there is little scientific understanding of what is "sustainable" (or "allowable") for a species, even less understanding of the effect it will have on interacting ecosystems, and no accurate understanding of how many target fish are actually caught, as well as bykill, worldwide on a daily basis. There is no system in place to prevent population or ecosystem collapse. Knowledge of devastation occurs after the fact, when it is often too late for recovery.

Rapid deterioration of marine ecosystems began in the late 1800s with the growth of industrial-scale fishing, which incorporated the use of large, mechanized fishing vessels equipped with advanced technologies to find and catch fish. Since then, there has been significant decline in targeted and non-targeted fish and serious impact on marine habitat. Industrialized fishing and ineffective management continues. It becomes fairly easy to criticize the system that uses MSY and TAC from a theoretical and empirical standpoint. Setting accurate TACs is highly improbable, because it would involve a complex process with an infinite amount of factors and variables, of which we have little knowledge. Despite this fact, setting a species' MSY and TAC continues, with decisions of the fishing industry based roughly on these figures. Even if researchers were able to more accurately assess the comprehensive impact we exert on our oceans worldwide, only 7 percent of coastal governments employ rigorous scientific assessments as the basis for their fishery management policies. Only 1.4 percent of coastal governments use a transparent process to convert scientific recommendations into policy, and less than 1 percent provide for strict enforcement of fisheries regulations.[150,151]

Most marine animals are negatively impacted by our activities in more than one way. As an example, many species of whales have been hunted and killed to near extinction. The ones that remain are now caught and killed as bykill in our pursuit to eat fish, and their habitat is negatively impacted by increased traffic (more fishing vessels), pollution, loss of food supply (we are now extracting massive amounts of krill), and adversely modified ocean water by way of acidification and warming due to climate change.

Coral reefs worldwide are in serious trouble. The Great Barrier Reef has lost more than half of its coral cover since 1985. The primary cause of coral reef death throughout many regions, especially in the Caribbean, is not pollution or climate change—it's overfishing. Unsustainable fishing and loss of apex predators like sharks results in shifting of fish size and species composition within coral communities, which precipitates large-scale ecosystem changes.[152]

This can happen as a single threat or in combination with other threats such as climate change. With an absence of large predatory and competing herbaceous fish due to overfishing in the Caribbean reefs, the long-spined sea urchin became the primary control of macroalgae levels on those reefs. The increase in population density of this urchin left them vulnerable to a disease that killed off over 90 percent of the species in the Western Atlantic in 1982, which led to overgrowth of algae and eventual decline of reefs in the region without recovery. The loss of sharks as bykill and direct fishing is one of the direct factors responsible for coral reef loss in the Caribbean and elsewhere in the world.[153]

An opposite example can be found in the Queens Islands off the southern coast of Cuba, where commercial fishing has been banned since 1980 and resident fish species have increased by as much as 50 percent. There, coral bleaching is minimal, and recovery occurs rapidly. Predator fish are abundant, and all ecosystems are healthy.

Bycatch, bykill

Bykill occurs at every level and with every type of commercial fishing. Many types of marine life are affected at the ocean surface, and there is severe damage to vulnerable deep-water ecosystems on the ocean floor. Bykill includes nearly all fish species as well as seabirds, sea lions, all seven species of endangered sea turtles, porpoises, dolphins, and even whales. Billions of corals, sponges, and starfish in fragile reef ecosystems are also lost as bykill.

A few of the bykill numbers occurring each year and fishing methods involved:[154]

- Over 300,000 small whales, dolphins, and porpoises (purse seine)
- Over 250,000 critically endangered leatherback and endangered loggerhead sea turtles (longlines and shrimp trawling operations)
- Over 300,000 seabirds (longlines)
- 89 percent of hammerhead sharks and 80 percent of white and thresher sharks (all fishing methods)

An estimated 500 miles of nonbiodegradable fishing nets have been cut loose from fishing vessels each year for the past twenty-five years, which catch countless numbers of sea creatures and essentially become depots of coagulated dead marine animals.

The current and future problem: sustainable certification

It was inevitable that someone would develop an organization and labeling system by which we could all feel comfortable in continuing to consume sea life taken from the ocean. This makes sense—to our habituated palate and economically. An example of this is the Marine Stewardship Council (MSC), created in 1997 out of a joint venture by the World Wildlife Fund (WWF) and Unilever to certify which fish populations and fishing methods are "sustainable." Their combined objectives are to "work with progressive seafood companies to harness consumer power in support of conservation." They tell us, "Sustainable business is good business." In fact, they were right. Sustainable business *is* good business, but that only applies if there is a clear understanding of what "sustainable" means. Unfortunately, there is not. As of 2012, MSC has awarded blue eco-labels of certified sustainability to over 130 fisheries. It is interesting to note, though, that with each certification, MSC is paid between $30,000 and $100,000 and thus far, all fisheries seeking certification since 1997 have been approved.

Certain fisheries are able to display the MSC's "Fish Forever" label, signifying to the public that their product was caught using socially responsible and environmentally sound management practices. So this becomes an interesting prospect.

There still will be two types of consumers of sea life: (1) those who do not understand or care about where their food is derived; and (2) those who are aware that we must start thinking about the origins of our food choices, but they want to rely on a trusted entity to provide assistance and justification in purchasing and consuming that choice. Customers relying on MSC or any mode of certification to validate their demand to eat fish are being misled. More importantly, it ultimately furthers the decline in numbers of various fish species and the effect on other ecosystems. Although it may seem like a step in the right direction, certification organizations such as MSC are improperly designed and have, at best, conflicting intentions. MSC was not established to be a steward of our oceans; their principal focus is how to continue fishing and appear responsible during a time when consumers' concern for our environment is on the increase. The conscientious consumer has a desire to feel justified in eating fish and the process of catching and killing them. MSC and other certification labels provide them with this, so the habit can and will continue.

The Monterey Bay Aquarium Seafood Watch (MBASW) is another certifying organization. Since its establishment in 1999, their vision of sustainability is to encourage consumers and businesses to purchase seafood that is fished or farmed in ways that do not harm the environment. MBASW states, "When there is scientific uncertainty, we err on the side of conservation." However, with the limited pool of knowledge we currently have regarding the complexity of various oceanic ecosystems and our effect on them, "scientific uncertainty" is a given. Therefore any guidance provided by MBASW and our subsequent decisions regarding sustainable seafood are questionable and without accuracy. They have a rating system that easily guides businesses and the general public to purchase and consume what MBASW recommends as sustainable. As an organization, they are well linked and influential, with distribution of over 40 million pocket guides and affiliations with over 200 partnering businesses and the two largest food service companies in the U.S. Their rating system is separated into three categories: Best Choice, Good Alternative, and Those to Avoid.

The Monterey Bay Aquarium Seafood Watch states that their recommendations consider the fishery, habitat, species, management, and "a host of other factors that affect each species." "Host of other factors" means support of the fishing industry and economic factors that are driven by the demand to eat specific species. MBASW has also shown a limited and biased regard to the effect fishing has on other oceanic wildlife. As an example, for many years they have recommended lobster from the Gulf of Maine as a "Good Alternative," directing millions of individuals to consume them. However, lobster harvesting is not at all sustainable for three reasons:

1. Declining number of lobster in that region
2. Inefficient trapping mechanisms, catching and killing more lobster and other sea life than needed
3. The tragic effect lobster trapping has on the 400 critically endangered North Atlantic right whale remaining in the world

The long-standing recommendation for lobster as a Good Alternative remains as a symbol of a major disconnect and that the fate of many species is in the hands of a community of scientists, businesses, and consumers who are not aware or who do not care.

Seeing through clouded corporate pledges

Partnerships are now being developed between large players in the food service industry such as Aramark, and certifying organizations such as MBASW. One such alliance occurred in 2008 with a commitment by Aramark to "preserve the world's oceans" by partnering with MBASW, which will guide company practices of supply, purchasing, and consumption of sustainable seafood for as many as 260,000 Aramark employees and tens of millions of consumers in businesses, universities, schools, sports and entertainment facilities, parks, and many locations in twenty-two countries where they operate. The transition to purchase seafood species listed only in the Best Choice or Good Alternative categories is to be completed "by the year 2018," as stated by respective corporate officers. Information about this grand proclamation was made public and can be found in a conspicuous area of information titled "Environmental Stewardship" on their website. This is good business and superb marketing.

This appears to be like so many other claims of apparent concern for our planet, so I felt it important to contact both the Monterey Bay Aquarium Seafood Watch and Aramark to clarify their commitment and ascertain the degree of progress—important information for consumers who rely on words turning into action. I proposed the following questions to both corporations regarding their 2008 agreement:

1. What quantifiable progress has been made by Aramark in regard to this commitment? For instance, what percentage of all Aramark seafood products was considered MBASW sustainable (green or yellow) in 2008, and what percentage of all seafood products are now sustainable (in 2012)?

2. Is your agreement to reach 100 percent compliance in your green or yellow designation for all their seafood products (by the year 2018) or simply working toward that goal by then?

3. What is Aramark's total amount in tons of seafood products sold per year (most recent yearly figure), to give your customers an idea of just how much seafood (sea life) will be affected with this commitment?

Alison Barratt, communications senior manager with MBASW, deferred to Aramark, stating, "Aramark is best placed to respond to the progress made to date." The response from Aramark's communications senior manager, Megan Haney, was that all my answers could be found on their public website. Such answers were not available, so I fired off the following communication to Ms. Haney and three other senior members of Aramark's executive staff:

I find it both interesting and disconcerting that you directed me to a comprehensive public marketing site for your company, rather than answering the questions specifically and in an up-to-date fashion. The only subtitles found under the search for "sustainable seafood" on your website were:

1. An outdated public announcement about the 2008 agreement with Monterey Bay Aquarium Seafood Watch

2. Two additional links to generalized statements about Aramark's "commitment to help preserve the world's oceans ..."

Additionally, the links would not open; there was an indication of all three being a "bad request."

Ms. Haney, what I am asking is for specific

information, essentially validating your company's commitment with Monterey Bay Aquarium Seafood Watch to these prior public statements. It would seem as if a company as large as yours, making such environmentally important statements, would/should be more than happy to provide specific answers that would substantiate commitments and objectives claimed to be part of your corporate responsibility. Transparency and ease of retrieving this information would seem to be prudent and mandatory, rather than asking a researcher to filter through your generic website used more for public marketing, branding, and image strengthening. This is not the time for that.

Someone within Aramark should have the answers to my questions right at their fingertips and be more than happy to provide them to me—unless, of course, there is something to hide. Please direct me to the person who would be best suited to answer the simple and few questions I posed. I sincerely appreciate your understanding and assistance with this and look forward to hearing from you soon. Many thanks.

The corporate response to this was: "We stand by our commitment to the Monterey Bay Aquarium Seafood Watch and are making progress toward that commitment. The information you request is proprietary and as a matter of corporate policy, we will not disclose this type of business information."

Obviously, something remains hidden behind the fluff of corporate environmental concern, as they are simply not proud about their progress. I offered them a great opportunity to let their many customers know just what environmental stewardship really means to them. Of what value are corporate pledges, partnerships, or commitments without definitive action?

Walmart and Wegmans have followed suit with public announcements of use of the MBASW recommendations, and Whole Foods has pledged to eliminate all MBASW red-list seafood by Earth

Day 2013. Compass Group joins Aramark as the two largest food service corporations in North America, pledging to phase out seafood on the MBASW red list. In the final analysis, it is not about a pledge proclaimed by big business. It's about how accurately the word "sustainable" is defined and used (or abused) by the certifying organizations and how the pledges are translated into tangible actions by the multinational corporations who are publicly committing to environmental stewardship in this regard.

Another avenue corporations have taken in order to appear concerned about our oceans is a public alignment with Seafood Choices Alliance, an international program of the nonprofit ocean conservation organization SeaWeb. Seafood Choices Alliance isn't able to accomplish its stated objectives, due to lack of properly defined interests by stakeholders (i.e., most are involved in the *business* of fishing, not the conservation and protection of fish) and the general lack of ability to monitor or enforce.

With these examples, we can find difficulties on two levels. First, certifying organizations are not entirely precise or credible. Second, large corporate entities aligning themselves with these certifying organizations do so for obvious marketing purposes, enhancement of public opinion, and ultimate economic gain—all at the expense of the continued demise of our oceans and the life they contain.

Killing machines

Commercial fishing has an enormous arsenal of tools, using technology such as GPS, radar, satellites, and computerized information that enables them to locate which fish are left in an area to be captured. Once located, there are many methods used to catch fish, including purse seine, trawling, gillnetting, and longline. All of these methods are destructive by any definition of the word—they *catch* and *kill* fish. The Marine Stewardship Council, the Monterey Bay Aquarium Seafood Watch, and other organizations allow nearly every fishing method, including bottom trawling. Only explosives and poisons are banned, but these methods are on the rise worldwide because the ruling is unenforceable. The world is turning to these organizations because they are the respected certifiers of what is considered sustainable sea life. Yet they all allow fishing of heavily depleted stocks, massive bykill ratios, and the killing of endangered sea mammals, directly or indirectly, in the process.

Trawling of all types is damaging but most severe is bottom trawling, which is similar to clear-cutting forests. With bottom trawling, ocean floors as deep as 2,000 meters are bulldozed, killing everything in its path, leaving scars miles long, and sending up raised plumes of polluted sediment that can be seen from space. Many trawling operations catch nine to ten times more sea life as bykill than the targeted fish they catch.[155]

Many of the larger purse seine operations are able to take 150 tons of fish in one catch. They find and track a large school of targeted fish with sophisticated location equipment, circle the school, and then pull them in, somewhat like a large bag catching every single fish in that school—sometimes 7,000 or more fish—leaving no young or juvenile fish. This is the method used for tuna fishing, which is an $8 billion per year industry, with 4 million tons caught per year. This is four times more than was caught in 1970. Purse seine tend to catch every fish and sea life that were with the targeted fish, including dolphins and endangered sea turtles. Turtles are able to only hold their breath for thirty minutes, and many times they drown, being unable to escape.[156]

Longline fishing extends a line from the boat, 25 miles on average, with some known to exceed 100 miles. With thousands of barbs and hooks, longlines snag any species of sea life and birds that happen to swim near the lines, including birds such as the albatross. With nineteen of the twenty-two species of albatross endangered due to longline and other fishing, some countries like New Zealand have mandated the use of plastic bird ties on longlines to scare them away.[157]

Certain poisons such as cyanide are on the increase, where fishers spray sodium cyanide into the water to stun fish without killing them for easier harvesting. Originally used to supply fish to the international aquarium trade, now cyanide and other poisons are used to supply live reef fish to restaurants in Southeast Asia, such as in Singapore and China.

More than 22,000 tons of live fish are eaten annually just in the restaurants of Hong Kong. For every single fish caught using cyanide poisoning, one square meter of the respective coral reef is killed. Dynamite and other explosives are also used, being set off under water, and the dead fish (and all sea life in the area of the explosion) float to the surface for fishers to net. The underwater habitat involved is decimated. This form of fishing is on the rise, especially in Southeastern Asia, where massive coral reef destruction has occurred over the past twenty years.[158]

One of the most blatant examples of lack of regulatory control in our oceans is with shark finning. Over 100 million sharks are killed each year, with more than 90 percent of many shark species gone—many as bykill; others taken for shark fin soup, where the dorsal fin is cut off the shark, and then the shark is thrown overboard to die. This is because there are no strict or consistent international policies to protect sharks and no policing of the oceans, even if policies were in place. Sharks play a critical role in balancing reef, seabeds, and other vital ecosystems and have done so for more than 400 million years. The health of our oceans depends on the health of shark and other predator species, which is currently being lost over a bowl of shark fin soup. It is interesting to note that as of 2012, five states in the U.S. have banned shark fin soup.

But nearly half of the 100 million sharks killed each year are caught in fishing nets and lines as bykill. If we are truly concerned about sharks, banning shark fin soup is not enough. We should ban fishing.[159,160]

Only 1.4 percent of coastal governments use a transparent process to convert the recommendations based on limited scientific knowledge into policy and less than 1 percent provide for strict enforcement of fisheries regulations.[161]

The Exclusive Economic Zone (EEZ) is a strip of water allowing for a 200-mile extension from the mainland of each country to claim as its own, managing the waters by way of nation jurisdiction. This leaves all the rest of our oceans, or high seas, vulnerable to international use without regulation or monitoring.

Many conservation organizations, such as Greenpeace, WWF, and the Union for Conservation of Nature, advocate establishment of marine protected areas (MPA) but of the 5,880 that currently exist in the world (1.1 percent of our oceans), all are poorly regulated, without strict enforcement. At the most recent meeting in Nagoya, Japan, in 2010, the Convention on Biologic Diversity set forth an agreement by 196 nations to preserve 10 percent of our oceans by the year 2020, which can only be viewed as an embarrassing display of stewardship.

Despite lack of ambition by the global community, the few marine protected areas (MPAs) that have been in place do form the beginnings of refuge oases for wildlife. An international team of scientists found that 35 percent of the world's endangered green sea turtles are found within MPAs—a remarkable and surprising statistic considering that only a small portion of shallow oceans are designated as protected areas. Credit should be given to the turtles for finding their way to the very few and small sanctuaries.[162]

New Guinea was the first Pacific island country to propose that the high seas become off limits to global commercial fishing in order for sea life to regenerate. Because there is no monitoring or enforcement, our high seas are being pilfered by selfish fishing vessels, individuals, countries, and industries that care only about their immediate needs, without concern for the ecosystems and species they are destroying or for future generations of humans.

Sustainable certification may occur under the guise of science, but many researchers unaffiliated with the Marine Stewardship Council or the Monterey Bay Aquarium Seafood Watch admit to not fully understanding the complexities and interrelationships of all ecosystems found in our oceans. Indeed, there has been a very clear pattern established of certifying a fishery as sustainable and then witnessing the decline of that very same species, as well as other species of sea life including fish, mammals, birds, plants, and entire ecosystems.

Five species of salmon are listed as sustainable, despite loss of numbers or being caught by methods that are quite damaging to ecosystems. Considered sustainable by the MSC and MBASW, the Fraser River sockeye salmon are considered "endangered" by those biologists who are intimately studying them, such as the Committee on the Status of Endangered Wildlife in Canada, and considered "critically endangered" by the International Union for the Conservation of Nature, whose scientists consider overfishing a key threat to the stocks' health.

Coho and Chinook salmon, whose numbers and habitat we have devastated, are allowed to be "sustainably" caught by gill net, troll, and seine methods in many areas including the Annette Islands Reserve.[163-166]

In early 2010, the MSC was criticized by many environmental groups, such as the Sierra Club, for certifying these salmon as sustainable. In 2011, the MSC came under fire by several European World Wildlife Fund chapters for certifying the Denmark North Sea plaice fishery for similar reasons, opening the door for exploitation of stressed species. Many of the assessments upon which the MSC certification is made are conducted by commercial contractors, paid by the fisheries, which creates an obvious conflict of interest—the assessors have a financial incentive to recommend fisheries as sustainable and get more work and profits from the resulting annual audits.[167]

Antarctic krill, the most abundant animal species on earth, has seen its numbers plummet by 78 percent since 1980, which has affected the decline of certain penguin species and the food supply of endangered blue, right, and fin whales. Yearly quotas for krill are 1.5 million tons, yet researchers admit "production and total biomass of krill is still very uncertain."[168]

The most heavily harvested fish in the world is the Alaskan pollock at a rate of 3 million tons per year. The stock levels of Alaskan pollock in the East Bering Sea fell 64 percent in just the period of time between 2004 and 2009. They are caught by industrial trawl methods that have proven to seriously damage ecosystems and create large amounts of bykill. Pacific hake saw their biomass suffer an 89 percent decline since 1989, without recovery. Both pollock and hake fisheries are under the watch of the Marine Stewardship Council and are labeled "sustainable."[169]

Swordfish numbers have declined by over 90 percent, yet in the northwest Atlantic, it is certified "sustainable" to kill them by harpooning and by hooks on longline. Numbers are so low that up to 70 percent of captured swordfish by commercial and recreational fishers are below approved minimum size. Despite this, the MBASW has listed swordfish as a "Best Choice" if harpooned anywhere in United States or Canadian waters, the North Atlantic, the East Pacific, or the waters off Hawaii.[170]

Most types of tuna (e.g., bigeye, yellowfin) are in "assessment," meaning we do not have accurate numbers or know our precise effect on them, but they are deemed as sustainable if caught anywhere in the southeastern U.S. Atlantic waters by longline methods.

For centuries, cod was the fish in most demand worldwide, with seemingly inexhaustible stocks, especially from the Grand Banks off Newfoundland, Canada. Internationally agreed upon quotas began in the early 1970s, and fishing continued under scientifically established limits and with a national declaration by Canada of an exclusive fishing zone. But by 1992, cod had been overfished to 1 percent of their original numbers. The fishery collapsed, and a moratorium on fishing in the area was imposed; the fishery was closed indefinitely in 2003. Despite this, recovery of cod has not happened and after twenty years, researchers have found the ecosystem has changed substantially, indicating that cod may never make a comeback. This is a sad example of our stewardship failure on many levels:

1. Extraction and killing of a species and ecosystems of which we have little knowledge, thinking it is inexhaustible, or not thinking at all about that possibility
2. Lack of recognition of our limited knowledge in this regard
3. Lack of respect for that species and involved ecosystems
4. Inability to act appropriately when first recognized
5. Inability to learn from this experience and to apply to current and future ocean management policies

And the same scenario is occurring in the North Sea. In 2006, the UK and European governments reduced quota numbers because North Sea cod were nearing an extinct status. This occurred because there were serious miscalculations of what fishing industry analysts and regulators felt were sustainable in that region. Also, there was no accounting for cod becoming bykill. In 2007, researchers realized that cod bykill totaled at least 50,000 tons per year, which happens to be almost double the established quota limit of 26,000 tons. They were killing and throwing overboard more cod as bykill than was allowed by going after cod by itself.[171]

The New Zealand hoki (blue grenadier) is now used by McDonald's in their fish sandwich because we have decimated the cod species, which used to be everyone's fish sandwich. Hoki was the third fishery to achieve "sustainable certification" status by the MSC in 2001. The quota for harvesting hoki was 300,000 tons from 1995 to 2001, but the MSC had to do a quick reversal to 100,000 tons per year, because catching hoki causes significant trawling damage, obvious loss of hoki, and the killing of thousands of seabirds and sea lions. Thirty percent of the hoki from New Zealand is exported, with most of it routed through China, where it is processed into fish sticks and filets for the U.S. and Western Europe markets. Chile and Argentina quotas for hoki were reduced by more than 25 percent due to similar findings of rapidly declining numbers of fish and inaccurate initial estimates of "sustainability" by organizations such as the Marine Stewardship Council. The MSC by itself, however, cannot be viewed as the principal offender of misusing the word "sustainable" with regard to our oceans. The international fishing industry is in a constant drive toward increased extraction of sea life, as influenced by a number of interests including a vast number of governmental agencies, subsidies, corporate concerns, and cultural factors. But none is as powerful as the global demand to eat seafood and the economic benefits of meeting that demand.[172]

Orange roughy, a species found in the waters off New Zealand, was discovered in the 1970s but by 2008, the species had already been overfished, down to 10 percent of its original numbers, becoming the first commercially caught fish to appear on Australia's endangered species list.[173]

Because it's running out of fish, the industry has turned to the Southern Ocean, despite the objections of a number of organizations concerned about conservation. In 2011, the MSC awarded its eco-label of certified sustainability to the Ross Sea Antarctic toothfish fishery, despite its being considered "exploratory," with very little known about stock numbers, breeding, or how the fish has been affected since opening the fishery in 2005. Nevertheless, 3,000 tons of toothfish are now taken from our oceans each year. As of 2012, researchers have never seen a juvenile toothfish and still do not know even where they spawn.

Scientists are just now beginning systematic study of these fish and their remote habitat. Age at maturity, life history, population structure, effects on and by other species, and ecosystems remain unknown. Most toothfish are taken by bottom longlines, with some taken by trawling. The rapid expansion of toothfish fishery has been linked to new longlining techniques, which allow fishers to work deeper and rougher waters. Seabirds, including petrels and albatrosses, are routinely attracted to these longline baits and get caught on hooks, dragged underwater, and drowned. Several of these species are internationally endangered. The Commission for the Conservation of Antarctic Marine Living Resources (CCLAMR) has stipulated requirements for reduction of longline use but as typically found in the industry, there is no means of enforcement. Australia has led efforts to ban illegal fishing methods, installing satellite tracking devices, imposing steep fines and strict enforcement within its Exclusive Economic Zone, and chasing down offenders to help curb illegal fishing in remote areas.

A team including the Antarctic and Southern Ocean Coaltition (ASOC), Last Ocean Charitable Trust, and Greenpeace stated that the certification by the MSC ignores forty scientists from seven countries who argue that there is too much uncertainty surrounding the health of the Ross Sea toothfish population to call it sustainable. Nevertheless, harvesting of toothfish continues in what is considered to be the last area of intact oceanic ecosystems on the planet.[174,175]

Next to pollock, menhaden is the most widely fished species in the U.S. Over 400,000 tons of these fish are extracted from our eastern coast each year. Menhaden, like many heavily harvested, small pelagic fish (e.g., herring, anchovy, sardine), form a critical link between the lower and upper levels of the oceanic food web.

They are a key food source for larger fish, mammals, and birds at one end, and at the other end, menhaden are filter feeders, grazing on various planktons and algae that are responsible for oxygen and carbon exchange of our oceans and feed for other sea life. Although menhaden were considered "sustainable" for the past twenty years, scientists independent of the certification process in 2011 concluded that declining stocks of menhaden were now worrisome, and quotas have been reduced by 30 percent.[176]

It becomes an improbable task for researchers and sustainable certifying organizations (e.g., MSC, MBASW) to exhaustively study and accurately and comprehensively understand the effect that extracting pelagic or any other fish has on all of the dependent wildlife and their interacting ecosystems. There is an infinite line of connection, of intertwining ecosystems. *Has the fishing industry and sustainable certification organizations accounted for and devised a calculation of this infinity?*

The case of bluefin tuna

The National Oceanic and Atmospheric Administration (NOAA) announced in May 2011 that bluefin tuna would *not* be listed as endangered, despite losing 96 percent of its numbers. This endangered status would have provided the much-needed legal protection in hope of recovery. The tragic decline of this beautiful fish is due to overfishing and illegal practices, poorly designed and ignored "quotas," and false reporting, lack of understanding the species' complex life, and our inappropriate choice of food and the demand for sushi. Even though numerous countries, including the U.S., actively harvest bluefin tuna, Japan purchases 80 percent of the world's supply and vehemently opposes any ban or restrictions on tuna. As stewards of our planet, this is certainly not a logical decision. It also is embarrassing because we have relentlessly caught and killed bluefin tuna to the point of near extinction, strictly because we want to eat them—essentially due to an unnecessary, acquired taste and habit, and of course, due to economics. By not granting an "endangered" status, we have missed an opportunity to right a wrong; we are being oblivious and apathetic to what we are doing to another living species on earth. Total catch of all tuna (Atlantic, Pacific, and southern bluefin, bigeye, albacore, and skipjack) species has grown steadily since the 1960s, with skipjack making up 51 percent of the global catch, with over 70 percent of all tuna caught by purse seine. All types of tuna are at risk of becoming overfished. China developed a distant-water tuna fleet, catching over 100,000 tons per year across the Pacific, Atlantic, and Indian Oceans.

Bluefin tuna grow up to 14 feet in length, weigh up to half a ton, and can swim 50 mph for long distances, which is why their stocks are governed by an organization composed of many countries, the International Commission for the Conservation of Atlantic Tuna, based in Spain. The tuna are managed as two stocks—the western Atlantic and eastern Atlantic, which includes Mediterranean blue fin tuna. For the past forty years, blue fin tuna have been caught and eaten without regard to potential extinction. Although many are harpooned and caught by big-game fisherman, most commercial vessels catch them by using longline and purse seine techniques, dropping a mile-long net and circling a large school of tuna with a boat, and then catching the entire school and all other sea life that happen to be present, such as dolphins, seabirds, and endangered turtles. Many more bluefin tuna are killed each year than are reproduced—with up to 150,000 tons of total tuna killed in just one year alone. Annual cumulative "declared" catch amounts by tuna fishing vessels from 2006 through 2009 ranged from 21,000 tons to 35,000 tons, although the International Commission for the Conservation of Atlantic Tunas (ICCAT) admits now that "catches of bluefin tuna have been seriously underreported," with catches in the Mediterranean area alone now more realistically estimated at 61,000 tons per year. The current recommended yearly "sustainable" catch rate by the ICCAT is 13,500 tons—but this is absurd, since there already has proven to be no accurate reporting methods and no enforcement protocols, thus leading to the decimation that is seen today. Committee members admit that "given the quantified uncertainties, the bluefin tuna stock would not be expected to rebuild by 2019, even with no fishing," and some scientists predicted that without protection, the species would become extinct in the Mediterranean by the end of 2012. They have already been fished to extinction in the Black and Caspian Seas. Most researchers without economic ties to the tuna fishing industry agree that they do not fully understand the complex life of the bluefin and associated ecosystems. Many are concerned that their numbers are under further duress because of the BP oil spill and longline activity throughout the species' spawning grounds in the Gulf of Mexico. Many longline fishing operations in that area use multibarbed nets that can extend up to 25 miles, catching bluefin tuna and other sea life as bykill.[177-180]

Despite all of these facts, the ICCAT and NOAA feel that this fish needs no protection. For months, a review process was established to help determine whether to grant an endangered species status to the bluefin tuna. This review was conducted by the National Marine Fisheries Service (NMFS) and then submitted to the NOAA for final determination. Much of the final decision was based on the result of interviews requested by the NMFS of the tuna fishing industry itself—those fishermen whose livelihood depends on catching these fish. The following is an excerpt taken directly from the formal correspondence to all commercial tuna fishermen with regard to a determination meeting about the bluefin tuna:

Questions attendees may consider include the following: What are your general impressions of the abundance and distribution of Atlantic bluefin tuna over time? If you have experienced a decline or increase in bluefin tuna catches, what do you attribute this to (abundance, distribution, availability, gear changes, regulatory effects, etc.)? Are there particular areas where you typically encounter larger numbers of bluefin tuna? If so, where are they (e.g., inshore or offshore)? Do these areas change on an annual basis? What is the average size of bluefin tuna being caught by different gear types or fisheries? Written comments may also be sent to National Marine Fisheries Service, Northeast Regional Office, Protected Resources Division, 55 Great Republic Drive, Gloucester, MA 01930.

Unbelievable, isn't it? This series of questions essentially asks the bluefin tuna fishermen if they think what they catch every day for their income and food should be taken away from them. Brilliant.

In January 2012, one single bluefin tuna—just *one* of these fish— sold for $736,000 (56.49 million yen) at Tokyo's Tsukiiui fish market auction. Caught off northeastern Japan, this bluefin tuna was purchased by the president of a sushi restaurant chain who said he wanted to "liven up Japan." One year later, in January 2013, another single bluefin tuna sold for $1.8 million in Japan. This certainly will not help the bluefin tuna's cause for achieving protection and fighting back extinction while in the firm grasp of media hype, public demand, and economic motives.

Rich Ruais, executive director of the American Bluefin Tuna Association stated, "There are over 5,000 commercial and 15,000 recreational tuna fishermen just in the U.S., stretching from Maine to Texas, and they are relieved NOAA didn't give the fish an endangered status." And if you still wonder if politics ever plays a role in decisions about food choice and eventual loss of biodiversity, consider this statement from Senator Olympia Snowe of Maine: "Listing the bluefin as threatened or endangered would have jeopardized the livelihood of tuna fishermen." What else needs to be said?[181]

Loss of 90 percent of global stocks of large predator fish like the blue fin tuna, swordfish, and sharks will have negative cascading effects, most likely more widespread than what we are able to predict. Exacerbated declines in both commercial and noncommercial fish species and deaths of coral reef ecosystems are already attributed to our overkilling and eating of large fish.

The effect on other sea mammals

In January 2012, the MBASW placed a new Good Alternative status on Atlantic haddock, pollock, and cod. All have seen significant declines in number, and cod fishing, as we discussed, has been banned in some areas of the world since 1992 without recovery. All three species happen to carry the highest consumer demand. A new ban was placed in January 2011 on mackerel and Pacific cod fishing near the Aleutian Islands, due to the decline of the endangered western Steller sea lions, who lost more than 50 percent of their population from 2000 to 2008. By 2011, scientists were finally able to convey the dire predicament we were placing on this sea lion species because of our demand to eat their food. The message I pull out of this is that we have to wait for an endangered species to decline in numbers by 50 percent or more before we realize we are extracting too many fish from the ocean, and we really didn't have a clue as to what numbers of mackerel and cod we could take until it became embarrassingly obvious.[182]

Because of the ban on these fisheries and new imposition on the fishing industry in the Pacific Northwest, Alaska, Washington, and Oregon petitioned for de-listing (taking off the endangered list) of the eastern Steller sea lion. This will reduce the regulatory burden on some public and private sector activities and allow fishers to more easily meet their quotas.

Attorney General Dan Sullivan and state endangered-species coordinator Doug Vincent-Lang said research has not shown a connection between commercial fishing and nutritional harm to Steller sea lions (western or eastern species) and that the federal agency *"has not given sufficient consideration to the economic damage fishing restrictions would do to Aleutian communities."* Spokespersons for the fishing industry have said on the record that "biological opinion" concludes that current fishing practices were not having impact on sperm whales and humpback whales either. It's interesting that in the last discussion I had with sperm whale researchers, they admitted to not understanding the species very well—yet somehow people in the fishing industry do.

Mixed signals

"I love fish. ... Salmon is my favorite fish." Those words spoken by actor Ted Danson as he appeared March 22, 2011, at Climate One at the Commonwealth Club, a leadership dialogue based in San Francisco, California. It is interesting to note that for Mr. Danson—and 98 percent of all other individuals in the world—the words "I love fish" really mean "I love to *eat* fish." No offense to Mr. Danson and perhaps things have changed recently, but if he really loved fish, as he loved his cat or dog, for example, he certainly wouldn't kill and eat them. This misuse of words and perhaps sentiment is at the epicenter of how the world is now approaching solutions to very real ecological problems.[183]

With each of the specific topics of global depletion, there are a few organizations engaged in researching and developing strategies for resolution. Oceana is one of those organizations. Oceana is the largest international ocean conservation and advocacy group, campaigning to prevent collapse of fish populations, marine mammals, and other sea life. One of their primary objectives is to produce clear, identifiable policy changes, with a three- to five-year timeframe. Oceana was established in 2001 by a number of leading foundations, led by the Pew Charitable Trust, and then merged with American Oceans Campaign, founded by Ted Danson, to further address the mission of protecting and restoring the world's oceans. Mr. Danson remains their most visible spokesperson.

While Oceana has many accomplishments, with an array of ongoing campaigns, such as protecting sea turtles, pollution, shark finning, and offshore drilling, true definitive progress will be difficult until the connection is made to changing our eating habits. All of their projects reflect a defining objective to maintain cultural demand to catch and eat fish. For twenty-five years, since the American Oceans Campaign began in 1987, Danson has lobbied for protecting our oceans, while at the same time promoting fishing and the fishing industry. Frequently interviewed, he has been quoted a number of times making claims such as "This is about people being able to fish and eat fish forever. It's not save the fishes; this is save the fisherman." And that is what millions of viewers and listeners are hearing.

In 2010, Oceana and Ted Danson became most visible, with their mission of reducing worldwide fishing subsidies, now totaling $20 billion. This, according to Oceana, promotes overfishing. Most researchers agree that we are taking fish out of our oceans at a rate of 2.5 times what might be considered "sustainable," fueling a $110 billion fishing industry. But once more, Oceana and Ted Danson are missing the most important point—it isn't a loan or tax break that drives how many fish are taken from our oceans; it's our demand to eat fish.

Turning to aquaculture

Our oceans are running out of fish, so instead of simply not eating them (which would be a solution), we have turned to aquaculture—raising fish on fish farms. Now, 50 percent of all fish consumed worldwide is from fish farms, and it is growing faster than any other food sector. A reason for this tremendous growth is the false illusion of environmentalism. As with factory farms and grass-fed livestock operations, fish farms present their own set of ecologic damage—pollution with uneaten feed, chemicals, antibiotics, and feces; disease; and energy use. Although the intent is to move away from our dependence on catching fish out of our oceans, raising fish in factory fish-farm settings is actually depleting more of our oceans. That's because every fish raised in fish-farm settings still needs to eat other fish (in one form or another) in order to grow and obtain omega-3 fatty acids. Farmed fish are fed wild-caught fish in the form of fishmeal, fish oil, or the fish itself, usually ground up into pellets. Food and Agriculture Organization (FAO) reports from 2009 (the most recent data) indicate that 98 tons (89 metric tons) of fish were wild caught, with another 62 tons produced from aquaculture, or 39 percent of all fish produced. Fish farms are typically either marine-based, using ocean water either in open sea pens or just off coastal shores; or land-based, using large pens of freshwater, which constitutes over 60 percent of current aquaculture methods.

By volume as a nation, the U.S. is the third largest seafood consumer in the world, behind China and Japan. Eighty-six percent of the seafood consumed in the U.S. is imported, and at least half of these imports are farmed.[184,185]

The most widely consumed type of seafood in the U.S. is shrimp. While we eat eight times more shrimp than any other type of fish, 95 percent of it is imported, and most of this is farmed from Asia. U.S. imports of fish-farmed shrimp, Atlantic salmon, and tilapia totaled $7.5 billion in 2011, up 14 percent from the previous year.[186]

All types of fish farms are involved in global depletion of our resources due to continued stress on our oceans; use of fossil fuels, land, and water; feed; and energy, and they all create pollution.

A conventional salmon farm with 100,000 fish will produce and release waste equal to the raw sewage generated by up to 32,000 people. According to Scotland's World Wildlife Fund, salmon farms in Scotland produce nitrogen wastes equal to a human population of more than 9 million people.[187]

I have visited a number of fish farms, some operating in oceans and some on land. Land-based aquaculture uses thousands of gallons per minute of well water, and although this is funneled eventually back into the nearest surface water system (stream/river), such aquaculture essentially uses massive amounts of water from an aquifer system that does not become recharged instantaneously with their recycling of wastewater into the stream. Additionally, there is tremendous use of electricity to power all the pumps and water recycling mechanisms.

In terms of policy, aquaculture leaders are urging our government to deregulate their operations and classify farmed fish as "livestock," which also then would create tax incentives and eliminate current jurisdiction issues with many organizations such as the U.S. fisheries and wildlife and state officials. Basically, there are a number of different organizations looking over fish-farm operations in the U.S., and the fish farm industry doesn't want that. They would rather be classified as livestock, which has minimal regulation, especially when it comes to environmental concerns.

The largest global threat to our environment from fish farms as a region is from Asia, where they account for 91 percent of the world's supply of aquaculture. China alone is responsible for 64 percent of the global amount of farmed fish. Chinese exports of aquaculture products have been known to contain contaminants, including heavy metals, antibiotics, and other medicines and bacteria. With tuna species on the decline in our oceans and demand on the increase, China turned to tuna fish farming on a commercial scale in the 1980s and now is producing 60,000 tons per year. Production of tuna in this manner creates many concerns such as overharvesting of juvenile tuna in the ocean, use of highly inefficient feed conversions requiring up to 25 pounds of wild-caught fish to produce 1 pound of tuna, and pollution throughout the fish farms.[188]

China produces 40 percent of the world's supply of wild-caught shrimp as well as about 40 percent of the farmed shrimp. Diseases are of concern with farmed shrimp from China, reportedly affecting 20 percent of shrimp and causing the loss of 1 million tons per year. These operations are poorly regulated, contributing to overuse of antibiotics and pesticides, which leads to subsequent water pollution, but fish farms of all types (especially from Asia and developing countries, where there is lack of regulations) will continue because wild-caught shrimp and other sea life stocks are fully exploited, with some nearly collapsed.[189]

Currently, 73 percent of all salmon and over half of all crab and lobster come from fish farms. Carp dominate world aquaculture production with nearly five times as many tons as shrimp, followed by catfish, tilapia, and salmon. Nile tilapia growth is occurring faster than any other type of farmed fish, with China accounting for nearly 50 percent of the global production. Being more concerned about business aspects than providing proper habitat for the fish, China raises tilapia outdoors, dismissing the fact it is a fish species found in the tropics. In 2008, excessively cold weather and early snowstorms caused the death of 88 million tilapia. Although yields can reach 12 tonnes per hectare (12,000 pounds per acre), there is a tremendous toll on the environment by way of pollution, water waste, energy consumption, and potentially irreversible effects on nearby ecosystems if farmed in natural freshwater lakes.[190]

An extensive study and report of the methodologies of global aquaculture systems and the environmental impacts was accomplished in 2011 by authors Hall, Delaporte, Phillips, Beveridge, and O'Keefe, titled *Blue Frontiers: Managing the Environmental Costs of Aquaculture*. In it, thirteen sea-life species and seventy-five different production techniques were studied by evaluating the life-cycle assessments (LCA). Comparisons were made to livestock agricultural systems, where aquaculture methods were shown to still be very much resource-intensive and quite damaging to the environment.

This study was the first to provide a global picture of the demands of fish farming on our environment resources, using life cycle assessments.

While fairly thorough in the documentation of the damaging effects of fish farms, this study excluded infrastructure, packaging and processing of produce, and transport. With this omission, I feel the report greatly understates the full environmental impact of any species assessed, due to underreporting of the energy requirements for refrigeration and freezing during the processing, transport, and storage of the product.[191,192,193]

One of the largest concerns with fish farms is that feed is given to produce lives that are then slaughtered. (More about slaughtering can be found in chapter 8.) Significant resources are being used to produce feed for fish grown in aquaculture settings. This feed is derived from wild-caught sea life that continues depleting our oceans or from plants grown on land that could have otherwise been given directly to us to eat. There is strong interest in fish farms because it generally requires less feed to produce 1 pound of fish than of any other animal we raise and eat. Fish tend to convert a greater proportion of the food they eat into body mass than livestock, which then becomes a point of argument for supporters of the industry. For instance, it requires 13.5 pounds of grain or fishmeal to produce 1 pound of finfish meat, as compared to 61.1 pounds of feed for 1 pound of beef or 38 pounds of feed for pork. For carnivorous species such as tuna, however, the demand on fishmeal and fish oil is great, as these tuna still rely on wild-caught fish for feed. The aquaculture industry prides itself on what it perceives as a diminishing "fish in/fish out" ratio (referring to the pounds of fish food being fed to a factory-farmed species relative to the amount in pounds of that particular factory farmed fish produced). The industry is currently achieving rates of 9 for tuna, 5 for salmon, 4 for both eel and trout. The Global Aquaculture Alliance has advocated for certification of fish produced on fish farms, to adhere to the Best Aquaculture Practices program, where ratios will be below 2 to 1. Whatever the ratio becomes, it is too much. The ratio should not exist, because there should be no food derived from our oceans and any food grown as plants should be fed directly to us.[194]

Demand for wild-caught fish by fish farms is most notable for marine-cage and pen-cultured types. These are common methods used in aquaculture.

Since carp production is the greatest of all farmed species, it is the largest overall negative environmental impact, followed by eel. By contrast, commercial production of sea vegetables and plants (types of seaweed) places the least amount of demand on our environment and actually has been shown to reduce *eutrophication* (stagnation and pollution of water).

All fish grown on fish farms need artificial supplementation to obtain omega-3s. They do not produce these essential fatty acids on their own. Typically, factory-farmed fish require a diet of fish meal, fish oil, and whole fish—all wild caught.

Eighty-eight percent of all fish oil and 56 percent of fishmeal produced in the world is given to fish on fish farms. Another 20 percent of fishmeal produced globally is fed to pigs, 12 percent is fed to poultry, 1 percent to cattle, and 12 percent to other animals, such as mink.[195]

The amounts of fishmeal fed to various species of farmed fish as a percentage of their total feed per day are as follows:[196]

- 20 percent for shrimp
- 30 percent for salmon and trout
- 5 percent for carp
- 10 percent for catfish
- 55 percent for eel
- 40 percent for other carnivorous fish
- 15 percent for freshwater crustaceans
- 6 percent for tilapia

More information about fishmeal:
- Farmed shrimp consume 27 percent of all fishmeal given to farmed fish worldwide.

- Five tons of wild-caught fish are required to produce 1 ton of dry fishmeal.
- Peru supplies over one-third of the world's supply of fishmeal.

Two general types of fishmeal are produced: (1) waste from fisheries (e.g., salmon, tuna), from the processing of fish harvested for direct human consumption; and (2) from fish harvested for the specific purpose of producing fishmeal (e.g., herring, anchovy, menhaden). The vast majority of fishmeal is of the second type.

Although some suggest that the use of fishmeal and fish oil will gradually decline over the next twenty years due to lack of supply in our oceans and increasing costs to produce it, most researchers and fishing industry analysts agree that the use of fishmeal in domestic and farm animal diets "will remain a core and efficient practice, particularly for young, rapidly growing, and high producing animals like maturing fish, egg-laden shrimp, poultry, and lactating dairy cattle."[197]

The fishing industry, certifying organizations, and the Fishmeal Information Network (FIN) feel that since fishmeal and fish oil are produced primarily from small pelagic fish living in surface and middle-depth waters, for which there is little or no demand for human consumption, the production of these products is "sustainable."

Barramundi/Australis

Seafood has been called "the health food of the century." The American Heart Association now recommends "eating fish at least twice a week," while the USDA urges everyone to "double their intake of fish."

Television show host Dr. Oz states, "Full of heart- and brain-healthy omega-3s, barramundi is a shoo-in for one of my top five superfoods. Bonus: the white meat is light, flaky, and delicious." *Women's Health* magazine says, "Turn to barramundi: one of our top five go-to species that's low in mercury, packed with nutrients, sustainable, and a cinch to prepare. Go fish!"

They are talking about barramundi, the white fish produced on farms by Australis, an aquaculture operation launched in 2004. Barramundi are native to northern Australia through Southeast Asia. Australis farms these fish at their primary location in Turner Falls, Massachusetts, and in Vietnam. The Turner Falls location uses 120,000 gallons of freshwater per day on 4 acres of land, producing 1 to 2 million pounds of fish per year. The Vietnam location produces 2 million pounds of fish on a 10-acre piece of land.[198]

Argument for this type of food production lies in two broad areas:

1. It produces fish in an environmentally sustainable aquaculture manner, taking pressure off our depleted oceans.
2. The end product (fish meat) is considered a "health food."

Australis operations are less land-intensive than those producing livestock, but they use tremendous amounts of freshwater. Although they are quick to mention it is filtered water and discharged back to a river, it reduces an aquifer system much quicker than it can be replaced, even though it adds to a surface-water system. It also requires an exorbitant amount of energy to supply the pumping, filtration, cleaning, and maintenance.

Although Australis is "striving" for a 1:1 feed/conversion ratio and with less dependence on wild-caught fish, it still requires more than 1 pound of any feed to produce 1 pound of barramundi. The pelleted feed is composed of 8 percent fish oil and 15 percent fishmeal for their source of omega-3s, in addition to a wheat/canola/soy mixture. A better option would be to leave the fish oil/meal combination in the fish in our oceans, and give the plant-based items directly to us, which could occur without additional energy and water usage. Even though barramundi are advertised as saving our oceans, a significant amount of anchovy from Peru and herring from Canada must be harvested and killed to support their diet of omega-3s.

Whenever that many fish are confined in any aquaculture operation, there are health and pollution concerns. As in all fish farms, barramundi are prone to infection by parasites and protozoa, which are prevalent at both sites, especially in younger fish. Infestation is usually handled by "sodium manipulation" (changing their medium to freshwater, which kills most protozoa, and then changing back to salt water in a flushing style), treating the fish with an oxidant, or by potassium permanganate and antibiotics. Barramundi at Australis are harvested by crowding them into a purse seine, dumping them into brine ice, and killing by electrocution.[199]

I found similarities at all domestic factory fish farms. Most marine-based operations had the potential for issues with controlling pollution, disease within stocks as well as introduction of disease to wild species, and needless inhumane slaughter. Land-based aquaculture operations displayed resource depletion with water and energy. And even though there appears to be more efficient use of land (yield of product per acre) as compared to livestock operations, land-based aquaculture is still quite inefficient when compared to plant-based systems. This observation becomes more apparent when taking into account the life cycle analysis of any operation. Both sets of fish-farm production systems (on land or water) still deplete our oceans by way of their dependency on wild-caught fish for inclusion in fishmeal and fish oil.

In addition, overseas fish farms displayed a much higher degree of pollution, increased feed ratios, and lack of regulatory control.

The two largest types of aquaculture in the western U.S. both feel they are the future of food and are sustainable. One is American Gold Seafood/Icicle Seafoods, a marine-based operation located off the shores in the Pacific Northwest. It is depleting our oceans by way of pollution, use of space, and land and food use due to the pellets fed to these fish.

The other, a land-based aquaculture operation, SweetSpring/ AquaSeed, in Washington State, uses freshwater from an aquifer at the rate of 2,000 gallons per minute for each of its many tanks used for raising fish. And similar to the Australis operations, this well water is funneled back into the nearest surface water system (stream). They are essentially using massive amounts of water from an aquifer system, which required hundreds to thousands of years to develop. Additionally, there is tremendous use of electricity to power all their pumps and water recycling mechanisms.

Instead of being a "health food," the end product of both types of aquaculture—marine-based and on land—contribute to global depletion of our health by producing a food that has cholesterol, saturated fat, endotoxins, and no phytonutrients or fiber, and produces substances such as heterocyclic amines and polyaromatic hydrocarbons when cooked.

Lastly, there is a question of humaneness. Fish farm operations of all types kill billions of fish yearly by a combination of suffocation, freezing, electrocution, and cutting and bleeding them. If this seems to be the way of future food production, it will be surely carrying a large load of ethics with it.

Many organizations are positioned to provide guidance for businesses and consumers as to the most sustainable seafood and production practices. These include Global Aquaculture Alliance, WWF, MSC, MBASW, FAO, National Fisheries Institute, Seafood Choices Alliance, Guide of Aquaculture Certification, Aquaculture Certification Council, and hundreds of other organizations that are species-specific. Problems encountered that create futility in their efforts are related to traceability, disparate standards between countries, lack of enforceable regulations, lack of accurate definition of sustainability, and the ubiquitous concern for economics (seafood, wild caught/aquaculture's contribution to GDP, businesses, and livelihoods) that take priority over the environment. All of the above-mentioned organizations may be legitimately concerned about the state of our oceans—but not concerned enough.

Here comes aquaponics

Since we are running out of fish in our oceans, running out of land to raise livestock, and running out of freshwater to use to raise fish in aquaculture settings, soon animal agriculture will be churning out fish by way of aquaponics—systems that combine producing fish via aquaculture and plants by way of hydroponics.

There are many businesses in the U.S. now snatching up abandoned industrial warehouses in urban areas, raising fish in tanks, growing green vegetables with the wastewater, and then cycling the water back to the fish. These systems rely on plants to filter the waste created by fish, thereby reducing freshwater needs. Regardless of how attractive these systems may seem to investors and consumers, all still have three major sustainability concerns:

- Massive energy requirements
- Production of animal products, which are less healthy for us to consume than plants
- Requirement of feed for the fish, creating an inefficient step for food to reach us

And of course, there is the continued raising and killing of life, regardless of this fact being lost in the shuffle of the concomitant growing of plants. Hydroponic vegetable and fruit production has, with a blink of an eye, become adulterated.

We will see and hear much more about these systems in the future, especially as we begin running out of our natural resources, and the operational loop of inputs and outputs for aquaponics becomes more closed (relying only on the resources it creates).

The omega-3 disconnect

We continue eating fish and exploiting sea life for many reasons. Along with strong cultural and societal influences, the recent impetus has been for their omega-3 content and protein. We all know that these essential fatty acids are very important—they're referred to as "essential" because they are necessary for proper functioning of various cells, organs, and systems. Because our bodies are unable to produce them, we must obtain them from our diet. It is how and from where we obtain them, however, that is even more important. For instance, a 3-ounce serving of unsustainable cod provides 150–200 mg of omega-3, whereas 1 tablespoon of very sustainable chia seeds provides over 2,000 mg of omega-3. Flaxseed has 1,200 mg of omega-3 per tablespoon, and walnuts and hemp are also exceptional sources of omega-3 as well.

Some may want to know about the conversion ratios of alpha

linolenic acid (ALA, the type of omega-3 found in plants) to docosahexanoic acid and eicosopentanoic acid (DHA and EPA, the two primary forms of omega-3 found in fish). When we consume ALA from plant sources, our body converts this ALA to DHA and EPA at a rate of 1 to 9 percent. The 2010 U.S. Dietary Guidelines has recommendations for ALA at 1.1–1.6 grams per day because your brain only needs 3.8 *milligrams*, and your body can store and assimilate DHA/EPA (converted from ALA or otherwise) for up to two years—with a half-life of two to five years. Just 1 tablespoon of chia seeds has over 2,000 mg of omega-3s from ALA. Even at 1 percent conversion rate, one tablespoon of chia seeds would provide you with 20 mg of usable omega-3 fatty acids—five times the amount your brain needs daily. There is no need to worry about your omega-3 intake if you stop eating fish.

No fish produces omega-3s on its own. Omega-3 fatty acids are found in microalgae or plants, which every fish has to eat in order to obtain them, or it needs to eat other smaller fish that have consumed plants and microalgae along the way.

So in addition to finding omega-3 in plants, we could go right to the source ourselves and eat microalgae, like spirulina or chlorella, or plants and skip past eating fish and the ecological baggage that comes with producing and harvesting them, as well as bypassing the health issues of consuming them.

If we eat fish primarily because we think it's healthy, then we should take a closer look at what those "health benefits" are. *Every* fish has saturated fat and cholesterol and can form cancer-causing chemicals when cooked, such as heterocyclic amines and polycyclic aromatic hydrocarbons.[200]

No fish has phytonutrients or fiber, both of which are some of the most beneficial substances you can consume. Phytonutrients are substances that will improve your immune system, reduce the likelihood you'll develop cancer, and provide you with anti-inflammatory properties. All of these properties are extremely important and can be found only in plants. Predatory fish higher up on the food chain, such as tuna, and those living the longest lives have a large probability of containing higher levels of mercury and other heavy metals, as well as chemicals, such as dioxin and PCB contamination.[201] And *all* fish caught anywhere in our oceans will contribute to bykill and the loss of ecosystems.

Our country consumed 5 billion pounds of seafood in 2010. Instead of inflating the human health benefits of eating fish, it would make sense for the USDA to inform consumers of all the health benefits of eating plant-based foods and the many and significant advantages of these foods over eating fish, as well as emphasizing the continued global depletion that occurs with every bite of fish we take. We all must understand the full impact that eating fish has on the health of our planet and on our own health. It is time to become aware. Instead of mass producing, harvesting, catching, killing, and eating fish, just let them live.

Rhetoric, policy making, and the future of our oceans
In 2010, the USDA recommended that Americans consume "twice as much seafood" per year as the 16 pounds they currently do. With our oceans collapsing, availability of land and freshwater resource systems in decline, and rising rates of Western disease and health care costs, this is not the message we need to hear. Increasing the demand to eat fish, wild caught or from fish farms, will escalate global depletion on many fronts. The toll paid in numbers of lives we slaughter each year to support our seafood habit is difficult to precisely measure. This is primarily because statistics of wild-caught fish taken from our oceans and freshwater systems, combined with those raised and killed in fish farms, are tracked by weight, not individual lives. Additionally, there are many millions of tons of bykill, illegally caught, and unreported sea life. It is estimated that 1 to 3 trillion wild-caught fish are caught and killed each year globally, with an additional 120 billion fish raised and slaughtered in fish-farm settings. This involves only FAO-recorded fish capture, so the number could be easily twice this range if it included all other sea animals killed as bykill and illegally caught.[202-205]

The global seafood industry generates over $190 billion annually.[206] In the mid-1960s, the average person ate 22 pounds of seafood each year, whereas in 2011, the global average was 38 pounds per year. The demand for seafood is expected to grow by at least 10 percent annually over the next decade. This is an additional 15 million tons per year.[207,208]

While the oceans are suffering, Americans are spending more on fish ($90 billion in 2011) and catching more fish (4 million tons in 2010) than ever before. More than 520 million pounds of fish were landed at just one of our U.S. fishing ports in 2011 (Dutch Harbor, Alaska).[209]

I am not so sure this is consistent with President Obama's proclamation for National Oceans Month of June 2012: "Let us celebrate our heritage as a seafaring nation by instilling an ethic of good ocean stewardship in all Americans."

Since the 1990s, China's involvement with world fisheries and trade in aquatic products has dramatically increased, making it the world's largest producer, consumer, and exporter of seafood. Because of this, any efforts at improving the health of our oceans and achieving a higher degree of relative sustainability will have to include a link to their production and harvesting systems. There is now a geographic complexity of global seafood supply chains, which creates a great challenge of connecting sustainability impacts to specific species, stocks, and ecosystems. Many countries are catching many fish and destroying many ecosystems under their own jurisdiction, in oceans shared by all. Regulations are established in the best interest of the fishing industry, not sea life. Even if appropriate protective global fishing regulations were enacted, illegal, unreported, and unregulated fisheries throughout the world and in the open ocean would remain.

Efforts are in place by the International Institute for Sustainable Development, WWF–China, and others to work with Chinese market supply chains in order to integrate sustainable systems into China's seafood production policies. We do know there are a number of issues with certain practices: overfishing of the Patagonian toothfish, sharks, rays, reef and shrimp fisheries, and in waters off Africa, as well as lack of regulations across all their aquaculture operations. As with our lack of understanding the ocean itself, we have a limited understanding of the full picture of China's involvement in world fisheries—other than realizing it is significant.[210]

Globally, $20 billion are given as subsidies to the fishing industry, which further perpetuates overfishing and is thought to be one of the "causes." However, if there were no demand, it wouldn't matter how many economic incentives governments were providing to the industry—overfishing wouldn't exist.[211]

Greenpeace is one of a few environmental organizations that feels no fully credible certification program for sustainable wild-caught or farmed seafood currently exists. Certification specialists created an evaluation tool for Greenpeace to establish how well various certification programs can help realize Greenpeace's vision for healthy oceans. This vision would be a network of marine reserves, untouchable by commercial fishing, covering 40 percent of the world's oceans, and sustainable and fair use of the remaining 60 percent. This is a genuine and calculated effort by Greenpeace, but the ratio of only 40 percent is not ambitious enough to ensure adequate recovery and conservation, while allowing continued subjectively interpretive use with an economic lens for the other 60 percent. It will not work.

The Convention on the Law of the Sea is a case in point for an attempt at international policy making. It is accepted as the legal framework that guides every aspect of our management of the oceans and seas and the activities that take place on and beneath them. When the convention was opened for signature in 1982, it was rightly characterized as a "constitution for the oceans." It is a living monument to international cooperation—negotiated by more than 150 states—and is among the world's most significant legal instruments. That, however, was 1982. Look at the condition of our oceans today.[212]

The restoration of our oceans and establishment of enforceable (and functionally appropriate) regulations may be in the hands of businesses, as governments have proven to be unaware and apathetic to our oceans' demise. It may reach a point where it will not be perceived as good business by the public or by multinationals to continue providing seafood products, at least in some capacity. Indeed, environmental groups are now joining businesses to find solutions. A collaboration of more than a dozen leading U.S. and Canadian organizations, called the Conservation Alliance for Seafood Solutions, has developed a path that businesses can take to incorporate sustainable seafood in their corporate policies. Some of the largest U.S. retailers have signed on in support, with policies in place. The difficulty is with who has defined "sustainable seafood" for them, upon which their entire platform is based.[213]

From Captain Paul Watson, sea shepherd:

I was raised in a fishing village. I was raised on fish, lobsters, scallops, clams, oysters, and even seaweed. I don't eat fish anymore. I view it as an ecological crime, because I have seen their numbers diminish, and I've seen the eco-systems go from bountiful to lifeless in my lifetime and it horrifies me that we can be so insensitive and so ecologically stupid. To look at the fish market there seems to be no shortage of fish, yet to keep those shelves full, the largest assault fleet ever conceived, with over 2 million ships and boats, ravage and rape the oceans every day, literally vacuuming life from the sea. From every port in the world these boats head out to deploy weapons of mass destruction in the form of drift nets, seine nets, drag nets, longlines, [and] troll lines, and in some case they literally use a large vacuum to scoop up fish from the sea.

This armada ranges from massive multi-million-dollar drag trawlers and purse seine clippers to decrepit scows with longlines and rusty hooks held up with empty bleach bottles.

This kind of merciless hunt-and-destroy approach would never be tolerated if we were to pursue terrestrial wildlife in this manner. We contemptuously call the meat from giraffe, elephant, gorillas, and hippos by the name of "bushmeat" and dismiss the Africans in the Congo who eat it as being a part of the problem, contributing to the diminishment of wildlife in what is left of the African wilderness.

Yet large predators like tuna, shark, swordfish, and mahi mahi are simply "aquatic bushmeat."

Hunting down a lion and slaughtering it is no different than hunting down and killing a shark. Slaughtering an elephant on the savannah of Africa is no different than slaying a large bluefin tuna in the North Atlantic.

When poor Africans kill a giraffe to eat, we complain [about it] over a meal of swordfish or between bites of tuna at the sushi bar.[214]

The WWF lists six reasons why overfishing is occurring: poor fisheries management, pirate or illegal fishers, massive bykill, subsidies, unfair fisheries partnership agreements allowing foreign fleets to overfish in waters of developing countries, and destructive fishing practices. Reducing or eliminating fishing industry subsidies by all governments will certainly help matters. Increasing fishing efficiencies may help reduce total catch and bykill. Setting aside marine preserves or conservation areas (marine-protected areas, such as the Save Our Seas programs in the Maldives and Keeling Islands) in combination with strict policy change and enforcement would provide the most immediate gains toward restoring the health of our oceans—but it is relative to the ratio set aside and degree of policy enforcement. A "no take" set-aside program of all ocean waters (at least in all high seas) in combination with comprehensive enforcement may still not provide full recovery in our lifetime, but it's the best we can do—regardless of how unrealistic it may seem. Asking customers to purchase only "sustainable seafood" obviously is not the solution if we do not know how to accurately define "sustainable."

The underlying reason for the demise of our oceans is our demand to eat fish and the lack of affixing appropriate economic pricing to the cost of sea life, ecosystems, and our oceans as one entity—a life-sustaining resource—that needs to be enforced until we stop eating fish altogether.

When we sit down to eat fish, do we know or care about where it came from or anything about the fish itself or its life? Most likely not, which is one of the dissociation mechanisms that allows us to eat seafood. It may matter if we knew more about the ecosystems damaged, bykill thrown overboard, or how the fish died while it was being caught in order to get to our plate.

Whether labeled "sustainable" or not, we need to always remember the motives at play here. It must be kept in mind that every step along the way in the chain of producing that fish for you—the fishing vessel, wharf, processor, sustainable labeling company, retailer—is driven by economics. *The only reason anyone within the fishing industry has become concerned about the health of our oceans is to maintain a pool of sea life from which more can be extracted.* If the world, as a whole, were truly concerned about repairing what we have done to our oceans and all the lost numbers of fish and destroyed ecosystems, we would leave it alone—and hope that it heals itself in the next 100 years.[215,216,217]

What we need is complete and immediate restoration of all oceanic ecosystems to a balanced state, where pluses and minuses occur naturally instead of being controlled and manipulated by our wants or by organizations influenced by money and by scientists who don't know what they need to know. We *want* to eat lobster or pollock, so therefore they're considered sustainable.

There are four key points to this chapter: (1) healthy oceans are necessary for our survival on this planet; (2) our oceans are not healthy at all—they are, in fact, being destroyed, in many respects irreversibly and rapidly; (3) we are destroying our oceans because of our insatiable desire and demand to eat fish *and* by raising and eating animals on land; (4) it doesn't have to be this way. There is no physiological mandate for us to eat seafood. There is no reason for us to extract, kill, and eat billions of fish each year and destroy the intricate ecosystems in our oceans. *No* seafood can be commercially taken out of our oceans in a "sustainable" fashion. From an ecological standpoint, harvesting from our oceans or from fish farms will never be as sustainable as producing plants for us to eat, but it also is a question of ethics—what are we "sustaining"? What becomes "sustainable" when we slaughter 1 to 3 trillion fish every year?

Three billion people on our planet depend on fish as a primary source of protein, with nearly 4 billion people relying on fish to supplement other protein sources.[218] It's time we introduce those people (98 percent of the global population) to another, plant-based source of protein and to the fact that protein isn't our only dietary need. Two hundred million livelihoods depend on the fishing industry. It's time we introduce them to another livelihood that will be associated with production of purely plant-based source of protein—a livelihood that doesn't destroy and doesn't kill. In doing so, we will all be one step closer to becoming sustainable.

4

The World of Food Choice Disconnects and Becoming Connected

HOW DOES YOUR breakfast, lunch, or dinner have anything to do with a shaman from the Amazon area, or with any of the 1 billion people in the world without water, or with the imminent extinction of a number of species on Earth, or with the plight of a starving child in Ethiopia, or even with the taxes we pay to our government? What could you and the food you choose to eat possibly have to do with these things? Why should you even care? These questions pertain to the disconnection we have regarding food choices. One distinct reason for our disconnect can be found in how we use certain words and what we perceive them to mean—and our reliance on others to define these words.

Use of the word "sustainable," for example, can be seen nearly everywhere—and it has now been morphed into many different meanings to suit many different needs. For most people, the word "sustainable" refers to our energy sector—how many miles per gallon of gas your car will achieve, how many energy-efficient lightbulbs you can use to save electricity. Sustainability also refers to waste—how, what, and when to recycle. Often, we even think about economic or social sustainability. But in most areas of the world, no one really knows much about the effect that our food has on our environment, particularly with regard to the animals we raise, kill, and eat. I believe that's because most of us are unaware—and are comfortable being that way. It's simply too challenging for us to consider—culturally, socially, even economically.

Many authors, lecturers, and advocates strive to raise our understanding of the dangers of the commercially produced food we have consumed since the 1950s (and are still consuming). Individuals such as Michael Pollan, Mark Bittman, and Jamie Oliver have guided us away from high-fructose corn syrup (HFCS), packaged and processed food items, industrialized agriculture, and factory farms and toward eating "less" meat. But is this all good? Not entirely, because while it moves us away from some forms of less healthy food, at the same time the messages of these food advocates have opened a new era of pseudo-enlightenment, pseudo-sustainability, and continued global depletion due to food choice. On one hand, these individuals and their messages have reached millions, and in doing so they have accomplished much. But these issues are just fragments of the picture, creating paths to follow that are based on incomplete or inaccurate information. Because of the profound implications of global depletion, it is time to understand the entire picture of food choices and sustainability—it's time to see and hear the entire story and have it delivered through an unfiltered lens.

Although one can find the dissemination of inaccurate information and many incongruent aspects related to it within our society, there appear to be three fundamental levels of disconnect related to food that can be seen in the way we perceive our role or relationship with our planet. All three must be addressed and eventually corrected in order us to reduce global depletion and ensure the health of our planet for future generations.

First, Earth does not have an infinite amount of resources, and many of the daily choices we make impact these resources in a negative, sometimes irreversible manner. It's the consumptive factor. We typically live in a bubble, often unable to understand, recognize, or appreciate that what we consume may have a profound impact on something else in the world. Second, our daily choices and decisions regarding what we eat will most likely have a greater long-term impact on the planet than any other. And third, there is a general lack of understanding that of all the food choices we make, a decision to eat animals or animal products will have the largest negative impact, and therefore it needs to be changed—and in an expedient manner—in order to restore health to our planet. It is quite simply unsustainable for the world's population to continue raising more than 70 billion livestock each year and taking 1 to 2 trillion fish out of our oceans—it's unsustainable to our planet and to us.

Unfortunately, the gap (the difference between the total world population and the number of those actually making the connection on a conceptual and functional level) seen at each subsequent disconnect becomes proportionately larger, from the first to the third—meaning that the number of individuals, communities, or institutions in the world that understand the basis of the third disconnect and who are eating solely plant-based foods is a very small fraction of the world's population, less than 1 percent.[219]

Current food movements—what's wrong with them?

Today, many notable organizations and movements are positioned to create healthier food choices and implement food production systems. Institutions and communities are beginning to rally around concepts such as "real food," local, farm-to-table, farm-to-campus, organic, biodynamic, cool foods, sustainable seafood, grass- and pasture-fed, free-range, cage-free, traceable, fair trade, small family farms, community supported agriculture (CSA) and urban agriculture, and humane—all of which are fueled by the desire to move away from agribusiness and the past fifty years of industrialized, profit-driven food production systems. However, none of these concepts or movements will be successful long term if it includes raising, slaughtering, and eating animals or harvesting fish out of our oceans or on land by way of aquaculture. Beyond the primary reasons implicit to their effect on global depletion, nearly all of these movements have precepts embedded in misinformation and inaccuracy as it relates to animals. While operating with inherently good intentions, the results of these movements and organizations never will be optimal. They are disconnected from certain realities.

Although there are many reasons for this, it essentially is an issue of definition. What entity or individual is capable of deeming a food or production system as "sustainable"? What food can be referred to as "sustainable"? In the case of grass-fed livestock, for instance, it is clearly not a sustainable practice in many geographical regions or on a collective global basis, long term, from the standpoints of land and water use, contribution to anthropogenic greenhouse gas production, and contribution to climate change, food security, and human health. Yet there is that stamp of approval for grass-fed animal products, though it's given primarily by those stakeholders in the meat and dairy industries—all the producers, the National Cattlemen's Association, National Dairy Council, American Grass Fed Association, all businesses and organizations associated with the meat and dairy industries, and by individuals such as Michael Pollan, Bill Niman, Joel Salatin, and others who are now serving as "experts" or advisors to many organizations but who also consume beef, tuna, and other unsustainable animal products and raise grass-fed cows themselves.

Have you ever been lost and had to ask someone for directions? Maybe that person gave you those directions quickly and decisively—he or she appeared to know. You then followed those directions perfectly but found yourself more lost than you were before—and also frustrated because you were running out of time. Your decision to follow those directions was based on the person's confidence in giving them to you. He or she presented a base of expertise for that information. Otherwise, you would have asked someone else. The same scenario holds true today with our food choices—what to eat, what is affected by those choices, what will be solved. Every decision we make regarding food has been influenced by many factors around us— by individuals or organizations that have their own base of definitions. We assume they must be correct and comprehensive. They're not.

A common and dangerous misconception is that we are "going in the right direction" with sustainability and food choice by taking "baby steps"—going "meatless on Mondays," eating "less" meat, supporting local and organic food markets, and consuming grass-fed animals or "sustainable seafood." Superficially, these all may *appear* to go in the right direction because they go away from factory farms and away from processed foods, and they are easy-to-accept alternatives. But under the surface, these movements are, in many ways, not going in the right direction at all, because they create justification for the continuation of raising, slaughtering, and eating animals, which is certainly not sustainable. The danger lies in the fact that a confident complacency is created, while in reality, global depletion and the unnecessary slaughtering of billions of animals continues.

The word "sustainable" and what it really means in terms of food choice
Sustainability is the more subjective version of global depletion. In many cases, we can measure or quantify that which is being taken away (depleted) more easily and accurately than proclaiming something is fully sustainable. The word "sustainable" has become ubiquitous—it's applied to every aspect of nearly everything we do. Businesses and institutions of all sizes and types recognize the need to project an association with this word, at least on paper, as a point of validation of integrity. Every college, university, non-governmental organization (NGO), and for-profit organization and corporation must now reflect sustainability in its statement of responsibility in order to be taken seriously. But there is a large distinction between establishing written objectives of sustainability and actually attaining the state of being sustainable throughout all aspects of a particular business and the life cycle of all products and services it may provide. There is a difference between achieving economic sustainability and achieving environmental sustainability. Recent use of the word "sustainable" has allowed the shaping of its definition to fit just about every aspect of life and, more important, it has allowed for placement of a positive connotation to quite unhealthy practices. After all, if something has been labeled "sustainable," it is a good thing, right? Unfortunately, with food choice, the word "sustainable" has been severely misused.

Pseudo-sustainability

Regarding our path toward sustainability, there are two points in space and time. Point A represents where we are currently, how sustainable (or unsustainable) we are, and the systems we have in place today. Point B, on the other hand, is where everyone would like to be, where we all would like (or need) to go—to a destination of being fully "sustainable." Now, the thing is, we're very far away from Point B, but being far away is not entirely the problem. It's how we're traveling there—which ship we've boarded to transport us there. Of great importance is who we have directly or indirectly chosen as our navigator and the direction we are taking. If food choice—specifically, the effect of eating animals—is never factored accurately into the equation on our trip toward sustainability, we're never going to reach point B, and we'll be faced with perpetually inaccurate recalculations in direction. Instead, we are reaching various points somewhere out in space—in an area of pseudo-sustainability. It is a significant problem because not only are we *not* reaching our goal of becoming sustainable, but also, the wheels of motion of this particular ship are very large and powerful, and there are very influential navigation systems in place, no matter how wrong they are. Therefore, turning this large tanker in the right direction becomes exceedingly difficult, and it has over 90 percent of the world's population on board, dragging everyone else along with it.

Everyone is connected, even if a few of us are on a different, smaller ship with a more astute navigator, and with a more direct line to point B. Reaching sustainability of our planet ultimately becomes a collective effort.

Most businesses now have "sustainability" emblazoned on their corporate responsibility statements. It eventually will become an economic necessity associated with success and will be a common, interwoven thread of ethics, connecting businesses, governments and nations, communities, and people. To reach this new state of the planet, though, we must realize and apply a more consistent definition. Regardless of the fact that nearly every organization and institution in the world has sustainability concerns written into their statement of intent, I have yet to find one of these entities that properly addresses eating animals in their quest to become "sustainable." By excluding an objective to eliminate eating animals and animal products, it is impossible for any organization of any type to achieve "true sustainability"—casting them into this state of pseudo-sustainability. This is an insidious place to be—having the perception that you are sustainable, when in reality you are not.

There are two concerns with regard to use of the word "sustainable" in the corporate world. The first is that corporations, institutions, organizations, and governments use the word quite indiscriminately, without being aware of proper definitions, especially as it is applied to food. It may be intentional, knowing the façade of integrity that the word "sustainable" provides, despite its blatant misuse. Or it may be unintentional, as these entities simply hop on the bandwagon of what is hip or even culturally mandatory (as far as the business world goes), without understanding what the word really means.

The second concern is the effect that the nonstandardization of the word "sustainable" has on public perception, which of course leads to ill-informed decisions on purchasing and consumption, which perpetuates global depletion. After all, without a proper grasp that eating grass-fed livestock or "sustainable seafood" is *not* sustainable, the public will continue making poor food-choice decisions, based on advertisers' claims or carefully crafted public images, fabricated by economically driven businesses that have limited knowledge of what is and is not sustainable.

McDonald's Corporation, for instance, in its 2012 statement of sustainability proclaims: "From the start, we've been committed to doing the right thing. Our sustainability efforts ensure that our business practices and policies continue our rich heritage of making a positive impact on society." Guided by its "company values," McDonald's now has "five focus areas," in which it purports to make progress: "nutrition and well-being, sustainable supply chain, environmental responsibility, employee experience, and community." To further establish its symbol of concern for sustainability, McDonald's combined a corporate responsibility statement and sustainability reports into a "scorecard" format in 2011. My point is that with $27 billion in revenues ($70 billion total sales) from 33,000 unit restaurants worldwide,

McDonald's is achieving financial success by way of focusing on their "5 P's: People, Products, Place, Price, and Promotion"—with sustainability now thrown in the mix as a theme within the 5 P's. Although 68 million people may visit McDonald's units on a single day throughout the world, sustainability is likely not on any of their minds; if it was, they would be eating somewhere that didn't serve meat or any other animal product.[220]

McDonald's now has a new "Sustainability Library," where one can "come take a look and peruse the shelves." One should first peruse McDonald's food products and follow the trail back to how all those animals they purchased were raised and killed and the resources it took to do so, and compare that perusal to what would be found if McDonald's served only plant-based products. Then, perhaps the word "sustainable" would be viewed in better context and could actually apply to at least one component of their operations.[221]

Similar to all other large businesses, Unilever (a British-Dutch multinational consumer goods company) feels that corporate responsibility "underpins our strategy." In 2010, they introduced the Unilever Sustainable Living Plan, which was a set of targets to help combine growth of their business while minimizing their impact on the environment. Here is an excerpt from their introduction to Unilever statement:

> *To embed sustainability into every stage of the life cycle of our products, we're working with our suppliers to support responsible approaches to agriculture. We're also learning from NGOs and other organisations, recognising that building a truly sustainable business is not something we can do without expert advice. We believe that as a business we have a responsibility to our consumers and to the communities in which we have a presence. Around the world we invest in local economies and develop people's skills inside and outside of Unilever. And through our business and brands, we run a range of programmes to promote hygiene, nutrition, empowerment and environmental awareness.*[222]

This is a fairly bold, sweeping statement, one that makes you feel that Unilever really has a grasp on sustainability and the need to make it a priority in their primary corporate objectives. Such a statement is necessary in order for the public to see the corporation as responsible for economic viability. The difficulty becomes one of definition and who the corporation relies on to make that definition for them. Who is guiding Unilever and other businesses and institutions to the most accurate and unbiased assessment of sustainability? Does this sustainability-consulting entity have a full understanding of the role of food choice and, more specifically, the true impact that eating animals has on sustainability of our resources and on us? For instance, looking more closely at Unilever's statement above:

- What are "sustainable approaches to agriculture"?
- What is their definition of "building a truly sustainable business"?
- Which "NGOs and other organizations" are they "learning from" as they seek "expert advice"?

Are the eggs and egg yolks used in Unilever's Hellmann's mayonnaise "truly sustainable"? How about the beef, chicken, ham, and shrimp or other seafood they use to produce all their Knorr brand products? Were the cows, chickens, pigs, and sea life all raised (or extracted from our oceans) and slaughtered in a "truly sustainable" manner? What about all the massive support Unilever provides to the dairy industry with their line of Slim-Fast, Becel, and Flora brand items? Are these to be considered "truly sustainable"?

Most likely not. But their introduction to Unilever statement is convincing, so perhaps they, like so many other corporations, are simply ... unaware. We will return to this subject later in "Reconnects."

The importance of "optimal" or "relative" sustainability
In lieu of there being no universally accepted and accurate formula for determining the "true" sustainability of any particular agricultural system—

meaning it would be improbable to accurately state that any implemented agricultural food system is *fully sustainable* throughout the entire range of impacts (land and water use, effect on biodiversity and our atmosphere, world hunger/food security, sustainability of our own health, fresh and saltwater quality, and oceanic ecosystems, etc.), projected out over an infinite amount of time—we must recognize that we can only view a food product and production system as sustainable in a relative sense (deciding what is *more* sustainable than something else). Additionally, it makes sense that we begin gauging what is sustainable by adopting a more global and geographical perspective, instead of within our own narrow field of vision. For instance, just because California was given 82 percent of the Lower Basin states' flow of the Colorado River for its use since the 1922 Compact, shouldn't mean that this water be used in a manner excluding a more responsible national or international perspective and without maximizing efficiency of use—which currently is not being accomplished. With over half of California's allocation of the Colorado River used for livestock, California could certainly find a more "sustainable" method to produce food.

From a chronological standpoint, for instance, using Ogallala glacier water to support the corn-fed cattle industry of our High Plains states has been quite "sustainable" for the past fifty years (meaning it has been used without running out), but scientists predict this ancient aquifer will become depleted by 2030 at the current rate of use. The water from the Ogallala will then be "sustainable" for another eighteen years, will it not?

We also must view the word "sustainable" from a human health standpoint. How "sustainable" is it to raise a product, such as livestock, that then contributes to our national health crises, increasing the risk of contracting one or more of the four leading causes of disease and death in the United States, the five most common cancers, as well as many other disease states. How "sustainable" is this type of food from an economic standpoint when factoring in the percent of contribution eating animal protein and animal products has on the $3 trillion health care costs incurred by our country in 2011? Consider, too, the subsequent loss of productivity that should be factored into any discussion about "sustainability," health, and food choice.

I feel it's critical to introduce the concept of *relative sustainability*—how our land, air, water, and other resources could be *best used* to obtain a more sustainable food product. The sustainability issue (or more appropriately, the "relative sustainability" issue), as it relates to food choice, begins and ends with an equation that can be expressed as follows:

> *We use resources to grow plants, which are then given to animals (that are taking much more of our resources to simply live), which are then slaughtered (taking even more of our resources), processed, packaged, and transported (that, again, takes more of our resources) to get to us. We then use more resources to refrigerate, wash away pathogens, and cook (in order to kill more pathogens that we were unable to wash away). After consuming the animal products, we either become sick immediately from various pathogens or endotoxins we were unable to kill, or we contract a disease later in life from chronic consumption of the animal product, which used this massive amount of resources to produce.*

That equation needs to be changed to this: *We produce more plants for us to eat directly.*

Although in some instances, resources will be used for transportation and washing, that is the way our food equation should be written. Please notice how much simpler and less resource-driven it becomes. So the question becomes, how "sustainable" is it to raise and eat *any* animal product in a *relative* sense, as compared to plant-based foods? How can we best use our resources? What foods will have the least effect on climate change? Which foods best promote our own human health, and which are the most compassionate? Do we really have to slaughter another living being in order for us to eat? This is the way we need to start viewing things, in a relative sense, from this day forward.

Animal agriculture systems keep a keen eye on the Feed Conversion Ratio—how much feed must go in to an animal as compared to how much body weight that animal will gain. This relationship can also be measured as residual feed intake (RFI). As we have seen, examples of common FCRs are as follows:

2:1 feed to weight for salmon (considered having the "best" FCR of any animal)

8:1 for tilapia

2:1 for chicken

5:1 for pork

8:1 for beef (combined grain and grass fed)

30:1 for beef (grass fed)

Even a turkey will eat 1 pound of food per day (less for smaller turkeys, more for large turkeys close to slaughter). It becomes an indirect and quite inefficient method of attempting to produce food: use land, water, and energy to grow crops that are then fed to animals (instead of directly to us), which are then slaughtered. The FCR then becomes a tool of measuring how absurd this concept really is—by the simple fact of having to measure and be concerned about this ratio.[223,224]

When discussing relative sustainability, it is also important to know how much water livestock drink, without factoring in the amount used for irrigation of crops that feed them. Turkeys average 1 liter (34 ounces, .27 gallons) of water per day. Chickens require half a liter of water per day. Dairy cows average 32 gallons per day, with some heavy milk producers requiring up to 43 gallons of water per day. Beef cows, whether grazing or not, average 15 gallons of water per day, with some reaching an average above 20 gallons per day. Pigs require 2 to 3 gallons of water per day.[225]

With our global drinking water supply becoming scarcer, the following questions should be posed:

If any of us were fortunate enough to have 43 gallons of drinking water at our disposal on a given day (more than 1 billion people in the world do not have this luxury), should we supply it to a cow, in order to produce a glass of milk (which is implicated in numerous disease states and which 75 percent of the global population can't digest properly)? Or, alternatively, should we drink 32 ounces of that volume of water ourselves and then give the remaining amount of the 43 gallons to 172 other human beings who have none, providing all of them the amount needed to live one more day (43 gallons, or 5504 ounces, divided by 32 ounces per person)?

Therefore, is milk or any dairy product "sustainable," "fully sustainable," or even "relatively" sustainable?

And the same thought could be applied to global land use, grain production, and the impact that raising animals has on climate change.

As mentioned earlier, many food movements now are in the public eye. All of them seem to make sense on a superficial level, because they make us feel as if we are going in the right direction. They're going away from factory farms, away from processed foods, and away from high-fructose corn syrup. That seems to be a good thing ... but maybe it isn't. Do any of these movements actually mean "sustainable" or "healthy"? Many would want you to think so. Even the word "humane" is now used synonymously with sustainable. Does "humane" (as it's now used by organizations and the general public) even *mean* humane? And who is it that tries to define humane for all of us? Thus, there is the introduction of skewed subjectivity into definitions that ultimately shape our food-choice patterns and the health of our country and planet.

All livestock operations in the world, as well as any organizations affiliated with them, have a completely different definition of the words "sustainable," "healthy," "humane," or "ethical" than I do. We will explore much more about "humane" in chapter 8.

The world hunger/food choice connection: a summary

World hunger, as it relates to our food choices, is a very serious and complicated issue. The United Nations predicts that by 2050, the world's population will reach 9.1 billion, 34 percent higher than today. Most of this population increase will occur in developing countries and in cities. It is estimated that 70 percent of the world's population will be urban, accelerating from the 49 percent seen today, and income levels will be many times what we have now. Many researchers feel that in order to feed that many people—people who are wealthier and living in cities—the world will have to increase annual meat production by over 200 million tons (to reach an estimated 517 million tons needed). But increasing annual meat production is not the answer, and it instead will escalate many other issues related to global depletion, such as climate change and water scarcity concerns.

Fertility rates of African countries announced by CIA World Factbook in 2012 increased to an average of 5.2 births per female. The country of Niger saw an increase to an average rate of 7.52 children per female. Clearly, there is a concern for escalated birthrates in countries where, at the same time, food security is an issue. Although there are those who point their fingers at "overpopulation" as the overriding reason we see so many hungry and poor, in a global context, other factors come into play.

Nearly 1 billion people in the world suffer from hunger, and 6 million children died from starvation in 2012, as they did in 2011. We all seem to have difficulty understanding how our choices, particularly regarding items we consume, such as food, could possibly have an impact on something or someone elsewhere in the world. It is so very difficult to see, feel, or extend beyond our own sphere. For many, if it is not directly in our sight, it must not be real.

Although there are many layers of complexity, most observers would think the reason we have world hunger is because of poverty. While on its simplest level this is true, animal-based food production systems are directly responsible for many factors affecting hunger, starvation, and even poverty, which then cycles itself back to hunger.

This correlation between animal (livestock and fish)-based food production systems and world hunger is, of course, fueled by the demand for these products and can be found in generalized global factors, as well as on a very local basis or regionally within countries where hunger rates are high. Together, these two categories of factors (global and local) insidiously manifest themselves in many ways.

Two primary groups of people suffer from this poverty/hunger cycle—about one-third live in more urban settings (this is the case with those found in the United States and other developed countries), while the other two-thirds are those in rural and more undeveloped nations. For both groups, the raising and eating of animals (livestock and fish) by our global community ultimately affects food prices, food availability, policy making, and even education to improve agricultural systems in those developing countries. Global factors include control of seed manufacturing and pricing, primarily for livestock feed crops by large companies such as Monsanto and DuPont (Pioneer), buying and selling of grain, including futures by Archer Daniel Midland, and Cargill, and through the processing/slaughterhouses and packaging by Cargill, Swift, Tyson, and JBS. These few but very large and powerful companies control over 65 percent of all seed and grain and over 80 percent of all final animal products in the world. It is a very monopolized production and economic system, manufacturing seeds at one end and spewing out meat at the other. Because of the global demand for meat (all livestock), cultural, social, political, and economic influences remain strongly supportive of the continued dominance of these large companies and of the meat, dairy, and fishing industries in general. This then drives how global resources are used (land, water, rainforests, oceans, atmosphere, biodiversity, etc.), how money is spent, and how policies are determined. The demand for animal products in developed countries drives resource depletion in developing countries as well as exacerbating poverty and hunger.

Realize that 82 percent of the world's starving children live in countries where food is fed to animals, which are then killed and eaten by more well-off individuals in developed countries like the U.S., UK, and in Europe. One-fourth of all grain produced by third-world countries is now given to livestock, in their own country and out.

Globally, even with climate change issues and weather extremes, we are producing enough grain to feed two times as many people as there are in the world. In 2011, there was a record harvest of grain in the world, with over 2.5 billion tons, but half of that was fed to animals in the meat and dairy industries. Seventy-seven percent of all coarse grains (corn, oats, sorghum, barley) and over 90 percent of all soy grown in the world was fed to livestock. Clearly, the difficulty is not *how* we can produce enough food to feed the hungry (nearly 1 billion), but *where* all the food we produce globally is going, in addition to the other factors of pricing, policy making, and education. This certainly will become more of an issue as our planet's human population reaches beyond 9 billion before the year 2050.[226]

On a local basis, specific animal-based agriculture simply perpetuates both poverty and hunger. This is true whether in urban, industrialized countries, which are affected by all the factors mentioned above, or in rural developing countries. As an example, in Ethiopia, over 40 percent of the population is considered hungry or starving, yet the country has 50 million cattle (one of the largest herds in the world), as well as almost 50 million sheep and goats, and 35 million chickens, unnecessarily consuming the food, land, and water.[227,228]

The argument for livestock—and specifically, cattle—to remain strongly fixed in African countries is that it is a cultural practice, strongly associated with their history. But history has shown us that animal agriculture has failed there from a resource use standpoint, and it is time for a change to a much more efficient organic, plant-based production system. In the other direction, a simple argument could be made that if the agricultural land in the world were used more efficiently to grow crops for us to eat directly, more people could be fed, less land and other resources would be needed, and therefore world hunger would be significantly lessened. Following conversion to full plant-based agriculture and more sustainable farming techniques those impoverished countries more likely would be able to solve their hunger situation. If they still had difficulty meeting the needs of their people, then it would be no great difficulty for the United States or other countries who also have made the conversion away from animal agriculture to export some of their plant food surpluses to those countries, instead of, for example, to Mexico to provide for the growing number of cattle or pig operations across our border. It needs to be remembered that

6 million children will die this year from lack of food. Either way, directly or indirectly, the meat you choose to eat likely will have a large impact on global food supply—which ultimately affects world hunger.

In addition to periods of drought and other weather circumstances, lack of knowledge about sustainable plant-based farming techniques has affected the plight of various developing countries, where high percentages of hunger are found. This is especially true in Africa. But most of these issues can be overcome with teaching and implementing proper organic techniques and placing all land used for agriculture into growing plant-based foods. There basically are two types of farming in the world: commercial and subsistence. While less than 2 percent of the U.S. population makes their living from agriculture, nearly 45 percent of the rest of the world does. Of this 45 percent, most— approximately 150 to 250 million—subsistence farmers use a slash-and-burn method of agriculture, called *swidden*. This technique is prevalent in the majority of developing countries in Latin America, Southeast Asia, and Africa. In the areas of Africa most stricken with hunger, swidden methods are employed, where land is cleared and burned, crops are grown for only one to three years, livestock are raised, and then this land is rendered useless so the process repeats itself on a new patch of land. This results in not only poor crop yields and less than optimal food from animal products, but also the more insidious loss of land fertility due to overgrazing, compaction, erosion, depletion of soil nutrients, and eventual desertification. With an emphasis on education for these subsistence farmers, more sustainable farming techniques could be employed, replacing livestock and swidden methods with plants used directly for human consumption, which would improve long-term soil health and eventual yields. In Kenya and other areas of East Africa, where water availability is limited, farmers using drought-resistant leguminous cover crops (those crops planted to increase soil fertility) without raising livestock have already seen yields tripled.[229]

More than two-thirds of Ethiopia's topsoil has been lost due to raising cattle. An estimated 2 billion metric tons of soil each year is lost. Less than 3 percent of their land remains forested, as compared to 40 percent in the 1960s.[230]

Many countries elsewhere in Africa and in the Amazonian region that suffer from hunger raise cattle inefficiently, at the expense of their soil and other resources, while producing a fraction of the food they could if they converted to plant-based foods. This is because of their local cultural factors to raise cattle, as well as global demand for animal products and by neighboring countries.

More than 66 percent of the world's poorest people (those living on two dollars or less per day) live in rural areas and rely on natural resources for their existence. Global demand and production of fish and livestock has reduced traditional fishing stocks and decimated coral reef systems for indigenous people living on coasts and islands and has shriveled and segmented million-year-old forests. This will only exacerbate world poverty and hunger, because while remote from those who consume animal products, these ancient coral reefs and forests are what constitutes the world of the indigenous and the very natural resources they have relied on for centuries.

How would conversion to plant-based, local agriculture systems change this? Hunger and poverty is, in many cases, a circling phenomenon, whereby each perpetuates the other. Addressing the hunger issue will help solve the poverty issue. Growth in the agricultural sector of a developing nation is two times more effective than growth in any other area, including economics. This is because in Africa and most other developing countries where there is poverty and hunger, over 75 percent of the working force is engaged in agriculture. Ninety-five percent of Ethiopia's income depends upon agriculture. However, at the same time that agricultural growth is needed, it must be in organic plant-based systems, because this would be the most efficient use of their resources, many of which are critically diminished, such as water and land.[231]

Drought, hunger, and famine have occurred in Ethiopia since the beginning of civilization there. As in other areas of Africa, poorly managed cattle grazing has cause severe overgrazing, deforestation, and then subsequent erosion and eventual desertification. Much of their resource use must be focused on these cattle. Instead of using their food, water, topsoil, and massive amounts of land and energy to raise livestock, Ethiopia, for instance, could grow teff, an ancient and quite nutritious grain, grown in that country for the past 2,000 to 3,000 years (teff seeds were found in a pyramid dating back to 3359 BC). Teff is one of the smallest grains in the world (one-thirty-second of an inch in diameter) and is high in protein, with an excellent amino acid profile, is high in fiber and calcium (1 cup of teff provides more calcium than a cup of milk), and is a rich source of boron, copper, phosphorus, zinc, and iron.[232]

Seventy percent of all Ethiopia's cattle are raised pastorally in the highlands of their country, where less than 100 pounds of meat and a few gallons of milk are produced per acre of land used. Researchers have found that teff can be grown in those same areas by the same farmers at a yield of 2,000 to 3,000 pounds per acre, with more sustainable growing techniques employed and no water irrigation—teff has been shown to grow well in water-stressed areas and it is pest resistant. This would begin to build soil and improve fertility and provide a much greater amount of much-needed nutrients for Ethiopians and, with proper marketing efforts, could even stimulate improved economics with business opportunities to sell teff (as well as many other types of produce) to other countries. Therefore, conversion to plant-based food systems for local regions in developing countries would feed more people more nutritiously with more efficient use of their resources, improve long-term soil fertility, and create economic opportunities, all of which would provide a path toward breaking the poverty and hunger cycle.[233,234]

The Machakos district of south Kenya is one example of how education plays an important role. This is a poor area, economically as well as in soil fertility, and the people frequently find themselves in the midst of an unstable, if not repressive, government. Nevertheless, a program was implemented to teach the women farmers (more than half of the farmers in African countries are women) techniques such as erosion and rainwater control with terracing. They began focusing on organic, plant-based foods instead of livestock or animal-feed crops, and their yields improved by more than 50 percent. They now use produce to feed more people and even have created business opportunities that are selling items, such as green beans, to other countries.

In developing countries elsewhere, organic plant-based agricultural systems have been shown to improve yields by as much as 400 percent, with an average of 150 percent.[235] Most researchers and organizations involved in the plight of nations suffering from hunger feel that efforts and dollars should be spent on improved information technologies, increasing intensified livestock operations, and fostering the continuation of cultural practices. I can see many difficulties, however, with that approach and feel that the emphasis should be placed on education, redefining the word "yield" beyond short-term consumptive gain, and providing guidance for the implementation of fully organic plant-based agricultural systems. This is the best way to improve soil fertility for the future, provide the most nutritious food at the least cost to their environment, while opening the doors to economic opportunities, thus "feeding themselves" and creating a food, economic, and environs security net, despite what repressive forces may surround them or that they may encounter.

The 2011 world hunger report (*The State of Food Insecurity in the World* 2011) projected high and volatile food prices and called for "forceful" action. The heads of three agencies—Jacques Diouf of UN Food and Agriculture Organization (FAO), Kanayo F. Nwanze of International Fund for Agricultural Development (IFAD), and Josette Sheeran of World Food Programme (WFP)—warned in the preface of the report that such drought and weather crises as seen in the Horn of Africa "are challenging our efforts to achieve the Millennium Development Goal (MDG) of reducing the proportion of people who suffer from hunger by half by 2015." However, even if that goal were achieved by 2015, there still would be 600 million people in developing countries hungry and undernourished. The emphasis of that report and the three organizations' heads was to reduce food waste while increasing farm productivity and "more sustainable management of our natural resources, forests, and fisheries." That will be difficult to achieve when livestock remain in the equation, as waste of resources—land, water, food, energy—and waste of food is generated from every bite of any animal product. This is true in any setting but exaggerated in developing countries, where someone starving is looking for help, while their country and the world continues to churn out resource-depleting animals.[236]

We must remember that although climate change and extremes of water conditions, from floods to droughts, do obviously exist, much of the soil fertility issues that developing countries face, in Africa and elsewhere that have high rates of hunger and malnutrition, are derived from how they have been managing (or mismanaging) agricultural systems over the past 100 years. It would be difficult to blame any other reason than their use of livestock—their complete cultural dependence on cattle. In many areas of Africa, poorly managed cattle herds have caused severe overgrazing, deforestation, and then subsequent erosion and eventual desertification. On average, half to two-thirds of all the topsoil has been lost across the entire African continent, with some areas experiencing complete topsoil loss. It would help eradicate hunger (as well as address many other concerns) to allocate the 2.5 billion tons of grain produced globally to people instead of animals, eliminate livestock-based agricultural systems globally and locally, educate all small stakeholders in developing countries for furthering organic plant-based systems, and of course, increase global awareness of these issues and develop a collective consciousness.

According to the University of Colorado and the National Center for Charitable Statistics, there are now approximately 1 million nonprofit organizations worldwide providing food and other humanitarian relief, including UNICEF, Action Against Hunger, Oxfam America, and Ethiopia Catholic Relief Services, and many others. It would make sense for part of the relief efforts to countries suffering from hunger to educate the farmers, citizens, business leaders, and policy makers of the suffering country as to benefits of plant-based food production systems and the need to transition away from raising animals—immediately.[237]

Quoting the World Hunger Service, the Food and Agricultural Organization of the United Nations, 2011: "The principal problem is that many people in the world do not have sufficient land to grow, or income to purchase, enough food."

And therein lies the difficulty, which explains why there has been no progress. This vividly illustrates the very narrow view of the institution that is leading the efforts to solve world hunger. The World Hunger Service should recognize the "principal problem" as food choice, and focus its efforts on that.

We can do our part in reducing world hunger and poverty by increasing awareness about changing to a fully plant-based diet and then moving the change forward.

A word about buying "local" food

There has hardly been a food movement (or any movement, for that matter) so widely accepted and so quickly spread as the call to buy "local." Unfortunately, buying food that's produced locally has little to do with sustainability, other than from an economic standpoint. Why should you support a product economically if it is unhealthy for you or our planet? There happen to have been meth labs (illegally producing the drug methamphetamine) within 15 miles of my home in Michigan, which by definition are "local," but we certainly wouldn't buy this product because of that criterion. And so it is with locally raised and slaughtered animals. The only difference between the local meth lab and local livestock is that one *is* illegal and the other one *should* be.

The local phenomenon most likely began with a somewhat limited study conducted by Rich Pirog, the associate director of the Leopold Center for Sustainable Agriculture at Iowa State University, in 2001. In this study, he and his researchers analyzed the transport of just twenty-eight foods (fruits and vegetables that were not grown anywhere near Iowa) to Iowa markets by way of their respective food distribution systems. They found that these twenty-eight foods had to travel via semitrailer trucks (food traveling by railway, though, uses one-tenth the fossil fuel of trucks), an average of 1,518 miles per item from where they were produced to reach the retail outlet where they were sold. Although this was among the first studies in the United States to show this particular version of food-to-miles relationship, it was an incomplete study at best and left much to clarify.

Nevertheless, this did begin a wave of localism. Everyone was interested in becoming a "locavore" (voted word of the year in 2007 by the *New Oxford American Dictionary*), reducing "food miles," and basically supporting everything made or found locally (excluding meth labs, I suppose). One should eventually ask, from how many miles away would a food item be considered "nonlocal" and cast off as an unworthy edible? Readers of books such as *Coming Home to Eat* and *The 100-Mile Diet* began to interpret "local foods" as those produced within a 250- and 100-mile radius, respectively.

However, we need to be concerned about food *choices*, not food *miles*. And here's why: we now know that transporting food from the producer to retailer is responsible for only 4 percent of all the fossil fuels used and all the greenhouse gases emitted in the entire food production process—*only 4 percent*.[238]

Indeed, it was found that eating a total "local" diet (a typical omnivore U.S. diet) would reduce greenhouse gas emissions per household equivalent to 1,000 miles per year driven (with a 25-miles-per-gallon automobile), while shifting to a purely plant-based, but *nonlocal* diet (vegan) reduces greenhouse gas emissions equivalent to 8,100 miles per year. Even factoring in the greenhouse gases and fossil fuels used in the production and transportation process for nonlocal food, switching to a completely plant-based diet would have nearly the same effect on climate change as not driving a car for one year. And this reality was supported by studies in other developed countries. In the UK, it was found that transport accounted for only one-tenth of the food system's greenhouse gas emissions and that this pattern held for Europe as a whole. We should certainly encourage our communities to eat something made locally instead of being transported from 1,500 miles away, but only if it's plant-based food.

A more accurate method of assessing the impact a particular food item would have on our environment is by way of a life-cycle analysis (LCA). This, if performed properly and comprehensively, provides a more complete understanding of the journey of that food item, from the cradle to the grave (seeds, planting, growing/raising, harvesting, cleaning, packaging, transporting, storage, cooking/refrigeration, consuming, and post-consumption effects), and the full impact along the way (water, land, and fossil fuel consumption, type and amount of greenhouse gases emitted, pollution created, effect on biodiversity, and overall impact on human health). While greenhouse gas emissions and the carbon footprint are important, an LCA is a better indicator of all greenhouse gases created and the full effect on climate change, as well as all other impacts.

By employing the LCA to animals and animal products, then, one would see quite quickly that eating meals consisting of *all* nonlocal but plant-based foods has minimal sustainability concerns, as compared to eating animals produced by your next-door neighbor. Yes, anyone within 100 miles of you who is raising and slaughtering animals or producing animal products is a major contributor to global depletion. So before you proudly proclaim that you are a "locavore," are deeply concerned about "food miles," and eat "only foods that are produced locally," you should at least have a better understanding of the effects:

Eating "local" equates to 4 percent GHG emissions for just the food production process. But eating animals equates to 18–51 percent of *all* GHG emissions, 45 percent of all land use on earth, 23 percent of all agricultural water used in the world, 100 percent cause of overfishing and of all species and ecosystems that are now endangered or nearing extinction in our oceans, 50 percent contribution to biodiversity loss, 77 percent of all coarse grain use globally, 70 percent of California's diverted Colorado River water use, *13,000* percent more urine and feces waste created by livestock in the U.S. than by the entire human population of the country, and 15–35 percent increased risk factor for the four leading causes of death and disease in the United States.

We (and our planet) will be much better off if we eat organic asparagus, blueberries, beans, or just about any plant food, instead of local meat products, even if those plant-based foods have to be carted from 1,500 miles away to get to our plates.

Clearly, it's time a new, more accurate, and more appropriate movement gets under way and takes charge—one that's inspired by awareness. Title it whatever you want—local herbivore, vegan, relatively optimal sustainable eater, compassionate consumer, peaceful palate—but put it into perspective for yourself and for those around you. Live by and express the whole story—the *real* story—that food miles or eating local is a very small fragment of our GHG problem and that the GHG problem is just one component of the much larger global depletion picture. We need to address the type of food, *what* we eat, and the animals and fish that we kill and consume, not the miles traveled.[239]

Let's refocus and start solving the real problem.

The cage-free movement

We couldn't have a meaningful discussion about current food movements without examination of cage-free, but let's first look at the essence of its disconnection. Many colleges, food companies, and the general population are becoming aware of the atrocities and health concerns that occur within the egg industry. Because of this—and the belief that we need to eat eggs— there has been a movement toward creating a more humane environment for the egg-laying hens, away from the barbaric confinement of battery cages used in over 90 percent of all egg production. On paper, the words "cage- free" sound inviting. Many of the universities where I speak have made a change to all cage-free eggs. As with most consumers, they really do not know where or how the eggs were produced. The following is an example of my findings at one of the universities I visited, where I traced back an order of "cage-free" eggs from their campus.

None of the students or leaders involved in the campus change knew where the eggs came from, nor did the dining director of purchasing, who told me they came from "Eggs America," of which the USDA and all registered egg-producing organizations had no record. The carton I traced (using the USDA processing plant code on the carton) actually came from M and R Eggs—an egg-packaging plant in Fort Recovery, Ohio. Kelly Evers, the food and safety inspector for their parent company, Fort Recovery Equity, stated that it is a cooperative with forty member farms in the surrounding 30-mile radius. Nine of their farms are cage-free and American Humane Certified, and twelve are organic, with the rest conventional white eggs. Kelly Evers conveyed to me that my access to visit any or all of the nine cage-free farms was denied due to "bio-security" concerns. I told her I had no difficulties at any other livestock operation in our country—or in the world—and simply followed their own protocol of attire and disinfection. She was adamant and denied my access, even though the reason for my visit (as I conveyed to her) was to document the origins of eggs for a university—a validation of being "cage-free" and "humane," consistent with their reason for purchasing them. After all, if the hens were not cage-free or humane, why were the students buying these eggs? Still, no access.

I then contacted the USDA and the Food Safety and Inspection Service (FSIS), the supervisory departments for ensuring food safety in the United States, requesting data that showed a connection between a visitor who follows a particular farm's disinfection and cross-contamination protocols and transmission of pathogens. I wanted to see documentation of bio-security breach, essentially providing justification for Kelly's denying my access and confirming a reason for her concern. Well, of course they could not provide me with any data, not one incident, because if a visitor followed a farm's own established procedures for entering an area where animals are raised, that visitor would be doing what all the other staff do daily at that farm, every time they enter the area. Obviously, Kelly was simply being argumentative or didn't want me to see it because she didn't want my report of the realities of their operation to get back to the students.

The decisions you make every minute are ultimately affected by the information you've taken in. If the information is wrong, the decisions you make may be wrong.

The "Real Food" movement. What is *"Real* Food" anyway?

Whether defined by chef Jamie Oliver or the Real Food Challenge (RFC), I have issues with precepts. "Real Food," as associated with Jamie Oliver and his "Food Revolution" as well as the Real Food Challenge, is becoming a very large movement in the United States, and it's defined as being "local, fair, sustainable, and humane," which on its surface is appealing. There are serious flaws, however, in the base of definitions upon which the entire movement is structured. On one level, just because a food item was produced more than 100 miles away from you doesn't at all imply that it is not healthy, sustainable, or humane, as we have discussed already. On another level, *any* food item produced from an animal locally does not mean that it is fair, sustainable, or healthy. In my lectures I occasionally illustrate these facts with a comparison of two food items.

I begin by showing a Vega Sport Endurance Bar (by Sequel Naturals), holding it up for the audience to see and then explaining that it is not "real food" because it's not local. And worse, it's processed—it had to be produced from the mixing of numerous ingredients. It doesn't fit the definition of "real food," even though it does contain sacha inchi seeds (a powerful source of omega-3s and phytonutrients), four different types of plant protein, and is quite beautifully formulated. The other food item I show, in comparison, is a graphic photo of a slaughtered whole chicken, lying in its blood on a cutting board. I then explain that the dead chicken *is* considered to be "real food" because it's local (you can find a dead chicken within 100 miles of just about anywhere in the world), and the Real Food Challenge folks will tell you that it is sustainable, fair, and humane—to round out their own definition of "real food." It is none of those things, aside from being local. I also remind the audience that if I were to bring in an actual dead chicken, I would have to don gloves to handle it and then wash the podium, table, and everything else nearby with a powerful contact surface disinfectant, because 75 percent of all dead chickens carry, at minimum, three to four different pathogens (salmonella, shigella, campylobacter, viruses, and parasites). Then I explain that the chicken—or being local—doesn't mean that it's sustainable, fair, sustainable, or humane. Local doesn't even mean that a food item should be eaten. The only thing "local" means is that it's not very far from here.

Nevertheless, the Real Food Challenge is becoming a strong movement, especially on U.S. college and university campuses. Quite similar to the "local" movement, "Real Food" is off and flying, but it is not going in the right direction. It is going away from factory farms but not toward sustainability.

The Real Food Challenge organization is made up of national and regional field teams, grassroots leaders, steering committee, advisory board, and partners. Its goal is to "leverage the power of youth and universities to create a healthy, fair, and green food system" by shifting minimally 20 percent of the over $5 billion national campus food budget (that's $1 billion) by the year 2020 from "industrial farms and junk food" toward what they define as "real food"—again, food that is "local/community-based, fair, ecologically sound and humane."

And now we begin to see the problem. Real Food, similar to many other movements today, is gaining momentum and national attention—without a clear and accurate definition of the very concept that guides them. They provide information, such as the Real Food Calculator Guide (a list of criteria that determines what qualifies as "real food"), Pre-Calculator Baseline Survey (assessing how far from "real" a food purchasing entity may be), Appendix, and Spreadsheet, along with protocol for counseling a university, institution, or community toward what they feel is more just and sustainable food choices. This is a beautiful idea, and their efforts should be applauded, but since many of the food choices in the Real Food Calculator Guide involve animals and animal products, the RFC organization needs to reexamine the definitions on which the campaign is based. It's much like a ship that has left a hostile port or country of industrialized and factory farming. The Real Food Challenge ship has recognized the need to leave port and go in a different direction, and they are well stocked and strongly armed—but they are going in a wrong direction, guided perhaps by a navigator who is unable to read the compass correctly or chart the proper course or even know which is the right direction. Sure, they left agribusiness and high-fructose corn syrup behind, but their ship will reach Iceland when their intent is to reach Costa Rica.

Nina Mukherji, director of programs for RFC, recognizes this. When I raised the question of accuracy of definition, her response was:

"I wonder if you might be interested in chatting about some of the issues we've come up against in trying to define 'real food.' We frequently consult advisers to negotiate thorny questions, and you might know of resources or frameworks that we've missed." Nina's recognition of potential disparities is a good sign, and I immediately conveyed this to her and to two other national directors, inviting further discussions by the Real Food Challenge team. I never heard back from her or anyone in her group, despite my repeated attempts.

As seen on the University of California system-wide Real Food Calculator Guide, there are numerous issues with regard to definitions. Green Light status (food that meets the RFC's highest standards for real food) has been applied to any "unprocessed food within 250 miles, small farm, biodynamic, Marine Stewardship Council (MSC)-approved or Seafood Watch "Best Choice," Food Alliance, USDA organic, certified humane, pasture raised" (meaning, all meat, dairy, fish, and any animal or animal product that fits those labels), and a Yellow Light status (food that doesn't clearly meet their standards but is okay to eat while RFC conducts "further research") to local food within 250 miles, with a designation of American Grass-Fed Association (AGA), USDA organic, cage-free, humane raised, 100 percent grass-fed, and Seafood Watch "Good Alternative." Obviously, those who created the Real Food calculator are unaware or chose to ignore the fact that food miles are irrelevant if any of the food involves animals. They also seem to ignore that all the items in their Green and Yellow Light designations that have any animals or animal products are not at all sustainable in a relative sense, as compared to plant-based foods. The designers of this calculator apparently eat animals themselves and chose to selectively mold information into the calculator that supports their own eating habits. Still, the RFC is quick to point out that "the criteria in each of the green, yellow, and red categories has been thoroughly researched and reviewed by experts."

In the Red Light section (denoting food items to stay away from, considered *not* real food) they list, among other things, a "vegetarian diet." This might be accurately positioned under certain circumstances—

consuming processed, nutrient-deficient, unhealthy vegetarian food, for example—but this is a distinct inconsistency. By placing vegetarian diets in the "Red Light" section, the directors and "expert" council of RFC made a decision to view real food with human health consequences in mind but without concern for the sustainability of our planet's resources. In reality, the RFC directors should consider *all* vegetarian food as Green Light material as it relates to sustainability of our environment, even though some vegetarian foods are not supportive of our own health.

High-fructose corn syrup (HFCS) can be found at the bottom of the Red Light area (just below but, amazingly, in the same category designation as "vegetarian diet"), where RFC has applied the statement "No way. If any of these ingredients are found, they are considered health concerns, and the food item does not count in any category." So, this begs the question of why the RFC council was compelled to apply human health parameters on some food items such as these (HFCS and "vegetarian diet"), but chose to blatantly ignore any and all health correlations to other food items designated as "real food"—such as all meat and dairy products.

The Real Food Challenge directors and their advisors (led by Michael Pollan, Ann Lappe, Vandanna Shiva, Daveda Russell, John Turenne, Tom Kelly, and Greg Gale) apparently have dismissed the findings of hundreds of physicians and organizations (among them, Dr. Neal Barnard, one of America's leading advocates for health and nutrition; Dr. John McDougall, best-selling author and plant-based diet guru; Dr. T. Colin Campbell, author of *The China Study* and biochemist at the forefront of nutrition research; Drs. Esselstyn, Greger, Ornish, and Furhman; and the position statements of the American Dietetic Association, the American Heart Association, the American Cancer Institute, and many other institutions), all of which have concluded that consuming animal products, including all meat and dairy (whether or not it is locally grown, grass- or pasture-fed, or humane raised), carries with it an increased risk of contracting any of the four leading causes of death and disease in the United States today (coronary heart disease, cardiovascular disease, diabetes, cancer) and the five leading causes of cancer (lung, colon, breast, prostate, pancreatic) and precipitating factors, such as hypertension, hypercholesterolemia, and obesity, as well as many other disease states and types of cancers. I wonder how much longer the RFC advisors can comfortably reconcile this inconsistency found in their support of eating animals—food that "truly nourishes" and "respects human dignity and health," as stated in their "What is 'real food'?"[240]

Who's to say that reaching a goal of "20 percent sustainable of real food shift by the year 2020" is even sustainable itself? Would that be sustainable to our planet? To our own health? Not likely. It appears the RFC did not determine that goal by using the global footprint data and calculations of the Global Footprint Network or any respected research-oriented organization. The RFC advisors seem unaware of the irreversibility of climate change projected at 2017 if our greenhouse gases aren't kept in check, nor do they seem to understand the relationship of eating animals to this problem. Unfortunately, the RFC movement is already well under way, coming to prominence even with the lack of appropriate information regarding food choice.

RFC is positioned—leveraging the power of youth and universities—where it could generate great change. As of mid-2012, 363 universities and colleges had committed to the Real Food Challenge program. But the RFC campaign will fall short of its own goals ("to build a healthy, fair, and green food economy") if its definitions, which form the very nucleus of their philosophical and operational systems, do not accurately address and eliminate the raising, slaughtering, and eating of animals. Potentially significant food movements such as RFC must begin recognizing this, seek more accurate definitions, and begin charting course for the right change in food choice.

A case study, University of California System: self-perceived but unattainable sustainability, and a look at why this is happening

The University of California (UC) system, with its ten statewide campuses, is governed by a Sustainable Practices policy, which was originally issued in 2004 and last revised August 22, 2011. Its scope involves all campuses, medical centers, and Berkeley National Laboratory, essentially impacting a substantial number of individuals. As of 2011, UC had a combined student body of 234,464 students, 18,896 faculty, and 189,116 staff members. This policy establishes goals in eight areas of sustainable practices—green building, clean energy, transportation, climate protection, sustainable operations, waste reduction and recycling, environmentally preferable purchasing, and sustainable food service. By developing a fairly comprehensive policy, establishing a commitment to examine and improve each of these eight areas, and including food service as a priority, UC is to be commended.

However, the food service section of this policy is riddled with inconsistencies, grounded in lack of proper definitions, because much of it is based on food movements (with heavy influence from the Real Food Challenge), organizations, and individual consultants that do not fully comprehend global depletion as it relates to food choice. The development and implementation of this policy is a perfect example of how the efforts of well-intentioned individuals and institutions can be far out of alignment with reality because of the definitions used. As such, it deserves a more detailed examination. In doing so, we will be able to see the origins of the chain of inaccuracies upon which systems like UC rely, and it will serve as a base of understanding for solutions.

The policy's section on "Sustainable Food Services Practices" states that "sustainable food is defined as food and beverage purchases that meet one or more of [nineteen] criteria." The policy then lists these criteria, and if a food product meets just one of them, UC defines it as "sustainable." The following is their list of "sustainable" criteria:[241]

1. Locally grown
2. Locally raised, handled, and distributed (Resulting from regional constraints, campus definitions of "locally grown" and "locally raised, handled, and distributed" may vary; however, locally grown and locally raised, handled, and distributed cannot be defined as over 500 miles.)
3. Fair-trade certified
4. Domestic fair-trade certified
5. Shade-grown or bird-friendly coffee
6. Rainforest Alliance certified
7. Food Alliance certified
8. USDA organic
9. AGA grass-fed
10. Pasture-raised
11. Grass-finished/100% grass-fed
12. Certified humane raised and handled
13. Cage-free
14. Protected Harvest certified
15. Marine Stewardship Council
16. Seafood Watch Guide "Best Choices" or "Good Alternatives"
17. Farm/business is a cooperative or has profit sharing with all employees
18. Farm/business social responsibility policy includes (1) union or prevailing wages, (2) transportation and/or housing support, and (3) health care benefits
19. Other practices or certified processes as determined by the campus and brought to the Sustainable Food Services Working Group for review and possible addition in future *policy* updates.

It's easy to see that UC's definition of "sustainable" is, at best, subjective and relegated in most instances to the base of definition fabricated by a particular organization or certifying entity to which UC has turned for advice. The nineteenth item is a statement of future inclusion/allowance for modification and therefore should not be part of this list, and items 17 and 18 are related to more social sustainability issues. They have relevance but not to sustainability of resources or human health.

Of the remaining sixteen criteria, **fourteen are not sustainable**. They are not relatively sustainable as compared to plant-based alternatives and should be considered less than optimal—without proper direction or guidance.

It is interesting that the UC system is unable to differentiate "humane" (meaning compassion) from the word "sustainable" by their inclusion of number 12 in this list. However, number 12 (certified humane raised and handled), if accurate in definition, would essentially preclude nearly all others on the list, simply because they all include raising animals. In other words, if UC continued to define "sustainable" by whether an animal or product was raised, handled, *and slaughtered* in a humane manner (in a manner that everyone could agree was without psychological, emotional, or physical harm to an animal), then it would, by definition, necessitate the removal of all other criteria from this list, except numbers 3 (Fair Trade) and 5 (shade-grown or bird-friendly coffee). Items 1 (local) and 8 (USDA organic) would be valid as "sustainable" criteria only if they did not include animals or animal products and therefore should specify this.

It is difficult to structure a set of precepts or an entire doctrine around a term (in this case, "sustainable") that was defined by individuals or organizations that lack full understanding themselves. This merely sets the stage for ultimate failure. One such example can be found in the subject matter of item 12, "certified humane raised and handled," which brings to light a number of questions and disparities. What supervisory entity defines and then certifies that an animal's life was "humane raised and handled," and what criteria does it use? What monitoring mechanisms are in place? When did the word "humane" become synonymous with "sustainable"? And just because an animal was raised in a kind and cruel-free manner doesn't imply that it was killed in a kind and cruel-free manner.

There are two other major issues of concern with defining humane and sustainable. One is that certifying organizations such as the American Meat Institute (AMI), Humane Farm Animal Certified (HFAC), Animal

Welfare Approved (AWA), and American Humane Certified all admit to lack of proper monitoring during the transportation process of animals to slaughterhouses, with the Director of Certification of HFAC calling it "tricky." Second, the trail of the definition of "humane" used by all these organizations leads directly to one individual: Dr. Temple Grandin. When a leading educational institution such as the UC system associates "humane" raising and killing of animals as "sustainable," it potentially makes three mistakes:

1. There is a separation of the killing process from "raised and handled" references within the "humane" definition created by these organizations and therefore implemented by UC. In reality, there is no separation.

2. The Sustainability Steering Committee's reliance on various organizations' platform of "humane" ultimately relies on one individual's interpretation of what constitutes and can be defined as kind, compassionate, and not inflicting pain (emotional, mental, spiritual, or physical). The guidelines accepted as "humane" management of animals we raise and eat then becomes a manifestation of what one person *believes* is humane—not what *is* humane. This is unnecessarily subjective at best.

3. UC improperly equates the word "humane" with sustainable and improperly interchanges the word "sustainable" for "grass-fed" or "pasture-fed." If anything, I would tend to think the opposite would hold true—that the word "sustainable," if applied correctly, should mean that you "sustain" the life of an animal, not kill it.

From the list of UC criteria of sustainability, 1 and 2 ("locally grown" and "locally raised and handled") raise the following points:

- Neither would equate to "sustainable" from the standpoint of land or water use, contribution to climate change by way of GHG emissions, effect on biodiversity loss, fossil fuel use efficiency, or any other components of global depletion.
- Neither would equate to "humane."
- Neither would equate to "healthy for human consumption."

Regarding 7 ("Food Alliance certified"), the following disparities are found in that particular organization and certification process:

- Emphasis is on nonuse of GMO, prohibited pesticides, growth hormones, and subtherapeutic (feed additive) antibiotics, which is good, but not all inclusive of being "sustainable."
- There is a glaring inconsistency of this organization's stated ability to "identify natural areas suitable for endangered species" and "protects the habitat," while at the same time promoting loss of habitat by way of agricultural land use inefficiencies as the certified farms are raising animals and producing animal products. Also, this organization has no realistic monitoring system in place for loss of natural predators, past or present, due to livestock operations.
- With regard to "humane animal treatment," their organization states "Food Alliance producers are trained and competent handlers minimizing animal fear and stress during handling, transportation, and slaughter." However, they condone the use of conventional transportation and USDA slaughterhouses, which are not humane.
- It purports to adhere to strict "soil and water conservation" measures, but the use of livestock directly contradicts this.

Regarding 8 ("USDA organic"), sustainability for soil fertility is possible but contribution to all other aspects of global depletion remains with all organic livestock production.

Items 9, 10, and 11 ("AGA grass-fed"; "pasture-raised"; "grass-finished/100% grass-fed") are not at all synonymous with "sustainable," especially not "relative sustainability."

Regarding 15 and 16 ("Marine Stewardship Council" and the "Seafood Watch"), food items in these categories are not sustainable.

Once again, then, this leaves only two criteria, 3 and 5, remaining on UC's list of food items that could be considered "sustainable."

Until recently, Rain Forest Alliance certified only applied to plant-based food products. However, in 2010 a new standard was adopted, allowing Rain Forest Alliance certification to be granted to cattle. Regardless of their *intent* to "combat social, economic, and environmental problems with cattle farming," only two of those three problems are arguably attainable. By certifying cattle, Rain Forest Alliance certified ignores the facts and adds to global environmental issues with the creation of another certified sustainable façade.

In addition to having inaccurate definitions and criteria for specific food items regarding sustainability, further review of UC's policy reveals flaws in proposed strategy.

The "Procedures" section of their policy states the following (beginning with number 3 as it appears in the policy, since numbers 1 and 2 are not applicable):

3. With the goal of achieving 20 percent sustainable food purchases (by the year 2020), all Food Service Operations should track and report annually the percentage of total annual food budget spent on sustainable food.

4. If cost-effective, each campus and medical center will certify one facility through a third-party green business certification program through one of the following: (1) city or county's "green business" program, (2) Green Seal's Restaurants and Food Services Operations certification program, or (3) the Green Restaurant Association certification program.

5. Campuses, medical centers, and retail food service operations will provide an annual progress report on these goals. Annual reports should include the individual campus and medical center's goals as well as the progress and timelines for the programs being implemented to reach those goals.

6. Campuses and medical centers are encouraged to form a campus-level food services sustainability working group to facilitate the campus goal setting and implementation process.

7. The stakeholders who are involved with the implementation of the Sustainable Food Service section of this *policy* will participate in a system-wide working group to meet, network, and to discuss their goals, best practices, and impediments to implementation.

8. Campuses and medical centers are encouraged to implement training programs for all food-service staff on sustainable food-service operations, as well as, where applicable, on sustainable food products being served to patrons, so that staff can effectively communicate with the patrons about the sustainable food options.

9. Campuses and medical centers are encouraged to participate in intercollegiate and national programs that raise awareness on dietary health, wellness and sustainability (e.g., the MyPyramid. gov Corporate Challenge, and the Real Food Challenge).

10. Campuses and medical centers are encouraged to develop health and wellness standards for food service operators, including eliminating the use of trans-fat oils or products made with trans-fat.

11. Campuses and medical centers are encouraged to undertake additional initiatives that encourage healthy and sustainable food services operations. Examples include tray-less dining, beef-less or meat-less days, and preservative minimization programs.

If UC is concerned about sustainability, why is the goal only 20 percent? Why not 100 percent? Is "20 percent by the year 2020" sustainable? Many researchers who are not affected by thoughts of "realistic expectations" of the public or by cultural influences but who understand the more accurate timeline think differently.

Seeking green-business certification by a third party is a good idea, but only if that third party is fully aware of global depletion and uses it accurately in assessment protocols—Green Seal's Restaurants and Food Service Operations as well as Green Restaurant Association certification programs are not aware and therefore are not accurate in their certification process.

As evidenced by items 6 through 11, UC clearly encourages campus and medical centers to participate in training and education regarding sustainable food practices, yet there is no specification of where they are trained and by which organizations or programs. And so we begin the process over again:

1. Who is defining the word "sustainable" for those organizations from which UC is obtaining their "training and education"?
2. What are the motives and the educational base of the "national programs" they rely on? And are they fully aware of global depletion related to food choice?

If these training and educational sources upon which UC relies are ingrained with cultural influences that perpetuate the eating of animals and animal products beyond just one day, then UC will not achieve "sustainability."

Item 9 states: "Campuses and medical centers are encouraged to participate in intercollegiate and national programs that raise awareness on dietary health, wellness, and sustainability (e.g., the MyPramid.gov Corporate Challenge and the Real Food Challenge)." While this may appear to be a step in the right direction, the USDA's "My Pyramid":

- has no reflection of sustainability (no association with or base of sustainability anywhere in its design); and
- lists many animal products in the "protein" area of the plate that are, in fact, not sustainable for the planet and for our health. Blatant inclusions in this category are all land animals and swordfish, tuna, and salmon, with no regard to sustainability.

"Campuses and medical centers are encouraged to undertake additional initiatives that encourage healthy and sustainable food services operations. Examples include tray-less dining, **beef-less or meat-less days**, and preservative minimization programs." Why is UC advocating going "beef-less" or "meat-less" on only one day a week if it is a "sustainable" initiative?

Within the "Definition" section of their policy, there is a curious set of objectives:

> **Climate neutrality:** in the context of this policy, climate neutrality means that they will have a net zero impact on the earth's climate, and that it will be achieved by minimizing greenhouse gas

(GHG) emissions as much as possible and using carbon offsets or other measures to mitigate the remaining GHG emissions.

Strategic sourcing: a process designed to maximize the purchasing power of large, decentralized organizations, such as the University of California, by consolidating and leveraging common purchases.

Recycling and Waste Management

1. The university prioritizes waste reduction in the following order: reduce, reuse, and then recycle.
2. The university adopts the following goals for diverting municipal solid waste from landfills:
   - 50 percent by June 30, 2008
   - 75 percent by June 30, 2012
   - Ultimate goal of zero waste by 2020

The goal of attaining "climate neutrality" by the year 2020 is noteworthy, but without eliminating animals and animal products from their food service purchases, it will likely never be reached. While "strategic sourcing" is a wonderful tool to leverage purchases, foods must be included in the mix—and it must be the *right* foods: organically grown plant-based foods for direct human consumption. Food purchasing must be treated in the same manner as "recycling and waste management." If UC has no difficulty proposing an "ultimate goal of zero waste by the year 2020," why is it content with adopting the goal of "20 percent sustainable food purchases by the year 2020"? Of course, the food they consider "sustainable" really isn't, but nevertheless, the goal should have at least been on par with that of recycling and waste. If UC or any school system really wants to be climate-neutral instead of just talking about it in a document, they would begin with not eating animals—and that should begin now. With any continued support of the meat, dairy, and fishing industries, the UC school system will, in fact, not be "minimizing GHG emissions as much as possible," so they are going down the wrong path.[242]

The UC policy also states the following:

> Resource sustainability is critically important to the University of California, the state of California, and the nation.
>
> The university is committed to stewardship of the environment ... "Through its teaching, research and public service, UC drives California's economy and leads the world in new directions."[243]

It appears that UC has everything in order for a progressive move toward sustainability, but as we've seen, there is a rather large disconnect between their stated goals related to sustainability and the reality of what is being accomplished on their campuses. Indeed, their Sustainability Practices policy is more a set of baby steps that happen to affect nearly 500,000 students, faculty, and staff, millions of animals, and our planet.

In summary, the five major issues found in this example at UC are as follows:

1. The base of definitions upon which UC has structured its entire food service section within the Policy of Sustainability is flawed. Education about global depletion—what should and should not be considered "sustainable" food and food production systems—needs to be initiated immediately throughout all campuses, including board of directors, provost, all administrators, sustainability committee members, food service staff, and students. A plan to refresh and update the base of knowledge with appropriate and accurate information about global depletion needs to be adopted and set into motion for implementation every year.

2. Proper prioritization must be given to food items in terms of the magnitude and urgency of the issue of global depletion/ sustainability, and therefore a proper timeline must be in place.

3. UC must eliminate baby steps, meatless Mondays, and all information provided by those with ulterior motives, conflicting agenda, or lacking the educational base of understanding about all aspects of global depletion as it relates to food choice.
4. UC should adopt policies immediately to utilize an outside organization with a better grasp on issues of sustainability related to food choice in order to receive periodic assessments and guidance to achieve the highest level possible of "relative sustainability" and then create initiatives to better position UC as the world's leader in this regard, being a model for others to follow.
5. UC should understand and appreciate the relationship between true stewardship related to food choice and the ensuing attainment of prosperity for their campuses, the communities they serve, and the world.

In order to appear to be sustainable, many campuses in the United States today seek to be evaluated by a series of questions and then graded with the "College Sustainability Report Card." One of the questions asked is, "Do you offer specifically labeled vegan entrees on a daily, weekly, or other regularly scheduled basis?" And then it asks the campus to "specify the number of options and the frequency with which they are offered." It is interesting to me that this question would appear as a passive criterion for "sustainability" of a campus and yet there is no further delineation or emphasis on serving *only* vegan options at *every* meal, *every* day. Why would it be important for a campus, striving to be sustainable, to offer vegan meals occasionally—either in the grade received on this report card or in its own functional initiatives found on campus?

The problem with eating "less" meat

Many of the most widely accepted and fastest growing food movements seen today have at their epicenter the thought that we need to simply eat "less" meat than we are now and that will provide instant resolution to any detrimental effect caused by eating animals. Aside from gratification for the consumer and industries involved, these food movements do the opposite. The terms baby steps, Meatless Mondays, "less meat," grass-fed, local, etc., provide a shield of justification for the perpetuation of global depletion of our planet's resources and our own health, as well as the slaughtering of billions of living beings. There really is no other way to look at it.

In May 2012, the *New York Times* posted an article written by Mark Bittman that mentioned some of the ill effects associated with eating meat, such as the contribution to greenhouse gas emissions, the taxing of our natural resources, and effect on our own health. It was a fairly well written article about a very important subject and seen by a large audience. Mr. Bittman, unfortunately, believes that eating "less" meat is "a good thing," that "we Americans need to eat less of it," and "we can begin eating less meat tomorrow," instilling his thoughts that everything we are doing now is perfectly fine; we should just do less of it. This method of management was mentioned no less than three times in his article.

But what this does is essentially create a subjective and complacent route, one that has no realm of quantification—one that will not work.

When I spoke at a conference a few days after Bittman's article first appeared, I summed up my thoughts on the "eat less" movement by stating the following:

Just in the one hour I am speaking here this morning, over 8 million animals were slaughtered. In that one hour, 114,000 tons of grain were fed to livestock we're raising, but during the same one hour, 684 children in the world have died from starvation; 6,000 acres of tropical rainforest were destroyed and replaced by cattle; and another 4 million tons of greenhouse gases dumped into our atmosphere by livestock. So I'm advocating a quite different approach than what Mark Bittman suggested in his recent NY Times article, where he stated numerous times that we should eat "less" meat. Because with that approach, of eating "less" meat, only 7 million animals will be slaughtered in the next hour and only 113,000 tons of grain will be wasted, leaving only 683 children in the world that will starve to death in that one hour, and only 3 million tons of greenhouse gases will be emitted by livestock.

Therefore, unlike Mr. Bittman, I think those numbers should be zero. And it is easily attainable. There's no magic involved; nothing has to be invented; you won't have to consult with your financial or legal advisor; no new technologies have to be employed—it's simply with what you choose to eat.

And quite contrary to Mr. Bittman's position that "we can begin eating less meat tomorrow," I strongly urge everyone to begin eating *no* meat, effective *now*. To do anything less would be an admission of being still comfortably unaware or apathetic. Either way, it's a display of irresponsibility.

Meatless Mondays, supporting local farm markets, and voting with your forks

Whenever I mention that our global depletion due to food choice is not a "go meatless on Monday" type of problem, I mean that approach is not enough. We need to be constantly aware that if your choice of food involves animals—that means all livestock, grass-fed or not, and fish. It's the driving force behind global depletion and it is very, very real. And therefore, it needs to be dealt with correctly.

For instance, for years and from numerous advocates, we have all heard that we need to "vote with our forks." I'm telling you not to do that. Voting with our forks is something we have done for the past fifty years— and look where it has gotten us.

Let's give ourselves much more credit than that by becoming more aware of our food choices. Then we should actually vote with our *minds* first and let our forks follow.

There are now over 7,000 local farmers' markets spread throughout the United States. When you go to one of these markets, let the local farmers know that you support them. Let them know you want organically (or biodynamically) produced food and nothing that came from raising animals, because that uses too much land and water and affects our atmosphere and our health. Guide them. Influence them. Again, you will be voting with your minds, not your forks.

And about the "Go Meatless on Monday" campaign ... if you do this, if you go meatless on Mondays, you'll be contributing to climate change, pollution, global depletion of our planet's resources, and your own health on only six days of the week instead of seven. You'll be creating a false justification for your actions on the other six days of the week. It is essentially waking up Monday, saying, "Today I care about myself and our planet," while on Tuesday, Wednesday, Thursday, Friday, Saturday, and Sunday—well ... you don't. In other words, *don't rest on the laurels of what you're doing right only one-seventh of the time.*

Traceable food, so what's the point, if it's not the right type of food?

Traceable food has an objective of allowing a customer to track that particular food item backwards from the plate to the farm, where it was originally produced. However, that objective for the traceable food agency, organization/business/producer, as well as the customer, most likely entails *the path it took*, not necessarily *the resources it took to produce it.* In other words, what good would it do to only know *where* a food item came from if you don't also know *what* it took to produce it?

Let's take a pair of shoes or silk goods, for instance, which were made in a factory in Karnataka, India. Perhaps this is a factory that employs bonded child labor, disregarding all international labor laws, but has escaped detection. If this product was "traceable," you would know *where* your shoes were produced but not how they were produced or with what materials.

Similarly with food, you may be able to track down the farm your product was produced from, but will you know how many gallons of water or acres of land it took to produce it? Or how much carbon dioxide or methane that animal produced during its life and thus its contribution to GHG emissions and global warming?

It doesn't matter if the process of raising animals has a new title (grass-fed, local, traceable, Real Food); its effect on GHG is the same if it involves livestock. And most important, remember that climate change is but a fragment of the picture of all the global depletion caused by raising and eating animals. If you got in an accident and totaled your car, why would you talk about one flat tire that needs to be replaced when the whole car needs to be fixed?

"Pink slime" made headlines in early 2012. Pink slime refers to extruded or mechanically separated beef products, treated with ammonium hydroxide, which was approved as an additive or filler to ground beef and processed meats. There was general public disdain generated from the newfound knowledge of this process—the national descriptor, echoed everywhere, was "Gross!" Although banned in the UK and now even at McDonald's, pink slime can be found in over 70 percent of all ground beef in the United States, according to Beef Products, Inc. Nevertheless, immediately following heavy media coverage, the USDA purchased 7 million pounds of pink slime to place in the school lunch program, rolling it out a few months later in the spring, as it has done routinely over the years. The USDA commented that all of its ground beef purchases "meet the highest standard for food safety."

The Food Safety Inspection Service explains that ammonium hydroxide is used to kill pathogens such as E. coli and salmonella in meat. Consumers should be concerned about the entire process of slaughtering, cutting body parts off the bleeding animal, and then serving it as food to eat. E. coli, salmonella, and many other pathogens can be found on all animals and in all animal products. Blood and body fluids are associated with all meat. That's what we should find disgusting, not a chemical used in an attempt to reduce public risk of contamination from naturally contaminated muscle tissue taken from a dead animal. Consumers ask for ground beef; the USDA is simply trying to find a way to get an inherently unsafe product safely to them. How about asking for organically grown adzuki beans instead?

Is the world really eating less meat? Meat projections globally vs. U.S. perception

In early 2012, National Public Radio aired coverage of a survey they conducted about meat consumption, with results indicating it was dropping in the United States. The NPR-Truven Health Analytics Health Poll of 3,000 adults nationwide found that 39 percent were eating "less" meat than they did three years ago, which is consistent with USDA statistics of per capita meat consumption. Websites began to project this as great news, but there is a clear disparity between perception and reality of our changing diet. This may have seemed to be good news, but it is certainly not enough change— or soon enough—and the survey's findings are misinterpreted because it is vastly out of global context.

Although this NPR survey concluded that meat consumption in the U.S. has dropped, it did not include chicken, turkey, and fish, or animal products such as eggs and dairy items (milk, cheese, yogurt, ice cream, which, combined, is on the increase. Additionally, it did not divulge the fact that animal production, total imports and exports, in the U.S. are increasing, and global animal production and consumption are increasing as well.

Global meat production increased by 2.6 percent in 2010 to 290.6 million tons, and worldwide meat production has tripled since the 1970s. The increase continued the steady growth of the past decade. Since 2000, global meat production has risen by 20 percent. At 110 million tons per year, pork is the most widely produced meat in the world, followed by poultry (98 million tons), beef (66 million tons), and then sheep (13.5 million tons). China has half the world's pig market, even with the effects of loss of government subsidies and outbreaks of diseases, such as foot-and-mouth disease and swine blue ear disease. Reduced Asian supplies are expected to translate into record exports by the U.S. to feed rising demand in traditional Asian markets (South Korea, Japan, and China).[244]

By the end of 2011, the United States overtook Brazil as the largest exporter of beef in the world, followed by Australia and then Brazil. The United States is also the second largest importer of beef, following Russia, importing more than 3.7 million tons (6.8 million tons "carcass weight"). India has 324 million cattle, Brazil has 198 million, and the U.S. has 93 million. There are over 1 billion cattle in the world and 2 billion pigs. Less than 9 percent of the cows are grazing. In 2012 and beyond, however, it is predicted that Brazil, Australia, and India will lead the world, along with the United States, in beef exports, with a steady increase in beef consumption by 2–5 percent per year over the next twenty years. The expected rise in beef consumption is due to a 10–20 percent increase in demand from the Middle East, Southeast Asia, and North Africa.[245]

While NPR and others are reporting that Americans are eating less beef or "red meat," the rest of the story is that the U.S. is seeing higher consumption of every other type of animal product and becoming the world's leader in raising animals for export. Total red meat exports (beef, pork, lamb) hit a record $11.5 billion in 2011.[246]

There are two primary reasons that we, as a society, have not evolved properly or quickly enough to stop eating meat:

1. The institutions we rely on for education or guidance simply are not aware of the connection of food choice to global depletion or of the magnitude and urgency of the problem—they are comfortably unaware.

2. The influences that surround us have been too great—culture, social, political, economic—to allow change to occur.

Any food movements that promote the raising, slaughtering, and eating of animals or animal products suffer from a form of confirmation bias. Although this phenomenon can be seen in many areas of life, confirmation bias is a common theme running between all food movements, and it is displayed by individuals who follow one of these particular movements as well as by those who organized it.

Followers and organizers alike tend to favor food choice information that confirms their own beliefs. Each of them has created a tidy little box of cognitive function that allows entry and interpretation of only that information that *affirms their existing personal views and interests.* That's why any evidence presented to them that refutes their existing view is typically met with emotion or even manipulated irrationally in some manner to support their position—at least in their mind. Deeply embedded beliefs such as those involving eating meat often are buried under so many layers of influences that the effect of confirmation bias can be more extreme, leading to emotionally charged discourse and belief perseverance (hanging on to a belief after clear evidence is presented showing it to be false).

Worse, I think, is when this phenomenon occurs on an institutional or organizational level and thereby has a much more profound impact, with mismanaged and poorly disseminated information. Historically, confirmation bias has led to poor if not outright wrong decisions that affect millions and sometimes billions of people. And so it is with the food movements we see today. Any of these movements that include the raising and eating of animals are either comfortably unaware or wallowing in a form of confirmatory bias, which then slows down our evolutionary journey toward a more relatively sustainable state, especially as it relates to eliminating animals from our diet.

Becoming connected

According to most scientists and radiometric age-dating, Earth has been around for more than 4 billion years. Modern humans came into existence about 200,000 years ago. Whether you consider the origins of Earth or of humans, our own seventy-six or so years on Earth can be considered no more than a true flash in time, a fleeting moment in our planet's history.

It is an alarming thought that within merely the last fifty to one hundred years, our species has done so much damage to our planet—some of it irreversible—to something that has been in existence for billions of years. I don't believe that we would want to be judged by the generation following us as the group of humans who had the necessary information but were so short-sighted that our Earth and its atmosphere, harboring life for 4 billion years, was set on its way to destruction in only one hundred years.

Our anthropocentricity did not negatively affect our planet until the mid-1900s, when the number of people on Earth and our collective actions reached the point of having a significant and measurably negative impact. Raising and eating animals is the single largest component of our continued self-centered approach to life.

It is a new era, where awareness is mandatory, and acting responsibly, relative to our global impact, should be standard practice. It's time we make positive change with food choice. We need to take care of our home—and it begins with connecting.

To our credit, there is a growing awareness of the detrimental effects of eating animals and the benefits of plant-based diets. The number of vegetarians has increased to over 3 percent of the population in the United States and to over 500 million people in the world. Relative to the magnitude of global depletion caused by eating animals, however, this growing interest in vegetarianism is not enough. Quite bluntly, the rate at which we are depleting our planet's resources is far greater than that which can be compensated by the current rate of global change to a fully plant-based diet. We need to step up increased awareness of what we are doing to our planet and how eating animals is involved and then create initiatives to ensure our compliance. To be sure, many problems will be solved. Citizens will become healthier and more productive, health care costs will go down drastically, insurance premiums will decline, and government deficits will diminish. Additionally, new industries will arise, agriculture will flourish and be profitable, new jobs will be created, and we will ensure the long-term sustainability of our planet and its resources.

What has happened to the typewriter, stagecoach, pony express, abacus, and bloodletting? Their time has come and gone; they have been replaced by other, more efficient alternatives—word processing, Boeing

787, e-mail and electronic funds transfer, computers, antibiotics. As we evolve, methods and technologies evolve—our understanding of where we are in history and where we need to go improves and creates the impetus for change. It begins with awareness and, perhaps, an appreciation of how things can be done better—and learning from our mistakes. We now know that eating meat is not healthy for our planet, for the animals involved, or for us. We also know that many of our activities and industries are causing global depletion—using our natural resources and causing climate change at an unsustainable rate. One of those activities has been unequivocally identified—the raising, slaughtering, and consuming of animals and animal products. If we are to move forward into a more relatively sustainable position as a global community, then we must eliminate this obstructive factor. We must eat all plant-based foods, and it must begin today, not tomorrow or the next day, or whenever we get around to it. The planet cannot wait.

We need a grassroots approach (bottom up), but we also need to have imposed regulations and laws (top-down approach), because without such regulations, some will inevitably not comply. For those individuals and businesses, we need to invoke reprimands.

There are many reasons we have such a general disconnection with our food choices as they involve animals—where it comes from, what resources it took to produce it, how eating animals will affect our health. Mostly, though, we seem to be immersed in layers of cultural influences— social, psychological, political, economic, and even our media. Culture molds and shapes our preferences and holds us back from making changes. It can distort realities and create unnecessary bias. Culture usually will even trump religion. (Regarding food choice, for instance, many religions have made modern-day modifications to the ethos found at the core of all religions, "Thou shall not kill," to now interpret it as "Thou shall not kill, unless it is an animal that you want to eat.")

More thoughts on baby steps

When faced with the need for imminent change, we often employ an interesting approach: taking "baby steps." I've never really understood this approach. When we need to correct something, why not just do it? What's the point of taking "baby steps"?

There appear to be three different reasons propelling people's decision to begin eating "less" meat:

1. Health—to prevent or manage disease, lose weight, or simply feel better
2. Ethics—making the connection that meat comes from animals that are not treated so well
3. Environment—concern for the environment and hearing that eating meat damages the earth

Does it make sense to take baby steps here—to eat "less" meat, even when you know that eating *any* meat has dire consequences? What does "less" mean in this context? That you have decided it's okay to kill animals—but just *fewer* of them? That you've decided to ruin *less* of the environment and damage *less* of your own health? Is it your approach to be healthy and feel good *one* day of the week—by having "meatless Mondays," for example—and that you now will risk contracting any of a number of diseases on only six days of the week and reduce your risk of contracting various cancers by one-seventh? That's not such an ambitious goal.

Additionally, unless you completely eliminate meat and animal products from your diet, every day for more than four weeks, it is likely that your acquired taste preferences for meat and the strong urge to eat it will still be present.

If you've made the connection that meat comes from animals that are not treated well (because you now know about factory farms), you likely will find alternatives—and there are many to choose from. Any of the new food movements support eating animals but now they allow you to feel better about keeping meat in your diet, because you are eating animals only on Tuesday through Sunday. Not Monday, though. That's your meatless day—your non-killing day. If you make the decision to eat less meat and only that which is "certified humane" or grass-fed, then you are condoning the continued inhumane slaughtering of animals, regardless of how well they were treated while alive.

Many astute dieticians and physicians who advocate small steps (one day a week or one meal a day) in changing to a plant-based diet do so because the majority of their patients simply will not switch entirely to a plant-based diet—ever. Indeed, the vast majority of physicians do not advocate dietary changes to plant-based alternatives because of anticipated "lack of compliance."

However, in addition to human health perspectives, my concern is also from a time and environment aspect and with the impact on animals—both the ones we raise as well as in the wild—time is of the essence. Global change to a plant-based diet when we "get around to doing it" is not the prescription that is required to achieve sustainability.

Time is running out with respect to environmental concerns, and that's why the compromise of simply *reducing* meat consumption will not work.

Why procrastinate? I see a combination of factors that inhibit us from changing our meat habit—lack of awareness or full understanding of the problem or its severity or magnitude; unwillingness to act appropriately/ responsibly; and lack of our culture to place the proper emphasis on making a change. Nevertheless, we all have the ability to move faster in the right direction, particularly as it involves eating only plant-based foods.

I frequently hear, "What's wrong with baby steps? It's not realistic for us to quit eating meat in one day." People often say, "Everyone is different, and we need to take our time in cutting meat from our diets."

It's true that everyone has the *ability* to take their time eliminating animal products from their diet, but in the face of advancing global depletion and continued slaughtering of animals, do they have the *right* to do so?

I fully understand that most individuals will not adopt a plant-based diet overnight, despite its being a healthier and more peaceful choice. But that observation alone shouldn't make it the accepted standard by which we pattern ourselves. It's time we reach for a higher bar. The clock is ticking.

It is time to redefine what is "realistic." Instead of being dictated by patterns of emotional acceptance, we'd be far better off to concern ourselves with what is "realistic" for our planet.

Worldwatch and sustainable solutions
Founded by Lester Brown, Worldwatch has been at the forefront of providing information, having a "vision for a sustainable world," since 1974. I have supported them as well as applauded most of their efforts. You can imagine my interest when one of their brief e-mail updates from Danielle Nierenberg, an expert on sustainable agriculture and director of the Nourishing the Planet Project for Worldwatch, reminded us that she had spent eighteen months traveling across twenty-five countries with more than 350 projects in sub-Saharan Africa, "documenting innovations that are helping to alleviate hunger and poverty." She and Worldwatch generated "unprecedented" media attention.

It was also encouraging to see that the information Worldwatch gathered on this journey already was disseminated as a resource for local farmers in those African countries and other associated agricultural groups, scientists and researchers, academics, and journalists. Ms. Nierenberg and Worldwatch will accomplish the same objectives with a series of two-week trips to over twelve countries in Latin America through 2012. Knowing that their findings and conclusions will serve as a strong reference point as they meet with many stakeholders, it was very important for me to hear that food choice and production systems were being addressed adequately. They were not.

Most of their conclusions from this trip were summarized in Worldwatch's *Innovations That Nourish the Planet, 2011,* but I felt clarification was needed. During ensuing conversations with Ms. Nierenberg and Worldwatch in March and April of 2012, this is what I found out: they held hundreds of meetings and outreach sessions with local farmers and their projects. According to Ms. Nierenberg, the "major innovations to alleviate hunger and poverty" were:

1. Preventing food waste: in the field, in transport, by using solar dehydrators, better food storage, low-cost improvements
2. Innovations in urban agriculture
3. Helping youth get more involved: making rural areas more stimulating and more vibrant with increased IT (for example, cell phones, technologies)
4. Helping with climate change: working with plants that are more resistant to drought, providing information to help farmers predict and manage weather conditions

According to Ms. Nierenberg and Worldwatch, "These are the things that have the most potential and deserve the most funding for research. ... These innovations can really apply all over the world, and they are not getting the attention they need."

In order to understand and perhaps find solutions to world hunger and poverty, research such as this particular Worldwatch project is critical. But there was an obvious omission from their conclusions. I explained to her that while those "innovations" might be important, that's not what I have found to be the most critical factor in poverty-stricken nations; it's food choice itself, how it is being produced, and if it involves animals. That, I feel, is the single most important topic, and education about the elimination of livestock is the single most important innovation that will help eliminate world hunger and poverty. The effect of raising livestock—something that was completely omitted from her report—needs the most attention: the serious agricultural land-use inefficiencies, resource allocation, food-production systems, and cultural constraints found in these countries, where more than 50 percent are hungry and poverty-stricken. I pointed out the stark ratio imbalances of producing less than 100 pounds of meat on 1 acre of land, instead of 3,000 pounds of vegetables, fruit, and grain on that same acre. We also discussed the disturbing fact that while the majority of people are hungry or starving, food, water, land, and energy are inefficiently used for cattle, not people, in all of the countries she visited. Because eating meat and dairy products is a cultural "norm," it is left out of the equation when attempting to analyze or find solutions for world hunger. Ms. Nierenberg admitted that Worldwatch and other researchers generally feel that cattle are an important part of the agricultural systems of developing countries in Africa and elsewhere with "proper management."

Hunger, poverty, and resource use are all interrelated in the countries she visited (and others like them); they are heavily impacted by food choice, climate, water scarcity, and clear resource-use inefficiencies. The information needed to understand the relationship of food choice, resource use, hunger, and poverty is data-driven and can be found or determined. So whether it is Ethiopia, Eritrea, Sudan, or any country in the world, especially those caught in a hunger/poverty cycle, I feel the following questions should be routinely posed by anyone attempting to find solutions:

1. What percentage of all arable land is used for livestock in that particular country being researched?

2. What types of crops are planted on the other arable land? What percentage of this is for feed-crops, and what percentage is for produce/grain for direct human consumption (and which type of plant is in each category)? What percentage of feed-crops is exported? What percentage of the crops for human use is exported?

3. What percentage of livestock is exported? What percentage is exported illegally across borders?

4. What percentage of total water consumption is used for livestock (feed crops and direct use)? What is the source of this water (e.g., aquifer or surface water)?

5. What percentage of crops is irrigated? (What percentage of feed crops irrigated and percentage crops for human consumption irrigated?) What are the rates of irrigation and total gallons used per year for this purpose per crop?

6. What percentage of all crops is raised organically with soil-building/long-term fertility techniques in mind?

7. What steps, if any, have been implemented, and by what organizations, to improve education of farmers and villagers to more efficient plant-based systems of agriculture? (Teff is grown in

the highlands of Ethiopia at an average yield of 600 to 1,000 pounds per acre, yet under certain test circumstances, with better organic techniques, yields of 2,000 pounds per acre can be achieved in the same area.) Has there been any attempt at converting grazing land to planting food for direct human consumption?

8. What steps, if any, have been implemented and by what organizations to raise awareness levels regarding the human health benefits of plant-based foods? And what reinforcement measures are in place and by whom for this education?

9. What are the eating patterns of the country's citizens? What are the numbers and percentages related to animals and animal products (i.e., how many pounds of which animal and animal product are eaten annually per capita)?

10. What strategies are implemented to increase business opportunities for farmers regarding plant-based foods, especially the women farmers?

The point to this discussion is that as much as I appreciate Danielle Nierenberg and the work she and Worldwatch are accomplishing, they are missing the underlying elements of world hunger and poverty—food choice and production systems, specifically those involving livestock. The single "innovation" that is so desperately needed to help eradicate hunger and poverty, while rebuilding soil and providing much-needed optimal human nutrition is a transition to purely plant-based farming systems. Inherent in conveying this single life-changing innovation is providing the people with the education and micro-financing to accomplish it and increasing the awareness levels of the rest of the country to appreciate and fully adopt this change.

With this one research trip by Worldwatch, many in the world will know that information technologies need to be improved in developing countries and that these countries need to waste less food in order to combat world hunger and poverty. However, until raising animals and animal products are eliminated from their and our agricultural practices, it is highly likely that rates of hunger and poverty, poor nutrition, and infertile soils will remain miserably high, despite pursuing other suggested "innovations." Additionally, contributions by these developing countries to GHG emissions, climate change and all other aspects of global depletion will continue.

Reconnection at Rio+20

The possibility of becoming reconnected can occur in many areas of business. One such occurrence, on a rather large international stage, was during the most recent United Nations Conference on Sustainable Development ("Rio+20") held in June 2012, where some steps were taken in the right direction to place sustainability into a more proper priority context. There is still a lack of precise definitions and clear direction or timeframe for policy making and change, but a major shift in dialogue was observed, especially when looking back at the previous meeting in 1992.[247]

The overall objective of the Rio conference (or "Earth Summit") was to secure political commitment for sustainable development and to assess remaining problems in implementation of initiatives resulting from major sustainability summits. New and emerging challenges also were reviewed. The conference focused on the two themes of green economy in the context of sustainable development and eradicating poverty and the institutional framework for sustainable development. As with its predecessor in 1992, Rio+20 brought policymakers and scientists together from many countries, as well as other interested stakeholders, such as business executives and corporate leaders.

In order for proper change to occur regarding global depletion from all factors but especially from food choice, four levels of consciousness must be in place:

- Recognition that there is a problem
- Awareness of why the problem exists
- Commitment to resolution
- Implementation of initiatives to foster change

Although Rio+20 didn't accurately address our global food choices—specifically, eating animals—within the context of sustainability, there was progress in the general approach toward sustainability and how businesses perceived their role in achieving it. No longer is it an afterthought, one left to our governments. There is certainly a long way to go before it becomes apparent to all those in attendance at Rio that they need to look much more seriously at food choice if they hope to be successful in their attempts regarding sustainability. But Rio marked the beginning of a new era, whereby establishing and working within a model of sustainability became clear as a corporate priority. Business leaders urged governments to support policy related to sustainable development. Some of the many examples of this seen at the conference were from insurance giant Aviva, which led a group of financial institutions in asking UN members to introduce mandatory reporting on sustainability issues alongside conventional financial data.

Understanding that business has a critical role in the process, Unilever's CEO, Paul Polman, urged government leaders of many developed and developing countries to support the establishment of a global set of sustainable development goals, in order to guide government policy on sustainability. With its policy manifesto at Rio+20, Unilever asked for "collaboration between policy makers, business leaders, and civil society to develop a set of Sustainably Development Goals (SDGs)" by way of a UN SDG committee. These SDGs would then succeed the Millennium Development Goals set to expire in 2015. The five "key areas" described by Unilever that need to be addressed are deforestation, food security, water, waste and recycling, and sustainable consumption—with a 2030 deadline for SDGs to be created and implemented. Given this display of concern for achieving global sustainability, Unilever should immediately establish, implement, measure, and report its own SDGs. It is insufficient and even hypocritical for Unilever to urge governments to move forward with sustainability development when it hasn't even accomplished it itself. If Unilever is truly committed to sustainable development, only plant-based food items would be offered at all corporate facilities and functions, with no animals or animal products found anywhere throughout their product or service line. Additionally, statements to this effect would be found within their corporate social responsibility documents, and Unilever would effectively urge all staff and employees as well as their communities to support only organic plant-based food systems in their own food choices. To do anything less is to not address Unilever's "key areas" of sustainability development. Yes, sustainability is the new metric of business integrity and success, but it begins with the correct definition of sustainability, the inclusion of food choice, the elimination of all support for animal products, and adoption of these principles in their own house first.[248]

As shown in some of the conference's briefs, there was a clear disconnect between intent and what is actually happening. An example of this can be found with Brief 4—Oceans, UN-DESA (Department of Economic and Social Affairs), which was aimed at providing an overview of international commitments, implementation successes, remaining problems, and challenges in the area of oceans. In 1982, the United Nations Convention on the Law of the Sea set out legal framework, within which all activities in the oceans must be carried out, establishing three institutions: the International Tribunal for the Law of the Sea, the International Seabed Authority, and the Commission on the Limits of the Continental Shelf.

Brief 4 stated that the work under the watch of the Law of the Sea and the Commission on Sustainable Development has become more closely linked as they applied sustainability goals to the oceans and marine life. Other UN agencies such as the FAO, the IOC, UNESCO, and the UNEP all have now begun work to promote sustainable ocean development and to protect marine resources. Brief 4 failed to highlight the fact that with the immense time, money, and efforts all these agencies and individuals within them expended, the way we currently use our oceans is not sustainable—at all.

What does that tell us? It is a matter, again, of definition. The definition of "sustainable" was no more accurate in 1982 than it is today. Businesses today, though, realize they need to include this powerful word in their objectives. A necessary step, however, is to include in their written statements the global depletion caused by food choice as it involves the raising, slaughtering, and consumption of animals. Only organically grown, fully plant-based food and production systems should be supported, and this needs to be applied within the operational protocols of business to any related products or services they provide.

I mentioned in my first book, *Comfortably Unaware,* that since Kyoto and the beginning of the climate change summits in 1997, there have been no initiatives, directives, or policy changes involving the lessening of eating meat. Despite the general consensus that livestock now has a substantial effect on climate change, there remains a hands-off approach to dealing with it. Various influences are so strong that meat actually is on the menu during important conferences on climate change. Rio+20 was no exception.

When all was said and done at Rio+20, perhaps the most important message was that although meat was served at the world's most significant sustainability conference, many observers took note, realized the hypocrisy, and communicated it to the public—and the *Washington Post* thought it important enough to publish this observation. Change is upon us.[249]

I believe the future success of a nation will be based on ethical and ecological values, rather than entirely on military and economic strength. Wealth will be measured in natural resources, not economy. It will become more viable economically for businesses to establish ecological integrity. The highest relative sustainable practices will be rewarded, stewardship of our Earth will be a priority, and long-term views will become more important, regarding yields rather than short-term gains. Instead of thinking "what's in it for me?" there will be a more thoughtful manner of conducting business, maintaining a consciousness about those who come after us.

Sustainability as a growth opportunity for businesses

Rather than its being a word to impress or serve as a reflection of perceived awareness, real and functional sustainability presents itself as a growth opportunity and a risk-management strategy. Achieving a level of sustainability will become more of a method for businesses to continue to be profitable but with a humanitarian/social and ecological commitment. Current consumption and population projections, when added to the mix of a short-term view of profits by businesses, certainly do not ensure a sustainable future. In fact, this apparent discounting of the future suggests to me that a paradigm shift is necessary—one with more accurate and consistent definitions and a more global perspective and with future generations in mind.

Many analysts are concerned with predicting which new idea will create drastic changes for the world. Their lists include such ideas as new nanotechnology, robotics, and tradability within businesses. Nowhere, however, is there mention of food choice.

The emphasis currently of what might transform us and be the next big change is renewable energy—solar, wind, biofuels. I believe, however, this will be simply one component of the much larger change, which will be the recognition that we, as a global society, must transform our entire archetypical mode of thinking and acting. The necessary change I envision is that of moving away from a consumptive, immediate-gain emphasis and a primarily economy-driven society to a recyclable, renewable, long-term view, with ecological and social responsibility components added to the equation of our daily lives and decisions. We are at a peak oil reserve as well as many other of our natural environs, such as land, water, our oceans, and our atmospheric tolerance of human-induced GHG emissions.

The only way we can ensure a sustainable future (and profitable businesses) is with proper food choice and a quick departure from our current demand for animals and animal products, moving entirely to a plant-based diet.

The Gaia Survival Theory suggests that the earth will take care of itself, and it is most likely true that the planet can live well, perhaps better, without us, but we cannot live well without a healthy planet. Lord Robert May of Oxford, previous chief scientific advisor to the UK and past president of the Royal Society, once referred to his understanding of the environmental damages we inflict on our planet by saying, "Mankind only has a 50-50 chance of surviving the twenty-first century." Appreciation of this possibility should incite us to act accordingly—the easiest and most profound way for us to act is by way of food choice.

Wellness and eating are themes now occasionally included in discourse related to solving loss of our natural resources and frequently when discussing health problems (such as obesity and diabetes) and health care costs of the world's population. But rarely is there discussion about resolutions involving purely plant-based food systems. Therefore, the real challenge we face may be more adaptive. Many strategists and futurists feel solutions exist for the most serious problems we face, but the primary challenge is that the most powerful, influential individuals have little appreciation of the urgency and magnitude of the problems, limited understanding of the most viable solutions, and no incentive or will to change. This is clearly the case with global depletion and food choice. Because of this, there needs to be a rethinking of "wealth" from strict economic strategies to ecologic and social strategies. There will eventually be an economic value factored into every new business model, mandating accountability by assigning economic value to anything taken from any ecosystem or natural resource used. Instead of a negative, reprimanding connotation, incorporation of this model of accountability will be translated into profitability and be viewed fundamentally as the right thing to do. Yes, transformation of the way we do business and accounting for what we consume needs to take place. Food choice will be at the epicenter of this transformation, accompanied by retooling of our food production systems. There, of course, will be continued focus on waste management and renewables, recycling, and energy use, but not more so than what we decide to eat and how it is produced. Businesses and the collective will of the people hold the key to change.

The future and division of two types of individuals

I predict that eventually, perhaps as soon as the year 2030, there will be two sets of individuals in the United States, and by the year 2050, in the rest of the world:

1. Those individuals who have become aware and eat all plant-based foods. For them, change has occurred from the bottom up, by way of education and grassroots efforts. They have stopped eating meat or any animal product (livestock, fish, dairy, eggs) from a health, environment, or ethical standpoint or combination of these reasons.

2. Those individuals who are not aware or who are aware but simply do not care. These individuals should be appropriately taxed; they should have regulatory measures imposed on them. Change, for them, has occurred from the top down. These individuals had the opportunity to become educated but still ascribe to a self-centered, consumptive view and therefore should pay extra for animal food items. This will apply to producers as well as consumers of all animal products. And of course, if taxed appropriately, it would be improbable that anyone would be able to pay the amount.

The first group described above will gradually grow in number and ultimately comprise the majority of the people in the United States. They will evolve to becoming the group that will dictate legislation, mandating that all production systems and food choices be plant-based, because they will not accept the effect that raising and eating animals has on our planet's resources or on health care costs. I believe that by the year 2030, those individuals who eat only plant-based foods will not tolerate the economic and environmental burden imposed on them by those who eat meat—including water, land, and energy costs; effect on climate change; and increased health care costs. *We will reach a point when those who do not eat animals will no longer subsidize those who do.*

"Cool Foods" aren't so cool

In 2008, Santa Monica was the first city in the country to sign on to the Cool Food Pledge, a promise to promote awareness about the effects that food choices have on global warming. The pledge, established by the Center for Food Safety, with their plea to "stop climate change," is to eat fresh, unprocessed foods; buy local; choose organic; select pasture-raised meat and dairy and local wild-caught seafood; and plan ahead to prevent food waste.

The pledge, unfortunately, does very little to "stop climate change." And the promise to "promote awareness" stops short of providing any awareness of the primary cause of GHG emissions. With expenditures of 3–4 tons of methane and carbon dioxide, trampled and deforested land to accommodate pasture, and up to 2 million gallons of water usage for just one pasture-raised dairy cow by your neighbor, your "Cool Food" local, organic milk is not so cool.

Promoted by their Office of Sustainability and the Environment, Santa Monica has their own version of the Cool Food campaign: eat organic; reduce conventional meat and dairy consumption; opt for organic, local, and grass-fed alternatives; avoid processed foods; buy food grown locally; and say no to packaging.

The primary difference is that the community of Santa Monica is advocating to "reduce conventional meat and dairy consumption" by opting for "local and grass-fed alternatives." This, of course, displays a lack of understanding—"reducing" consumption of factory-farmed animal products but switching to local and grass-fed meat and dairy really doesn't change the global footprint at all. It would be best if they created a more accurate Cool Foods campaign that eliminated all animal products, which would then be consistent with their goal of minimizing their community's impact on greenhouse gas emissions, climate change, and all other aspects of sustainability.

It is encouraging to see that Santa Monica is one of the more progressive cities in the country by recognizing the need to include food in the discussion of sustainability. They have also created a "Sustainable Food Commitment," which is great to see, but their definition of "sustainable" food needs to be more accurate, particularly as it relates to animal products. Their objectives to become more sustainable are well positioned, but their inclusion of livestock, seafood, or dairy products will not allow them to reach their goal.

Advancing communities

Grassroots or a bottom-up approach to increasing awareness about food choice and creating change can take place in many ways. A common problem I see is that even the most environmentally conscious communities and their governments will follow a path of pseudo-sustainability. This is because their efforts typically are directed at managing waste and energy, and *if* food is mentioned, it is always with the same thought—eat organic, local, grass-fed, and "less meat" alternatives. Energy and waste reduction are simply easier topics for everyone to grasp and for municipalities to discuss and create change. The connection needs to be made between eating animals and the environmental damage it creates. Often, however, when presented with this awareness, community leaders do not want to address creating change. The entire process of educating community members and establishing initiatives targeted at the elimination of eating animals and animal products seems unrealistic and unattainable in their eyes—it's easier to recycle, reduce waste, drive hybrid cars, and change out lightbulbs.

The framework that many communities follow to become more sustainable is that set forth by Urban Environmental Accords—a road map and assessment plan that was signed into action June 5, 2005, by "the world's largest and most visionary cities." The Accords were drafted in recognition of World Environment Day, a project of the United Nations Environment Program, and it frames twenty-one specific actions for sustainable urban living, addressing seven environmental areas common to all large cities: energy, waste reduction, urban design, urban nature, transportation, water, and environmental health. As of August 2012, 100 cities worldwide have signed on to the Accords, including Delhi, London, Melbourne, Moscow, Rio de Janeiro, Copenhagen, Zurich, Dhaka, Kampala, Seattle, and thirteen cities in California. A "City Green Star program" assigns stars to each participating city in recognition of how many of the twenty-one actions a city has implemented after seven years of following the Accords. The three actions in the environmental health area are:

- Action 16: Every year, identify one product, chemical, or compound that is used within the city that represents the greatest risk to human health, and adopt a law and provide incentives to reduce or eliminate its use by the municipal government.

- Action 17: Promote the public health and environmental benefits of supporting locally grown organic foods. Ensure that 20 percent of all city facilities (including schools) serve locally grown and organic food within seven years.
- Action 18: Establish an Air Quality Index (AQI) to measure the level of air pollution and set the goal of reducing by 10 percent in seven years the number of days categorized in the AQI range as "unhealthy" or "hazardous."

Clearly, those who were responsible for drafting the Accords had no understanding that "locally grown foods" have little to do with sustainability or that ensuring "that 20 percent of all city facilities serve locally grown and organic food within seven years" is not the prescription for achieving a sustainable future in any of the three parameters they projected (20 percent, seven years, or type of food). Unwittingly, the Accords composers may still have provided the key action for a city to follow in order to become more relatively sustainable. Regarding Action 16, "identify one product that is used within the city that represents the greatest risk to human health, and adopt a law and provide incentives to reduce or eliminate its use by the municipal government." If all cities would apply this action to livestock, fish, and all animal products, then progress toward sustainability by using these Accords could be made.

The objective of the Accords is to have participating cities achieve zero waste and to reduce GHG emissions. By not clearly addressing the role of livestock, however, this objective will be impossible to achieve. Yes, the Accords are an important part of a much-needed grassroots movement focused on cities, but it is mandatory to place the role of eating animals in proper perspective—at the top of legislative agendas.

Since 1972, World Environment Day has attempted to promote understanding that communities are pivotal to positive change related to environment. The United Nations Environment Program (UNEP) has encouraged partnership in caring for the environment by educating and enabling nations and people to "improve their quality of life without compromising that of future generations." It's time the UNEP became more specific with this wonderful goal. In addition to initiatives directed at managing waste and energy, the route for the UNEP is education about the benefits of plant-based food, while supporting the elimination of animals as a food choice—as an addendum for participant cities of the Accords, as well as for all other cities and nations to follow.

Any food-related solution is usually managed by a statement such as the following, found in a city in California: "Eating local, organic food can significantly reduce emissions." This is not true if that "local, organic food" has anything to do with livestock. Additionally, there is never mention of all the other aspects of resource depletion associated with eating animals. A few cities go a step further and have created a Healthy and Sustainable Food purpose statement. One of these statements reads "Purpose: To support the local agriculture economy and reduce negative impacts from food production, distribution, and consumption." This is a perfect purpose statement, but there is no other information offered for community members beyond this, which presumes the intended audience already knows which foods are sustainable and which are not. I offer the following suggestions and modifications:

1. Reword the title to read "The Role of Food in Sustainability"
2. Express what that title means
3. Clarify and expound on the purpose statement

With these changes, the page would read as follows:

The Role of Food in Sustainability

Your own individual health and the health of our environment are intertwined inextricably and both comprise true sustainability for life on earth. The food you choose to eat and the systems in place to produce it will affect how well you and our environment are sustained and, therefore, will ultimately impact the long-term health of our home, our city, and our planet.

Purpose: To support the local agriculture economy and reduce negative impacts from food production, distribution, and consumption. In doing so, we will accomplish the following:

a.   Provide education to our community (residents, businesses, and farmers) on the most optimal (relative) sustainable food production systems

b.   Encourage the production and consumption of foods shown to be the most beneficial to our health and that of our planet—organically grown, plant-based foods

c.   Discourage the production and consumption of foods shown to be the least beneficial to our health and that of our planet—livestock, fish, and animal products (including "grass-fed livestock" and "sustainable seafood")

d.   Create initiatives to accomplish these objectives

e.   Measure and track the results for parameters of success

A city in California has a pie chart on their website showing the results of a survey to determine the number of vegetarians in their community. That is truly a great idea. But with no other information provided for their community members or visitors to their website, it begs the questions: Why the survey? Why post the results? Why was this important? The survey is only relevant if it is presented and used as an educational tool. Although a good start, this survey was taken only once, over a decade ago and only presenting the "number of vegetarians." My suggestions for city leaders are as follows:

1.   State why the survey was taken and how a vegetarian diet relates to reductions in climate change and global depletion.

2. State all the known and documented health benefits for community members.

3. Let everyone know the difference between "vegetarian" and "vegan" and that the community supports only a purely plant-based diet ("vegan"), which is the most beneficial to our planet and people.

4. Conduct follow-up surveys annually, and include the number of vegans (not just "vegetarians") and why the person surveyed adopted that diet (environment, health, or animal welfare); this will elucidate a better understanding of motive.

5. Post the results in as many places as possible, and use it as an educational tool.

6. Promote, convey, and be proud of the increases in percentages seen each year of those who are vegan.

7. Convey why this survey is important to all community members, businesses, and local farmers (who should know that they should be growing produce and grain instead of animals)

8. Note the "increase" in vegans from 1983 or 1993 to 2003 and then from 2003 to 2013.

9. Each survey should ask the question "Are you aware that a vegan diet is healthier for our environment?" Otherwise, the meaning is by inference and subject to interpretation, which leads to less than optimal gain in positive change.

This is a template that every city can develop, place on their websites, and begin to make a real difference, rather than wallowing in lack of awareness and misdirection, believing they are becoming "sustainable" when they are not.

There is no question that proper changes in food choice and an appropriate timeline for change will require the effort of community leaders—those few individuals who have the awareness level and vision as well as a viable plan, with or without the Accords to implement. There is a strong need for progressive cities to form coalitions, whereby two or three representatives from each city serve as a liaison between the political arm of those communities and informational sources related to sustainability. Attendance at a conference two or three times per year, where cutting-edge information is presented, is advised. Using information gathered at these conferences, the representatives then could assist their local government in developing and adopting policies, as well as establishing educational protocols for full dissemination to their communities.

Representatives should be selected carefully, because food change is quite subject to bias. These should be conscientious, open-minded individuals, with vision for environmental perspective—progressive individuals who are critical thinkers and are interested in enlightening themselves as well as their communities. The success of biannual conferences is dependent upon two important factors: (1) achieving awareness from an organization, institution, or individual who is capable of providing conference attendees with the correct definitions and terms, upon which they can establish a base of better understanding; and (2) ensuring that attendees are able to take that new base of understanding to a level of awareness and actually create initiatives for their respective communities—appropriately designed initiatives that would be adopted, followed, and monitored. A time-activated metric would need to be applied in order for meaningful interpretation of the effort and evaluation of the degree of success. Additionally, there should be a high level of formal commitment established to continue educating themselves biannually. Once communities are on the path with accurate definitions related to food choice, and initiatives are in place with accounting mechanisms, they will serve as models, effectively setting the standard for other cities and communities to pattern themselves.

Connecting through the "high price of organics"

When discussions arise about how expensive it is for the U.S. consumer to purchase organic plant-based food, I would suggest viewing it with a more comprehensive perspective.

Latest statistics reveal that organic produce typically costs the consumer between 10 percent and 40 percent more than its conventionally grown counterpart. This is simply the "price" of the produce, but all consumers should consider other major factors when buying organic plant-based foods. One such factor to consider is the *real cost* savings to our environment and our own health. Organic produce, especially when compared to nonorganic or organic animal products/meat, is less costly to our planet, saving valuable resources, such as our atmosphere, fossil fuels, water, land, biodiversity, rainforests, and others. When compared to any type of animal product, organic plant-based foods are much less costly to our own health, as they substantially reduce our risk of various diseases.

Very soon, though, retail prices of organic produce will come down, simply from economies of scale—once demand increases, production systems have improved, and the industry expands with large quantities of organic produce in the supply chain, the price per item will decrease, fulfilling a fundamental law of economics.

The campus connection

For me, one of the most encouraging aspects of this journey to increase awareness has been the involvement of college students. With my research, lectures, and workshops, I have had the privilege of interacting with many campus communities, where I consistently find large numbers of students who care about the planet and are eager to learn and become active participants in the change that is necessary for their future.

Although I am frequently in dialogue with campus administrators, staff, and faculty, it is the *students* who are interested in creating change—and often are at odds with those in supervisory and decision-making capacities. But the students are our future and happen to be at that point in their lives where family, societal, and cultural constrictions ease just enough to provide a small opening for them to formulate and ask questions. Unfiltered answers and information become more easily available, and exploring the profound impact their food choices have on our planet and on others now has become a priority. Most students are demanding healthier food options and have been involved in movements to accomplish it. This is absolutely wonderful to witness.

Unfortunately, there are problems associated with this, primarily in the reluctance of college administrators to change (because of their own lack of awareness) and with what I have seen as a rather large issue with definition of terms—the students are mobilizing, but they are following the wrong lead.

Let's examine just one movement, cage-free eggs, which happens to be the most widely found food movement on college campuses in the United States today.

Many universities I visit receive an A grade on their College Sustainability Report Card (a data collection and evaluation service initiated by the Sustainable Endowments Institute). One of the reasons a high mark is frequently bestowed on them is because of the efforts of the dining services for eliminating trays, reducing waste, incorporating composting, and increasing recycling efforts. Regarding specific efforts related to food purchasing, the high grade reflects buying and supporting local, "preserving open space," and reducing fuel use and greenhouse gas emissions. So once again, in some areas, such as recycling and food waste on site, they are indeed moving in the right direction. However, with their food purchases, by their support of local animal products, livestock, and fish, universities are contributing to climate change and global depletion. The Report Card grading system furthers pseudo-sustainability—and it needs to be changed.

As of 2011, 41 percent of the 322 academic institutions surveyed by the College Sustainability Report Card had changed from eggs produced by battery-caged hens to serving only cage-free eggs. Each of these academic institutions also participates in the green report card's efforts to survey and provide a metric of "sustainability." The organization behind the report card, as well as the colleges and universities involved, is to be generally commended for orchestrating such a large movement for change. However, the report card itself and efforts of the colleges have serious inaccuracies and insufficiencies related to their base of definitions, understanding, and therefore expectations. While they are concerned about "animal welfare, health, and sustainability," as can be found in many of their goals related to the cage-free movement, the victory they achieve with this specific movement is lost by their following the *wrong* movement.

Sadly, they have been led down the wrong path in two different ways. First, by shifting all their egg purchases to cage-free, they have stamped their approval for the continual support of inhumane treatment of the egg-laying hens and the nearly 300 million male chicks per year that are killed, as well as the continued misuse of our resources and further global depletion. Second, while the focus of attention is placed on cage-free eggs, all other areas of global depletion related to eating animals still remain—these colleges still serve meat and dairy throughout all food service operations. They essentially are saying, "Let's take care of cage-free eggs because other campuses are doing so, and it sounds like the right thing to do. But let's ignore all the other unsustainable and unhealthy and inhumane practices we support, campus-wide."

These well-intentioned activists are spinning their wheels, putting out a small fire in their backyard, while ignoring the forest fire that is consuming the entire neighborhood. These campuses can claim to serve cage-free eggs, but they need to address the fact that they still serve chicken, turkey, cows, pigs, fish and other sea life, and dairy products. They rest their hats on a movement such as cage-free (which actually perpetuates all those things they wanted to correct) but then continue to support the raising and slaughtering of animals by serving animals as food, along with animal products.

According to the 2011 Highlights of the Green Report Card, "schools are offering food to encourage sustainable diets." The report proudly pointed out that "vegan options are offered on a daily basis at 87 percent of the schools." This strongly infers that plant-based diets are the most "sustainable" choice for everyone. If that's the case, however, the organization should extend its survey to ask if the campuses serve any animals or animal products of any kind, and then grade accordingly. There cannot be a meaningful sustainability "report card grade" to a campus that serves vegan options only one day of the week, while contributing to climate change and all other forms of global depletion on every other day of the week (because of the animals they purchase and make available to their campus community).

One example of many misinterpreted findings on this report card caused by lack of awareness of the parent organization is a statement by the Sustainability Endowment Institute itself, concluding that the surveys of report card-participating institutions have "shown dramatic increases on 52 green indicators since the first publication in 2007." For example, 64 percent of surveyed schools had a "commitment to carbon emissions reduction" in 2012, as compared to only 23 percent in 2006, and "95 percent of all schools now have a sustainability committee," as compared to only 40 percent in 2006. These numbers are quite meaningless, because even though a university may have a sustainability committee and has made a "commitment to carbon emissions reduction," it still contributes heavily to GHG emissions and further depletion of resources because of the livestock, fish, dairy, and eggs they procure and promote campus-wide every day. Having a "sustainability committee" that is unaware of the detrimental effects of eating animals or that is unwilling to eliminate animal products from its campus does little for the advancement of "sustainability." A "green indicator" is meaningless as well. Only when awareness levels are raised will the "dramatic increases" shown by a report-card survey become relevant and something to be proud of.

The Sustainable Endowments Institute has worked with the Association for the Advancement of Sustainability in Higher Education (AASHE), *Sierra* magazine, and the *Princeton Review* to develop collaboration on collecting college sustainability data, developing and launching innovative items such as the Campus Sustainability Data Collector, a web tool designed to streamline survey methods. In May 2011, executive director of the institute, Mark Orlowski, announced this collaborative effort by stating, "For the first time, the four organizations are working together to develop common sustainability survey language." If these organizations fully understood the role of raising and eating livestock, fish, and animal products in achieving optimal or higher relative sustainability, then their "survey language" would be instrumental in creating positive change—without such understanding, their "survey language" is inadequate.

Founded in 2005 as a special project of the Rockefeller Philanthropy Advisors, the Sustainable Endowments Institute has a purposeful vision of increasing interest in and attainment of sustainability by colleges. It is in a unique position to advance this cause, but not by handing out "A" grades to universities, encouraging them to continue eating animals and thereby contributing heavily to GHG emissions, climate change, and global depletion. Their survey mechanisms and definitions may be appropriate for accurate assessment of a university's recycling efforts, waste management, and even energy efficiency, but with food service, it is deficient. Once the Sustainability Endowment Institute and the collaborating organizations have become more aware of the global depletion caused by eating animal products, and they establish a more accurate base of definitions for their survey, then their report card will become the tool it is intended to be.

As of midyear 2012, the Sustainable Endowments Institute announced it would lead efforts to facilitate investment in energy efficiency with its newly launched "Billion Dollar Green Challenge." This "challenge" is a beautiful concept, whereby colleges, universities, and nonprofit organizations invest in self-managed green revolving funds, or GRFs (funds that loan money to projects, and repayment is made from savings achieved in the utility budget), which finance improvements targeted at energy efficiency. The objective is to reduce GHG emissions and operating expenses for participating institutions, while creating more funds for future projects. *Greening the Bottom Line*, written by principal author Dano Weisbord and published by the Sustainable Endowments Institution, examines the results of GRFs established in fifty-two institutions, allowing better understanding of this emerging trend. Since energy use and savings can be easily quantified and tracked, initiatives such as the Billion Dollar Green Challenge are attractive, especially from an investment standpoint. As of August 2012, the challenge has forty-two participating colleges and universities and $88 million committed. While recognizing the tremendous effort they have put forth to date in addressing sustainability as it relates to the energy sector, one would have to ask the challenge's eleven funders, two sponsors, fifteen partner organizations, and thirty-seven distinguished members of their advisory council how they plan to manage the unsustainable contribution their universities are making to the 51 percent GHG emissions and the many aspects of global depletion caused by livestock, found in uncontrolled food service purchases by unaware institutions.[250]

The problem I find at every university is this: the students sincerely want to effect change for the better but are relying on other "experts" or organizations to guide them and therefore, the campuses are not going in their originally intended direction. To more fully understand this phenomenon, let's look at one specific campus I visited on the East Coast. On paper, the campus appears to have all bases covered, but in reality, it doesn't. Worse, those involved *believe* their campus is doing all the right things, which then deters them from making full progress. This is similar to the person who is 80 pounds overweight and believes she is moving in the right direction because she has a personal trainer and works out for three hours a day. But of those three hours, that person takes thirty minutes to change clothes, floats in the pool forty-five minutes, walks on a treadmill for thirty minutes but with frequent breaks, sits on a bench to lift a small barbell a few times, and then the three hours are up and another day of working out is complete. Then the person proceeds to eat lunch, which consists of animal products, refined sugars, and fats—typical of all her meals every day. So although this person believes she is doing the right thing, she is not—actually, she is *contributing* to the problem—just as those "progressive" universities that are concerned about being "sustainable" are doing, even those that include food choice in their policy.

The following few paragraphs offer a summary of an East Coast university that has a sustainability policy, sustainability committee, and even a sustainability director of dining services established on their campus.

Economic overview:

- $12.2 million spent on food 2011
- $3.14 million, or 26 percent, of the total food expenditure was local

- Of the $3.14 million spent on local food, *9 percent was for fruit and vegetables; the rest for meat and poultry*
- $1.55 million for dairy
- $2.3 million spent on "meat," local and nonlocal
- $206,000 for seafood (not including canned tuna, which is used and offered frequently)

This campus, ascribing to the philosophies of the Real Food movement, is already ahead of all other universities in the country in terms of reaching the "20 percent Real Food purchases by the year 2020" and with their campus-wide conversion of eggs to cage-free. Is this good enough?

With just 9 percent of all local purchases for fruit and vegetables, they are effectively contributing to global depletion and unsustainable food purchases, with 91 percent of all dollars spent on local food. Further, this campus spends minimally 32 percent of their entire $12.2 million annual budget on unsustainable meat and dairy products, excluding seafood.

Kudos to the student activists who raised the 1,500 signatures and created campus-wide change to cage-free eggs, but while this is clearly a step in the direction of change, is it enough? The students likely do not recognize the full set of issues and aspects of global depletion that they still support by eating cage-free eggs. For instance, have they sent a representative, unannounced, to the farms where these eggs are produced? Have they researched the entire chain of production for loopholes in their understanding or conformity of expectations by the industry? Their understanding should include issues such as:

1. Conditions of the farm and henhouse, ratios of hens to space, etc.
2. Feed and water used per year and sources
3. Breed of chicken, hatchery where purchased, how long kept, whether they are debeaked
4. What happens to hens when they are finished producing.
5. What happens to male chicks at the hatchery where hens were procured.
6. Regulations of the American Humane Certified (or the certifying organization involved)

7.   Guidelines of monitoring and enforcement, and adherence by the farms

Even though switching to cage-free eggs is a tremendous accomplishment, I see it more as a stamp of validation that the students at a university can succeed at creating positive change. They can be proud of it and to use it as a platform of empowerment to continue the movement toward a healthier, more peaceful planet. But it should not stop there.

This particular campus also had established a "make a difference Monday," for vegetarian offerings to be the only food on campus, one Monday each month. With a Make a Difference Monday policy, this campus essentially is saying they only want to make a difference on one day of the month. I asked them what were they doing on the other days of the month—were they consciously *not* making a difference? If you know you can make a difference in the world by your collective actions on just one day of the month, why not extend that to every day? You, indeed, have that opportunity.

I suggested to the leaders of campus activist groups to seek more accurate definitions and to not be satisfied with their cage-free success—they need to keep moving things forward, funneling their energies toward:

- Increasing the "local" effort from 9 percent fruits and vegetables to 100 percent of all campus local expenditures
- Increasing the "Make a Difference Mondays" to every Monday and then to phase in twice a week, etc., until every day is met
- Reducing "sustainable seafood" and all seafood to zero purchases
- Educating the entire student body and campus community, including decision makers, to the global depletion issues with grass-fed and seafood offerings
- Understanding and being sympathetic to the challenges their sustainability director confronts with any movement toward sustainable plant-based foods

Allowing that complete and immediate change away from all seafood on campus arguably will be difficult, I proposed the following:

1. Begin with a phase-out of Marine Stewardship Council–certified sustainable seafood, moving toward Monterey Bay Aquarium Seafood Watch at 100 percent of purchases, immediately eliminating flounder tartar sauce and canned tuna.

2. Understand and create strategies toward substitution of seafood with plant-based alternatives, with a definitive timeline established, eliminating all seafood within one year.

3. Educate with regard to why change is in order (using lecture video segments from my website as a template), similar to what they have done with suggestive statements about moving away from "beef and pork," which is found in all sources of campus information. (Statements can be found on their website that they "strongly recommend sustainable seafood and poultry over beef and pork," so why not do the same with something like this: "strongly favor plant-based foods over any animals or animal products.")

4. Examine why the sustainable food service director and staff feel we can devote resources to certain animal species but kill others, such as some selected fish species, chickens, and turkeys.

5. Form a better understanding of what "local" really means in terms of sustainability, land and resource requirements, greenhouse gas emissions, and fuel costs caused by locally grown meat and animal products.

It is critical that all students at all colleges and universities continue becoming more aware about their food choices, specifically animals and animal products, and the effect it has on global depletion and then seek positive change. They should not blindly follow a food movement or its advisor or proponent until all terms, words, and concepts are accurately defined and understood. If change is sought as the most sustainable and most humane and with the health of our planet and the students themselves in mind, then the change can only be to plant-based foods.

"You're asking us all to be vegans."

Following one of my lectures at a university campus, a graduate student said to me, "Many of us will be teachers, and I am teaching sixth grade now. Are you saying we should teach our students that they should be vegans? Do you know how many problems that would create?"

My response was that she should strive to teach *truth* to her students. Let the children know the reality of their food choices and the impact on them and our planet. Teach children about the realities of global depletion and all the things that were presented in my book, *Comfortably Unaware*, and in the lecture that I just presented to them. Some may wish to place the title "vegan" on it, but classroom lessons should be more about clarity and truth than placing labels.

A label of food choice isn't as important as the translating of the stark realities of raising and slaughtering animals. I suggested a class field trip to a slaughterhouse. "Tell them the truth," I said, "that these animals being slaughtered for us to eat are every bit as smart and lovable and sensitive as their own dog or cat. Then ask your students if they think shooting those cows, pigs, chickens, or turkeys in the head, hanging them upside down, and slicing their throats is a cool thing to do. Instead, we could eat all plants, which are infinitely healthier for your students to eat and for our planet to grow— and they could just pick their food off a plant and more can grow back."

Then I suggested that she give them each one-seventieth of a glass of water and tell them that's all they could have for the day, because the rest of the glass of water went to **just one** of the cows that were killed at the slaughterhouse. Let them know about the 6 million other children in the world that will starve to death while we eat meat. Tell them the connection of where all of our grain is going. Tell them about all the rivers and streams that are polluted (over 70 percent of all waterways in the U.S.) because of the animals we raise to eat. Tell them we are ruining our oceans because of our desire to eat fish (they need to know that over 80 percent of all fish species are gone because we ate them), and explain that we do not *need* to eat fish—or any animal, for that matter. I urged her not to impose her beliefs or lack of awareness on her students—they need to hear truth.

Finally, I encouraged her to ask her young students if eating meat is a smart thing to do or even makes sense to them. No, I explained to the university student who is a teacher of children, it's not really about the word "vegan."

The role of ecotourism

One solution to our rapidly diminishing resources is the development of ecotourism (socially responsible travel in support of threatened, natural environments, wildlife, and local people), which may prove critical to preserving biodiversity. In many instances, ecotourism would serve to protect wild species as well as inhibit the use of land and water for raising livestock.

There are many examples of ecotourism today. Sperm-whale watching is now available off the coast of small Caribbean islands, rather than allowing the Japanese to hunt and kill them.

In the Virunga Mountains, visitors pay $750 an hour to see the last of the mountain gorillas—about 480 gorillas remain in these mountains, and about 300 live in Uganda's Impenetrable Forest. Efforts there have been aimed at strengthening gorilla habitat protection by way of education and working with local communities to develop livelihood strategies. Much of the gorilla habitat was destroyed because of slash-and-burn agricultural techniques, combined with pastoral livestock grazing.

The south coast of Mombasa, Kenya, was once the scene of hostile human/animal conflict, but now has the Mwaluganje elephant sanctuary, a successful preserve.

These are just some of the many examples of conservation efforts that were tied to ecotourism in a manner that provided resolution to habitat loss, due to agriculture or outright hunting of the species. In all examples, education was critical to bring awareness to the importance of maintaining habitat and the life of wild animals. Additionally, the local community members and farmers were able to realize many benefits by

242 // FOOD CHOICE AND SUSTAINABILITY

adopting conservation and ecotourism strategies. The same can hold true with domesticated animals used for livestock. Awareness levels could be raised regarding the benefits of plant-based agriculture (in developing and developed countries), using fewer of our resources, and economic incentives could be structured to invite change.

How we use information

The dissemination of accurate, unsuppressed information is a beginning step for positive change to occur. The next step is what we do with that information.

On June 19, 2012, Drs. William Rees and Mathis Wackernagel received the Blue Planet Prize, one of the world's most prestigious environmental awards, for their work in creating the ecological footprint—a measurement of the impact we have on our planet. Since 2003, Rees, Wackernagel, and their Global Footprint Network have used a data-determined metric as a monitoring device, tracking how sustainably we are living. Their group and global partners now span six continents and apply the impact of the footprint to many projects. As of 2012, they report that humans are in overshoot mode, because we are using the equivalent of more than 1.5 planets to provide the resources taken and to absorb our GHG emissions. One of their goals is to "increase international media outreach to broaden our message." The work of this group is remarkable and can serve as an important tool as we assess and then correct the detrimental effects we impose on our planet. They are to be truly commended.

But *knowing* that we are in an overshoot, unsustainable mode and actually taking the right steps to correct this are two separate issues. How we can best use this tool becomes the question. The Global Footprint Network makes it perfectly clear that it is "not anti-trade, anti-technology, or anti-GDP." It is information-based only and "makes no judgment about the value of technologies" or "the benefits, disadvantages, or fairness of trade." As such, it is left up to our nations' leaders, policy makers, business leaders, and individuals to first become aware of the information provided by the ecological footprint and then to create change—if sustainability is the goal. The Global Footprint Network has come to the same conclusions as many other organizations, in that "climate change, deforestation, overgrazing, fisheries collapse, food insecurity and the rapid extinction of species are all part of a single, over-arching problem: humanity is simply demanding more from the earth than it can provide."

However, as with other organizations, the Global Footprint Network stumbles with providing specific reasons and a viable direction for resolution—we need a pathway toward sustainability, not reciting observations that show we are not sustainable. Change is in order, and it begins with conveying realities.

I can help with the clarification: our global demand to eat animals, without proper economic reflection of resource use, has caused food production systems to become the largest contributing factor to our unsustainable ecological footprint. The raising, slaughtering, and consumption of animals—livestock, wild-caught fish, and aquaculture— is the primary cause of global depletion. Our demand to eat animals is responsible for 30–51 percent of all anthropogenic GHG emissions and climate change, 80 percent of the deforestation of tropical rainforests, 100 percent of the overgrazing, 100 percent of the fisheries collapse, 100 percent of the food insecurity issues (with factors we can control), and at least 50 percent of the rapid extinction of species. So Drs. Rees and Wackernagel are quite right in stating that "climate change, deforestation, overgrazing, fisheries collapse, food insecurity and the rapid extinction of species are all part of a single, over-arching problem: humanity is simply demanding more from the earth than it can provide." They, and the world, need to identify the reasons and spell out the fact that although there are other contributing factors, our food choices, as they involve animals and animal products, are the largest. We need to use this valuable information to create change, not simply point our finger at a generality. Although specifying the major cause of our ecological overshoot appears to be difficult for everyone to do, it is the easiest to identify and correct. Simply begin eating *all plant-based foods*—no animals—now.

I encourage everyone to take the information Rees and Wackernagel have so skillfully assembled, assign the major causative factor, make the change to a fully plant-based diet, and then inspire others to follow suit. We have the information. Let's do something with it.

A new metric for success and an organization to help achieve it

Going one step further, our demand to eat meat and animal products is causing global depletion of our planet's resources and loss of our own health, which impacts nearly all aspects of life on earth. By an immediate and comprehensive change to a fully plant-based diet, nations would see an increase in sustainability (not pseudo but more optimal relative sustainability) manifested throughout many systems—improved environmental balance, enhanced health and well-being of all citizens, decreased health care costs and health insurance premiums, increased worker productivity, decreased national deficit, increased job opportunities, and improved economics of agriculture and food-producing operations (if engaged in plant-based food). New farmers or those who transition to plant-based foods will prosper, and so will the nations and their citizens who support them.

It is time that the wellness of a country or nation is measured by the health of its natural resources, its people, and with respect for animals and caring for biodiversity, and by the fact that truly sustainable systems, particularly those for producing food, are properly defined and in place. This, then, becomes our civilization's new metric of success.

The concern for sustainability has finally reached a level where mobilization of ideas and initiatives can occur. The obvious difficulty is that food choice involving animals has yet to be properly included in the front seat of any mobilization—it is not recognized as the major contributor to reaching "sustainability." In order to correct this, an organization of reconnect—serving as an institutional nucleus to ensure proper prioritization of sustainability factors and to ultimately facilitate appropriate change in an expedient manner—was formed. It's called Inspire Awareness Now (IAN), a nonprofit educational organization, and it is a critical tool for reconnection.

The model of a tool for change

The overriding objective of IAN is, through education, to improve the health of our planet by way of food choice, solving many interrelated issues along the way. IAN will create awareness and initiate sustainable systems where food is involved, reducing global depletion on all possible fronts. To accomplish this mission, IAN will assist institutions to achieve their goals of "sustainable" or will incorporate "sustainable food practices" into their Policy of Sustainability. With some initiatives, IAN will provide educational assistance in the form of technical and public communications expertise to facilitate and enhance projects and services already undertaken by the particular institution we are working with. Other initiatives will demand that IAN serve as the primary provider to institutions that have new or no policies or programs in place. Inherent in this goal is to develop more accurate definitions of what can be considered sustainable and then facilitate change, based on these more accurate definitions. IAN will provide educational assistance in the form of technical and public communications expertise to four categories of institutions and organizations:

1. Institutions such as universities, school systems, communities and countries, and businesses that strive to incorporate sustainable systems within their operating policy or business model, having already demonstrated the need to involve food practices as a relevant component. These entities most likely will have an existing policy.

2. Organizations that seek to assist another entity (organization, school, community, and country) and have funding and objectives in place but need to incorporate "sustainable food practices" and systems as a priority. IAN will create an education and then networking service to assist them in achieving their goals. Examples would be a nonprofit group with initiatives in place to provide information or assistance to areas in the world where there

are food production and security concerns and in countries where hunger is rampant. IAN will redirect or refine some of their efforts to better position the campaign for long-term sustainability.

3. Supervisory organizations that are seen as experts or certifiers of sustainable food products and practices.

4. Businesses or institutions that have no knowledge of, or commitment to, food choice as a component of sustainability. IAN will provide first-line educational materials to these groups. Some may not have a sustainability policy drafted or in effect, and they may not even recognize the need for one.

IAN plans to provide education and creative ideation, advocating change and administering services to hasten the intelligent transition of our food systems into biodynamic operations, which will result in much more efficient use of water and land to reduce global depletion, while producing more healthful and safe foods.

In all instances, IAN realizes the need to strengthen each particular institution. Its goal is to "make the institution more prosperous by our efforts."

Institutions and organizations benefiting from the educational services provided by IAN share the following characteristics, goals, and desires:

- Lack critical technical expertise regarding issues of "relative sustainability"
- Lack critical communications skills required to gain traction regarding public communication of their efforts in the area of "relative sustainability"
- Need to lessen their global footprint regarding resource use and contribution to climate change
- Aspire to provide the healthiest environment for the constituents they serve
- Want to strengthen their competitive position and marketing agenda among their peers and constituents

- Seek recognition from their customers, stakeholders, community members, etc., as leaders, operating at the very forefront of sustainable practices
- Want to establish themselves as role models

Why is an organization like IAN needed? Why now?

Inspire Awareness Now (IAN) views global depletion and all disconnects discussed in this book as disconnects in levels of awareness and policy. Therefore, we help correct or solve these problems by educating, advocating change, and administering services to transition our current meat and dairy farming, as well as fishing systems, into organic or biodynamic plant-based operations, which will result in much more efficient use of our nation's water and land and food supply, while drastically reducing pollution, greenhouse gas emissions, and fossil fuel use.

This important transition will result in the increase of many more job opportunities in skilled labor, management, and education, all of which span the academic and previous job experience spectrum. By providing more green jobs, our initiative ultimately will have a positive impact on the 9 percent unemployment rate and the current 3 percent "structural" component of those who are jobless in the United States. The envisioned goal is for a healthier economy, healthier and more productive population, a truly more sustainable food production system, a healthier country, and ultimately, a healthier and more peaceful planet.

In developing countries, Inspire Awareness Now will work with other organizations to educate and implement farming and marketing systems to improve long-term soil fertility, yields, health of the community members, and economic strength. Recognizing there will be strong cultural challenges, it is a goal of IAN to create positive change by increasing awareness of the local farmers and communities as to the multiple benefits of plant-based systems and provide ongoing support to ensure success of the transition away from livestock.

As my astute colleague, Dr. David Bebiak, once pointed out so eloquently, "Regarding agriculture broadly as a technology, there are signs that it is on the declining slope of the normal 'technology maturity lifecycle.' When marginal advancements in the application of science yield diminishing benefits, even when deployed in the face of significantly increasing risk, we are witness to a dated technology. When even the ingenuity and heroic effort of our nation's farmers can no longer hold balance against the rising prices of their products, the diminishing health of our planet, or the depletion of resources on which they depend, we owe them a new edge with which to lead."

That "new edge" is the transitioning of all U.S. farms and associated agricultural businesses to plant-based food production systems and providing them with the educational and funding resources to do so successfully.

There are over 2 million farms in the United States; 98 percent are family owned. We have an aging population of farmers—more than 25 percent of all farmers over sixty-five years old. It's time we develop incentives for young individuals to enter this vocation by creating jobs, technique guidance for rebuilding soil fertility, education regarding sustainable resource use and plant-based systems, and funding to ensure success.

A 2011 report to the United Nations by Olivier de Schutter, its *Special Rapporteur on the Right to Food*, concludes that ecologically based farming requires both greater knowledge and more human labor. But that can be an economic advantage: "Creation of employment in rural areas in developing countries, where underemployment is currently massive, and demographic growth remains high may constitute an advantage rather than a liability and may slow down rural-urban migration."

Job creation in the United States must be on the table when discussing advancement of any technologies.

Sponsored by Rep. Chellie Pingree and Sen. Sherrod Brown, the Local Farms, Food, and Jobs Act supports regional farm and food systems but does not support proper nutrition education or the most sustainable food-producing systems, which are plant-based.

Instead of promoting conventional food choices and small-farm systems that produce those conventional foods and therefore perpetuating global depletion, IAN supports only those foods that use the least amount of our resources, cause the least amount of ecological footprint, and that provide superior health benefits while diminishing the risk of human diseases and death. Therefore, IAN promotes and supports only organic, plant-based foods and food systems.

IAN provides assistance regionally and locally to farmers, producers, and distributors for production, processing, administration, marketing, distribution, and education to increase business opportunities while improving the sustainability of systems. IAN creates new and enhanced markets for locally grown products.

IAN increases the overall availability of food, creating regional production systems and centers where "food deserts" currently exist. For instance, for each state, especially those in the Midwest and northern states, where the growing seasons are minimal, IAN will promote the development of growing centers and greenhouses, where cool-weather/short-season, highly nutritious plants can be grown on a large scale. Inspire Awareness Now will establish numerous regional centers by either retrofitting existing buildings (specifically, greenhouses) or building new ones that would be able to produce plant-based foods year-round, such as lettuces, spinach, broccoli, tomatoes, and nutrient-dense plants such as kale, collard greens, Swiss chard, and mustard greens. Retrofitted existing buildings would require minimal economic investment, while realizing immediate returns in energy savings and revenues from production. Jobs opportunities would be created in the planning, education, and administration aspects, as well as within the management and production processes. Where necessary, new greenhouses would be built, especially where there is limited or no access to fresh plant-based produce. Many of these new regional greenhouses could be established on existing farms where transitioning has begun from traditional beef and dairy operations to organic plant-based systems under the guidance of other IAN departments. IAN will provide marketing assistance for growers to increase their economic strength and growth. IAN recognizes the critical need to strengthen each individual community by the development of regional growing centers, providing education and job training for displaced, unemployed, youth, or otherwise disadvantaged workers—essentially, an integration of sustainable systems within a community and then networking one community with another, creating locally driven food, as well as a system positioned for global sustainability.

IAN will provide assistance to consumers by producing healthy plant foods and by increasing access to and education of the importance of these foods. IAN will increase viability of direct farm-to-table systems and farm-to-school systems, which combine food access with educational protocols to increase awareness for the consumer.

Education is, of course, key

The basis of all endeavors is to increase awareness. IAN will provide education to governmental agencies, committees, and legislators for them to properly structure bills, legislation, and overall policy changes. IAN will provide education to women farmers, creating long-term solutions to depleted soils, reducing hunger, and land/resource use inefficiencies in Africa and globally.

IAN encourages and supports the long-term health of our planet and all living things, realizing that true sustainability must include a symbiotic inclusion and relationship of environmental, economic, and social concerns (locally and globally) by way of plant-based food choices. IAN will impress this upon legislators, educators, business leaders, and all policy makers/leaders.

It's time we recognize and create a positive image and association with IAN-certified corporate responsibility statements, IAN-certified food policy, IAN-certified food movements that affect the public, and IAN-certified policies of sustainability (or at least the food service section of them and organizations, institutions, and businesses). This would be very similar to the recognition given to Platinum LEEDcertified buildings, whereby those who are IAN-certified are held in a higher esteem from an environmental awareness or sustainability perspective.

A question I am frequently asked is "What is the one tip you could give to someone for finally taking the 'plunge' to be a vegan?" My answer is that there is no "tip." It's not about finding taste substitutions or ways to make certain dishes or sandwiches smell and taste like meat or adding salt or fat to your cooked vegetables. There should never be food fads or "diets" that come and go, because eating the right type of foods and adopting a purely plant-based diet is actually a lifestyle, and it all begins with awareness. It begins with knowledge.

For instance, do you wear a seat belt when driving a car? If so, is it because you will get a ticket or be fined if you don't wear one, or is it because you know that you may become injured or die in an accident if you're not wearing your seatbelt? You have the knowledge—you are aware—that there are potential consequences for your decision to wear or not wear that seatbelt. Well, the same applies to not eating animals. The more aware you become of all the detrimental effects of eating animals—to our planet, to ourselves—the more likely it will be that you will not eat them.

The last piece of the puzzle—taste

The factor that propels global depletion is, of course, demand. And the demand for beef, fish, dairy, or any animal product comes from what we have learned to eat and the influences we have around us. None of us was born with the need or desire or taste preferences to eat meat. It is something that we acquired; it was taught to us and then reinforced by society and our culture, which is also shaped by politics, economics, and even the media. All those factors have played a part in making us want to eat animals. We don't *need* to eat animals; we *want* to eat them—there's a big difference.

One of the driving forces we have today regarding our food preferences is the widely held myth that vegan or vegetarian dishes don't taste very good, or aren't satisfying, or aren't even fully nutritious. It appears that fish and poultry will be the last strongholds as we move away from "red meat," and of course we have an unwavering demand to eat eggs and dairy products, which for many are not even associated with animals. Even if you decide you could do without eggs and dairy, because they are not so good for our environment or for the animals behind the scenes, how do you make the food you love without including them—especially desserts?

Many wonderful plant-based cookbooks are now available that provide working models on how cookies, cakes, and your favorite desserts and all other dishes can be made without eggs and without milk or cheese. Chocolate, the hub of food decadence, is now more delicious—more chocolaty—without dairy than with it. If given the opportunity, it's easy to see how all food actually can taste better than if you used animal products.

Author and chef Chloe Coscarelli was a guest on the radio show I hosted called *Vital Signs*. She was the first vegan chef to win on television's Food Network competition, taking the top prize on *Cupcake Wars* as well as other contests, proving that vegan dishes can, in fact, taste much better than the same dish made with animal products. Chef AJ from Los Angeles has been an inspiration with her delicious recipes and passion for plant-based nutrition. Lindsay Nixon has written great cookbooks with many accessible dishes, and Julieanna Hever, "The Plant-Based Dietician," blends her unique experiences as a registered dietician and a certified personal trainer, while creating wonderful and easy-to-prepare recipes in her thoughtful cookbooks. Colleen Patrick-Goudreau has been inspirational with her insights that blend the spiritual, social, and practical aspects of a vegan lifestyle, while connecting us to delicious recipes. So regarding taste preferences, the last piece of the puzzle, I must ask, what are you going to miss? The fat? The cholesterol? Needing to modify the taste of a dead animal part with salt, pepper, or A-1 sauce to make it palatable? Will that be missed?

Plant-based food tastes fresh, flavorful, varied, light, and wonderful. There are so many incredible vegan cookbooks and recipes available now, making it that much easier for the world to change to a healthier, most sustainable, and compassionate way of eating and living.

Food choice, specifically our demand to eat animals and animal products, and those operational systems involved are the most important issues of our time. No other single collective act by individuals has such a profound impact on our health and that of our planet. The raising, slaughtering, and eating animals or their products has negatively impacted our water supply, land, oceans, atmosphere, other species on Earth, and climate. Many of these effects are irreversible in our lifetime. We have the information, and we have the intellectual, informational, and technical tools to create change. Our food choices affect us every day on so many levels. Connection is really about funneling all the many avenues to the most sustainable choices.

Once I was asked if my book or lecture didn't seem "like brow-beating or telling us we're going off a cliff." Yes, there is certainly a fair share of information that could be considered as negative, particularly as I relate it to the responsibility we have to our planet, to ourselves, and to other living beings. If someone is about to drive off a cliff, wouldn't you point out the end result first and then show him an alternate route down the side of the mountain? There is certainly death and destruction in my message, but there is also an overriding sense of positivity, because I point out that it doesn't have to be this way. There happens to be an easy fix. I view my message as informing, educating, projecting realities, and providing solutions—better possibilities. The movement is under way; it's just fragmented and using an inaccurate base of definitions. We need to realize the reality of our driving off the cliff but understand there is another direction down the side of the mountain. I provide navigation for that alternate route and the appreciation that it exists.

It's time to make that connection, to realize that the health of our economy, resources, citizens, and society are inextricably connected—connected within our own country as well as with other countries on a fully global basis. We cannot make progress in one of these areas or aspects while ignoring others.

Making progress in our health and the health of our planet begins with unfiltered and comprehensive awareness. It begins with dissemination of truth and the uniting of those willing to make a difference in advancing peace and health. The furthering of any environmental movement will ultimately depend on our evolution as a society, beyond the anthropocentric manner in which we currently view things. We can no longer afford to exclude what we decide to eat from social, economic, and environmental reform and true wellness. A paradigm shift is necessary by all those individuals and organizations seeking positive change as we move forward.

Collectively, all of our efforts must include food choice.

Remember that almost everything we do, every decision we make every day, is based on our culture and what we've learned. By breaking down those constraints that bind us with regard to food choice, we can then create a new culture—one that is aware, compassionate, logical, and ethical. Instead of multiple food movements, each on a path of continued apathy and pseudo-sustainability, there could be one movement—organic, plant-based. Instead of followers, we all could be leaders. One hundred years from now, we could be remembered as the generation that set the world on a new course of health and healing.

Throughout history, many innovations, movements, individuals, and leaders have made significant contributions to life on earth. Ultimately, though, it will not be aviation, computers, the Internet, technology, or even medicine that will be the single most important advancement we have ever made. It will be our collective and swift evolution, globally, to a purely plant-based diet.

5

Why Should I Pay for What Everyone Else Decides to Eat?

THERE ARE LITERALLY an infinite number of ways to become ill; any of us can fall prey to sickness and disease. Many of the reasons for becoming ill are external factors, such as exposure to pathogens (bacteria, viruses, allergens, parasites); internal factors (weakened immune system, genetic predisposition to disease or condition); or a combination of factors, such as being exposed to contaminants, pathogens, or disease-causing agents at the same time as a drop in our body's defense mechanisms.

I began to eat only plant foods while in graduate school, primarily from a health, wellness, and environment standpoint but also because of the animal research with which I was involved at that time, working in various laboratories with funding from the medical school. The need to switch to a purely plant-based diet just became obvious to me on so many levels.

A wealth of information by trusted researchers and practitioners
This subject of food choice and depletion of our own health—or sustainability

of our own health—is a tremendously important topic. It has been made more medically credible, and information has become widespread by the work of many tireless researchers, such as Drs. John McDougall, Neal Barnard, T. Colin Campbell, Caldwell Esselstyn, Michael Greger, Dean Ornish, Joel Furhman, and many others. They are covering the topic so very well that I highly recommend reading the many books they've authored, attend any of their lectures, and visit their websites for the wealth of information offered. Because of the enormous volume of work from these individuals, I will simply highlight certain aspects and add a few new perspectives.

Increasing life expectancy and improved medical technologies in the U.S. and developing world brings a shift of disease patterns from infectious diseases toward chronic, degenerative disease, inflammatory conditions, and cancer—all of which are impacted by the food we eat—animal products in the negative direction; plant-based foods in the positive direction.

Every highly respected health organization in the world today has a position statement regarding the many health benefits of a purely plant-based diet, because the science is convincing, with an exhaustive amount of supportive studies and documentation available.

So why are we, as a society, still eating animal products? Because we just don't want to make that change. Our health practitioners provide weak support for the elimination of eating animal products, if they support it at all, and we keep trying to figure out ways to justify eating animals, continuing the unhealthy habit.

Of the four leading causes of death and disease in the U.S. today, animal products and animal protein are implicated in all four—coronary heart disease, cancer, cerebrovascular disease, and diabetes, as well as their precursors, hypertension and obesity. Eating only plant-based foods prevents and reverses these diseases, as well as lowering one's risk of contracting numerous other conditions, such as kidney stones and gallstones, kidney disease, osteoporosis, Crohn's disease, Parkinson's, multiple sclerosis, Alzheimer's disease, osteoarthritis, and many other degenerative diseases, gastrointestinal conditions, and asthma.[251-254]

We need to clearly understand that the link between eating animal products and many different diseases is as strongly supported by scientific literature and case studies as the link between cigarette smoking and lung cancer.

Of the five most common cancers—lung, colon, breast, pancreatic, and prostate—consuming animal products has been linked as a significant risk factor in all five, as well as many more. I need to emphasize that this is about animal products and the type of protein, which does not change if the animal is grass fed.[255,256]

A clearer view of protein

What does "type of protein" mean? All protein is not created equal, and animal protein has a detrimental effect on our health in two ways: by association (what comes or doesn't come along with it) and intrinsically (its chemical composition). We derive animal protein from meat or other animal products, of course, which brings a package of fat, cholesterol, hormones, endotoxins, and pathogens, as well as a lack of any fiber or disease-fighting substances, called phytonutrients. But animal protein, the protein structure itself, is also damaging to your health. Although inflammation is a natural healing body response, chronic inflammation of tissue, organs, and body systems is problematic and is a major contributing factor to nearly every degenerative disease, including heart disease, many cancers, arthritis, and Alzheimer's disease. Animal protein causes inflammation. It is high in arachidonic acid and high fractions of the sulfur-containing amino acids, methionine and cysteine, all of which increase levels of inflammation. Protein from animal sources causes excessive loading of kidneys, liver, and pancreas as well as metabolic acidosis (imbalance and lowering of the body's pH), which leads to additional inflammation. Filtration of increased urea (a waste product) because of animal protein creates imbalances in calcium and other minerals. If eaten raw, meat will transmit disease-causing organisms, yet when cooked, the protein type in meat has a high likelihood of producing cancer-causing agents (heterocyclic amines and polycyclic aromatic hydrocarbons) and transmitting endotoxins. Casein, one of the protein types in milk, is associated with increased risk of numerous diseases. In general, animal protein (the amino acid profile and general composition) is an upregulator of inflammation, which is a common component of many Western disease states.[257,258,259]

Some of the many studies to consider

Although there are thousands of peer-reviewed publications displaying the human health advantages of eating plant-based foods, one of the more recent analyses was conducted by researchers led by Dr. Frank Hu, professor of medicine at Harvard University. His study of over twenty-six years and 121,000 people factored out such tendencies for sedentary lifestyle, tendency to smoke, higher body mass index, and other poor eating habits. Even after controlling these and other variables, researchers still found that *each **daily** increase of 3 ounces of red meat* was associated with a 12 percent greater risk of death overall, including a 16 percent greater risk of cardiovascular death and a 10 percent greater risk of cancer death. The increased risks linked to processed meat, like bacon, were even greater: 20 percent overall, 21 percent for cardiovascular disease, and 16 percent for cancer. Interestingly, the study found that if people cut the amount of meat they ate per year by half, deaths would have only declined by 7 to 9 percent—the other 91 percent still obviously negatively impacted by consuming meat, despite eliminating half from their diet.[260]

Researchers at the University of Maryland's School of Medicine published an article in the *American Journal of Cardiology*, describing their study of the effect of a single meal on endothelial function (the lining of blood vessels) in healthy patients. They found that just one meal with an average amount of meat and dairy created inflammation of the lining of the entire vascular system for up to five to six hours. With meat or dairy consumption, there is essentially a low-grade chronic inflammatory condition established throughout the circulatory system.[261]

A recent thirty-five-year follow-up to the Harvard Nurse Study (a large study conducted on the relationship of diet and disease) revealed that consuming meat, dairy, and eggs is the largest causative factor to developing heart disease, while eating fiber is the most protective lifestyle measure one can take. Researchers found that eating just a single egg per day cut the person's life short as much as smoking five cigarettes per day for fifteen years.[262]

The American Dietetic Association perhaps stated it best in their position statement in 2009:

"It is the position of the American Dietetic Association that appropriately planned vegetarian diets, including total vegetarian or vegan diets, are healthful, nutritionally adequate, and may provide health benefits in the prevention and treatment of certain diseases. Well-planned vegetarian diets are appropriate for individuals during all stages of the life cycle, including pregnancy, lactation, infancy, childhood, and adolescence and for athletes."

Meat, dairy, and eggs have chemical residues, natural and synthetic hormones, and pathogens. They produce cancer-causing agents, such as heterocyclic amines and polycyclic aromatic hydrocarbons when cooked, and increase our intake of dioxin-like compounds (DLCs). DLCs are considered human carcinogens by numerous world health organizations, and 95 percent of our exposure to these compounds comes from meat, dairy, fish, and shellfish.[263,264]

New findings on Alzheimer's disease
We are only recently beginning to understand the relationship that diet has with immunological conditions, exacerbation of inflammation, and debilitating diseases such as multiple sclerosis and Alzheimer's disease. As is the case with other aspects of food choice and sustainability, the vast preponderance of information to which we are exposed by the media may not be accurate. Many institutions and organizations are not aware of the significant role of eating only plant-based foods, or they simply can't move beyond their own bias for

eating animals. A good example of this can be found with our understanding and current management of Alzheimer's disease.

The following statement is from the Alzheimer Association's website, a seemingly reputable site and currently the most widely used source of information related to that condition:[265] *"Alzheimer's disease is the only cause of death among the top 10 in the United States that cannot be prevented, cured, or even slowed."*

Alzheimer's is becoming a major health concern in our country, but information about it is mismanaged and suppressed when plant-based food choices are involved.

Alzheimer's disease (AD) has become the sixth-leading cause of death in the United States (2011 data). There are 5.4 million Americans living with AD, with one out of every eight older Americans having the disease. Payments for care of AD are estimated to be over $200 billion for 2012 in the United States.[266]

Quite contrary to the statement made on the Alzheimer's Association website, numerous studies show that plant-based diets reduce the likelihood of contracting Alzheimer's—it can be prevented and managed. There are many reasons for this. One of the more generalized reasons is that plant-based foods provide numerous phytonutrients, which are powerful antioxidants and anti-inflammatory substances. Researchers found that individuals who drink fruit and vegetable juice regularly had a 76 percent less chance of developing AD. One of the reasons for this is because of the high phenolic (a type of phytonutrient) content of plants. There are over 5,000 types of phenols found in plants; none is found in animal products.[267]

Additionally, increased homocysteine levels contribute to the risk of contracting AD, and the primary reason for these increased levels is the consumption of meat. As far back as 1998, researcher C. G. Gottfries, working with the Institute of Clinical Neuroscience in Sweden, reported, "We found serum-homocysteine to be an early and sensitive marker for cognitive impairment. In patients with dementia, no less than 39 percent had pathological serum-homocysteine levels."[268]

This study displayed that blood levels of homocysteine correlate strongly with Alzheimer's disease, but it also showed that elevated levels of homocysteine were useful in predicting who might contract the disease.

The only source of homocysteine in our body is that which the liver creates by using the amino acid methionine, as a building block. **Animal protein contains 20 to 30 times as much methionine as plants do.** One hundred grams of cod, salmon, or tilapia contains 700 mg of methionine; 100 grams of beef (grass fed or not) contains more than 900 mg of methionine; whereas 100 grams of kale, for example, contains 32 mg.[269]

In another study, reported at the World Alzheimer's Congress in July 2000, researches looked at 5,395 individuals, aged fifty-five and over, who were free from dementia. After examining subjects in 1993 and again in 1999, researchers reported the following:

"On average, people who remained free from any form of dementia had consumed higher amounts of beta-carotene, vitamin C, vitamin E, and vegetables than the people in the study who developed Alzheimer's disease."

Of importance, when considering a potential for genetic predisposition, the researchers also noted that in this study, family history or the presence of a genetic marker called the ApoE4 allele (both considered risk factors for Alzheimer's) did not alter their findings. In other words, high consumption of vegetables and fruit appears to offset one of the other known genetic risk factors for Alzheimer's.[270]

Another study, published in March 2012, found that curcumin, a substance found in the turmeric plant, known to have powerful phytonutrients, significantly reduced the risk of Alzheimer's.[271]

With nearly 6 million individuals in the U.S. affected with AD and another 15 million providing unpaid care (valued at $210 billion) for persons with AD and other dementias, it behooves the Alzheimer's Association to provide accurate statements regarding the role of food in prevention and management. Instead, the Alzheimer's Association highlights the five FDA-approved drugs—Aricept (donepezil), Razadyne (galantamine), Namenda (memantine), Exelon (rivastigmine), and Cognex (tacrine)— currently used to "manage" the disease, while admitting that none of these medications will prevent or cure the disease. In fact, Aricept, for instance, lists *187 adverse reactions/side effects*; many of these excessively numerous side effects are quite serious.[272]

Since 1982, the Association has been awarded billions of dollars for more than 2,000 research projects. Current funding (2010 and 2011 data) reached $529 million per year, in support of over 700 ongoing projects.[273] When I asked specifically what dollar amount has been spent on research related to plant-based nutrition as a preventative or treatment/ management regimen for AD, the associate director of the Alzheimer's Association responded, "We are unaware of any research of that kind related to Alzheimer's disease." In fact, my team of researchers couldn't find even one funded project related to plant-based nutrition from 2009 through 2011. With increasing incidence of AD in our population and mounting scientific evidence, consideration should be given to the importance of integrating plant-based diet schemes into the prevention of AD and also for treatment and management modalities. Not doing so is negligent and provides further support of the meat, dairy, egg, and fishing industries, as well as the pharmaceutical companies that do damage control for these industries.

Health-risk tax

The demand to eat animal products contributes heavily to global warming and global depletion, and in doing so, it affects everyone on earth. In the U.S. and other developed countries, eating animals is one of the most significant risk factors found in nearly all of the most common diseases. It is, therefore, heavily implicated in rising health care costs, health insurance premiums, foods prices, and even labor costs for businesses. Those who eat animals are driving up all these costs while driving down productivity.

More than $3 trillion dollars were spent on health care in 2012 ($2.83 trillion in 2009, growing at 6 percent per year) in the U.S.[274]

Of that, minimally $130 billion dollars spent were due to dietary choices related to livestock.[275] I believe this figure is quite conservative and could be as high as $350 billion due to eating animals, because this is how some of the $3 trillion was spent:[276]

1. $300 billion—heart disease
2. $200 billion—diabetes
3. $190 billion—obesity
4. $124 billion—cancer
5. $88 billion—food-borne illness

These figures are truly staggering and are for just one single year. They also do not reflect loss of productivity. For obesity alone, it is estimated that the annual cost of the workdays missed is $30 billion, with employers losing, on average, $3,800 per year for a single obese person.[277]

These are not just figures or statistics to me; they're patterns that tell a story about what we choose to eat as a society and what happens to us afterwards—the stark and very real consequences. Eating animal products increases risks of contracting diseases that contribute to all of these health care costs. Eating plants, on the other hand, will take you in the other direction, protecting you from developing these diseases. All of this should be factored into our national health insurance plan and the premiums and taxes we pay. I often pose the question *"Why should I pay for what everyone else decides to eat?"*

My health care costs for the past forty years have been zero. I've never taken one aspirin, ibuprofen, or antibiotic. I've certainly prescribed quite a few medications over the years, but I have not taken any medications of any type. I have been at the same weight since I was sixteen years old. Thus far, I have not missed one day's work for the past forty years from being ill, and I'm certainly not special at all. It's because of what I eat.

Even with suggestions or new guidelines for eating healthier food, most people don't comply. With an average diet of 2,000 calories per day, one should eat 2 cups of fruit and 2.5 cups of vegetables per day (relative to age, physical activity, and gender). However, 94 percent of the U.S. population does not consume this minimum target.[278]

According to the Organization for Economic Cooperation and Development (OECD), a thirty-four-nation grouping of advanced economies, the average person in the U.S. spent $8,433 (public and private spending) on health care in 2011.[279]

On average, an obese person spends $5,500 more on medical costs than a person of average weight in one year. In 2011, 36 percent of all adults in the U.S. were considered obese, and by 2018, it is estimated that will increase to 43 percent.[280]

It is estimated that eating purely plant-based foods provides the following protective benefits, as compared to individuals eating the average amount of meat:

- 50 percent less risk of coronary heart disease (CHD)
- 40 percent less risk of cancer (breast, colon, prostate, ovarian, pancreatic, lung)
- 70 percent less likelihood of adult onset diabetes
- 50 percent less likelihood of developing hypertension[281]

As an example of what effect a purely plant-based diet would have on health care costs, let's look for a moment at hypertension. Worldwide, $500 billion was spent on hypertension in 2011—twice that amount if indirect costs are included. A 50 percent less risk factor in developing hypertension, simply by a change in food choice (elimination of all animal products from the diet), would save billions of dollars as well as improving the lives of millions.[282]

If additional money is needed to help reduce our national debt (implemented along with a reduction in federal spending) as well as a way to increase revenues in Washington, it can be obtained from eco- and health-risk taxes.

Developing strategies in drafting, voting into action, and implementation would require increased awareness and a much more serious and progressive approach to policy reform.

A 10 percent idle or empty calorie food tax has been studied and proposed, which would apply to soft drinks and eventually other highly processed unhealthy foods. This level of taxation is far too lenient for animal products, however. Although many more factors could apply, a surcharge of 320 percent on all meat and dairy products could be justified as the beginning point for a health-risk tax, given the increased risk percentages for animal products versus plant-based foods, as they relate to the four most common and costly chronic diseases and five most common cancers. A 320 percent health care tax on just beef products (which is only one-quarter of all meat eaten per person in terms of pounds) would yield $2 trillion per year, or $10 trillion in just five years. Additional revenues could be generated by way of an eco-tax, likely to be significantly higher than the 320 percent health-risk tax, if proper values are applied to resource use.

Let's look at how this could be applied.

U.S. national debt exceeded $16 trillion in September 2012 ($11 trillion public debt and $5 trillion intragovernmental debt), which is very concerning on a number of levels. Fully two-thirds of that debt is owed to the U.S. government by American investors, the Social Security trust fund, and pension plans for civil service workers and military personnel—the debt is owed by us. Even though China is the largest foreign owner of U.S. debt, it holds less than 8 percent of the money borrowed by the U.S. over the years. Nevertheless, the national debt has been increasing an average of $4.89 billion per day since September 2007.[283,284]

Taxing meat and other animal products with a health-risk tax and eco-tax (in addition to controlled government spending) would accomplish the following regarding economics and our national debt:

- Decrease health care costs by way of dietary measures
- Increase national wellness/productivity (reduce obesity, diabetes, CHD, and other chronic diseases)
- Increase revenues to help offset the national deficit (national health insurance, Social Security, new Farm Bill, etc.)

Of course, these benefits would be in addition to the many others that a transition to purely plant-based foods would provide, such as decreasing the production of unhealthy foods, increasing economic viability of small farms that produce organic plant-based foods, and decreasing all aspects of global depletion, including rampant pollution and our national contribution to global climate change.

Obesity, hypertension, diabetes and the myth that they are caused by HFCS

It is easy to point our finger at high-fructose corn syrup (HFCS), processed foods, and the government's role in subsidizing those unhealthy foods as the causes of many Western diseases that affect developed countries today. Highly industrialized processes take corn or a potato and turn it into an unrecognizable, commercialized caricature of what it once was. Eating foods that are high in fat, sugar, and empty calories does contribute to ill health and increased risks of many diseases. Processed foods containing HFCS, however, are not the only foods that increase our health risk.

One-third of children and two out of every three adults in the U.S. are overweight. Over one-third of all adults in the U.S., or 90 million people, are obese. Globally, 400 million are obese, and 1.6 billion are overweight.[285] Known risk factors for obesity are empty-calorie processed foods and lack of regular exercise—but so is eating animal products. All have similar risk factors, at somewhere between 25 and 30 percent.[286] Even though eating animal products has the same risk factor associated with obesity as does consuming processed foods containing high levels of fat and HFCS, it's simply easier for organizations, authors, health care practitioners, the general public, and the media to launch campaigns to stop producing and eating HFCS than to stop producing and eating meat. The meat, dairy, egg, and fishing industries and accompanying cultural hurdles present a much larger, more complex mountain to climb than the little bump that HFCS presents.

And the same is true with adult onset (type II) diabetes, now affecting 25 million people in the U.S., with another 85 million in a prediabetic state.[287] From a cultural and political standpoint, it has been so much easier for us to treat diabetes by blaming fats and sugars and taking medication. The newest studies by Dr. Neal Barnard with the Physicians' Committee for Responsible Medicine (PCRM) and George Washington University have shown that elimination of animal products from the diet and eating a balanced, nonprocessed diet of plant-based foods will decrease a diabetic's need for medication by increasing the insulin sensitivity of the beta cells of the pancreas. This is quite a breakthrough in the prevention and treatment of adult onset diabetes.[288]

Research by Dr. Dean Ornish and Caldwell Esselstyn, as well as others over the past few decades, has shown that coronary heart disease (CHD) not only can be prevented but reversed with a purely plant-based diet and changes in lifestyle.[289,290]

Many of the reasons that degenerative diseases respond so well to plants are because animal products have a type of protein that creates an acidic environment predisposed to inflammation, while plants provide many anti-inflammatory and anti-oxidative substances in the form of phytonutrients and anti-angiogenic substances. With any food movement or meaningful discussion of policy change regarding processed foods or HFCS, there should be inclusion of all significant risk factors to our ill health—beginning with eating animals and animal products.

Why phytonutrients? What are those?

All animal products contribute to all aspects of global depletion. All animal products have the type of protein that dramatically increases risk of many diseases. All animal products have unwanted cholesterol and saturated fat. Animal products do not have, however, very many vitamins or minerals. And not one animal product will give you fiber or phytonutrients—those are only found in plants. An optimal state of health and wellness is achieved when adopting a purely plant-based diet because of two reasons, both significant:

1. The elimination of animal products eliminates inflammation stressors, contaminants, and cancer- and disease-causing substances.

2. Consumption of plants provides many healing and preventive agents, primarily by way of numerous phytonutrients.

So what are phytonutrients, and why are they important? They are substances that play a very significant role in preventing and controlling disease, as well as improving longevity by increasing your immunity and providing antioxidants and anti-inflammatory properties. Phytonutrients have five main categories of actions:

1. Apoptosis (programmed cell death)
2. Repair DNA
3. Increase immune response
4. Anti-inflammatory
5. Antioxidant

Antioxidants scavenge free radicals (molecules that contain charged oxygen; essentially they are chemically active atoms with plus or minus an electron). Free radicals bombard your other cells and can be formed from stress, either endogenous (respiration, inflammation, disease) or exogenous (pollution, stress factors, chemicals, and even sunlight). Free radicals can damage DNA and cause acceleration of the aging process and cancer. Plants contain hundreds of these antioxidant-scavenging phytonutrients to help them survive from sunlight, chemicals, insects, and stress. When you consume plant-based foods, these phytonutrients will protect you in similar ways that they protect plants. Most plants have a number of different phytonutrients. Polyphenols, such as flavonoids (quercetin and kaempferol), are powerful antioxidants and can be found in many fruits and vegetables. Catechins are found predominantly in tea, with the highest concentrations in green and white tea. Beans contain lignans, and anthocyanidins can be found in brightly colored berries. Carotenoids (b-carotene, lutein, lycopene) are found in high amounts in orange- and red-colored vegetables, and green leafy vegetables contain isothiocyanates. High amounts of rutin are found in buckwheat.

Raw foodists will tell you that eating raw plant foods provides many benefits. This is quite true, but lightly steaming most vegetables actually increases phytonutrient availability. An article in the *American Journal of Clinical Nutrition* found that by lightly steaming (without overcooking), the antioxidants in many foods were raised substantially—broccoli by 654 percent, spinach and asparagus by 100–200 percent, tomatoes by 150 percent, carrots by 291 percent, and green or red cabbage by 250–450 percent.[291]

Rooibos is an important plant to examine for a number of reasons. Tea made from its small leaves and needles provides significant health benefits. It has measurable amounts of minerals and electrolytes, and a high polyphenol profile. Rooibos contains the polyphenols quercetin and rutin and is the only known natural source of the powerful antioxidant aspalathin. Rooibos has no caffeine and low tannins. Researchers in Bethesda, Maryland, have shown that rooibos has significant protective and antimutagenic properties with certain cancers, such as colon, liver, and skin cancer. Rooibos is grown mostly in South Africa and has adapted to nutrient-poor, hot, dry, and even acidic soil.[292]

All health care costs are not created equal—universal health care in the U.S.

The U.S. Congress passed a law in 2010 that put into motion a universal national health bill, a $1 trillion plan paid by our government for health insurance and Medicaid called the Patient Protection and Affordable Care Act (PPACA) to be in full effect by 2014. On its surface, the law seeks to provide coverage for more than 30 million previously uninsured Americans and to slow down soaring medical costs. This means more people will have access to health insurance and therefore, we will be a healthier nation. But it is not as simple as our policy makers, insurance companies, and the general public all tend to think. That's because a significant factor in our health status—and therefore with the costs incurred—is what we eat. Herbivores are predictably healthier than omnivores, and only 2.5 percent of the U.S. population eats as healthily as they could by way of a purely plant-based diet.[293]

All individuals who have health insurance do not conform to the same diet and lifestyle. So someone eating only plant-based foods will have a 20–70 percent less likelihood of contracting nearly all diseases and conditions that would require insurance payouts, yet these people have to subsidize the health care costs of everyone who eats animal products. This is neither fair nor ethical.

Prior to the Patient Protection and Affordable Care Act, many people could not afford insurance or cover the costs of becoming sick or injured, whether because health care coverage was too expensive from the various companies offering it, or the individual was not employed by a company offering health insurance. Under President Obama's plan, these individuals will have insurance subsidized by money raised by the government. The principal way money will be raised is with $430 billion in new taxes over the next ten years, mainly from high-income taxpayers and fees on the health care industry. This is consistent with Obama's pledge not to raise taxes on the middle or lower classes. It's essentially a $940 billion bill, meaning it will require the raising of $940 billion over the next decade to pay for the 32 million people in the U.S. who currently lack health insurance. An increase in Medicare taxes paid by businesses, including those small businesses that are currently struggling in the economic downturn from 2007–2008, will provide $230 billion, and there will be an annual fee on health care providers, providing another $100 billion. So while all the attention has been on *where* the money is coming from, there should be more focus on *who* will be the recipients of this health insurance program.

None of us should have difficulty with the concept that everyone is entitled to health care. Of concern is what I would call an *insurance predictability factor.*

Our health insurance system is supported by those who pay health insurance premiums, which then pays for medical care when they become injured or sick. These are the insured. The annual premium paid by the insured is often calculated by claims made by the similar age group over a one-year period, divided by the number of insured. Basically, the cumulative premium pool must be able to pay for the calculated and projected costs of all claims filed by that particular group of insured. With some companies, there are a few lifestyle considerations, such as smoking, for which a nominal discount may be accounted for and offered for nonsmokers, but for the most part, all premiums are similar for all insured. This is where a significant inequality occurs.

Let's just look at my particular age group, the 60- to 65-year-old individuals. Statistically, over two-thirds of this group are overweight, and 35 percent are obese and are suffering from one or a combination of cardiovascular diseases, type 2 diabetes, hypertension, heart disease, diverticulosis, kidney disease, one of three or four types of cancer, gallbladder concerns, and many more conditions.[294]

This fact substantially increases their predisposition to becoming ill and needing medical attention, services, and most likely expensive hospitalization. This is a frequently played-out scenario. Does it happen to every 60- to 65-year-old? No, but there is a clear and predictable pattern as to why most in this group need medical care, and very few do not. Remember that individuals who consistently and predictably do not need medical care do not use any of the pool of insurance money created by the premiums paid each year. Why, then, should those who do not need medical care and are in a lifestyle that can predict this lack of need for care pay the same premium as all those others? With the Obama Health Care Plan, we will be paying on two different levels for those seeking medical care. On one level, we will pay premiums that are based on the poor health of others, and on the second level, we will pay (by way of taxation) for mandatory insurance based on the lifestyle of a nation that generates poor health. We are essentially being penalized twice by a system that places more emphasis on after-the-fact care than on education, enlightenment, and mandating proven, data-based, and irrefutable lifestyle changes.

What, then, should really be considered when discussing fair and just health care coverage or insurance for U.S. citizens? Certainly, somewhere in the equation should be these considerations:

1. No one should receive arbitrary subsidized health care insurance coverage without receiving some form of mandatory and accurate

lifestyle-reform counseling, based on prevention and true sustainability of health (not culturally biased taste preferences or agricultural systems proven to be unhealthy).

2.   No one should have to pay directly or indirectly for another's health care if the recipient of that paid care is blatantly not doing the right things to optimize his or her own health risk factors.

Policy makers and industry leaders who draft health care insurance parameters need to carefully analyze and then effectively account for variations in lifestyle when underwriting this form of coverage—beginning with food choice. Why should I have to pay thousands of dollars in premiums or from taxation for a stranger who purposely and repeatedly runs out in front of a car? This is what happens when we who consume only plant-based foods pay for those who consume animal products. This type of insurance reform on a national or private basis is long overdue and will ultimately save billions of dollars each year, while serving as a catalyst for improvement in other areas affected by global depletion. Awareness will be increased, which will widen demand for plant-based products, which will then support the change needed in our current antiquated agricultural and food production systems.

You can't make people become humane or compassionate, but you can make them pay for the loss of land, air, water, and health that are direct impositions on you. Often, people will fail to recognize or accept a truth until they are hit in their wallets. Health insurance reforms are in order to reflect premium rates based on lifestyle, particularly diet. This would be no different from rate adjustments made for nonsmokers, having a smoke alarm in your home, good driver incentives, and age/occupation factors. If you exercise regularly and consume only plant-based foods, there should be changes in insurance coverage and a health-risk tax in place to reflect this.

Foodborne illness
Many human diseases have their origins in animal products because they

carry a number of pathogens. Forty-eight million Americans (one in six) contract foodborne illnesses each year, with the vast majority of cases going unreported as the victim battles being ill without seeking medical attention. According to the Centers for Disease Control, over 3,000 people each year die from foodborne diseases.[295] The following are only a few of the many pathogens carried by meat, eggs, and dairy products:

- Avian flu
- Nipah virus
- Creutzfeldt-Jakob disease (mad cow)
- Bovine encephalitis
- E. coli
- Salmonella
- Shigella
- Campylobacter
- H1N1 (swine flu)
- Listeria

It is important to note that none of these diseases *originates* from plants; this only happens if the pathogen is *transmitted* from an animal to the plant. Whether it is salmonella from peanuts or E. coli from spinach, an animal, typically livestock or human, is *always* the contaminant.

Campylobacter is the most common foodborne infection in the U.S., and most cases are associated with eating poultry and handling chickens. Listeria is present in soft cheese and many meat pastes. E. coli and parasites are spread by contaminated meat products. Salmonella spreads primarily through raw or undercooked eggs, poultry, and milk and accounts for the greatest proportion of foodborne illness in the developed world.

Many of these pathogens are found living naturally in all animals, but they are never in natural settings for plants.[296]

Meat and other animal products are also carriers of many pesticides, herbicides, hormones, and drugs. Realizing the severity and increasing incidence of foodborne illnesses and contaminants in the U.S., the USDA was quoted in an article of *Agriview* in late 2011 as saying it was "committed to supporting research that improves the safety of our nation's food system." In that same month, the U.S. meat and milk exports failed to pass the European Union's standard for drug residues.

Deborah Cera, leader of the drug compliance team at the FDA's Center for Veterinary Medicine, admitted there were many violations involving scores of drugs in U.S. livestock.[297]

The FDA announced in January 2012 that it would finally ban the use of cephalosporins in livestock by April. But this is one small group of antibiotics, representing less than .00032 percent of the 29 million pounds fed to livestock each year. Less than 20 percent of antibiotics in the U.S. are used to treat human disease; the other 80 percent are used on livestock to make them grow faster, which creates the evolution of antibiotic-resistant pathogens that cause concern and now plague hospitals. Antibiotic use is just one of the many negative human health aspects for which the animal-product industry is responsible.[298]

There have been many outbreaks of the bacterium E. coli, which is a naturally occurring microbe in all animals. Infection at some level has most likely been with us since we first began eating animals. But frequency of incidence, strength of virulence, and numbers affected are thought to be associated with modern meat production. One of the more recent outbreaks occurred in Germany in 2011 and caused massive confusion, hundreds of millions of dollars lost in the economy of numerous EU countries due to illness, at least thirty deaths, and over 3,000 individuals becoming ill. Every media source reported the story in the same fashion—that bean sprouts produced by an organic farm in Lower Saxony were responsible. With heavy media coverage and lack of accuracy in awareness, the world believed that bean sprouts caused this outbreak. But similar to other E. coli outbreaks over the years where a plant was accused as the culprit, bean sprouts weren't the cause. No vegetable, fruit, nut, or any plant could ever be the primary cause of E. coli outbreaks, because this pathogen comes from animals—specifically, cattle.

Food pathogens—a broader view

A number of articles and opinions were written about this E. coli incident, but one in particular reveals the depth of our misunderstanding. In June 2011, Dr. David Katz, director of the Yale Research Center, wrote an article titled "Blame the Meat, Not the Sprouts."[299]

On first glance, I thought how wonderful it was to have someone expose the real culprit in this story. But after reading his article, I realized we need to achieve another level of awareness. We are still very far off the mark as a society with interpretation of our delusionary "need" to eat animals. Dr. Katz is no doubt a caring, intelligent author and medical practitioner with a rather large audience, who brought to the forefront the real source of this E. coli outbreak—that is all good news. But at the same time, Dr. Katz also perpetuated the misconception that this outbreak and other similar woes were issues with roots in industrialized farming (CAFOs or factory farms). As I finished reading his article, I realized that readers would walk away with the understanding that E. coli originated from cattle, not bean sprouts, and that they would feel quite comfortable continuing to eat meat—as long as it was not from factory farms. That's a problem. So we need a clearer perspective on foodborne illness.

My difficulty with Katz's article is with one of his concluding remarks: "I am not intending to indict meat consumption. We (humans) have always included meat in our diet. We must concede it is an appetite for large quantities of meat derived from abused, drugged, mass-slaughtered cows that is responsible for E. coli …"

That is the wrong message. Actually, we *do* need to indict meat consumption for many reasons and not just meat from factory farms—all meat consumption.

I find his justification interesting that we "have always included meat in our diet." As I've previously mentioned, we used bloodletting for more than 3,000 years as an approach to ailment. Does that mean we should still slice our forearms to cure an infection? Our modern society has done fairly well at evolving from other forms of barbaric and obsolete practices that now are known to be unhealthy—it's time we do the same with eating animals.

Let's look more closely at the E. coli and contamination issue. Very few would dispute that there is less potential of the development and spread of disease-causing pathogens in pasture-fed operations than within factory farms. However, E. coli, campylobacter, salmonella, and other disease-causing pathogens *are found naturally on and in all animals that we raise and kill to eat*—it doesn't matter whether they are grass-fed. Cattle specialist Dr. Stephen Hammack at the Department of Animal Science, Texas A&M University, sums up the findings of numerous researchers with his statement "There are no differences in intestinal levels of E. coli 0157:H7 between organic grass-fed cattle and factory farmed grain-fed cattle."[300] As a consumer, you risk contracting E. coli from eating any type of meat from cattle—grass fed or not. Salmonella is carried naturally in the chicken's body and transferred to or through the shell as the egg is being laid. Salmonella causes nearly 2 million cases of foodborne illness in the U.S. per year, and over 80 percent of these are directly related to egg consumption. Salmonella are found in cage-free, free-range chickens, and organic eggs also, since it is naturally occurring in all chickens. Campylobacter is another organism found naturally in all healthy poultry, pigs, and cattle. In a 2011 report, the CDC estimated campylobacter to be responsible for 845,000 illnesses, 8,400 hospitalizations, and 76 deaths in the U.S. each year.[301]

Whether pasture fed or not, improper handling and undercooked beef, pork, and poultry are sources of contamination and subsequent illness. Based on CDC, USDA, and independent research reports, the Consumers Union estimated that up to 88 percent of all chicken carcasses were contaminated and concluded, "Any poultry—chicken, turkey, duck, goose, game fowl—meat and its juices may contain campylobacter, including organic and 'free range' products."[302] According to the U.S. Food Safety and Inspection, other identified vehicles include milk, and meats such as beef, pork, shellfish, and eggs. It is not a matter of "abused, drugged or factory farmed cows," as Dr. Katz stated in his article. E. coli and many other types of disease-causing organisms can be contracted from *all* animals raised, slaughtered, and eaten by humans.

How does this relate to the larger picture? Although Dr. Katz's article intended to focus on the source of outbreak of E. coli in Germany, it clearly gave the reader the false sense that CAFOs or factory farms were the problem, and if we move away from those entities, meat consumption can continue. He stated, "[F]eed animals are raised as an industrial commodity, rather than as creatures … their natural diets are disregarded," and "we, and our resultant health, not only are what we eat, we are to some extent what we feed what we eat."

The difficulty I have with this is that even if cattle and other livestock are "raised as creatures" without being "an industrial commodity," the end result will be further perpetuation of global depletion of our planet's resources and our own health. The continued eating of any animal, grass fed or not, and E. coli or not, will contribute to our national health crises, increasing the risk of nearly all major diseases found in developed countries. This has nothing to do with the animal being "an industrial commodity." It has everything to do with the fact that all animal products are unhealthy to consume.

Regarding global depletion of our planet's resources, only concentrated pollution may be improved with a move away from factory farms. All other areas of global depletion remain—continuation of greenhouse gas emissions, water scarcity issues, depletion of land due to agricultural land-use inefficiencies, world hunger, massive loss of biodiversity (loss of other species on earth), and devastation of our oceans and fish species. Additionally, if cattle and other livestock were raised as creatures instead of "a commodity," then it would make even less sense for us to slaughter them by the tens of billions—essentially, the willing global participation in the unnecessary killing of over 133,000 lives per minute. Again, choosing to eat animals is much more of an issue than simply stating that "cattle eating grasses have a healthy gastrointestinal tract that is not conducive to the growth of this particular E. coli germ," as pointed out by Dr. Katz. This is misleading to the public, who need to hear that *eating cattle is the problem*, not what the cattle eat.

Finally, instead of the audience hearing that "the mutant germs in our food have everything to do with how we raise and feed the animals by which we feed ourselves," they need to hear that the mutant germs in our food have everything to do with the fact that we eat animals—nothing more, nothing less.

And this is similar to all other areas of global depletion that impact our planet's health where the issue is not *how* we raise animals to eat or *how* we massively extract them out of our oceans. The issue is that we do it at all. Dr. Katz made a wonderful point about the origin of this E. coli pathogen in Germany; for that, he is to be applauded—but he should have painted the entire picture. We all need to raise our awareness to the next level, stop blaming factory farms, and start blaming the fact that we eat animals. That's the indictment we need to make.

The restricted argument of animal welfare

There are many reasons to not eat meat or any animal product and conversely to adopt a purely plant-based diet. The primary factors are (1) animal rights or welfare concerns, (2) environmental reasons, and (3) concern for one's own health. Most recent surveys indicate that many people adopt a plant-based diet for a combination of these reasons, and over half (53 percent) of current vegetarians eat a vegetarian diet to improve their overall health. Environmental concerns were cited by 47 percent, 31 percent cited food safety, and 54 percent cited animal welfare.[303]

Food choice has always been a personal decision, linked to cultural influences. After all, it's your life, and what you eat shouldn't have anything to do with anyone else, right? Now we know that is not right. What you choose to eat *does* affect many things—our planet and its resources, the lives of many species of animals (domestic and wild), other humans indirectly (by way of global depletion, food availability, and economically), and your own health (which affects everyone else by way of health care costs and food availability). Advocates of plant-based diets typically demonstrate one of two management approaches: aggressive and confrontational, or a passive, "everyone needs to take his own time," baby-step approach. The confrontational approach rarely is successful when trying to encourage someone to change his or her eating habits from eating animals. This relegates most advocates to the passive approach. As an avenue for change, however, this is appropriate only as it applies to animal welfare or ethics of animal rights. It is *not* appropriate for any argument that includes environmental or human health concerns—those perspectives are on a much different time line. They cause an imposition on the sustainability of others, and we all pay for this lack of awareness or irresponsibility. I've found that most authors, lecturers, and advocates who are in a position to create change are simply unaware of this delineation of timelines and therefore unknowingly perpetuate the raising, slaughtering, and eating of animals. Many wonderful individuals are speaking on behalf of plant-based diets and are increasing awareness, but in effect, they are empowering those who eat animals to continue doing so until they are ready to make that decision on their own terms.

Discussions should not separate out animal rights as the single or primary focus regarding food-choice change. Consider the following:

In the fall of 2012, Dr. James McWilliams, professor of history at Texas State University, best-selling author and long-time advocate of plant-based food, wrote two related articles regarding the ethics of eating animals. One was a brilliantly composed open letter to Whole Foods, asking them to consider taking meat off their shelves. The second article, written a couple of weeks later, was a call for vegans to be more patient and tolerant of individuals, businesses, or policy in the process of changing to a fully vegan lifestyle and to unite in this cause. With the second article, Dr. McWilliams' case is strong for a coalescing of animal welfare advocacy and adopting universal tolerance of individualized timelines for change. The point that is sorely missed, however, is that a well-conceived and effective movement toward purely plant-based food choices is about understanding and seeking choices that are in the best interest of our *planet* (wild animals included), not just what is in the best interest of animals. It is a journey toward choices that affords the highest level of peace and health—not just peace. Of course, Dr. McWilliams understands that all three objectives (animal welfare, our health, our planet's health) are intertwined. But I don't believe there should ever be separation of these goals, as it creates a false and inaccurate timeline for change. Dr. McWilliams' article quoted longtime advocate Dr. Melanie Joy in stating that asking people to stop eating animals is "*asking for a change in behavior or a profound shift in consciousness that people make only when they're personally ready to do so.*" But with an overfocus on animal rights, it becomes the base of reasoning for people like John Mackey (CEO of Whole Foods) in his economy-driven response to Dr. McWilliams' Open Letter, which appeared on numerous websites such as Free from Harm. And an overfocus on animal welfare becomes the single base of reasoning for anyone else who is simply unwilling to change. Mackey responded to McWilliams' request to take all meat off the shelves at Whole Foods by stating they would in no way do so, admitting that their high welfare meat offerings are largely responsible for the overall economic success of the company. Mackey went on to proclaim that Whole Foods is making great progress in prompting real change in the meat industry by pursuing more animal products (a "full array") that are humanely raised and "slaughtered with minimal stress."

For me, it was a very predictable response. Mackey and all other proponents of eating animal products would have more difficulty arguing for tolerance for change of consciousness or defending the continuation of eating animals if being humane or animal welfare became just *one* of the factors, not *the* factor. Dr. McWilliams' article, though exceptionally well written, was an oversimplification of a complex problem that deserves more comprehensive discourse.

Our planet and the global depletion we are witnessing today is on a much different and objectively more calculable timeline than that of animal rights advocates. Although ethics may be the easiest, most noble, and most attractive topic to debate, by separating it out from all other areas of sustainability when discussing eating animals, the reality of impacts becomes lost, and the magnitude and urgency become diffused and difficult to quantify.

We need to ask John Mackey if he is aware that *none* of his grass-fed animal options are "sustainable," or if he is able to extrapolate his newfound knowledge of the unsustainable aspects of lobster and octopus (just removed from Whole Foods' shelves in 2012) to *all* species of sea life that his stores carry. Is he aware of exactly how many other species and ecosystems are lost as bykill or during the fishing method itself? Is he aware that *any* dairy product, including grass-fed, local, and organic, carries with it the largest amount of water use, pollution, GHG emissions, and land-use inefficiencies of any grocery product found anywhere in any store in the U.S.? Mackey and Whole Foods are selling products that cause planetary ill health—it's not about being simply devoid of compassion.

The loss of resources, the effect our choices have on our planet and on us, and the timelines we are on cannot be refuted. While Whole Foods may have made strong efforts to become more eco-friendly with energy efficiency, waste reduction, and business management systems, it's time they do the same with food choice.

The prescription for food-choice change can be more objectively projected than relegating it to animal welfare advocacy. Since economics was central in the response by Whole Foods to Dr. McWilliams, perhaps the only real solution to enforcing proper animal welfare lies embedded in an immediate national policy change to reflect the eco-tax and health-risk tax that I've discussed. If the true cost to produce animal products were accurately reflected, then *all* of Whole Foods' meat, dairy, and eggs would certainly be taken off the shelves, because no one could afford to buy them. Problem solved.

Clinton goes vegan

In August 2011, during an interview with Dr. Sanjay Gupta of CNN, former U.S. president Bill Clinton explained that he had become a vegan for health reasons. *USA Today*, the *Huffington Post*, NBC, and just about every media source ran the story, which began to turn the tide in mainstream media coverage of plant-based food choice and the many benefits it represents. President Clinton's decision to become a vegan came in 2010 following as series of procedures for heart disease—quadruple bypass surgery in 2004 and then angioplasty and stent placement in 2010.

Clinton's fondness of hamburgers, steaks, chicken, and other animal products was legendary, but after the second set of procedures in 2010, he decided to adopt a more strict approach. With the advice of Drs. Dean Ornish and Caldwell Esselstyn, author of *Prevent and Reverse Heart Disease*, both of whom have guided numerous patients through reversing heart disease by way of a vegan diet, President Clinton made the change to fully plant-based food. In one year, Clinton lost 24 pounds. Ornish called Clinton after his stent procedure to tell him that the moderate diet and lifestyle changes he'd made in 2004 after his bypass surgery didn't go far enough to prevent his heart disease from progressing and that Ornish's research proved that more intensive dietary changes could actually reverse it.

The media was not convinced. Author and professor of Nutrition, Food Studies, and Public Health at New York University, Marion Nestle, made the comment "A vegan diet may be good for President Clinton, but whether it is good for everybody is a subject of much debate. Whatever [vegans] do personally is fine, but I don't want them telling me that if I eat a little meat, there is something wrong with my diet. I think animal foods can have a place in a healthful diet." Dr. Nestle is highly respected, and so her thoughts influence many—and that is exactly the issue with publication of these comments. They represent her personal bias toward consuming animal products, and they represent the desire to suppress or detract from elucidation of strong evidence in support of a plant-based diet. Mr. Clinton represents the majority of all U.S. citizens who eat meat in the same manner as he did. He represents changing from an unhealthy diet to a healthy one, and it is unfortunate that Dr. Nestle was unable to restrain herself from submitting her own personal, emotionally and culturally driven food preferences when evoking comments that defy current scientific knowledge and even common sense.

On the other hand, it provides us with a perfect example of why only 1 to 3 percent of the entire population in the U.S. has chosen to eat only plant-based foods. It also displays the continued limited view by some of our leaders that the choice to become vegan is a personal matter, one related to one's own health or that of animal rights. Dr. Nestle, at some point, will need to expand her view of this topic to better understand that there is no "debate" and that by eating animals, she herself is imposing on our planet and the other occupants. In doing so, there is "something wrong" with her diet.

Claims of health from the supporters of grass-fed

Along with the façade of improved animal welfare, marketing efforts for the grass-fed beef industry are also directed at making human health claims. Because of this, we have heard the purported health benefits of grass-fed beef—higher in omega-3s and lower in saturated fat, which is quite misleading because the comparison is to grain-fed beef, not to plants. In 1910, when everyone in the U.S. was eating grass-fed cattle and long before the commercialization of food occurred, the leading cause of death (as it still is today), just ahead of tuberculosis, was heart disease. These earlier people succumbed to heart disease from eating too much saturated fat, cholesterol, and the type of protein from all the grass-fed animal products and not consuming enough fiber, nutrients, and phytonutrients, or even anti-angiogenic substances—all only found in plants.

While increased attention has been placed on omega-3s by grass-fed beef proponents, even the National Cattlemen's Beef Association executive director feels the claims are overstated, commenting that "if you feed cows grass, you can slightly increase the omega-3 content, but it's not a significant advantage to human health."[304]

The American Grass-Fed Association (AGA) certification program includes beef, bison, lamb, pork, poultry, eggs, and dairy products and assures the public that their certified animals are Animal Welfare Approved and healthy to consume. Those consumers interested in AGA-approved animal products should also be informed of all the detrimental effects of these products on human health and that the AWA program should not be equated with the word "humane."[305]

Ancient grains

As I've mentioned, land is being used inefficiently in the U.S. and elsewhere, as it is applied for raising animals and crops to feed them. Current agricultural systems are designed to use land, water, and energy inefficiently, to produce animal products that are unhealthy for us to consume. Certainly, we can do better. As an example, in 2011 the U.S. planted 56 million acres of alfalfa over 120 million acres for feed crops—all going to livestock and poultry— but only 50,000 acres in buckwheat, an exceptional plant that provides numerous health benefits and that we can eat directly. In 2011, there were 51,481 dairy operations using millions of acres for the cows, feed, and hay, as well as massive amounts of water and fossil fuel.

Intended corn plantings in 2012 were up nearly 8 percent, to 96 million acres.[306]

Replacing our current animal agricultural systems with any fruit, vegetable, nut, and grain combination would significantly reduce resource use, while improving our own health. There are many unique, vigorous plants that could be grown with minimal input and no imposition on global depletion, while bringing unusual health benefits. Examples of this with plants used as grain (replacing feed grain) are amaranth, buckwheat, quinoa, and khorasan—all extremely nutritious and efficient production models.

Amaranth leaves can be eaten like spinach, and its seeds can be used as grain in bread or eaten as cooked grain. Grown and harvested for thousands of years by the Incan, Mayan, and Aztec civilizations, amaranth was believed to have magical properties that gave them tremendous strength. When the Spanish made their way into the Americas, every crop of amaranth was burned, and there was severe punishment (chopping off hands) for possession of the grain. The grain was then lost for generations until recently, now appreciated for its high protein and balanced amino acid profile, lysine, fiber, and phytosterols (a form of phytonutrient), which have been shown to be effective agents that reduce the risk of cancer and heart disease. Amaranth is widely adapted, growing in many different climates but responding well to high sunlight and warm temperatures. It is drought-tolerant and can be grown in a variety of soil types, yielding up to 3,800 pounds per acre.[307]

Technically a fruit, buckwheat has an inner seed, or groat (after dehulling), that can be chewed and eaten directly, cooked and eaten as grain, toasted to make kasha, or ground into flour. Buckwheat has all essential amino acids, is high in lysine and rich in essential fatty acids and many B vitamins, is high in many minerals, and is one of the highest sources of rutin (a strong anti-inflammatory agent that strengthens circulation) of any food source found in the world. Importantly, buckwheat is a hardy plant, thrives in poor soil conditions, and continues to live through freezing temperatures, droughts, heat, and excess rain. It also serves as an excellent cover crop, increasing soil fertility. There are 50,000 acres of buckwheat planted in the U.S., and yields have been between 1,500 and 2,000 pounds per acre. Until the recent interest in buckwheat as human food, 75 percent of this grain produced was used for livestock and poultry.[308,309]

Like amaranth and buckwheat, quinoa is a plant with broad leaves and is technically a fruit, not a grain. It resembles the ubiquitous lambsquarters and has been grown for more than 5,000 years in and around the Andes Mountains in South America. The Incas referred to quinoa as the "mother grain," knowing that eating it tended to give a long and healthy life. Quinoa is high in protein and provides a perfect balance of amino acids. It is high in lysine, many minerals such as calcium and iron, vitamin E, and several B vitamins.

Quinoa is a rugged plant and can be grown nearly everywhere in every climate and can even grow at extremely high, dry elevations, where grass doesn't grow. In Bolivia, it has been known to grow at elevations as high as 14,000 feet.

Similar to amaranth, quinoa is a quite adaptable, disease-free, and drought-tolerant plant. It thrives in rich soil and will produce large harvests under dry conditions. Yields have been to known to reach 5,000 pounds per acre.

Khorasan (Kamut) wheat is another ancient grain thought to have come from either Egypt or Turkey, although it most likely originated from the Fertile Crescent area of Western Asia, kept alive only by small plots for thousands of years. It was lost from nearly all agricultural records and systems until it was resurrected in the late 1980s by a Montana agricultural scientist. It was said to be the grain that Noah brought aboard the ark with him. Similar to spelt, many people who have wheat sensitivities are able to eat khorasan, although it is not entirely gluten-free. It is 30 percent higher in protein than wheat and has more fiber and higher amounts of vitamin E, thiamin, riboflavin, phosphorus, magnesium, zinc, and pantothentic acid.[310]

Khorasan began in the U.S., growing on only 1.5 acres, in 1986, and now there are over 45,000 acres devoted to khorasan, spread over Montana, Alberta, and Saskatchewan. The plant grows well in all areas suitable for most grains, with yields usually exceeding 1,500 pounds per acre.[311]

Another ancient grain that is similar to wheat but without high gluten content is spelt. Therefore, the majority of individuals who believe they are wheat-intolerant are able to consume spelt with no difficulty. Spelt has been grown throughout Europe for the past 9,000 years and is referred to in the Old Testament of the Bible. Swiss immigrants brought it to eastern Ohio, where it was grown for a few hundred years but abandoned in the twentieth century and grown only for feed for livestock. In 1987, Purity Foods reintroduced spelt to the U.S. food market, and acreage planted has increased from 100 acres in 1987 to around 8,000 acres in 2011. Spelt is much higher in protein and fiber than wheat, has many vitamins and minerals, and has a higher solubility in water, making it easier to digest. It contains phytonutrients that aid in blood clotting and boosting the immune system. As a plant, spelt can grow quite easily in an organic manner, as it is resistant to insects and not impeded by weeds. It can grow on poorly drained, low-fertility soils and on sandy soils as well and is winter hardy, producing on average over 3,000 pounds per acre.[312]

The above are all considered low-input grains with no need for herbicides, pesticides, synthetic fertilizers, heavy irrigation, or excessive fossil fuel use. More than 121 million acres were used in 2011 to grow feed crops in the U.S. Another 157 million acres of public land were used for grazing cattle and sheep for 18,000 ranchers with permits and leases. It is important to understand how agricultural land is being used, the crops that are being grown, who eats them, and how to use land and other resources more efficiently to grow plants that are provide many health benefits. For every acre of land in the U.S. that is used for raising just a fraction of a cow (as each grass-fed cow requires more than 1 acre to graze), as well as the acre next to it used to grow corn, sorghum, or soybeans to supplement feed for that cow, we could grow ancient grains, beans, green leafy vegetables, fruit, nuts, and herbs and spices, providing us with literally thousands more pounds of food per acre—and that's food that gives us phytonutrients and fiber that simply is not found in any animal product.[313]

6

To Ponder:
Perspectives on Another Dimension

WHY IS IT that as a global society, we don't eat the healthiest foods that are produced in the most peaceful and sustainable manner? I believe it is largely because of lack of awareness. Often, our culture is to blame. We have inherited food preferences that are now known to be archaic and unethical on many fronts. Food choice can no longer belong to the group of culturally influenced actions we call trends, because now what we eat is more serious, having implications that affect all inhabitants on our planet.

Evolution is a fundamental necessity for survival of any species. A principal factor in the survival of humans will be the evolution to a plant-based diet. The difficulty comes with how long and at what cost that process will take. I've come to the conclusion that often, creating needed positive change in food choice is not so much the effectiveness of a grassroots effort, sparked by enlightenment and driven by a desire to make things better, as it is a need to first educate those in supervisory positions—our leaders, those with platforms of influence, consultants, decision makers, directors, so-called experts in various fields—and bring these individuals, institutions, and organizations up to speed. Then progress can be made with increasing general public awareness. Essentially, we need to begin the movement by educating the educated. In order to make a difference, we must move from the problem-solving mode on an individual/personal basis to the creation and implementation mode, while engaging those very leaders and institutions that are moving us in the wrong direction. This, then, becomes a daunting if not improbable task, There is an extra step now involved—to inject newfound awareness into our leaders by somehow penetrating the deep level of wisdom these individuals and institutions have or are supposed to have. It becomes another culture-coated veil to peel off before change can be made within the public at large.

Examples can be seen in many areas of leadership and influence, but four of the most commonly found and most frustrating are:

- High-profile, leading, and expert consulting organizations, funders/donors to sustainability programs and research projects
- Individuals with a high degree of visibility or large public audience due to media exposure, such as authors, actors, and television show hosts
- Policy makers, leaders of the Group of Eight (a forum for the world's eight largest industrial market economies), physicians, educators, hospital administrators, chairs of sustainability departments or decision makers for universities, and food procurement directors for institutions (universities, hospitals, educational facilities of all types)
- Businesses, major multinational corporations

We are a culture that follows the lead of the media, and proper food-choice change is a reflection of the base of knowledge of our leaders who, in turn, are impacting the media. Currently, that base is incomplete and inaccurate, particularly as it involves food-choice category differentiation (animal-based or plant-based) and the immense effect that simple choice has on our planet. The problem is amplified by the fact that many of the aspects of global depletion are on a timeline that doesn't allow for our collective complacency. The "eat less meat" approach simply doesn't fit with the course we've elected to take to climate change, extinction of species, or water and food insecurity. A grassroots enlightenment approach for the general public to effect positive change will be only as good as the effort toward educating the educated.

The principle of educating the educated on the realities of animal food products as it applies to big business seems rudimentary on its surface. Indeed, if those behind the wheels of motion at any large food production company (for example, the CEO, CFO, COO, and board of directors) were convinced that greater profitability would result from elimination of all animal products and replacement by purely plant-based alternatives, it would happen. Supported by a history of success and the promise of another 2 billion more meat-eating mouths to feed in the next thirty years, the wheels of motion are currently in the direction of producing more meat, dairy, and fish. Therefore, educating the educated translates to showing them—the manufacturers and purveyors of animal products—the money.

With the realization that there is an increased market demand for plant-based meat alternatives, these products are becoming more readily available and are produced by some large multinational companies. With the newly launched "The Future of Food" project, Bill Gates has now joined the campaign to encourage food production corporations to shift to plant-based items. On one hand, this seems promising; on the other, a voluntary, adequately timed transition to fully plant-based food products by those comprised by the meat, dairy, and fishing industries is unlikely to happen. While Mr. Gates is attempting to convince big business that there is a market-driven alternative solution to eating animals, global depletion on all fronts continues to be rampant and in some cases is becoming irreversible. Therefore, the timing for change shouldn't be left entirely in the hands of a system reluctant to change and reliant on interpretation of annual profit-and-loss statements. Recognizing, creating strategies, and then implementing as a collective business effort is clearly on a different timeline from that of environmental degradation by food choice. The planet, its inhabitants, and its ecosystems can't wait. For this reason, Mr. Gates' approach will need to be augmented by policy change, as well as a massive public education effort—all timed with the urgency it demands.

Genetics and the basis of disease

Have you ever filled out a health questionnaire at your physician's office and taken notice of the section about which diseases your parents and other members of your family may have had? Many diseases do have genetic predisposition. Genetic predisposition is somewhat like a road you travel— the genes you have inherited on specific chromosomes constitute the main road you are driving down. When you come to a fork in the road, one way to veer has a much larger, easier path, and the other way to turn is smaller and more of an angle. Your genetic predisposition or makeup is the larger path. It's the one you are more likely influenced to follow. The other, smaller path is the one guided by environmental, external variables. With eye and hair color, there is one path—no forks in the road. With your health and disease, there are forks, and the small path is an active lifestyle and eating lower down on the food chain with all organic plant-based foods. It takes you down a different route than the one you were more inclined to follow.

That family history section appears on the medical questionnaire because there is a likelihood that you'll contract the same diseases of others in your family—if you follow the same lifestyle and eat the same foods as they did. However, if you choose to exercise, lessen your stress levels, and adopt a purely plant-based diet, the chances of your contracting many of those diseases is significantly lessened. In fact, in the instance where an individual does all the right things with food choice, and his or her parents and siblings did all the wrong things, that part of the medical questionnaire may not even be relevant. It would be more appropriate for physicians to pose the query in a different manner altogether, by asking patients to elaborate on the food choices to which they and their family ascribe for any conditions contracted.

The common denominator of most disease states, especially the degenerative conditions we are witnessing today in developed countries, is a mixture of oxidation, mutation, inflammation, and reduction of the body's immune system, many times overlapping, and which foods enhance the mixture and which foods do the opposite. Often, many plant-based foods will have different factors as they relate to disease states but with the same overall positive effect. For instance, anti-angiogenic foods will reduce the likelihood of contracting diabetes, cancer, and CHD from a microcirculatory or vascularity direction, while phytonutrients in plants will reduce the likelihood of these same diseases but from an anti-inflammatory and antioxidant standpoint.

A number of researchers feel that cancer is not *caused* by bacteria, inadequate exercise, environmental contaminants, ionizing radiation, viruses, or heredity. Rather, it's caused by a series of mutations in DNA. The chances of these mutations occurring in enough number to result in cancer is affected by all the factors just mentioned—some factors increase the risk more than others, diet being one of them.

The Statin Concept

I have an issue with a commonly seen form of compensation behavior, where we choose to do something that may not be in our best interest and then try to make up for it later. This happens frequently with food choice and the volume consumed. "I'm going to eat all this food today, but then I'll make up for it by fasting or working out for 84 hours tomorrow." This rarely works—whether or not one can find 84 hours in the day.

I call this—eating or doing something that's not good for you and then trying to cover it up or deal with the repercussions afterwards—the Statin Concept. The most widely prescribed medications in the world belong to the statin family—Crestor, Lipitor, Pravachol, Lescol, and Zocor—garnering over 6 percent of all medication purchases. These drugs are meant to lower the level of cholesterol in the blood by reducing the production of it by the liver. Statins block the enzyme in the liver that is responsible for making cholesterol. Annual sales of statins globally have reached $26 billion. Every day, 38,000 sales representatives from Pfizer, just one of the many statin drug manufacturers, make their pitches and give free samples, convincing physicians, clinics, and hospitals to prescribe Lipitor more than it already is (it's the first prescription drug to reach $10 billion sales in one year in 2004).[314,315]

There are two ways in which excess cholesterol enters the body—it's produced by the liver or we ingest it through food. Only one out of 100,000 people have genetically transmitted or familial hypercholesterolemia (a condition where the body is producing hundreds of milligrams of cholesterol daily); these individuals need cholesterol medication. All the other 99.9 percent of people who are taking statins do so because they are consuming cholesterol every time they eat fish, or any other type of meat from livestock.[316]

The biochemical story of cholesterol, how it is used and stored in your body, its biochemistry, as well as its effect on other substances, cells, and tissues can be complex. In simplistic terms, cholesterol is good—a necessary substance—but excess amounts and in combination with saturated fats and less fiber intake is unhealthy and can lead to many disease states.

Your liver creates, on average, 100 milligrams per deciliter (100 mg/dl) of cholesterol per day. The American Heart Association advocates a total blood cholesterol level of less than 200 mg/dl. A quarter-pound burger has over 100 mg of cholesterol, as does a single serving of most other beef. Just two eggs will give you 850 mg cholesterol; 3.5 ounces of chicken has over 100 mg; a medium-sized pork chop has 118 mg; and most fish meat contain between 60 and 170 mg of cholesterol. The average American will consume 2,000 mg of cholesterol in just one week. Unlike certain water-soluble vitamins, such as vitamin C or the Bs, excessive cholesterol that your body doesn't use (or want) is not easily removed; it is taken up and deposited in the walls of your blood vessels.

Cholesterol is found in the lining of all animal cells. Plants do not have cholesterol. Plants' cells are lined with chlorophyll. Every time an individual eats any animal—cow, pig, chicken, turkey, fish—he or she consumes unnecessary cholesterol and saturated fat and increases the probability of falling victim to one of the four or five leading causes of death and disease. Researchers found that a vegan diet, emphasizing almonds, soy, and other healthful plant foods, was as effective at lowering cholesterol as a statin drug. It's time we encourage the world to spend that $26 billion each year on education to eliminate animal products from our diet and on purchases of cholesterol-lowering plant foods instead of statins. Our planet would surely be in a better spot. Rather than relegating oneself to taking a statin pill every day and being confronted with the possibility of stents, quadruple bypass surgery, and other procedures for cardiac and circulatory vessel collapse, it should be an easy choice to simply not eat animal products to begin with.[317]

Global depletion of our health is really an issue of what we decide to eat. Human health and wellness begins by eating the right foods—organically grown plant-based foods—not by continuing to eat contaminants and animals products that cause disease and then frantically attempting to find ways to mask the damage. It seems "easier" for people to line up their pills every day to manage various diseases or conditions than it is to change what they eat.

Angiogenesis

Dr. William Li, president and medical director of the Angiogenesis Foundation, is accomplishing some amazing work, bringing to light a medical advancement to combat cancer by controlling the blood vessels that feed them.

He points out that this advancement holds the promise of conquering more than seventy of life's most threatening conditions. Dr. Li's work is with angiogenesis, which is the process of the stimulation of new small capillary growth. This is a natural process that occurs in the body to help with healing and reproduction. Normal angiogenesis is managed by the body, producing a balance of growth and inhibitory factors in healthy tissue. Either too much or too little angiogenesis can occur when this balance becomes disrupted, and this is the case in many damaging conditions— cancer, skin diseases, diabetic ulcers, cardiovascular disease, and stroke, as well as many others. A good example of how angiogenesis works can be found with cancer. All cancerous tumors release angiogenic growth factor protein, which in turn stimulates the growth of tiny blood vessels in the tumor, allowing it to thrive with oxygen and nutrients. Dr. Li's efforts focus on angiogenesis-based medicine, how to restore the body's natural control of angiogenesis with medical treatments that either inhibit or stimulate the growth of blood vessels. Anti-angiogenic therapies starve cancer tumors of their blood supply by inhibiting the process. Dr. Li's work in this area has been promising and may even help prevent tissues and limbs from being lost to cancer or suffering from lack of circulation, including heart, nerve, and brain tissue.[318]

Anti-angiogenic drugs (aimed at starving or inhibiting the small blood flow and nutrients to the tumor), such as Avastin, can be prescribed, but Dr. Li's research has found that certain foods have powerful anti-angiogenic properties and may work nearly as well as the medications. At the same time as inhibiting blood vessel growth at the tumor site, these foods also strengthen the body's immune system, setting into play a number of support mechanisms, such as reduction of inflammation and stimulation of healing factors. Resveratrol in red grapes and red wine reduces angiogenesis by 60 percent. Soy, parsley, many types of berries, and tea have shown to inhibit angiogenesis to reduce the propensity toward developing cancer and improved management schemes once contracted. Researchers have also realized a synergistic effect where two anti-angiogenic foods added together are much more potent than either one separately.[319] Lycopene is another antioxidant, and it is a powerful anti-angiogenic.

Dr. Li's work is promising and with newly researched health benefits, it presents another validation for a change to a fully plant-based diet. Even though remarkable, however, Dr. Li's work has an emphasis on correcting rather than preventing. The Statin Concept applies here as well—instead of waiting for disease to occur by fueling it with a typical American diet (or one with less consumption of animal products) and then administering anti-angiogenic therapy (with medication or foods), I think the emphasis should be on establishing clear, preventive measures—don't consume foods that add risk of disease that will then need treatment. Anti-angiogenic foods are actually the same foods that have large amounts of phytonutrients, providing ongoing optimal wellness factors of anti-inflammatory, antioxidation, and overall boosting immunity—plant-based foods.

The future of medicine

For nearly all of our questions, concerns, and treatment regarding our own health, we most commonly seek the advice of a physician. Other health practitioners offer adjunctive but quite beneficial services as well—chiropractors, acupuncturists, nutrition specialists, massage therapists, naturopaths, homeopaths—but the vast majority of diagnostic and treatment procedures are carried out by a medical doctor. I feel this eventually will change. There will still be the need for adjunctive therapists and treatment modalities, but the discipline of medicine and the general public would both be better served if a paradigm shift occurred as to how we approach and manage our health care—with a preventive diet and lifestyle focus.

Our current health care approach is by way of a reactive treatment in a pharmacologically focused system. When we become ill, injured, or develop a condition, our physician typically prescribes treatment based on a diagnosis that is limited by the knowledge and experience of the practitioner and governed by existing legal and medical parameters. More often than not, illnesses and conditions are treated with a pharmacological solution—more than $320 billion was spent on prescription drugs in the U.S. in 2011.

A fair amount of waste occurs within our health care systems. Recent studies have shown there to be $750 billion dollars wasted each year in medical services. There is an estimated $395 billion spent on services considered unnecessary, like repeated tests and inefficiently delivered services, as well as missed preventive opportunities.[320] That is reason enough for reform, but I want to focus on the general process of how we have come to use our health care system.

If we don't seek advice from a physician when we're ill, we may try home remedies with a sprinkling of over-the-counter (OTC) medications. U.S. consumers spent $23 billion on these nonprescription drugs in 2011 alone.[321] Many of these medications are necessary, but many are not. That's because we have created a nonpreventive routine of care, with a poor base of consumer/patient knowledge. I feel all health care efforts would be best served using an optimal wellness approach with two divisions of care—the holistic advisor and the biophysical technician. There would no longer be a medical doctor or category of alternative medicine (because alternative has now become mainstream), and our health would be governed by more of a wellness umbrella that would encompass (1) increasing our own awareness, empowering us to understand and take better care of our own health; (2) employing comprehensive preventive and treatment measures prescribed and monitored by the holistic advisor; and (3) a biophysical technician to meet surgical needs, if deemed necessary.

Prevention would take the place of medicine for the majority of concerns, relying on prescription or OTC medications only rarely, when absolutely necessary or unmanageable by more natural treatment or reversal methods.

Practitioners of both types (holistic advisor and surgical technician) would find themselves in a much different educational frame than we have currently. Both sets would be required to attend four or five years of graduate studies in a generalized health program. as they do now, although the structure and focus for the course of studies would be much different from what we find today. Following the first term of introductory courses (history, geographical, and cultural variations of medicine) and observations in clinics and hospitals, students would then embark on a one-year indigenous studies interval. This is a critical component of their education, where the students would spend two to three months combining virtual and physical learning experiences from shaman or indigenous healers regarding more natural healing modalities and focusing on the preventive and healing properties of plants and spiritual and physical health. This year would also include learning about the preventive aspects of yoga, acupuncture, stress management, and similar disciplines. All other years in wellness school would integrate plant-based nutrition and ecological sustainability into their academic protocols. Upon graduation, holistic practitioners could begin practice as preventive advisors and healers of conditions with more natural means (relying on prescription of pharmaceuticals only when necessary), or some would continue into surgical technology disciplines (equivalent to surgeons of all types). This wellness approach to health care would accomplish the following:

1. Establish a more adequate base of education for practitioners regarding the health benefits of purely plant-based foods
2. Establish a set of management protocols for the way in which health care is approached in the U.S.
3. Position prevention by way of plant-based nutrition and lifestyle as the primary focus for attaining and maintenance of health and wellness
4. Create a better understanding of the role of plant-based food and health care in attaining sustainability
5. Eliminate medicine as the primary focus for treatment, using pharmacological solutions only when necessary
6. Integrate a working knowledge of and appreciation for forms of healing other than simply Western culture
7. Substantially reduce Western diseases such as obesity, type II diabetes, heart disease, etc.
8. Reduce health care costs throughout the entire chain
9. Increase national productivity
10. Provide alignment for proper policy reform in agricultural and food production systems, creating a medical/holistic alliance to combat global depletion

This would obviously mandate a significant shift in the way our current medical school educational process is structured and very progressive influential strategists to encourage the change. Although the suggested health care model may seem radical, the basic precepts are well justified— increase the public and professional awareness of the health benefits of a purely plant-based diet (attaining ecological as well as human health awareness), and create a health care system of education and treatment based on this awareness. Eliminate animal products from our diet and agricultural production systems, structure our individual health around prevention and scientifically supported purely plant-based foods, and let the healing begin.

When eating animals becomes stigmatized

Many in the vegan movement believe that eating animals and factory farms will be with us until the eating of meat becomes stigmatized. There is some truth in this. Consider cigarette smoking, which many now view as uncool. But I believe that two more critical factors are necessary in our evolution to the healthier and more peaceful food choice of plant-based options. First, let's take a closer look at the cigarette comparison. Smoking isn't allowed in many business establishments and institutions, not because the act has become stigmatized but because it is a wise *business* decision to prohibit smoking. Their decision was based on the bottom line. The prevalence of smokers in the U.S. dropped from 40 percent in the 1970s and 1980s to 24 percent in this decade. Although many teens do not smoke because of a negative connotation, the decline across all ages occurred principally for health reasons. In fact, most analysts agree that once smoking rates declined to 25 percent in the mid 1990s, it became difficult to drive the rate much lower, even with imposed taxation and negative advertisement campaigns.[322,323]

The other two factors playing more important roles in change are awareness or education, and economics. When speaking with anyone from the World War II era, most of them will tell you that they smoked cigarettes and started at a young age, perhaps beginning the habit because it was cool, but they stopped smoking because they became aware of the damage it was doing to their health. They saw their peers dying from lung cancer. It was because of awareness, education. This issue becomes more pronounced as it's applied to eating animals, because now it is not just our own health that is at risk; it is the health of our planet and all life on it—a much more significant issue than that of cigarette smoking and therefore a reason to stop the addiction.

The second factor is economic. Many of our decisions are based on economics, despite the need for a more intellectual or rational base. Therefore, by essentially making the producers and consumers pay for the true cost of the product to our environment and to our own health, we will at the same time create a much quicker change to a plant-based system.

Even if stigmatizing is a necessary step in our evolution away from eating animals, it will occur only on the heels of education and raising awareness levels and in a quicker fashion when consumers have to pay a heavily elevated price for the environmental and human health damages they are creating by producing and eating animals.

Luxury items

We also need to get a grasp on what we consider to be luxury items that are animal products. We find ourselves using animals in many ways but there are two general categories—for food or for fiber (fabric). As with nearly all consumer goods, some fabrics are viewed as being luxury items, garnering premium prices.

Leather is increasingly viewed as a luxury item. Recently, while conducting research for a new car to lease, a representative for one of the brands I was interested in stated, "We don't offer any nonleather options for that car, and the manufacturer will not consider replacing leather for you. It would be an exorbitant after-market expense." Then he asked, "Why would you want to cheapen a premium luxury car like this by taking the leather out?" Perhaps thousands of years ago, an animal skin was considered a luxury item, without the knowledge or technology to produce an alternative for one's needs. Today, it should be viewed as what it is and what it represents— part of a dead animal that we killed because someone wanted to eat it. Some would call that a curse, not a luxury.

There are many examples of items considered as a luxury in the food category. Meat itself is considered a luxury in many parts of the world. These are the same areas of the world where the water, land, and feed required to product whatever meat they happen to eat could have provided meals for ten people instead of for just the one eating the piece of meat that day.

Served at posh, expensive gatherings and special occasions, coupled with champagne and by those who want to impress, caviar has become synonymous with luxury. Caviar is the "luxury" name we apply to fish eggs—primarily those of sturgeon. Sturgeon have been on earth for more than 200 million years, yet we have fished them to near extinction over the past one hundred years.

With numbers plummeting to less than just 1 percent of original numbers, the Atlantic sturgeon was finally granted an endangered status along the East Coast of North America. The NOAA reports that there is no recovery program in place yet to attempt bringing back their numbers, if it can be accomplished at all, as gillnetting and trawling continues, and sturgeon are killed as bycatch. Traditional caviar comes from sturgeon from the Black and Caspian Seas, where they are nearly extinct. Sturgeon grow to be 18 feet long, up to 4,400 pounds in weight, and live to be over one hundred years old, reaching maturity only when beyond twenty years. Killing them and eating their eggs adds a twisted definition to the word "luxury."

Whether it is to do your share in optimizing the health of our planet or simply for your own health, there are more than enough reasons to stop eating animals and animal products. When we wipe the slate clean and take away all aspects of global depletion due to food choice, what might remain will be the final test of reasoning, judgment, and consciousness—do we really need to and is it right to slaughter and eat another living being, regardless of how we treated it while it was raised?

We can learn lessons from previous civilizations and a few present cultures regarding sustainability, but we will learn more from ourselves— looking outside of the day-to-day microcosm we find ourselves living in, looking at how our collective choices affect our planet. Five hundred years ago, the small Pacific island of Tikopia decided against eating second-generation food (animals that were fed grain and plants), knowing it wasn't sustainable for their "planet." They stopped raising and eating animals on their island. Fifty to one hundred years from now, those living on this planet will look back and comment about us, "In nearly destroying our only Earth, how could they have been so selfish, so consumptive, so myopic?" But they might also say, "Yet when the reality of global depletion from food choice became known in 2013, they did the right thing. They stopped raising, slaughtering, and eating animals—and here we are today, thanking them for it."

7

Agricultural Systems and Accountability

OUR CURRENT METHODS of producing food are failing miserably in many areas, globally and within the U.S. The principal reason for this is that production has been economically driven with no real regard for sustainability, as it is correctly defined, with our health and the health of our planet in mind. Governments have supported agriculture and food production systems that have been shown to be the most economically viable, but it's been at the expense of our resources and the health of our global population. The thirty-year Green Revolution from the 1940s through the 1970s, seeking higher yields, brought short-term annual gains in crop and livestock numbers but long-term losses of irreplaceable natural resources.

Intensive, industrialized animal-based agriculture has had its effects on world hunger, both in the short term, with droughts and heat waves, increase in food prices, and grain speculation sometimes driven by increase in biofuels; and the long term—inefficient land use and farming techniques with livestock and longer term effects of climate change. Two seed companies, DuPont and Monsanto, control three-fifths of seed production in the world. ADM, Cargill, and Bunge control and manipulate corn and grain prices and trade, and JBS

Swift, Tyson, and Cargill control 80 percent of the slaughterhouse and meat production in the world. Seed companies such as Monsanto enjoy more than 30 percent increase in annual profits, while poverty, world hunger, and food prices are on the rise in developing countries.[324,325]

Today, there are many associated influential corporations and industries with so much money behind them that it becomes increasingly difficult to make a change from the business-as-usual approach of industrialized and processed animal-driven agriculture.

With increasing numbers of people in the world and resources becoming scarce, researchers have good reason to be concerned. Livestock are already using 45 percent of all the land on earth, 29 percent of all freshwater withdrawal, and are responsible for 50 percent of all anthropogenic GHG emissions into our atmosphere. Of all the coarse grain produced in the world, an inconceivable 77 percent (*702 million tons*) is fed to livestock.

In 1962, China used 4.7 million tons of grain to feed livestock, which seemed at that time to be an enormous amount, given the degree of presumed austerity. Just fifty years later in 2011, they fed more than 151 million tons to livestock. The U.S., by comparison, gave 126 million tons of grain to feed its livestock in 2011. Globally, over 90 percent of all the soybeans produced are used as feed for animals. We are even feeding 22 percent of all wheat grown in the world to livestock (131 million tons per year), often thought of as only grown for human consumption—all this while 1 billion people in the world are starving.[326,327,328]

As we add more people to our planet, we are running out of the raw ingredients it requires to make the meat, dairy, and eggs to feed them.

We need to use our "raw ingredients" more efficiently by using a different recipe to make a different product.

According to the United Nations' FAO, "livestock production holds great importance for ensuring food security." That's because global demand for meat, dairy, and eggs is predicted to increase as the world's population increases. Yes, livestock does hold great importance—the less we raise, the more food security will be ensured. By the year 2019, beef, pork, and poultry consumption will all grow between 2.4 and 5 percent annually, with most of the increase (as high as 83 percent of the increase) occurring in developing countries. That may not sound like much growth, but the demand is already staggering. In 2012, the one-year figures for global production and consumption of meat looked like this:[329]

- 63 million tons of beef
- 116 million tons of pork
- 97 million tons of poultry
- 14 million tons of sheep and goat meat
- 154 million tons of fish (91 million tons wild-caught)

Think for just a moment about all the cows, pigs, chickens, turkeys, sheep, goats, and fish that were raised and slaughtered in order to produce this monstrous amount of meat—more than 70 billion animals on land and 1 to 2 trillion fish.[330,331]

Bringing about change is difficult in industries that generate vast revenues and are expected to grow substantially over the next few decades. It is even more difficult when confronting cultural-based food preferences that drive decision making.

Combined, the U.S. meat and dairy industries account for about $160 billion in annual sales. The U.S. beef and cattle industry takes in $80 billion per year, the dairy industry realizes $36 billion per year, and turkey, broiler, and eggs have combined revenues of $37 billion. Another $4 billion is made from commercial fishing. With this much money behind the meat and dairy industries, it is easy to see why there is strong resistance to any policy change that would slow down their well-greased machines.[332,333]

Even if the U.S. is eating less beef in 2012, consumption of all other animal products is increasing, and all meat products, including beef, are on the rise worldwide. Uruguay has been gradually increasing its beef consumption and now eat over 198 pounds per person each year. Interestingly, while the grass-fed movement is advocated by many, U.S. *grain-fed* beef imports from Mexico in 2011 increased by 46 percent over the year before. This trend confirms Mexico's preference to produce feedlot beef as well as the increasing demand by U.S. customers to eat grain-fed beef, despite trends to eat slightly less beef in general.[334]

In the U.S., pork, poultry, and farmed fish are picking up where beef left off. For instance, the U.S. consumes more turkey per person than any other country in the world and is projected to see a substantial increase in poultry consumption of all types per capita over the next decade. There were 1.2 billion broiler chickens slaughtered in 2010 in the state of Georgia alone. Poultry production and the number of chickens and turkeys raised each year are expected to double by the year 2020.[335,336,337]

According to the Wisconsin Milk Marketing Board, sales of milk have lessened in the U.S. but yogurt consumption is up 400 percent from 1982. The world dairy market is expected to reach almost $371 billion in 2014, representing nearly 24 percent expansion over five years, reports.[338,339]

At $274 billion revenues in 2011, the world fishing industry and seafood market, which encompasses fresh, canned, and frozen seafood products, is expected to exceed $370 billion by 2015.[340]

The U.S. egg industry has shown rapid expansion over the past few decades, meeting close to all commercial egg demand in the U.S. and producing around 75 percent of the world's eggs from caged layers. With increased urbanization and a mass exodus from rural areas, the percentage of those growing their own food has fallen dramatically, boosting demand for eggs and other farm-produced food products. The majority of egg producers in the U.S. are small farm-owning families. As few as two U.S. egg companies are publicly traded entities.[341]

Throughout the U.S., there were 110 million pigs slaughtered in 2011, with a projected 112 million to be slaughtered in 2012, due to a 5 percent increase in demand for export of pork. That's 213 pigs slaughtered *every minute*. The prospect of this brings two questions of ethics into play: (1) Is it morally right for us to slaughter any sentient being and in such massive numbers? (2) Is it morally right for us to use excessive and unsustainable resources to raise so many animals for us to eat when it is not necessary?[342]

Even with a decrease in small farms and less beef consumption, the U.S. still has 935,000 cattle farms, 69,500 pig farms, and 233,000 farms with sheep and goats. There are over 1 million pigs just in the state of Iowa.[343]

American farmers may be the single most productive human workforce on earth, but they are producing the wrong foods. A little over half of all the land comprised by the U.S. is used in agriculture. But an unbelievable *76 percent of all farmland in the U.S. is used for grazing livestock*—614 million acres in pasture and range, 157 million acres of public land, and 127 million acres in grazed forestland. When the 121 million acres of feed crops (planted in 2012) are factored in, livestock and poultry are using 97 percent of all land used for agriculture in the U.S.[344]

Just as unbelievable, less than 1 percent of all livestock is raised on pasture; the rest are factory farmed. With either method, it is a miserably inefficient manner to use land, topsoil, and all other resources involved.[345]

Although it has been shown to be problematic to the health of our environment and citizens, correction is possible by transitioning meat and dairy operations to plant-based farms and changing conventional growing of crops to organic methods.

There are slightly over 2 million farms in the U.S. Ninety-eight percent are considered family farms, with 60 percent of all those having gross incomes of less than $10,000 and receiving supplemental income from farm sources. Fifty-four percent of all farms are less than 100 acres; another 31 percent are between 100 and 500 acres. Ten percent of all farms in the U.S. are considered commercial and gross more than $250,000 per year, but the majority of these commercial farms are actually family farms that are considered businesses. While some think that food in the U.S. is produced by large industrial-sized farms, much of it is actually produced by many families.[346]

In 1910, 31 percent of the labor force were farmers, with an average of 138 acres per farm, whereas in 2011, less than 2 percent of the labor force in the U.S. were farmers. The production of healthy food and protection of our natural resources should be the foundation upon which policies are based and around which agricultural systems should be structured. With loss of farmers in the workplace and the importance placed on healthy food production, there should be incentives to attract and retain new farmers, who will produce the right type of food.[347]

Only 14 percent of the total food production in the U.S. comes from the less than 2 percent that are considered corporate farms, related to food of all types. However, just 2 percent of all livestock farms in the U.S. are raising more than 40 percent of all the animals produced. Eighty percent of all pigs in the U.S. are raised on farms with 2,000 or more pigs. Additionally, 6 percent of all dairy farms are producing 60 percent of our country's milk. With our new national awareness that factory farms and industrial farming are indeed problematic—pollution, use of chemicals, unnatural confinement and inhumane conditions, increased fossil fuel use—it's easy to understand the public yearning for another way to raise and eat animals, now by way of grass-fed (pastured) operations and fish, both wild-caught and produced by aquaculture. But as pointed out, that movement will simply perpetuate and in some ways increase global depletion. We need to strive to achieve another level of sustainability by eliminating eating animals entirely.[348,349]

Transitioning conventional farms to organic, plant-based operations
From a business aspect, there is great promise for operations to move to organic farming systems. Of all plant foods, organic fruits and vegetables experienced the highest growth (12 percent) in sales for 2010–2011. The organic movement, both the number of farms and number of total acres, doubled from 2006 to 2010, from conventional to organic. From 2004 to 2011, organic food sales more than doubled, from $11 billion to $25 billion, accounting for over 3.5 percent of food sales in 2011. Although encouraging, certified organic acreage still only represents 0.7 percent of all U.S. cropland.[350,351]

In addition to creating a much higher level of resource stewardship, transitioning of our farmers' land and talents to organic plant-based foods would increase job opportunities. This is because typical organic produce operations require more employees as fieldwork mechanization lessens.

Andrew Stout sits in a supervisory capacity for numerous boards for the furthering of produce in the Cascadian area of Washington State and owns Full Circle Farms, an organic produce-growing and distribution business northeast of Seattle. His vegetable operations are nestled in between small- to medium-sized livestock farms and produce over 2 million pounds of produce on 354 acres spread out over three locations in the county, which equates to 6,415 pounds per acre. While the livestock operations next door typically would use similar acreage for cattle and produce, approximately 250 pounds per acre of meat, and employ a handful of staff (usually family members), Full Circle employs 184 people. Eighty-two percent are full time and fill numerous positions, skill levels, managerial levels, and departments, ranging from field workers to marketing and administration. This is quite typical with organic plant-based operations, where there are many more job opportunities than with conventional animal-based feed-crop farms.[352]

Another reputable organic produce farmer for twelve years in the northwest Washington State area moved back to conventional farming because "it wasn't profitable," stating that "customers didn't want to pay the higher price of organic." She felt the reason for the price differential was due to "labor," whereas now she can just "spray fungicides and other chemicals to reduce loss of product and without anyone picking weeds. ... The public expects good food but wants to pay for cheap food." This is a common sentiment that I find among small farmers attempting to grow and sell organic produce, which can be solved with increasing public awareness and providing the tools to ensure success for the transitioning conventional livestock or dairy farmer.

As the transition from conventional farms to organic plant-based systems takes place, we will need to see a higher degree of support by our government in the form of policy revisions. There should be generous incentives provided for farmers who make the transition in the form of educational and economic assistance, until a favorable economy of scale exists for their products. For too long, our government has provided assistance to the producers of meat, dairy, and fish, allowing them to flourish. It is time to kick-start a better way to produce food.

Once all subsidies for animal products have been eliminated (allowing markets to establish an unbiased and natural balancing of supply/

demand/pricing), then the price of organic fruit, vegetables, grain, and nuts will decrease and animal products will increase. Less than 1.5 percent of previous Farm Bill subsidies (2008–2012) were paid to vegetables and fruit producers. These products are considered "specialty crops" by governmental definition. Even the highly supported Conservation Stewardship Program (originally the Conservation Security Program of 2002) is severely disproportionate, with 92 percent of all funds given to farms with livestock and farms growing feed crops.[353]

The livestock industry employs 1.3 billion people worldwide, with 82 percent of the rural poor in Asia, Africa, and Central and South America keeping some form of livestock. For those employed and the smallholders in developing countries, it is time for them to use their skills and land more efficiently, producing healthier foods and building soil. A transition to plant-based systems is in order.[354]

"Agribusiness" thoughts

Agribusiness—what does that word mean to you? If you're like most progressive thinkers, agribusiness may imply factory farms, agricultural systems, and products that are manufactured and controlled by large corporate entities; loss of the small, local family farm; and ultimately, food items that are unhealthy for our environment and for all of us. Some of these inferences are true; some are not. Many of the food movements today focus on the term "agribusiness" in describing what it is they want to move away from. Although there are many aspects of larger farming operations that are less than desirable, the principle component that we should be concerned about is if they involve raising and slaughtering animals.

For example, Cal-Organic is a food-producing business that owns over 30,000 acres, with a combination of organic methods and crops spread over five regions in California. Cal-Organic employs 6,500 workers and grows over seventy-five different varieties of vegetables. They don't use any animal products or any animal manure in their techniques—it's all plant-based. One would have to consider Cal-Organic as an example of agribusiness, as they produce more organic carrots than any other company in the world.[355]

So just what is the benefit of moving *away* from a working model of agribusiness like Cal-Organic, or larger industrial farming operations, if it's *to* a small, local dairy or beef farm that may not be large but is responsible for significant collective contribution to pollution, GHG emissions, and inefficient use of land and water? Our first concern should be with what and how a food product is grown before we worry about how large the company is that is growing it.

You and the 2012 Farm Bill/food policymaking—
time for a new perspective

The U.S. government's Farm Bill, in one form or another, has been the backbone of support for what we eat and how we grow it in the U.S. for more than seventy years. Even though we, as individuals, are ultimately responsible for what we decide to eat, the meat and dairy industries and our government, by way of policy, have great influence on our food choices— what food is more readily available for consumers and school systems, how it is produced, and education regarding food production and health aspects. When you hear the phrase "farm subsidies" or the word "commodities," it is the Farm Bill that they are talking about. Let's look briefly at the subsidies issue and why we should know and care about it.

The original Farm Bill most likely was once a good idea with humble beginnings. In 1933, it was used to help prop up farmers coming out of the Great Depression. The U.S. government decided that farmers, at that time, needed to have income support to keep them on the farm, without much respect for what they grew. This is where it all began—with the Agricultural Adjustment Act of the 1930s. Today, that governmental support has grown into a seriously flawed and disconnected system on many levels. Consider this:

We are giving a lot of money to our government for them to pay unaware farmers to produce food that makes us sick. That pretty much explains the U.S. Farm Bill.

That's not all, though, because we give a lot more money to our government all over again for them to pay for the health bills of all those people who eat all that bad food—which explains our national health insurance plan, unfortunately intertwined with our Farm Bill.

There are a few reasons we need to be concerned about the Farm Bill:

One is that we, as taxpayers, are paying for it—that should be reason enough, and it's pretty large, with the current bill (ending 2012) weighing in at $280 billion. Second, it is often misrepresented to the public and has many problems, but it is rewritten every four to five years, so if there is something wrong with the existing bill, we should be able to fix it—or so it seems, because there are very large agricultural forces at play (industries, lobbyists, and money).

The 2008–2012 bill was a plan with fifteen categories or "titles," each with its own set of funds. We have heard mostly about the $42 billion given as direct farm subsidies (these are for "commodities" or corn, wheat, soybeans, sorghum, barley, and five other crops) and also about the $40 billion for two other titles that provide various types of support, such as crop insurances and land-set-aside programs. These two are the grouping of funds that have supported industrial farming the most, in a direct fashion. But $190 billion, 70 percent of the entire Farm Bill, is given to the 43 million people enrolled in the food stamp program—and that title has issues as well, but you won't hear about them because it is more insidious and slides along unnoticed.

What about the other eleven titles? No one knows much about these because they have less money involved so they are not considered a problem. But I consider them extremely important. These titles pertain to such things as conservation and environment, forestry, renewable energy, and research. In fact, if our government would have devoted more of the previous Farm Bills, essentially more of our tax dollars, to just two of those categories—for instance, to environment and research—they may have discovered decades ago that we are growing our food all wrong. In fact, they would have found out that we are not growing food at all. We are growing livestock and now fish.

So, from the 2008–2012 Farm Bill, we have these issues:

1. There is no supervisory department managing our health, currently divided between the USDA, FDA, and EPA. There needs to be one FEED ("Food production for Efficient Ecosystem use Department) or some such umbrella department and acronym.

2. There is no emphasis on correct dietary education. There needs to be. It really does not matter how much subsidy support the government provides or where it goes if we, as a nation, do not fully understand the health implications of our food choices.

3. The Supplemental Nutrition Assistance Program (SNAP), better known as the Food Stamp program, is actually contributing to the perpetuation of current food production systems and escalating health care crisis. We need to involve education, incorporation of incentives such as "market bucks" and mandating use for proper foods, and put a monitoring system in place.

4. There historically have been no incentives for plant-based food production. We need to devote all subsidies to these only, leaving none for farms related to livestock production (either raising the animals themselves or growing crops that will be fed to livestock).

5. No incentives are in place for small, family-based farms, CSAs, or cooperatives. We need to have these available but only if no animal products are involved.

6. There are no current incentives for organic growers. We need to have support but only if it's plant-based.

7. Currently, there is no economic responsibility for depletion of resources or pollution.

In order to move forward with the redrafting of any Farm Bill, I think the following most important three issues need to be sorted out:

First, the Food Stamp program has no proper nutrition education or monitoring system, so the program itself is essentially contributing to our national health care costs and the perpetuation of producing unhealthy food, because those enrolled spend $190 billion on the cheapest and most readily accessible food possible—food produced with empty calories and from the meat and dairy industries. Since this will continue to be the largest part of the bill, it needs to be corrected at least as much as the other subsidy issues.

Second, we must clearly understand that government subsidies, by themselves, although a contributing factor, do not cause obesity or any other disease (contrary to what has been stated by a few authors and circulated through the media). Healthy food is available. You just have to find it and create a larger demand. If we all decided to stop eating candy bars or soft drinks today, manufacturers would stop making them. Again, it begins with education. It begins with awareness—and the Farm Bill needs to provide this awareness, before it does anything else.

Third, all government funding should be for only those foods that are factually the healthiest for our environment and for ourselves—organically grown, plant-based foods. Farmers that grow them should be heavily supported and obviously benefit the most.

That means there shouldn't be one penny going to any other type of food. Otherwise, we are simply perpetuating ill health for ourselves and for our planet.

Doing these three things would create the right environment for healthier food to be produced and for proper choices to be made. I encourage everyone to get involved with this. You have a voice, but carefully examine what is proposed, because the movement to restructure the bill is continually in motion and is quite strong but not in the right direction.

Less than 2 percent of the current Farm Bill is used to support vegetables, fruit, and nuts; most of the rest of the money is given to the meat and dairy industries, in one form or another.

Many of the major changes proposed for this bill are aimed at taking away economic support for factory farms and giving more to small farmers, thinking this will produce healthier food. Essentially, it will shift funds from large meat and dairy operations to small meat and dairy operations, which begins to solve the agribusiness issues, but then we will have many smaller farm entities still producing unhealthy foods. Because the Farm Bill is rewritten every five years and is being renewed for 2013, the political year 2012 presented a great opportunity for appropriate retooling.

Food choice guided by government:
how the 2013 Food Bill is being retooled

In 2011, President Obama established a Super Committee to recommend a deficit reduction plan of $1.3 trillion to span ten years. One of the many areas where the administration felt budget reduction was needed was with the Farm Bill. The reduction become the responsibility of the Senate committee for Agriculture, Nutrition, and Forestry (ANF), to establish recommendations for the Super Committee as to how and where government funding would be spent in regard to food production in the U.S. The ANF made its suggestion of a $23 billion reduction, but the Super Committee failed to agree on acceptance by the November 23, 2011, deadline imposed by the president. This threw into motion the need for ANF to come up with another plan, with the objective of passing and pressing into service a bill by the end of 2012, when the Farm Bill expired. Four hearings were set to discuss how to structure this next bill and create a budget framework and guidelines, new programs to stimulate growth, and hear witnesses who were stakeholders, such as producers/farmers, industry leaders, and representatives of pertinent organizations. There was much energy, time, and taxpayers' dollars spent in the process of drafting this bill and the budget for it.

Hearings were held, and then a plan had to be developed and passed by both Senate and House of Representatives. The Senate passed their version in June 2012, but after repeated delays, by late September, the House had not. Much of the drafting of the new bill was being accomplished by the ANF committee, which is headed by Senator Stabenow of Michigan. Although Chairwoman Stabenow has been an advocate for fruit and vegetable growers, successfully securing the first ever fruit and vegetable title in a Farm Bill in 2008, she has been a much larger advocate for the production of animal products. With more than 98 percent of the rest of the bill for animal agriculture, Stabenow allowed profound bias to the meat, dairy, and egg industries. In her home state of Michigan, animal agriculture plays a predominant role, with livestock and dairy products, hay, and feed crops occupying the top five farming revenues. Income from animal products rose by more than 15 percent from 2009 to 2010, strengthened by $185 million from government subsidies given to livestock operations in Michigan. Herbrouck's Poultry Ranch in Saranac supplies McDonald's Corporation with all of the eggs it uses east of the Mississippi. Herbrouck's uses significant energy, water, and feed in the form of corn and soybeans. Much of the feed production was subsidized by the government.

Throughout the hearings, there was significant discussion about the development of alternative fuels through agriculture and how to increase job opportunities and incentives for rural America, disadvantaged, and minority farmers, and provide healthier food for the country while protecting resources. Much like we have seen in other venues, the hearings displayed noble intentions based on inaccurate definitions that will preclude success.

Becky Humphries' definition of sustainable agriculture and conservation was made clear as she spoke before the Senate regarding how money should be allocated in the next Farm Bill. Her approach is for the bill to provide more funding for farmers to conserve land and set areas aside that involve wetlands. As the spokesperson for Ducks Unlimited, Ms. Humphries urged protection because it would provide economic activity through conservation, so that hunters and anglers could pursue their passions every year—amounting to $86.1 billion expenditures for rods and reels, guns, ammunition, boats, decoys, bows and arrows, tree stands, hotel stays and dinners in small rural towns across the country. She argued that in Michigan alone (her home state), 1.37 million hunters and anglers (people who shoot wildlife and catch fish) spend $9.4 million a day and that everyone benefits from their activities, which need support programs established for our environment in order to thrive. She voiced concern that farmers needed to be subsidized adequately to conserve land, protect the quality of our water, and ensure that the individuals she represents as well as her own daughter and son could "successfully hunt and fish." Ms. Humphries' reasoning that conserved farmland is important for hunting was echoed by Bruce Nelson (the Farm Service Agency administrator) and others. Her definition and that of the hunters and farmers she represents have a much different definition of sustaining life on earth than I do, but this is the logic presented throughout much of the hearings to revise our Farm Bill.

As policy makers continue wrangling over drafting of the new Farm Bill (and most likely future Farm Bills), it is generally agreed that direct subsidies by our government to farmers will be lowered, if not eliminated. Safety nets such as crop insurances and conservation measures will be maintained, if not strengthened. Dialogue will continue with use of the word "sustainable" found repeatedly as politicians modify policies for better use of our natural resources. Attempts will be made to increase markets for access to healthier food. The success of all these objectives is relative to how they define *healthy* and *sustainable*.

Farmers feel that Obama's suggestion of cutting crop insurance by $8 billion is unacceptable. This makes sense because farmers now are more vulnerable to catastrophic loss and economic failure, due to much less diversification. Many farmers only grow one type of plant—a monoculture farming system—so they are more susceptible to loss (weather, insects, etc.) than if they produced numerous crops, as was the case more than sixty years ago. Farmers are very concerned about needing a safety net as they continue producing mostly single feed crops for livestock.

Conservation has been at the center of the most recent Farm Bill and will become more important with future bills. Funding for conservation measures by farmers is based on current industry beliefs of what composes a sustainable food production system. It makes no sense to support farmers with land-set-aside programs (land that will not be used by a farmer for a period of time), soil tillage or water reduction techniques, or any other methods, while they are engaged in any form of producing livestock or animal products. We will be paying them for a small amount of identified resource reduction, while condoning significant and unnecessary resource use to raise livestock and feed. This lack of definition became more evident as the hearings progressed.

Witnesses were heard, such as Earl Garber, president of the National Association of Conservation Districts, who urged for continued strong government support for the conservation (land-set-aside) programs in order to "protect our natural resources." Garber is a rice, soybean, and hay farmer using most of his resources to grow animals to eat.

Darrell Mosel, a Minnesota farmer, owns a 600-acre "diversified crop" and dairy operation with 40 percent corn, 30 percent soybeans, 30 percent alfalfa, milking Holsteins, and operating a feedlot with 150 cattle. Nearly all of his crops (even the half grown organically) are used to feed livestock—his own beef cattle and dairy operation and to other livestock farms. A small portion of his corn is sold to a local ethanol plant. So when Mr. Mosel uses the word "diversified" to describe his farming operations, what he means is that he grows more than one type of plant. Everything he produces, however, aside from a small amount of corn targeted for ethanol use, is not so "diversified" because it is used for one purpose—to feed livestock. Despite the positive aspect of referring to his operations as diversified, it is not a positive picture for the impacts his livestock-driven operations have on our ecosystems. He was a witness providing testimony as a lobbyist: "I am here today as a farmer member of the Land Stewardship Project, or LSP, a nonprofit organization ... and also on behalf of the National Sustainable Agriculture Coalition, a grassroots alliance that advocates for federal policy reform to advance the sustainability of agriculture, food systems, natural resources, and rural communities."

Speaking from his personal experience with use of governmental funding programs, EQIP (Environmental Quality Incentives Program), and CSP (Conservation Stewardship Program), he related how using both allowed him to remain economically sound while helping him "protect and enhance natural resources on my land." The Conservation Stewardship Program has paid out more than 85 percent of its funding to meat and dairy farmers. This represents the fact that farmers need to be educated as to the true effects of their individual meat and dairy operations on our resources and their cumulative effect, and increase their awareness of the many conservation benefits—the much higher degree of relative sustainability—of growing purely plant-based systems. Safety nets such as crop insurance and conservation programs and funding through a Farm Bill should only apply to operations growing plants that are used directly for us to eat and in an organic or biodynamic manner.

In the summer of 2012, U. S. farmers faced the worst drought since the 1950s, and corn and soybean future prices were at record highs. The USDA declared 42 percent of all U.S. counties as disaster areas, making them eligible for low-interest loans, and fragile areas set aside as reserves were opened up for grazing and hay production to help reduce losses of livestock. The Conservation and Wetlands Reserve pays farmers to retire these lands. With imminent livestock and feed-crop stress, once set-aside lands are now used for grazing, and crop insurance will cover any economic loss the heat and drought were responsible for. It is interesting that one of the principal reasons for extremes of weather is from GHG emissions, many of which these farmers and their livestock are responsible for. Our government felt that the solution for these farmers' plight was to open fragile ecosystems to cattle grazing for more damage and increased methane production (40–50 percent higher in grass-fed cattle) and habitat loss, while insurances pay for the feed crops they lost, providing them with incentives to begin the whole process over again next season.

The Conservation Security Plan, originated in 2002, evolved to become the Conservation Stewardship Program (CSP) in 2008. In 2010, the CSP awarded 12,000 contracts to farms, of which 10,407 went to livestock producers (8,533 to beef, 1,047 to dairy, 827 to "swine and others"). With nearly 90 percent of the Conservation Stewardship Program funding applied to unsustainable livestock operations, the U.S. government should have a better understanding of the full impact and resource use by animal agriculture and the relative sustainable aspect, comparing animal agriculture to plant-based systems. With this mandatory new awareness, policy makers should support the awarding of conservation contracts to only those farms that are not depleting resources at the other end of their farm. It should be funding for true stewards, not for the façade of stewardship.

Over the course of one year's worth of testimonies before the Senate and House, there were only a handful of witnesses representing fruit and vegetable farming. The vast majority presenting their case urged continued government funding of animal livestock operations.

A perfect example of most witnesses and their testimonials regarding the need to continue funding their operations was Bill Grieving, from Prairie View, Kansas. He and his wife grow feed crops and alfalfa under irrigation, raise 500 cows, and have a licensed feedlot with 950 cattle. Their entire operation is livestock-based. The following statement by Mr. Grieving displays the testimony that was arranged to be heard throughout the hearings and the disconnect by farmers and policy makers from the realities of raising livestock as it relates to food and sustainability: "Farms like ours are proof that ethanol production, grain production, and meat production work together. In this synergistic system, we are growing feed, fuel, and food on my farm." He proudly pointed out that both sweet and grain sorghum can be grown now for feed crop and ethanol use. What he is growing on his farm are animals, not "food," and there should be no government subsidies pointed in his direction or any farms with similar operations.

The Local Farms, Food, and Jobs Act is a brilliant thought—to create jobs and spur economic growth by way of supporting local food and farms. Local and regional agriculture is a major economic driver in the farm economy. There are now more than 7,000 farmers' markets throughout the United States—a 150 percent increase since 2000—and direct-to-consumer sales have accounted for more than $1.2 billion in annual revenues. Now, on the heels of that expansion, we are witnessing the rapid growth of local and regional food markets that have scaled up beyond direct marketing. Together these markets represent important new job growth and economic development. Farm-to-school food programs can be found in every state. Using these opportunities, the Act will increase local and regional markets, increase access to healthy food, and provide training, information, and research to help farm operators become successful. This is a superb framework and one that would ensure growth in all areas intended, if the proper definitions are applied to the terms "healthy food" and "local."

The statements made by Secretary of Agriculture Vilsack at various times during the Farm Bill hearings made it clear there is a wide separation between what is perceived as being accomplished by our government and what is actually being accomplished. One example of this was his commenting that the USDA is focusing on "local" economies, equating this with "healthy" food and establishing "food hubs." Before focusing on local and healthy food, it would be beneficial for Secretary Vilsack to have a clearer understanding of what those words really mean, particularly since policies and funding are based on the application of these two words. During one of the hearings, Vilsack stated, "In 2010, the market entered into a cooperative agreement with USDA's Agricultural Marketing Service to expand the availability of healthy, local food throughout Detroit. The market is currently partnering with the Detroit Public Schools on their internal goal of converting 30 percent of their $16 million annual food purchases to Michigan-grown and minimally processed foods." This is a bit of rhetoric that presents a picture of progress. Once again, though, just because a food is "local" does not mean that is healthy. What his statement means to me is that in 2010, the USDA made efforts to make *food* more available for the Detroit area and for their public schools—not *healthy* food or sustainable food. The term "healthy," to him and to the U.S. government, doesn't mean it is factually healthy. Meat, dairy, eggs, and fish are all promoted as healthy food and therefore will be made more available in Detroit. That's not so healthy. The wheels of our government and policy change are moving forward quickly on the wrong definition base.

Secretary Vilsack's example of how the USDA's efforts are driving healthy food forward can be found in his discussion of one of these "food hubs," the Detroit Eastern Market. The following is offered on the retail directory page for participating food businesses in the Eastern Market: Al's Fish Seafood, Chicken, Butcher and Packer (where "the art of sausage making and meat processing is fun and enjoyable"), Capital Poultry, Cheech's Chicken, R. J.'s Meats, Ronnie's Meats, Wrigley's Meat Market (two locations), and Hambone's of Detroit (where they profess to serve "porky goodness").

Does this particular food hub (Detroit Eastern Market) have healthy food? Yes, but the fresh organic fruit and vegetable produce offered remains buried among many other unhealthy food vendors. I find it disconcerting to see just how much effort Vilsack put forth in promoting advancements and appearing as if the USDA has some depth of understanding of the food choice problem and to the direction it needs to steer our country. More from Vilsack:

> *"And the Detroit Eastern Market is a food hub, offering warehouse, storage, processing, marketing and retail functions to hundreds of Michigan producers, allowing them to participate in the state's biggest market.*
>
> *"In order to better understand the impacts of these projects and how we can further support local and regional food hubs, we have created a dedicated working group composed of representatives from the Agricultural Marketing Service, Rural Development, Economic Research Service, Agricultural Research Service, National Institute of Food and Agriculture, and Food Nutrition Service."*

Another example that Vilsack mentions is La Montanita Co-Op in New Mexico, serving 15,000 co-op members. Their objective is to provide food that is "local, fair, and fresh," none of which means that the food is healthy or sustainable. Just because their "organic beef, lamb, and other meats and cheeses" that they proudly offer are local, fair, and fresh, this doesn't mean that these products are healthy for our planet to grow, for us to consume, or for the animals (wildlife or the animals slaughtered) affected by the process. As a matter of fact, they are not.

It appears that this co-op is a model to be followed, which is precisely why it was represented during the hearings, because it carries "over 1500 *local* products from over 900 *local* producers, and *local* food purchases and sales accounts for 20 percent of their totals and the decades of demonstrated commitment make the co-op a regional leader in the *local* foods movement." However, touting this becomes meaningless if one looks further at the myriad of wasteful and truly unhealthy local animal products they offer, which should be viewed as a "demonstrated commitment" to unsustainable food production systems and the need to change. This is the point continually missed. Therefore, a proper focusing of definition accuracy and efforts by Mr. Vilsack and our government is in order.

An objective of this co-op is to educate their members and the community "on the importance of local foods for their nutritional value, safe secure food system, and good ecological stewardship practices for a sustainable future." That becomes the starting point for Secretary Vilsack and our policy makers—this co-op already has education as an objective; now guide them toward the real definition of nutrition, safe and secure foods, and preservation of our resources. Those parameters can only be accomplished with plant-based foods. Begin the educational process there.

More than one-fourth of all farmers in the U.S. are sixty-five years or older; the average age is fifty-seven. An estimated 70 percent of the nation's farmland will change hands in the next twenty years. With such a large segment of existing farmers at retirement age, it is important to have incentives in place to attract and retain young and beginning farmers. The Beginning Farmer and Rancher Opportunity Act of 2011 has been introduced to break down barriers that would impede new agriculture operators from starting a farming business. This act has no differentiation between highly sustainable plant-based operations and those focused on high-value feed crops, milk, pigs, poultry, and beef, which has been and is predicted to continue to be where most agricultural production will occur. If incentives are created for young entry farmers, they should be made only available for plant-based systems. We have enough unsustainable animal operations in existence already. Why fund more?

Many healthy food initiatives are under way with the 2008–2012

Farm Bill and likely will only increase in attention and funding with future bills. The definition of healthy obviously drives the true success of every one of those initiatives.

Initiative S.1926, the Healthy Food Financing Initiative, recognizes the relationship of certain diseases and availability of healthy food. Western diseases such as obesity and diabetes are more prevalent in underprivileged areas of our country, and there is a general lack of supply and access to healthy foods in those areas. Overall, the initiative is based on a solid premise, but there is general inaccuracy of the definition of the healthy food—the exact food type to which these areas need to have access.

The definitions section of this initiative is riddled with problems. There is no reference to ratios of food types, and meat is listed alongside fruits and vegetables as "healthy and fresh food." By their definition, healthy and fresh food means "food that is a basic dietary item, including bread, flour, fruits, vegetables, and meat." A healthy and fresh pear, apple, or spinach is certainly in a different category than a pound of ground round, which isn't healthy—and how can it be fresh? It's dead.

There are nearly 50 million people living within the U.S. that are food insecure, not able to find healthy food at prices they can afford to feed themselves or others in their household. To be sure, with this popular initiative, there is little assurance that anyone living in an underprivileged, underserved area of our country will lessen their likelihood to develop heart disease or diabetes, now that they have better access to hamburgers, hot dogs, pork chops, chicken meat, dairy products, and eggs. If anything, we will see a rise in Western diseases coming from these underprivileged areas. Maybe they will eat less candy and potato chips and guzzle fewer soft drinks. Perhaps these underserved people will consume a few more fruits and vegetables, but having meat anywhere in the lineup of options and without accurate food choice education, it will not be successful. It is a one-way ticket to illness for them and to another ill-conceived funnel of lost tax dollars for us.

This is a significant initiative, in that it has the ability to impact the health of millions of people and further the support of the agricultural systems producing the food types that are made more available. As such, it demands accurate defining of "healthy and fresh."

The Fresh Regional Eating for Schools and Health Act of 2011 (S.2016) has received great attention and support. It is a bill to amend the Food and Nutrition Act of 2008, the National School Lunch Act, and the Child Nutrition Act of 1966—to increase access to healthy food for families and increase access to credit for small and new farmers. Once again, throughout the act there are no proper definitions of "healthy." The act needs to incorporate a system by which nutrient density and lack of disease risk are valued and referred to. The inclusion of specialty crops (fruit and vegetables) has been made, although vague with percentage purchased. The term "local" needs better defining as well, by not associating it with "healthy."

The National Sustainable Agriculture Coalition (NSAC) is an alliance of grassroots organizations that advocates for federal policy reform to advance the sustainability of agriculture, food systems, natural resources, and rural communities. It is well structured, with strong membership, an agenda that appears to be in the best interest of U.S. agriculture, and a voice that is heard by our government regarding policy reform. NSAC has forty represented members (formally represented before Congress and government agencies) and fifty-four participating members (organizations not formally represented but are involved at NSAC gatherings, with issues, and grassroots activities).

NSAC has become a powerful and influential force in agriculture policy reform. Their vision is one of nutritious, affordable food, produced by family farmers who are protecting the environment while remaining economically viable. While their goal to give a voice to sustainable and organic farmers is consistent with their vision, their objectives can be met only with plant foods. At the center of all efforts by NSAC is sustainability and nutritious/healthy food. Economic sustainability can certainly be realized by this group's actions, but sustainable ecosystem resource use and human health cannot.

In the proposed agenda by the NSAC (outlining their primary areas of concern for the new 2012 Farm Bill), they do *not* address animal agriculture. Their focus is directed at economic growth and job development, strengthening American agriculture, enhancing natural resources while improving productivity, and driving innovation for tomorrow's farmers and entrepreneurs. While NSAC encourages the bill to assist new farmers, job growth, and organic farming, it includes all forms of livestock production in its agenda.

Without reaching an agreement for budget reduction and specific spending cuts, on March 1, 2013, the Obama administration and Congress saw a mandatory sequestration take effect—an across-the-board reduction of government spending with nearly all departments and programs affected. Because of this, any definitive rewriting and enacting of the 2012 Farm Bill was effectively postponed until September 2013. An enormous amount of time, energy, and taxpayers' dollars have been spent by our government as they wrestle with our impending fiscal cliff, health-care crisis cliff, and climate-change cliff. In many ways they are all the same cliff— interconnected and to some extent caused by our eating decisions and food production systems.[356,357]

Whether it is with our farmers, legislators, or consumers, the 2012 Farm Bill has been viewed as the foundation of food change in our country, perhaps lifting us out of many unhealthy eating habits we've acquired over the years. The overriding difficulty I see with this bill and our perception of it is that we really have no accurate awareness of the impact our food choices have on our health or that of our environment. Therefore, we are attempting to draft a Farm Bill and then criticize its efficacy, based on an imprecise and often distorted view of food and health. Further, many in our society are concerned about a limitation of freedom if the government establishes any policies to dictate what U.S. citizens eat—clearly complicating the effectiveness of any Farm Bill, as we have vividly and repeatedly displayed our lack of ability to choose truly healthy foods when they are placed right in front of us.

Since the 2012 Farm Bill will become a reality as a successor to the previous enacted bills while this book (*Food Choice and Sustainability*) is being published, there may be slight changes to the bill from what I have presented. Whether it with this or future bills, the government's insufficiencies, inaccuracies with definitions, and the money we pay to support them certainly need to be addressed. With lack of awareness and no motivation to become educated as to the benefits of plant-based agricultural systems, I see little hope for progress toward true sustainability coming from our government. Mobility for proper change in food production systems will be difficult to achieve without policy reform, but the impetus for such reform will likely arise from ultimate public outrage and progressive business strategies.

At some point in time, it seems the question of ethics will surface with regard to how we produce food. Ethics is already an issue frequently found with how we raise and slaughter animals, from an animal welfare perspective, but it also should apply to the effect our food choices have on the environment and to our own health. I have posed the question, with regard to health care costs, "Why should I pay for what everyone else decides to eat?" This is essentially a question of ethics. The same question can easily apply to environmental costs.

The topic of conscious eating has always been about animal rights and animal welfare—the life and death of other living beings that we consume and how they're treated. But it's time to view conscious eating or ethics in a much different and much larger context.

Is it ethical, for instance, for any of us to eat food that causes the extinction of other species if we don't need to eat it? Is it ethical for the vast majority of the humans on earth to cause, or contribute heavily to irreversible climate change, loss of ecosystems, and resource depletion, while 2 percent of us are living our lives to protect Earth? Is it ethical for any of us to use our planet in a way that exacerbates world hunger and extracts the potential for future generations to survive? Is it even ethical for 310 million Americans to impose their diet-related health care costs on the 5 million who choose to eat the right foods? It's time we rethink ethics. It needs to be framed much differently than with just animal rights.

Our government will—very soon, I believe—tackle these questions as costs begin to be affixed to ecosystem goods and services we use. It's time researchers and environmental groups begin asking these questions, fervently and repeatedly.

A report was issued from a working group established under the framework of the Ethics and Climate Change in Asia and Pacific project (ECCAP) beginning in 2009. The goal of this project is not to formulate economic or political plans but to increase awareness of the complex ethical aspects related to energy and the environment. The ECCAP gathers scientific data and available ethical frameworks of values for policy options that have been helpful with confronting challenges in communities and countries. They pose the question of ethics regarding raising livestock and harvesting fishing: is it ethical for individuals, communities, and nations to condone (or support) the use of agricultural systems that are not sustainable or that deplete our natural resources (contribute to any or all aspects of global depletion)? Their primary focus was on energy consumption. It requires thirty to forty times more fossil fuel energy to produce 1 pound of animal products, like eggs and beef, than one pound of grain. The conclusion of the ECCAP is that "intensive livestock production is not sustainable," and policy change is in order for each nation and internationally, and that ethics should be brought into the discussion when designing policy around agricultural systems that involve livestock.

Aside from fossil fuel use, other costs of producing meat that need to be considered are numerous and far-reaching, with large costs to society and the environment. These need an economic value attached, and include:

1. Impacts on climate change, locally and globally
2. Land degradation, topsoil loss, deforestation, and effects of desertification
3. Water use for irrigation, consumption, and processing
4. Loss of habitat and biodiversity
5. Production and distribution of antibiotic-resistant and bacteria and pathogens in the food supply
6. Introduction of synthetic and natural-occurring hormones and hormone derivatives into the food supply and the environment
7. Release of parasites

8.   Release and accumulation of organic pollutants in soil, sediments, water ecosystems, and in the food chain
9.   Socioeconomic costs affecting the poverty- and hunger-stricken
10. Increased risk of regional and global pandemics by spread of disease associated with meat production and animal transportation

These are some of the costs created by the consumers and producers of animal products, and they provide a strong case for applying ethics to agricultural policy.

An agricultural system to alleviate world hunger

It seems improbable that an easy-to-replicate blueprint to eliminate world hunger could be established that would fit every affected geographic region. There are simply too many variables. However, the best approach would be to create a framework that somewhat simplifies a complex situation into the primary components—a road map of sorts—that would address each component by focusing on the one factor that connects them all—food choice.

There are over 2 million NGOs in the world, with half of them involved in humanitarian efforts to developing countries. We are not at a loss for organizations attempting to do good things in the world by good-doers. With nearly a billion people suffering from hunger and 6 million children starving to death each year, one would have to wonder how effective our global efforts have been at eliminating the world hunger/food security problem.

Hunger and poverty can be found in every country on earth. In developing nations, the majority of efforts to bring aid to those afflicted can be categorized in two ways: direct supply of food, and investment in commercial agricultural development by various multinational entities. Only supplying food to these countries may be a very small, temporary patching of the much larger problem. The overriding reason there has been little improvement in the number and severity of hunger and poverty in countries in Africa, for instance, is because food supply has always been separated from the multitude of layered factors. Just give them food. But it's not that easy, and it is not working.

In order to create sustainability for these people, there first needs to be a more precise defining of the term "sustainable," and then there needs to be a stratified approach in its application, creating the opportunity for them to become sustainable through their own efforts, not by continually receiving aid. A constant reliance on food baskets will not bring back the two-thirds topsoil lost, provide multifaceted education and training, introduce them to economic opportunities, develop food systems that are the most sustainable for use of their natural resources and for their own human health, and ensure social equality.

Hunger and poverty form a cycle, both affecting the other and involving education and resource use. In many sub-Saharan countries such as Ethiopia and Eritrea, hunger and illiteracy affect 66 percent of their population. More than 75 percent are engaged in agriculture, but it is on topsoil that has become eroded (two-thirds lost), and what's left is infertile, after years of trampling and overgrazing of livestock. Low crop productivity; food insecurity; malnutrition; and inadequate farming knowledge, skills, implements, and inputs are characteristic of smallholder agriculture in most of Southern Africa. For years they have been engaged in farming techniques where much of the dwindling resources available are used for livestock. At over 100 million cattle, goats, and sheep, Ethiopia has one of the largest animal herds in the world. These are animals that require water, land, soil, feed, energy, time—little of which Ethiopia has. And in the end, livestock-driven agriculture produces animal products that their people can ill afford to consume, as compared to plant-based foods that would provide the most sustainable nutritional and environmental foundation for them.

In Mozambique, the ratio of those hungry and poor is high, but at the same time, 81 percent of the population is engaged in agriculture. The population is considered to be young (median age is 16.4 years old), growing, and rural. Generally, the young men move to urban settings to find work for which they are not well skilled and without adequate education. This leads to discontent and unrest. Some of this unrest manifested itself as riots in 2010, due to increasing food prices, and caused eventual development of the Action Plan for Reducing Poverty by the government (a plan to increase agricultural production and employment, which to date has yet to gather momentum or results).[358]

This exodus of young men from rural areas leaves women to raise their many children (fertility rates are 5.4 children per every female; over seven children per female in Niger) and manage all farm operations by themselves (50 to 60 percent of all Mozambique's farmers are women, typical of most sub-Saharan countries). With agriculture at only 29 percent of their GDP, 5.6 percent of all the country's land being cultivated, and most of their workforce engaged in farming, much growth in that sector is very possible. Instead of providing food for these people, it might be time to provide them with the necessary tools to become sustainable on many fronts—then *they will be able to provide food for themselves.*[359]

Subsistence, pastoral-swidden farming is most commonly practiced in nearly all sub-Saharan countries, including Mozambique, where an individual or family slashes and burns an area, then cultivates, harvests, and moves on to another tract of land they do not own. The soil is typically left depleted, eroded, and deforested, and any use of animals simply depletes their resource more significantly. All land in Mozambique is owned by the government, but leases can be arranged through them and kept for a period of time, usually five years but sometimes as long as ninety-nine years.

In the past twenty years, foreign investors have bought land (actually, they have established lease arrangements with the Mozambique government) under the guise of helping to eliminate poverty and hunger. However, it has been shown that many are simply using the land as an investment for shareholders or private sector investors (pension funds and private equity groups) or to establish commercial agricultural operations that will bring them a return. It is argued that this will eventually create a trickle-down effect to improve the economic status of the Mozambique people. Many observers, including many Mozambique citizens, have referred to this as simply "land grabbing." The practice has become so significant that the World Bank, IFC, and others have become involved and have even attempted to create regulatory measures and a rating system for these endeavors, referred to as "responsible agriculture investments." With mounting reports of dispossession, violence, and acts of ethnic and social injustice, land grabbing as well as a regulatory agency or system to control it is being met with skepticism and resentment from the locals— understandably so. There are numerous reports of promises made by land-grabbing entities that are never kept—agreements to economically reimburse the locals for the use of land and crops that were taken.[360]

Estimates of how much land in developing countries has been procured by foreign investors range from 150 million to over 400 million acres. The land in African countries is procured by large businesses to set up their operations for timber, mining, and agriculture that is predominately meat-based—pork, beef, poultry, dairy, and crops to feed them. Land O' Lakes International Development is just one of many examples where funding was provided by the USDA for them to implement a forty-two-month (2008 to 2012) dairy and livestock development program in Mozambique's Manica Province. This intent of this initiative was to build the dairy and beef industry in that country, but it was at the expense of the Mozambique people and their resources.[361]

Other projects include $32 million committed by AGRA for developing the Biera Corridor for produce but also livestock. This is part of a $165 million grant established by the Bill and Melinda Gates Foundation that provides seeds and fertilizer to areas in Mozambique and eleven other sub-Saharan countries through the year 2014. AGRA is promoting use of the Integrated Soil Fertility Management (ISFM), helping build the fertilizer supply chain to improve yields. The best methods to improve yields (as more properly defined with a long-term, soil-rebuilding view) are with fully plant-based food systems that employ cover crops, crop rotations, and agroforestry concepts. Although a portion of the seeds provided and sections of the ISFM are plant-based, a significant amount of their efforts (and the $165 million grant) are in support of seeds for feed crops, recycling of animal fertilizer, and continued livestock predominance.[362]

The short- and long-term solution to the hunger and poverty cycle appears to lie in connecting most of the dots for the people themselves. Commercial farming isn't "one" answer, as many suggest; it's "the" answer. Small farmers relying solely on the subsistence model find themselves cemented in perpetual poverty. Establishing for-profit agricultural protocols ("commercial farming") for smallholder farmers will need to be an integral part of any successful program in the developing countries of Africa but not with the use of livestock or as a subordinated appendage of some multinational corporation. It becomes an issue of *how* the commercial farming model is to be framed, regarding the following:

- Land tenureship issues
- What and how business enterprises and opportunities will be developed
- The role of the smallholder farmer, particularly the women farmers, for themselves, their communities, and as part of larger entities such as cooperatives
- How the land is best used
- The role of those providing support
- Who benefits from profits

The goal of any project involving land to reduce hunger and poverty should be to develop a program with all of the above in mind but emphasizing that the highest degree of relative sustainability cannot be achieved in Mozambique or anywhere else in the world without a commitment to fully plant-based food production systems. It also must be realized that either a top-down or bottom-up approach will likely not work long term. A top-down approach, advocated by Obama, many Western leaders, and large agriculture businesses of establishing (with G8 support) industrial, animal-based systems will not be resource-efficient, build soil, create healthy food products, or ensure social and economic justice. A bottom-up micro-approach was advocated in a 2012 APP report by Kofi Annan, one of the board members of the recently launched Alliance for Green Revolution in

Africa (AGRA), an organization dealing with development of agricultural products of the continent and supported by the Bill and Melinda Gates Foundation and the Rockefeller Foundation. This approach also would not likely be successful in lifting the veil of poverty, because it upgrades but keeps subsistence farming as the base and perhaps impedes vertical growth economically. One concern all African nations need to address is the fragmenting of trade that currently exists. A World Bank report in 2012 revealed that African countries are losing out on billions of dollars in trade earnings annually because of high-trade restrictions among neighboring countries. It is easier for most African countries to trade with the rest of the world than the nation next door. This will have to change.[363]

It makes sense to create commercial farming viability, but not in our conventional way of thinking. In the U.S., the method of commercial farming (industrialized, animal-based food production/agricultural systems) will not be in their best interest. It hasn't been in our best interest.

The people of Mozambique, and those of any developing country who find themselves in a hunger/poverty cycle while having the vast majority of their workforce engaged in farming, need to have a way to farm to make money, truly living off the land. The best manner in which to do this is to encourage local and foreign governments to create avenues of support by way of policy change and grant funding, education, and functional aspects—much of this provided through and by appropriately experienced NGOs and guided by the principles of IAN. This umbrella of funding by governments and NGOs, as well as the conceptual support by IAN, would supervise projects that would establish tracts of land, 5,000 to 10,000 acres in size, as cooperative farms, each divided into 1.5- to 2-acre lots of land (the optimal size for each family or individual to efficiently operate). Each 1.5- to 2-acre lot produces a variety of plant foods more intensively cultivated for a commercial purpose but also provides subsistence (much like the small family farm we see in the U.S. in this regard). All subdivided lots would operate under the same set of organic, plant-based (agroforestry) parameters, and the harvested food items would be initially bought by an organization that is aligned with the parent organizer and the ideals of the project. This would provide market assurances and sales. Following the establishment of a consistent chain of distribution and sales, this aspect of the program would be transferred to the locals, as would all functional aspects of the project. This would serve a greater purpose than an outside institution simply providing funding.

Inherent in this model is providing the communities with initial assistance with methods and technologies, supplies, seeds, and proper education. Farming techniques would be employed to rebuild topsoil and increase yields for short-term gain (immediate positive impact) and with a long-term vision. It needs to be kept in mind that organic methods of growing plants and building soil typically realize, on average, 150 percent increase in yields of crops within the first year of operation, with some areas experiencing 400 percent increases. Also, these methods will develop soil fertility, ensuring consistent future plant growth and high production for the longer term. Instead of extensive pastoral grazing, farming intensity could be increased by use of intercropping, multiple competing crops grown in an agroforestry manner, and reforestation. The primary goal of any project to eradicate hunger and poverty in developing countries should be to have created a tangible, lasting, positive impact to be realized by and for the citizens of that country. The model I am proposing will accomplish this.

A cooperative of this type could be owned by all members of the 10,000-acre tract and be operated in a manner that creates harmony and prosperity at all levels and for all growers—community capitalism.

Focus would be on developing product value chain, thriving family farms, economic incentive zones for added employment levels and opportunities for lateral and vertical growth, and training and broad-based education. Assured markets for the produce must be in place and can be arranged by the directing program and assisting NGOs. Types of produce grown can be both traditional and high-value crops (typical for that particular area and that have existing local and regional markets) such as cassava, yam, and coconut, and a small percentage could be a unique, niche, high-value products, such as gogi berries, chia and sacha inchi seeds, certain green leafy vegetables, coconut water drinks, or ancient grains. All products need to be adequately marketed and sold through fair trade and organic channels and with inclusion of international destinations. Physical and economic corridors for markets must be secured that would streamline and assure seed-to-plate (or farm-to-retailer) efficiencies and success. With such high incidence of malnutrition, HIV, and many illnesses, a nutritional subsistence program for the local community could be established, utilizing the crops produced and the many health benefits the plant-based foods will provide.

Local discipline experts could be developed for supervision of the project for all categories and layers—agricultural/environmental, administration, marketing, social, educational. Continuing education and improvement would be embedded into training for an added level of success and eventually, these experts would transition into leaders of the cooperative effort as the original program directors withdraw, once adequate traction has been realized.

With this project model, smallholders in any developing country will reap many benefits and realize short-term wins and long-term objectives—building soil fertility, improved education (agriculture, nutrition/health, business, and basic), improved status for women (currently at 60 percent illiteracy in many of these countries in Africa), open micro-financing and entrepreneurial opportunities, land ownership (ninety-nine-year tenureship with government), improved economic status, and improved nutrition. Stratification of the term "sustainable" will be realized by creating a higher degree of relative sustainability in the area of human health and wellness, economic, environmental, social, and agricultural and food security sustainability.

Unemployment is published at 27 percent in Mozambique (2012), but rates of labor force participation are three to four times that, indicating a willingness to work but not being able to find full-time employment and settling for one or many part-time jobs.

Approximately 75 percent of the Mozambique population is under thirty-five years of age, with 300,000 new entrants into the labor market every year, so there is great opportunity for rural youth food producers as well as women farmer associations in their country.[364]

The effects of increased global warming and climate change will be most felt by those in developing countries, where drought and heat waves exacerbate existing water scarcity and food security issues. It is predicted that as the global population reaches 9 billion by 2050, per capita meat consumption will rise (driven by much higher meat-per-person rates in developing countries), and therefore land and feed increases will be necessary to support the raising of additional livestock. It is generally agreed that crop yields have leveled off with limited land in developed countries leaving the burden of growing food to feed the world in the hands of land-rich developing countries—thus, the burgeoning interest in land grabbing and thrusting our mechanized, industrial animal-based farming methods into areas such as the sub-Saharan. Whether these countries remain farming with current slash-and-burn techniques or convert to Western agribusiness methods, their contribution to global GHG emissions will only increase. Nearly 100 percent of carbon equivalent GHG emissions from the agricultural sector in developing nations come from burning savannah, conversion of forest and grassland to pastures, and directly from livestock. In order to reduce further increases in anthropogenic GHG emissions, it will be mandatory to employ no-till, intercropping techniques, planting trees and eliminating livestock. Each tree seedling planted will typically take 110 pounds of CO_2 out of our atmosphere per year, times fifty years of its growth.

Improved productivity and economic growth and lessened effect on climate change could be expected with reforestation efforts included in a plant-based redesign of agricultural systems—benefits that should span rural to urban areas and encourage investment in this type of sustainable smallholder combined reforestation agriculture.

The Millennium Challenge Corporation (MCC) is an independent U.S. foreign aid agency providing assistance to developing countries to reduce global poverty. MCC plays a critical role in the U.S. government's approach to assisting countries in their efforts to achieve the Millennium Development Goals.

In July 2007, MCC signed a five-year compact with the Mozambique government that hopes to spur economic growth in four northern provinces of their country by way of a number of projects (sanitation, roads, business regulation, and agriculture). Many of the hunger/poverty reduction objectives of MCC and other organizations are based on the Millennium Development Goals (MDG), benchmarks set forth by the United Nations in 2000 to reduce those suffering from hunger and poverty to half by the year 2015. While the MDG agenda has garnered support to increase international assistance for basic needs of African countries, it has been relatively unsuccessful in achieved results and constructive contribution to development strategies. Inherent in poverty-reduction schemes must be the inclusion of for-profit ventures and improved labor markets into sustainable agricultural systems. These concepts and the statistical data to support them are generally lacking in the MDG and therefore in the efforts put forth by MCC and many other poverty-, hunger-, and eco-agricultural-driven organizations. Until purely plant-based production systems are positioned at the nucleus of a multidimensional approach like the one I have outlined here, it is predictable that attempts at eliminating hunger and poverty in the developing countries of Africa will remain futile. Any private or governmental-sponsored land acquisition used in an industrialized or otherwise livestock-driven manner will predictably make matters worse—ecologically, socially, politically, and from a human health perspective.[365]

One scientist with whom I discussed these model concepts asked me, "How do you know this is in the best interest of the people of a developing country? The people in that country may not want what you think they need."

My response was that we certainly don't want to impose our belief system on them or presume to know everything that may be in their best interest, given the subjectivity of that presumption. However, there are two precepts we can feel comfortable with when prescribing this purely plant-based agricultural model for a project in a developing country:

- All people have certain recognized inalienable rights—to food, water, and a just way of life, the security of which this project will provide.
- The people in developing countries (or anywhere on earth, for that matter) should not impose on us by emitting GHG, erosion

of soil, burning and degradation of forests or savannah, extracting scarce water out of aquifers and surface sources, or by excessive use of resources they may be "borrowing" from future generations. If there is another, truly more sustainable way of approaching agriculture, then it would be in everyone's best interest to have us assist them in implementation.

At the end of the day, if we are able to show them what foods are in their best interest to eat, how to rebuild their soil, and set them on a course of true multidimensional sustainability, then we have been successful. What they decide to do with this new knowledge and skill set is up to them. As my adapted version of the well-known Chinese proverb would say, *Give someone suffering from hunger some bread, and he will eat it for a day. Teach that person how to grow teff and kale, and he will eat for the rest of his life. (And most likely, so will his village.)*

Mozambique ranks 184th of 187 countries listed in the International Human Development Index, a rating system measuring development by combining indicators of life expectancy, educational attainment, and income into a composite index. Mozambique has a lower ranking than earthquake- and poverty-stricken Haiti, war-torn Afghanistan, and the largely starving, poor, and highly illiterate countries of Bangladesh and Ethiopia.[366]

The United Nations Human Development Programme states, "Understanding the links between environmental sustainability and equity is critical if we are to expand human freedoms for current and future generations." Perhaps the most critical of these "links" is a purely plant-based agricultural system. Once this link is recognized and acted upon, then improved human development and expansion of human freedoms can be assured.[367]

Wouldn't it be ironic if Mozambique, Ethiopia, Eritrea, or any of the other sub-Saharan areas could be an example for the rest of the world, showing a developing country such as the U.S. how to successfully develop a truly more sustainable agricultural plant-based food-production system and improve human development as a result?

Eco-tax and health-risk tax combination

As a civilization, we have gone too long without recognizing the relationship between economics and natural resources that we use. Land, topsoil, and many sources of freshwater are not easily replaced in our lifetime, certain energy and mineral resources are not renewable, our atmosphere and oceans are not indestructible, and biodiversity can be lost forever. Because of this, two questions of management arise:

1. Should these resources that essentially belong to the earth be considered free for anyone to use?
2. Is it right that individuals or businesses that implement the most energy and resource-efficient measures be penalized economically?

Since our resources are not inexhaustible, yet are indispensible for our survival, it is time they be treated as precious commodities and prices affixed relative to their use. If the full economic value of our ecosystems were reflected in the price of animal products, global depletion could be slowed or even reversed, because no one could afford to pay for these products. Instead of conservation measures costing more (higher prices for energy-efficient appliances, solar-powered items, organic food, etc.), incentives should be in place to reduce their cost while conversely, industries using the most of our resources should pay more—resource-intensive industries such as those that produce meat, dairy, and fish items.

When a corporate responsibility statement (CRS) includes environmental stewardship, what does that really mean? How is that translated into quantifiable, functional action, something meaningful to the planet? It seems rhetoric is all we have.

In the future, businesses will continue to find that it makes sense to address sustainability from a marketing view and, eventually, with functional aspects. Some enterprises will simply realize long-term benefits in energy-cost savings. It is improbable that all businesses and industries will convert to the most sustainable methods of practice on their own. The meat, dairy, and fishing industries, as I have pointed out, are the sectors most responsible for combined global depletion, yet they are the least likely to change over to the most efficient operations, because that would mean they wouldn't exist.

Economic and financial interventions provide powerful instruments to regulate the use of ecosystems goods and services. There are many opportunities for this to occur and then effectively influence human behavior, but economic tools and market mechanisms are effective only when supporting institutions and governmental policies are in place. I feel the most promising approach to externalizations of costs would include a combination or all of the following interventions, particularly as this relates to food choice and production systems:

1. Establish appropriate economic value to all resources and ecosystems services and "excessive use" norms.
2. Eliminate all subsidies that have the highest degree of promotion for global depletion.
3. Develop a payment system for resource use.
4. Create taxation for excessive use.
5. Create consumer and general public education programs, K-12, and academic institution enlightenment mandates as to true or relative sustainability.
6. Create market incentives and governmental support for fully plant-based foods, such as certification of "highest degree of sustainability," or "lowest global footprint," or "low resource impact," etc.
7. Increase subsidies to industries, growers, and developing countries engaged in fully organic plant-based food-production systems.
8. Once the above are adopted, there needs to be strong leadership, representation, and policy change by the United States and other aligned nations to influence and encourage similar reform globally.

What is the cost of the trillions of gallons of freshwater taken from ancient (essentially nonrenewable) water sources by the livestock industry each year in our country? What would it take to replace 2,000-year-old sections of Peruvian rainforest that were clear-cut for grazing cattle? If we all suffer from the effects of climate change, why shouldn't those who contribute to it the most pay for those excessive GHG emissions? Once economic values are affixed to ecosystem goods and services, then development and application of payment strategies can begin. Having a comparison to the most efficient plant-based food-production systems (some use no irrigation and minimal land) will lead to development of excess or overuse taxation schedules. Animal agriculture is responsible for 78 percent of all inland streams and river pollution and the majority of dead zones formation (especially the most well-known dead zone off in the Gulf of Mexico), so apply 78 percent of the entire cost of an expedited cleanup effort to the animal agriculture industry. I would guess this would amount to trillions of dollars, although it would be impossible to perform an immediate and 100 percent restoration to original status of the water and ecosystems. And similar taxation schedules should be applied for pollution on land, in our atmosphere, and with GHG emissions as well as for loss of terrestrial and oceanic biodiversity. The livestock and fishing industries are responsible for 45 percent of all land use and destruction of natural habitat on land and 100 percent of loss of all species in our oceans. Make the producers, businesses, and consumers of animal products all pay for "excess use" or damages beyond what the most efficient plant-based systems are generating. There needs to be a clear economic acceptance of responsibility for ecosystem/ natural resource pollution and overuse.

Government subsidies paid to agricultural sectors of OECD countries average over $400 billion annually, which contribute to the livestock and fishing industries leading to promotion of overuse of fertilizers, pesticides, land, water, and further global depletion.

Plant-based systems in the U.S. and developing countries should be assisted with economic incentives to help with initial traction, to moderate food prices (until scaled production increases occur to keep prices lower), and to ensure long-term viability. Carbon offset programs could be sped up and enhanced by encouraging growers to incorporate reforestation wherever possible.

Positive change in consumer food preferences can only be achieved with increased awareness, so educational protocols need to be in place, and then incentives created and supported for market expression of more sustainable plant-based options.

In order for the U.S. or any other country to attain a more relative sustainable position, I would encourage complete elimination of all subsidies that promote the raising and consumption any animal product (livestock, fish, dairy, eggs) due to the implication in global depletion on all fronts. We are currently paying money to our government so they can pay farmers to overuse our resources and abuse our environment. Establishment of an eco-tax would inhibit this abuse while at the same time generate revenues to reduce our national debt.

As we continue to demand more meat, dairy, and fish products to eat in our country, we are closing our eyes to the true costs to produce those animal products—whether here in the U.S. or in other countries. Until we recognize, appreciate, and affix the true value of the resources and health implications of eating animals, irreversible losses on many fronts will continue to occur. We need to impose an eco-tax and health-risk tax on all animal products that are produced, purchased from other countries, and sold to consumers who want to continue eating them. Accountability is long overdue.

Pet food

The majority of individuals in the world are comfortably unaware of the environmental impact of their food choices. Additionally, those who are dog caretakers aren't aware that the dog food industry is simply an extension of the human food and agriculture industries. The cows, pigs, turkeys, chickens, and fish that are raised and killed for us to eat are the same ones that end up in a bag of dog food. Therefore, a life-cycle analysis of the ingredients of commercially prepared dog food would reveal similar unsustainable systems and resource usage. With over 80 million dog owners in the U.S., it makes sense that we all pay more attention to where the food we feed our dogs comes from and what the real cost to our environment might be.

Over 98 percent of all livestock in the U.S. are given feed, every fish produced in aquaculture is given feed (fish farms, which are now responsible for 50 percent of all fish consumed in the world), and every dog is given feed. Nearly all of these feed types contain fishmeal, while dog food contains fishmeal, meat, and other rendered dead animal products. Thirty percent of all wild-caught fish from our oceans are ground up into fishmeal and fish oil that are then fed to other fish, poultry, pigs, cows, dogs, and cats. *Eight million tons* of fish each year are taken from our oceans for the sole purpose of using in our cat and dog food.[368,369]

Pelagic fish, such as menhaden, anchovy, sardine, and herring, are extracted from our oceans more than any other fish. Most of these fish are ground up and reduced to fishmeal and fish oil and used as dietary supplements, fertilizer, farm animal feed, and pet food. Last year, 44 percent of all fishmeal produced in the world was given to livestock and put into pet food. In the U.S., as well as elsewhere in the world, fishmeal and fish oil are typically used along with other dead animal products, such as ground-up bone, blood, feathers, and dead poultry and mixed into the pet food you are feeding your dogs. In the dog food industry, these ingredients are known as the "4 D's": dead, diseased, disabled, or dying. Each year, about 3 million tons of these ground-up animal parts, called "animal protein" or "meat by-products" by the industry, are put into commercial dog foods such as Purina, Pedigree, Iams, Science Diet, and nearly all others. Powerful and harmful preservatives such as ethoxyquin are used in these commercial dog foods to keep any dead animal products from becoming rancid. Iams is one of many such dog foods that requires ethoxyquin due to its use of high amounts of fish products.[370,371]

Because of the universal use of slaughtered or harvested animals and their parts, all commercial dog foods, excluding those made solely from plant sources (vegan dog foods), contribute to global depletion of our planet's resources in an unsustainable fashion. The individual animals that those parts originally belonged to had to be fed, watered, and given land directly or for feed crops to be grown. Fossil fuel was used and greenhouse gases were produced in the raising, slaughtering, rendering, processing, refrigeration, packaging, and transporting of those animals and their parts used in dog food. Whether it is "meat by-products" derived from cattle and pigs, "animal protein" derived from a combination of animal parts, or fishmeal, commercial dog food's contribution to climate change and unnecessary use of our natural resources is significant. Authors Robert and Brenda Vale calculated that feeding a medium-size dog has twice the environmental impact as driving a Toyota Land Cruiser over 6,000 miles per year, with the vast majority of this impact attributed solely to the meat used in the commercially produced dog food fed to the dog.[372]

The meat, dairy, and fishing industries have become quite powerful and are in a position to manipulate the political and economic aspects of our food systems. Many of the very same businesses that comprised by these industries—large corporations that produce and influence our food choices—are the very same ones that manufacture most of the global supply of dog food. Over 80 percent of the dog food industry is dominated by only a handful of players: Nestle (which bought out Purina), Del Monte (Meow Mix, Gravy Train, Kibbles 'n Bits, 9Lives), Mars/MasterFoods (Royal Canin, Pedigree), Proctor and Gamble (Iams), and Colgate-Palmolive (Hills Science Diet). With almost $20 billion sales per year in the U.S. alone, these companies have clear economic motives without much regard for optimal or relative sustainability as a metric for success. If they have such regard, they wouldn't support the use of any animals in any of their products.

The way to turn all of this around and minimize the impact your dog has on our environment, of course, is to feed him or her only plant-based (vegan) dog food. One example of this is V-Dog food, produced in California by a family-owned business. From a nutritional standpoint, V-Dog food is quite beautifully formulated, and it uses no animals or animal by-products of any sort and has no GMO. It is gluten-free and hypoallergenic (a large percentage of dog allergens can be attributed to beef, chicken, and other animal proteins), and it even comes in a compostable bag. By using only plant-based sources and production system, V-Dog food is the most sustainable and compassionately packaged food to feed your dog. I am very encouraged by the example V-Dog food sets for the rest of the world's pet food producers and by the genuine stewardship of the family producing this product.

Almost all of the 25 million tons of pet food made in the world each year uses livestock, fish, and animal by-products from unwanted carcasses, filler materials, and subsidized ingredients. If you have a cat or dog and feed it a commercially produced food, you contribute to unsustainable food production practices that are diminishing our resources on land and in our oceans, as well as to climate change.

It makes sense for everyone to consider purchasing and feeding only 100 percent plant-based (vegan) dog food to their faithful companions— for their sake and that of our planet.

Rendering dead animal parts

One component of our inefficient agricultural system that shouldn't go unnoticed is the concomitant business of rendering. It represents just another in the long list of steps of wasted resources that comes with raising and eating animals. Even the cute free-range chicken and happy, grass-fed cow have body parts that are inedible and dangerous if not disposed of correctly. But instead of disposing, the meat industry has figured out a way to use more of our natural resources to recycle body parts and make money at the same time. Rendering plants perform one of the most complementing and necessary functions for modern slaughterhouses. They recycle dead animals, slaughterhouse wastes, and rejected supermarket animal parts into various products known as recycled meat, bone meal, and animal fat. These products are sold as a source of protein and other nutrients in the diets of dairy animals, poultry, pigs, pet foods, cattle feed, and sheep feed. During the slaughtering process, 43–45 percent by weight of the killed animal is removed and discarded as waste—body parts including fat trim, muscle and ligaments, bone, organs, blood, and feathers of poultry. These materials are collected and processed by the rendering industry; treated to kill the many bacteria, viruses, parasites, and other pathogens; and then put back into the animal and human food supply, now called bone or blood meal, meat by-products, animal protein, or simply "natural ingredients." The rendering process kills salmonella, BSE (bovine spongiform encephalopathy) and other food pathogens, but researchers admit that post-process contamination can still occur with many pathogens as well as chemicals and hormones.

Although not established in all countries, rendering plants perform a necessary function of limiting the accumulation of unprocessed animal parts that would impede meat industries and pose more serious hazard than we already have to human and environmental health. Over 67 million tons per year of processed rendered animal by-products are fed back to animals in the meat and dairy industries, pet foods, and our own food and supplements. More than 3 million tons of bone and blood meal are used annually in the U.S., and it is expected to increase substantially as rendered animal by-products are fed to fish grown on fish farms. Rendering plants waste more of our valuable resources to manage the waste caused by slaughtering, which is a wasted endeavor itself, killing animals that have been vessels of wasted resources while being raised.[373,374]

Urban agriculture

Globally, there are over 4 billion people living in cities. Over 80 percent in the U.S. are considered urban dwellers, so urban agriculture is becoming attractive and an important system to develop—how to grow food efficiently within large city settings with limited space and resources. Individuals and businesses are already growing food on porches, windowsills, and rooftops in many metropolitan areas of the world. It is encouraging to see the innovations as they are being made. You can't grow a cow up there.

Melbourne, Australia, is home to an established urban farm operation called CERES (Centre for Education and Research in Environmental Strategies) Community Environment Park, which is successfully producing locally directed food and education, as well as looped, renewable energy systems. Not surprisingly, their success is based on growing plant-based foods. It began in 1982 at what used to be a garbage dump. The site needed major cleanup and soil-building efforts and now is a working urban agriculture model for cities worldwide, with an outreach program in India. The founder of CERES feels that although individual homeowners can learn things from their operations, the overall model is more for institutions such as schools to follow.

CERES grows high-value and fast-growing greens, leeks, and herbs all year, harvesting over 40,000 pounds of produce per acre per year, which is distributed through their market, café, and CERES Fair Food home delivery, reaching 15 miles into the community. CERES generates income by way of enterprise stacking (non-farm but related business endeavors) to cover operating expenses, while capital investment is covered by government and philanthropic grants.[375]

Joe Nasr, coauthor of *Carrot City: Creating Places for Urban Agriculture*, feels New York City is the leader in terms of rooftop commercial agriculture. Urban farming operations there have shown to be prosperous, with a rapid increase in markets and ancillary benefits for the city. Rooftop farms can capture millions of gallons of storm water, diverting it from the city's sewer system. Harvesting and distribution allows for fewer trucks on local roads, lessening congestions and GHG emissions. Gotham Greens, Brooklyn Grange, and BrightFarms are just some of the enterprises converting rooftops into thriving greenhouses.

Gotham Greens in New York City generates 100 tons of green leafy produce per year in a 15,000-square-foot area on a rooftop. They grow year-round by way of hydroponics and sell to local retailers and restaurants. At Hunts Point in the Bronx, plans are under way to build what may be the world's largest rooftop farm—200,000 square feet—growing plants. As cities become more populated, this type of innovative urban farming will become even more critical.

It makes no sense to integrate livestock into urban and rooftop settings. The only animal species necessary, as with rural agricultural operations, may be bees, to assist with pollination. All other animals will simply use space, water, and feed that could be used for humans directly, while creating waste and increasing the risk of contamination by pathogens. I view the successful agricultural systems found in urban settings as models, projecting an example of how we should manage food production with increasing concentrations of people in a finite amount of space—the planet, perhaps, as one large city.

Lisa Taylor, director of Seattle Tilth's Children Education Program and author of *The Urban Farm*, has a beautiful concept of teaching children, parents, and other Seattle community members about growing food within an urban environment. The program she and other Seattle Tilth team members have developed could be considered a model that other cities in our country should follow—all but one aspect. Through her book and program, she encourages the raising of animals, which then undermines her efforts. In doing so, Ms. Taylor has missed a perfect opportunity to create an awareness of global depletion. For all the good her book and program offers, it fails to address foodborne illnesses—there is no mention of the various pathogens her audience will be subjected to (salmonella, shigella, campylobacter, E. coli, etc.), as well as the inefficient use of any space, food, water, and air while raising the chickens, rabbits, and ducks that limit fostering advancement of a more sustainable food system in our country. And certainly all animals raised in an urban environment are not healthy for her readers to consume, and certainly it is not at all humane in terms of how those animals must be slaughtered. One of the many questions I posed to her was "Do you really wish for all your children readers to raise baby rabbits, name them, care for them on a daily basis, and then kill one of these rabbits, bleed and skin it, and then eat it?" Unfortunately, that process isn't the healthiest and most peaceful food-producing system that could be taught to our children. We need to move beyond the cultural constraints that cause academic restriction on books, authors, and community leaders.

We need to think seriously about what I call "Conversion Permaculture," which is essentially a form of "agroforestry" with chaotic plantings applied. Instead of a fertilizer dump and water drain, I think everyone's grass lawns should be converted to functional green spaces and natural habitats, centered around a food-producing garden. Just one row of bean plants would be fine, although growing many edible plants is preferred. This would mean, of course, no grass—unless it is wheat grass. In arid or desert settings, you could grow edible cactus or other desert plants that can be eaten and in other regions of the country, simply grow any of many food-producing plants that could naturally grow in that location. Since awareness and motivation for adopting the most sustainable food practices is weak, let's encourage policy makers to create incentives for compliance to a purely plant-based permaculture conversion.

There has been tremendous progress lately with increased public awareness of the ill effects of factory farming. As a start, this is a good thing. But for every bit of progress this seems to be, there is an equally strong message tagging insidiously along with it, telling everyone that it's still perfectly fine to continue raising, slaughtering, and eating billions of animals, only now instead of with factory farms, we can accomplish it by using pastures, small farms, and our oceans—and we can conveniently hide behind the word "sustainable." That's the message we are hearing. What we don't hear, of course, is that we are still hurting the animals, our planet, and ourselves.

Our current agricultural systems are inefficient and need to be changed. That's because there is a demand to eat meat, dairy, and eggs that creates production methods that drain our resources, energy, and time, and our health is jeopardized after consumption. It will take a significant shift in awareness, policy change (with taxation and incentives), and effort by all stakeholders to complete the transition to organic and purely plant-based mode of producing and eating food. Current farms in the U.S. could change operations from animal-based to plant-based, supported by an appropriately modified Farm Bill and increased demand for plant foods by an aware and appreciative public. American farmers would wake up every morning, knowing they are rebuilding and restoring, rather than tearing down, depleting, and killing. Doing so, we would, in fact, be more sustainable on many levels.

By 2050, we will see 9 billion people in the world. It is predicted that meat consumption will dramatically increase, which will stress the ecosystem goods and services necessary to produce it, particularly in developing countries where growth is most expected but least capable of support. The movement for food is toward grass-fed meat, seafood that a few organizations are telling us is "sustainable," land-produced aquaculture, community supported agriculture, and locally grown. However, the only agricultural food-production systems that will achieve optimal relative sustainability are those adopting organic plant-based methods. Our survival may ultimately depend on our ability to recognize this.

8

Animals and Biodiversity

"Nonviolence is the essence of all religions." —Gandhi

MOST OF US know of the atrocities of factory farms—what happens to animals in concentrated or confined animal feeding operations (CAFOs). It is appalling. So it seems logical to move the animals we raise to eat away from factory farms into more "humane" settings—where, before we slaughter and eat them, these animals are allowed to breathe fresh air and live outdoors in as near a "natural" setting as possible. That would make us all feel better about how the animals live and would provide a form of emotional justification for us to continue eating them, wouldn't it?

What about killing them, though? How does that fit in to this new theme of being "humane"? Is it ethical for us to slaughter another living being, whether it lived in a comfortable manner or not? And what about the killing act itself? Even if we don't slaughter the animal ourselves, aren't we all, essentially, accomplices? Should we feel morally or ethically comfortable by asking someone else to kill an animal and cut it up so we can then eat it? Is this the right thing to do? Should we be eating animal *products* (such as eggs or dairy products) that were produced where the animal source was abused and slaughtered (or not abused and still slaughtered) and where heavy, unsustainable contributions to global depletion continued? Where do fish fit into this global depletion/humane situation? Clearly, it is no longer a factory farm issue; it's a raising-animals-to-eat issue.

About the words "humane" and "ethics"

What is the ethos by which our society lives, by which the few generations occupying Earth for the previous hundred years will be remembered? Is *ahimsa* ("to do no harm") possible for the world to follow? How each of us treats the other and all living beings should be fundamental to our existence—what we do, say, think. To not hurt, injure, or kill another living being should be at the core of that ethos. This rule of consciousness has been with us for thousands of years and has been the basis of spiritual ethics, regardless of which religion one follows.

When you eat any animal, there first was a raising process and a killing process. This has to take place with all animal operations and may seem obvious, but for those who support grass-fed, local, sustainable seafood, real-food, cage-free, organic, or humane animal products, it's as if there mysteriously becomes no resource depletion or killing involved.

Many organizations are attempting to use the word "humane" to market their animal products as sustainable. Indeed, from a branding and marketing standpoint, it is working. A USDA study revealed that 75 percent of meat purchasers indicated that their meat purchases would be influenced by the word "humane." In early 2012, I was asked to speak at the University of California, Berkeley, as part of a conference on "Conscious Eating." During my standard practice of researching the food policy at each university where I speak, I came across a perplexing statement in UC Berkeley's Policy on Sustainable Practices. Listed as one of the criteria by which the policy defined sustainable food was the designation "Certified Humane Raised & Handled."

So the definition at UC Berkeley of "humane raised" is "sustainable"—one and the same.

That is interesting news to me, because you can "raise" thousands of termites "humanely" in the privacy of your own home, but it won't be so "sustainable" when one day they have destroyed your house.

This confusion of such important food terms is disappointing when it occurs anywhere but particularly at an institution such as UC Berkeley, a university that prides itself as a leader and at the cutting edge of knowledge. Yet there it was, spelled out in the black-and-white of their policy. How could this have happened?

The words "humane" and "sustainable" obviously are not interchangeable, but use of these words does imply a more socially acceptable manner of eating food. Use of both words has become ubiquitous—we can stamp either word on just about anything and assume that provides us with justification for slaughtering animals, despite the fact that it may not be humane or sustainable at all.

The particular difficulty with these definitions is due to an information source dictating that a certain food choice is sustainable or humane. So the reference point and eventual actions based on that reference become dependent on this other source—on the informational and philosophical platform of another entity. UC Berkeley and other institutions and organizations simply are relying on advisors or consultant (e.g., organization, author, consulting firm), trusting that the base of information is accurate, when, in fact, many times it is not.

There are two primary categories for the source of information with regard to the word "humane." One category is the group of food movements (real food, grass-fed, local, cool foods, cage-free, humane raised) and those authors, lecturers, policy makers, and others of influence who advocate these movements and who, collectively, have convinced us that humane and sustainable are interchangeable concepts. The other category is from the group of organizations that are the genuine "humane" certifiers—Humane Farm Animal Care (HFAC), the American Meat Institute (AMI), the Food Safety Inspection Service of the USDA (FSIS), the Food Alliance, Animal Welfare Association (AWA). These are the organizations that are at the top of the supervisory hill that serve to govern "humane" standards as they apply to animals used for food. Each bestows its own certificate of compliance, but all of these organizations and their criteria for what is considered "humane" are based on the work—and therefore, belief system—of one person: Temple Grandin. Every animal raised and slaughtered that carries a certification of humane does so under the auspices of and philosophical doctrine conceived by Dr. Grandin. For instance, the HFAC is quick to point out that it is "endorsed by thirty-eight humane organizations," but the HFAC guidelines for animal handling and slaughter are based entirely on Dr. Grandin's principles and philosophies—and so are all thirty-eight of the organizations that endorse HFAC. This presents a significant display of subjectivity added to the already subjective topic of how one can kill another living being in a "humane" manner. Thinking that a technique to slaughter a pig might be *more* humane than another doesn't mean that it is fully humane. At best, it becomes an interpretive issue, based on many factors, including one's own belief system and acceptance of inflicting death or *degree* of suffering on another living creature. Temple Grandin's belief system regarding slaughtering and eating animals is quite different from mine—unfortunately, hers is the one that's universally accepted and followed.[376,377,378]

All humane-certification organizations, as well as food movements deferring to these organizations, use the term "humane raised" in their marketing efforts. Just because an animal was raised in a kind and cruel-free manner, however, doesn't imply that it was killed in a kind and cruel-free manner. In fact, how would you slaughter an animal in a "kind" manner? Many media sources have encouraged consumers to purchase meat products from humane-certified sources, with *USA Today* even referring to the Certified Humane Program as "the gold standard" for animal welfare. This, according to the program director, is because "producers that are certified meet our standards and apply them to animals from birth through slaughter."

I encourage everyone to follow a grass-fed animal as it's being led to slaughter, finish the act, and then tell me how "humane" it was.

When we all have agreed on the obvious need to include "humane *killed*" in this equation and that it really doesn't have anything to do with sustainability, then we will be able to move on to the next issue of subjectivity, which is how we allow the definitions and subsequent implementation to be so skewed.

And then, of course, there is the need to include fish in the discussion, which leads to acknowledgment of the existence of nociceptors (cells that detect pain). This, in turn, will lead to arguments related to how we define pain, which completes the circle of irrationality to why are we killing massive amounts of living beings, which clearly have sensory input and feelings but under the pretense that they don't. All this to create an anthropocentric form of justification for us to kill and eat something that eventually makes our planet and us unhealthy.

How did the words "humane" and "sustainable" become one and the same? First, there is the obviously improper defining and homogenizing of these two words by animal food-production industries and movements to further their products. Some of this improper defining is intentional (by the industry); some may not be intentional (by various food-movement leaders who simply aren't aware). Second, there is the actual definition of the term "humane" for the animal products used in the industry. Currently, the degree of humaneness is absolute and somehow measurable by organizations such as the American Meat Institute and Humane Farm Animal Care, which have developed and implemented humane certification programs. According to Jackie Sleeper, director of Certification for HFAC, all standards that their organization has set for compliance have been derived from AMI, which derived them from Dr. Grandin, as a one-person source. I find several problems with this:

1. Overall subjectivity of the definition of "humane"
2. A set of guidelines established and used as the gold standard for all methods and certification protocols that were derived from one person
3. Numerous flaws in the chain of steps, such as transporting, handling of the animals as they go off to slaughter, and the slaughtering process itself

The majority of all slaughtered livestock is sold across state lines, which mandates use of USDA-inspected and -governed slaughterhouses. Some large animals not destined for interstate commerce or resale and some small animals, such as poultry, can be slaughtered on the farm premises without USDA jurisdiction. Knowing then, that most of the 10 billion animals raised in the United States each year are killed in USDA plants, it is interesting to note that not one of the more than nine hundred slaughterhouses in the United States is HFAC-certified. According to Ms. Sleeper, HFAC does not certify slaughtering plants but will approve and certify the end-product "if the slaughterhouse used passes AMI guidelines at the time it is inspected." Additionally, when asked how a farm or meat product could be certified "humane" without monitoring humane handling during the loading, transporting, unloading, and pre-slaughter management of livestock, she responded, "You are right; transportation is pretty tricky right now."

Despite the presence of numerous inaccuracies in definition and monitoring systems, consumer interest and demand for meat that is "humane" is seeing tremendous growth. This is because there is a general misunderstanding of what "humane" means, and trust has been placed in the hands of supervisory certifying organizations (HFAC, USDA, and AMI), the food movements marketing that certification, and advocates of these movements. Ultimately, it ends up in sustainability policies of unsuspecting institutions such as UC Berkeley. HFAC began in 2003, certifying 144,000 animals raised by farms in accordance to guidelines established as standards and in their policy manual. In order to be certified as humane, meat has to be produced from animals raised, handled, cared for, and slaughtered in a manner considered humane by these certifying organizations. In 2011, HFAC certified more than 32 million animals, eighty-seven different businesses, and "thousands of farms," according to Ms. Sleeper. From 2010 to 2011, Humane Farm Animal Care saw a 20 percent increase in animal certifications and a 25 percent increase in companies being certified. I was told that any farm involved in the HFAC program would "welcome" a visit by nearly anyone interested in seeing firsthand how humane it is to raise a cow, pig, turkey, chicken, or other livestock. It makes sense that any supervisory organization, such as HFAC, as well as any farm that is certified "humane," would be quite proud of what it is accomplishing and therefore have no difficulty displaying its humane methods to everyone. Who wouldn't want to show or see a healthy cow, roaming leisurely around a lush grass pasture in the sun and fresh air? However, when I asked to see the last step of their "humane" process—slaughtering the animal—HFAC's answer was "I can't give you the names of any slaughterhouses our farms use. They do not want us to give that information out." Additionally, nearly all cage-free egg operations (such as the Ohio operations discussed in a previous chapter), or range-free turkey, pig, or grass-fed farms that I contacted or visited refused access to their slaughtering process, even though I presented myself as a writer interested in promoting sustainable and humane food systems in the United States. HFAC encourages visitors to see how humane certified animals are raised— no problem. But none of their member farms felt comfortable letting me see their humane transport and slaughtering processes.[379]

Although admirable attempts have been made to structure sustainable food-service practices at UC Berkeley (as seen in many other institutions worldwide), there is a clear problem with their **definition of terms**.

It is difficult to structure a set of precepts or an entire doctrine around a term (in this case, "sustainable") that individuals or organizations have defined when they lack full understanding themselves.

Those who see the "humane" raising and killing of animals as "sustainable" potentially make two distinct mistakes:

1. Accepting various organizations' platform of what is "humane." This ultimately relies on an individual's interpretation of kind and compassionate treatment and not inflicting pain (emotional, mental, spiritual, or physical). The guidelines accepted as humane management of the animals we raise and eat then become a manifestation of what one person *believes* is humane—not what *is* humane.

2. Equating the word "humane" with "sustainable." I think the opposite should hold true—that the word "sustainable," if applied

correctly, should mean that you "sustain" the life of an animal, not kill it.

In my first book, *Comfortably Unaware*, I mentioned that there is an eerie paradox when a farmer raises a pig (or any animal)—feeding it and lovingly taking care of it, calling the pig by name every day—and then takes a gun, points it at the pig, and shoots it in the head. Worse, Dr. Grandin somehow deems this act "humane," and therefore, every organization that has positioned itself in a supervisory or certification capacity (USDA, AMI, HFAC, AWA, etc.) now follows her lead. It is her opinion (and therefore that of these associated organizations) that all animals can be raised and killed for us to eat in a kind and compassionate manner by shooting them in the head. It is also her opinion that it is humane to lead them to slaughter, regardless of the process implemented. This is odd, because I do not know one pig, cow, chicken, or any other animal that, if it had its choice, would want to be shot in the head and killed. With grass-fed, humane-raised animals, leading them to slaughter becomes the ultimate act of betrayal.

That very same animal the farmer raised in a humane fashion would have become the farmer's best friend, relying on the farmer for food, shelter, a calming voice, and companionship, and even looking forward to seeing the farmer each day. That grass-fed, humanely raised animal would have come to trust the farmer. I am quite sure that trusted friends wouldn't consider it humane to shoot their trusting buddies in the head and then eat them.

Dr. Grandin, diagnosed with autism as a toddler, has a life story filled with amazing accomplishments, and her determination to excel is to be applauded. In her own words, she has been afforded the "advantages of an autistic experience," because she sees the world in ways that many of us cannot. Dr. Grandin may even be able to recognize some animals' "special talents," as she claims. But I question whether she actually is able to "understand" animals, as she professes. And more important, why should the world follow her beliefs and suggestions about animals, as well as her guidelines regarding the slaughtering of animals? It is not my intent to criticize Dr. Grandin; my criticism is for those who follow her. It really doesn't matter who Temple

Grandin is or anything about *her* life, because it is the animals' lives—and deaths—that are misunderstood. In following her advice, billions upon billions of animals are killed each year—as a result of our demand but clearly under her direction and those organizations that follow her lead.

New marketing factors, such as whether meat production is sustainable or humane, now drive the demand for meat in the United States. There are three categories of meat production on which the consumer relies for achieving a humane item:

- Are those products produced by the USDA under the Humane Animal Slaughter Act?
- Are those products derived from various recognized certification organizations?
- Are products assumed humane simply because they were raised and killed by small, local, organic, grass-fed operations?

The USDA has jurisdiction or regulatory control over the vast majority of slaughterhouses in the United States and has two levels of humane slaughter. The first was established in 1978, with influences by Temple Grandin, enacted as the Humane Slaughter Act. The second again was influenced by Dr. Grandin in 1996, whereby all slaughterhouses were to comply with new auditing measures, both self-regulated and with USDA auditors or auditors from restaurants, supermarkets, or other industries. Humane Farm Animal Care (HFAC) and the Animal Welfare Association (AWA) take the humane aspect one step farther by implementing steps and an auditing system to ensure that the animal was managed in a humane manner as it was raised on the farm, through all periods of handling, and throughout the slaughter process. The guidelines of HFAC and the USDA all follow those of the American Meat Institute (AMI), which were written by Temple Grandin. The primary AMI criteria for humane slaughter can be accounted for by measuring these issues: percent stunned, percent rendered insensible, percent prodded, percent vocalizing, percent slip or fall. Regarding vocalizing, Grandin explains, "If you get a moo, you score. If you don't, you score that," which bases a measure of how humane a slaughtering process is by way of listening for vocalizations. Mooing is not acceptable. She also states, "I've been in a plant where a prod is weak, and it really doesn't hurt the animal."[380,381]

We all know individuals who vocalize much less than others; cows are no different. Just because a cow is not vocalizing certainly does not mean that the cow is not in pain. As with humans and all animal species, individual variation in response characteristics surely can be found in cows. How does Temple Grandin know that the prod does not hurt the individual animal?

Grandin also states emphatically that "animals are afraid of darkness and dark places and will not go into them." That is not necessarily true. In fact, pigs love dark places and have no problem at all going into them, as long as they know they are safe. Every one of the numerous rescued pigs that have lived at my animal rescue and sanctuary over the past thirty-five years has a routine of walking quite comfortably through a small opening in the barn in the evenings, when it is very dark, and into their bed areas, which are in near complete darkness. They look forward to doing this, having no fear whatsoever. But that is the point: *they are not afraid.* What Dr. Grandin has noticed with her studies and observations is that pigs (as well as many other animals) are afraid of whatever she is doing to them, the new situation with which they are confronted, or perhaps the smell and sense of killing that has occurred numerous times before them. That is what causes their fear, not "the dark."[382]

The American Meat Institute places acceptable scores for audits at not less than 95 percent proper stunning upon the first attempt, and not more than 25 percent of animals had an electric prod used on them. USDA audits prior to 1996 displayed that only 30 percent of all slaughterhouses scored acceptable levels of properly stunned animals on first attempt and prodding frequency. Following McDonald's Corporation's initiative to audit slaughterhouses in 1996, studies have shown that now 91 percent of slaughterhouses meet the AMI acceptable levels. One would have to raise the question of how the AMI conducts these audits. For instance, are these unannounced, spontaneous audits, made without the plant knowing of the visit or having a chance to prepare, which would allow for the most unadulterated measurements?

In her many presentations, Dr. Grandin makes a very strong, if indirect and unintentional, case for *not* slaughtering animals. She goes to great lengths to describe the sensitivities of pigs and cows, referring to things that "bother" them. She encourages us to "get down into the chute on [our] knees to see what they see, what's bothering them, and why they vocalize." The "chute" refers to the winding passageway that she designed, now standard in all "humane" USDA slaughterhouses, meant for pigs to be coaxed along in a less stressful manner (according to Grandin) toward their death. During the process of leading these animals down through the chute, she relates that the animals are prone to frequently becoming distracted—by shadows, drains, unfamiliar faces, new wind patterns—which then causes them to balk. She also describes these animals' sensitivities to noises, requesting that there be "no yelling," loud noises or high-pitched sounds by human workers as the pigs are led through the chute.

In one of her many livestock handling instructional videos, Dr. Grandin points out that cows and pigs will outright "refuse" to go into a dark place but that they will "move toward light." This is simply not true; what they move toward is the place where they feel they can escape. She also tells the audience to "fill the waiting pen not more than half," because the animals will be upset and become agitated if the pen is too full. All these characteristics should lead one to ask, "If pigs or cows or any animal are so sensitive and have so many highly developed feelings, then how can we feel good about killing and eating them?"[383]

Simply put, Dr. Grandin believes that animals are here for us to eat (and that a heaven does not exist for them, even though many of her slaughterhouse designs for cattle are referred to as "the stairway to heaven"). We should ask, however, why the Humane Slaughter Act and principles accepted and followed by all USDA slaughterhouses in the United States and many other developed countries—affecting billions of animals per year—is based on the presumptions and beliefs of one individual. The answer is that we have disassociated ourselves from pigs, cows, chickens, turkeys, fish, and other animals that we eat and no longer see them as living beings with senses.

It's clear that Dr. Grandin, lauded for her understanding of animals, has missed one very important overriding truth: there isn't one animal—farm/livestock, wild animal, or fish—that would choose (if it could) to follow her willingly to its death. Dr. Grandin, along with those who follow her guidelines and those who are eating animals and animal products, are killing animals. I may not possess the ability to "understand" animals, as Dr. Grandin says she can, but even I can be certain that these sentient beings don't want to die. Plain and simple.

It takes so much wasted energy, effort, and lives to produce an unhealthy animal part that someone calls food. Once you become more aware of the entire slaughtering process, the machines involved, and the barbaric manner of killing (even with mechanisms that attempt to create a humane slaughter), you, too, may ask why we go to all this trouble to produce something that likely will cause disease or kill us after we eat it, instead of simply going outside and picking a vegetable from the garden or an apple from a tree and eating that.

And then, there are fish.

Many problems are associated with eating fish and other types of seafood. Of course there's the ecological damage we inflict on our oceans, but what about all the sea life we are killing? By this I mean all the lives we kill each year in our pursuit to eat fish, including the target fish, the bykill associated with extracting that target fish from the ocean, and the other oceanic life, in or out of the water, that now has a diminished food supply.

There is an entire humane movement for the livestock that go off to slaughter, but fish and other seafood don't have a similar activist base. Up to 2 trillion fish are slaughtered each year by over 4 million floating slaughterhouses that we call fishing boats. This deserves attention—and it needs to be stopped. A research team from the University of Edinburgh, led by Dr. Lynne Sneddon, found that fish do, indeed, feel pain. This conclusion was based on the fact that fish have pain receptors and that they also responded to various painful stimuli in a manner convincingly indicative of feeling pain. Researchers found fifty-eight receptors located on the face and head of fish that responded to stimuli; of those, twenty-two could be classified as nociceptors (sensory receptors associated with feeling pain, such as from mechanical pressure, chemical stimulation, and heat). As Dr. Sneddon stated, "Profound behavioral and physiological changes shown by the fish after exposure to noxious substances are comparable to those seen in higher mammals." Eighteen receptors found in fish could be defined further as *polymodal nociceptors* (receptors that respond to more than one type of noxious stimulus), resembling those found in amphibians, birds, and mammals—including humans. But these were anatomical findings, simply verifying the presence of nociception. To be certain of their findings, the scientists employed various tests to confirm that a fish feels pain, rather than simply reacting as a reflex. After a number of tests, such as injecting bee venom or acetic acid into the lips of the fish—saline solution was used on control groups—it became clear that the experimental group felt pain. They showed signs of distress, such as a rocking motion similar to what is seen in higher vertebrates like mammals, aggressively rubbing their lips onto the gravel in the tank and on tank walls and taking three times longer to resume feeding than the control group. Dr. Sneddon concluded, "This work fulfills the criteria for animal pain."[384]

In separate studies at Purdue University, Dr. Jeff Garner, professor of animal sciences, showed that fish feel both reflexive and cognitive pain. His researchers' experiments revealed that fish consciously perceive pain by responding to painful stimuli with reflexes and then also change their behavior, showing signs of anxiety and becoming wary and stressed, indicating they have experienced an aversive situation and have been hurt.[385]

In a 1991 article for the *Institute for Animal Laboratory Research Journal*, Dr. Jane M. Smith voiced concern in the danger of our adopting a less critical anthropomorphic approach, which could then lead to incorrect conclusions about what life forms can feel pain. In other words, we might incorrectly assume that pain cannot be felt in certain invertebrates, simply because they are "so different from us and because we cannot imagine pain experienced in anything other than the vertebrate or, specifically, human sense."

She further states, "Although pain might seem less likely in the more 'simple' invertebrates than in the most 'complex' invertebrates, such as the cephalopod mollusks (and, perhaps, decapod crustaceans such as crabs and lobsters, not considered here), this certainly does not mean that the more 'simple' invertebrates ought not to be afforded respect."[386]

Because fish don't communicate in a manner that we can recognize, it is easy for humans to not respect fish or to accept our lack of understanding of what fish feel or do not feel. Unlike mammals, fish, for the most part, have been left out of any welfare movement because of our inaccurate perception of them. In the book *Do Fish Feel Pain?*, author Victoria Braithwaite contends that fish do feel pain and endure suffering. Professor Braithwaite is chair of fisheries and biology at Pennsylvania State University and has researched the evolution of animal cognition. In *Do Fish Feel Pain?*, she focused on fish learning, memory, and perception and raised the obvious ethical questions of how we treat fish, arguing that "the latest growing scientific evidence would suggest that we should widen to fish the protection currently given to birds and mammals." This is a noble thought—except that we currently do *not* afford proper protection to birds and mammals; we still kill and eat them.[387]

Of course, anglers and all those in the fishing industry would find some reason to disagree with these findings, because they would prefer that everyone share their opinion—that fish can't feel pain. On that pretense, it's certainly easier for anyone catching a fish to view the experience with a sense of introverted numbness. That's right—it's a game. You place a barbed lure into the water, tricking a poor individual into thinking it is natural prey, something it has comfortably relied on numerous times. Once the sharp hooks become embedded in the fish's mouth, pain and panic follow, while it fights for its life. This becomes the game for the angler—how much "fight" the fish had in it to try to get away, before it physically (and perhaps spiritually) gives up, with no more life in it. The larger the fish (sailfish, swordfish, tuna, etc.), the larger and longer the fight—and, presumably, the more satisfaction of winning the game by the one doing the fishing. It's what legends mounted over the fireplace mantel are made of. But try to remember that, similar to any livestock animal slaughtered on land, every single fish caught and killed will feel pain as it's hooked, as it's taken out of the water, while it's flopping around gasping to breathe, and when it's clubbed or stunned and slit with a knife as it bleeds to death. Not a pleasant thought, is it? But that's exactly what happens. It's time we stop turning our heads the other way. Whether fishing recreationally or simply demanding that it be caught commercially for our plate, we are killing 1 to 2 trillion fish each year. At best, it's irresponsible.

Often, I am asked what the difference is between eating animal products and eating the animals themselves. In other words, how do I differentiate the impact of global depletion caused by raising animals to eat from that of raising animals in order for us to eat their products, such as dairy and eggs. My answer: there is no difference.

As we become more aware of some of the problems with factory farms and management of livestock, many people prefer to distance themselves from this by eating an ovo-lacto vegetarian diet (abstaining from animal flesh but eating dairy and egg products). Although they might think it is a step in the right direction, the slaughtering most certainly continues. Various food movements today want to help solve problems surrounding our desire to eat animal products, but they simply do not address the real problem. Their thinking that there is a division of sorts between animals and animal products should give us a clue as to why these food movements will never reach the goal of being sustainable. There should be no differentiation made between raising animals to eat and raising animals for products, such as dairy and eggs. As long as animals are anywhere in the mix, there will be unnecessary depletion of resources, increased risk factors for our health, and inhumane slaughtering of billions of animals each year.

What goes on behind the scenes when raising animals for their products is not at all well known by consumers of those products—and therefore, the reason for the indifference of the general public. After all, milk is just milk, and eggs are just eggs. The consumer, having not eaten an animal directly, feels absolved of any ill doing. However, the cheese you put on your pizza tonight carries with it the veal and hamburger on someone else's plate.

Along with fish, eggs and dairy seem to be the most "out of sight/ out of mind" food we eat today. We just don't seem to care about however they are produced, as long as it gets to our plates. Why do we eat eggs and dairy products? For most of us, the answer is that someone told us to.

Let's face it: none of us were born eating eggs. We were not born drinking cow's milk. Whoever raised us gave us eggs, milk, and other dairy products to eat, and then they and everyone else around us reinforced the habit throughout our life. That cultural and social reinforcement was so strong that most of us will find it difficult to listen to someone like me, stating that eggs and dairy products are unnatural and unhealthy for us to eat—and they do very bad things to our planet and to the animals involved.

Let's begin by looking at milk. The consumption of milk and dairy products is on the rise globally, which is unfortunate.

Many problems are associated with milk, from a human health, environment, and animal welfare standpoint. All dairy operations use unnecessary resources—land, water, food. They produce massive amounts of greenhouse gases, and the dairy industry is one of the largest sources of pollution in our country. Just looking at water usage, every dairy cow will drink 25 to 40 gallons of water each day, and the cows will eat pasture or alfalfa and grain that usually require water to irrigate. So each dairy cow will use 1 to 2 million gallons of water per year. Then there is the water used for cleanup of the cow and also managing the milk. In all, it takes between 300 and 1,000 gallons of water to produce just 1 gallon of milk. And remember: yogurt, cheese, ice cream, butter—they're all part of the problem.

Buying local (being a locavore) doesn't solve the problem with dairy products. The depletion of resources and of our own health will continue, as will the slaughtering. Even if you buy milk or dairy products locally or from small farms, the cows still may be given antibiotics, still require massive amounts of land and water use, still contribute to greenhouse gas emissions, and still will live only four or five years of a normal twenty-five-year life before they are slaughtered. And for all that, they produce something that creates many human health issues. While cow's milk is still widely recommended in Western countries as necessary for human growth and bone health, scientific evidence spanning the previous twenty-five years displays the need for modifying strategies of public health involving dairy products. Osteoporotic bone fracture rates are highest in countries that consume the most dairy, calcium, and animal protein, and lowest in countries that consume the least. Studies of bone strength and fracture risk provide little or no evidence that milk or any other dairy product (yogurt, for example) have any benefit to bone or our overall health. On the other hand, there is mounting evidence showing that consuming milk and dairy products may contribute to the risk of various cancers such as prostate, pancreatic, breast, and ovarian, autoimmune diseases, allergies, many childhood ailments, and Parkinson's disease. Casein and other milk protein have been implicated in increased risk of diabetes as well. Cow's milk has been shown to be unnecessary, if not damaging for human health, and any nutrients it may contain can all be readily obtained from plant foods. Numerous publications have emphasized that bone health is better served by increasing fruit and vegetable intakes, eliminating animal protein, exercising regularly, obtaining adequate sunshine or supplementation with vitamin D from plant sources.[388]

Some studies have documented as many as seventy-three contaminants found in any one milk sample. Even organic, locally grown milk will have allergens and contribute to diseases, such as type I or II diabetes, heart disease, obesity, and others. For these reasons, the American Academy of Pediatrics recommended a few years ago that no cow's milk be given to infants under one year of age. I find this interesting, because with all the associated problems, why is anyone *over* the age of one drinking cow's milk?

The calcium found in 1 cup of milk or yogurt is 300 mg. Fortified tofu has 500 mg, collard greens 400 mg, spinach 300 mg, and many types of beans (kidney, adzuki, black, soy) have between 200 and 300 mg.[389]

The majority of individuals in the world, 75 *percent*, are lactose intolerant, meaning they are unable to digest milk and other dairy products (yogurt, cheese, ice cream). Many of these people experience upset stomachs, bloating, and distress due to lactose intolerance because they do not want to give up their milk—or they simply don't know that milk is the problem.

Why do we keep drinking milk? Because our culture has heavily ingrained it in us. We grew up not knowing any better, and the dairy industry has told us that milk is a "health food" and is necessary for proper growth and bone development—this is not true. In reality, the two countries that have the highest per capita rate in the world of hip fractures due to osteoporosis, or weak bones, are Switzerland and the United States, which also are the two countries with the highest amount of milk consumption. It's really more a matter of how to minimize your calcium loss than how much calcium you take in. All the nutrients you think you need from milk can be obtained from plants—and without the baggage.

Most of these issues with dairy products are the same, regardless of whether or not they come from organic, grass-fed, pasture-raised cows. Regardless of the dairy product you choose, the behind-the-scenes process is still the same. That dairy product had to come from a cow, which needed to go through a pregnancy, have a baby cow, which was taken from its mother within the first few hours of birth (and then that baby cow was slaughtered for veal), while the mother went on to develop mastitis by living in repetitive cycles of coerced reproduction and abuse of her body and spirit. She will be tired and spent at the end of just four years and then considered "humanely" slaughtered by shooting her in the head with a bolt gun. Nine million dairy cows in the United States go through this process every single year. *Nine million.* All this so you can consume dairy products made from a liquid (milk) that was originally intended for the baby cow that was slaughtered for veal. I find that a bizarre concept.

Unnecessary killing and resource depletion takes place with every dairy product. And for that reason, there is no differentiation between eating animals and eating products produced from animals.

And then there are eggs, which are equally a problem. There are 285 million egg-laying hens in the United States. Ninety-five percent of those hens are of the battery-cage type, meaning the hens are held in barren cages so small that they can't spread their wings, dust, or even move. These poor hens are kept in that confined space for fifty-two weeks, laying eggs around the clock until they are so wasted that they are then slaughtered and used for low-grade food or simply trashed—after just fifty-two weeks. A normal lifespan for a hen at, for example, my animal sanctuary might be ten to twelve years or more. These 285 million egg-laying hens are the most legally unprotected farm animal with some of the cruelest conditions that we have ever imposed on another living being. A visit by the Humane Society of the United States to one of the largest egg-producing operations in our country found the following:[390,391,392]

- Hens confined in overcrowded cages with the rotting corpses of other birds
- Dead hens trapped under their cages, with eggs exposed to the rotting corpse
- Birds with severely injured legs, unable to reach food or water
- Eggs covered in feces and blood

This is common and has been documented throughout the egg industry, including at Cal-Maine Foods and Rose Acre and Rembrandt Foods, which are the largest U.S. egg producers.

These conditions are just a few of many reasons why we have so many salmonella outbreaks with eggs. It's also the reason many people are asking for cage-free eggs (eggs produced by hens that are not kept in battery cages), which is becoming a large movement in the United States today. But there is a serious problem with cage-free eggs, which is found in the definition itself. What cage-free means to you, the compassionate consumer, is vastly different from what cage-free means to the egg-producing industry. Unfortunately, cage-free doesn't mean healthy or sustainable, and it certainly doesn't mean humane. Therefore, the cage-free movement is not so good at all.

Nevertheless, the natural progression of thought, in response to public concern, is to shift the egg industry to what could be imagined as something better—cage-free eggs. The industry is spreading the false illusion that cage-free eggs come from happy hens and are a good step in the right direction for the industry that has suddenly become concerned about ethics and their consumers.

Let's look at this a little more closely. Numerous undercover videotapings have recorded the hideous way we treat caged hens. Once these atrocities became known, there was a large public outcry to reform the egg industry. The latest movement is for cage-free and humane-certified eggs. Many college campuses are pushing their dining directors to offer only these types of eggs, and they are becoming successful in their attempts. Following the lead by California and its Proposition 2—to legally enforce all egg producers in their state to be cage-free by the year 2015—the United Egg Producers, the largest egg organization in the United States, signed an agreement with the Humane Society of the United States (HSUS) in July 2011 to encourage Congress to pass a law for all eggs in the U.S. to be produced in a cage-free manner.

So what do cage-free and humane-certified actually mean? There actually are two definitions of cage-free. Conscientious consumers of egg products and the organizers of this cage-free movement have one definition; the marketing and economic-driven objectives of the industry and producers have another. The egg producers' concern is not for the chickens; it's for their profits, so their motives are quite different from the cage-free activists. The egg farms and industry itself will do the very least to look the very best. The cage-free agreement between the Humane Society and United Egg Producers looks good on the surface, but a look behind the cage-free label reveals an entirely different story.

First of all, the agreement will not take effect until it is signed into legislation by our Congress. Then, following that, egg farms will be given eighteen years to become fully cage-free. Now, my count is that there are nearly 300 million hens living in quite inhumane conditions that will be slaughtered every year, multiplied by eighteen years, before this regulation goes into effect—that's quite possibly over 5 trillion hens that will be impacted.

There is also the repeated killing of the 285 million male chicks every year by the various hatcheries. For every one hen that goes on to become an egg layer, one male chicken will hatch. This breed of chicken—predominantly Leghorn—is not bred or used for meat, so these male chicks are killed, by way of throwing them alive in a grinder (wood chipper) or in trash bags. This happens whether the corresponding egg-laying hens are cage-free or not. And all cage-free hens still have their sensitive beaks cut off. Cage-free operations are essentially large buildings that hold as many as 50,000 to 100,000 very cramped hens that never see natural daylight or breathe fresh air, so there's more than a bit of stress created by the increased flock size and inability for hens to establish a pecking order.

Numerous studies have shown increased problems with cage-free operations. For instance, a number of investigative veterinarians and even cage-free operators themselves report increased pathogens, ammonia gas concentrations, and birds damaging themselves. In a statement released April 35, 2012, the United Egg Producers (who represent 88 percent of the nation's eggs) affirmed their support of consumer choice "in the purchasing of eggs, whether that be from conventional, cage-free, organic, or enriched colony-cage housing," but emphasized that "the scientific community always has documented that cage-free hen housing is not necessarily better for animal welfare, and in fact, hens producing cage-free eggs often have *more* health problems (skeletal, foot, and respiratory health) and higher mortality levels than hens in conventional egg housing."[393]

Nevertheless, most cage-free operations are American Humane Certified, which has some of the weakest guidelines. Inaccurate public perception of cage-free operations continues, fueled by those individuals and organizations who are in the industry and are concerned about profits— or by those who are simply unaware.

Documented problems with humane certification include integrity issues, vague and interpretive regulations, lack of strict enforcement, and allowing the continuation of inhumane treatment of chickens, even though they are not in a cage.

Consumers rarely are aware of the space requirements for the hens that produce cage-free and humane-certified eggs. Egg-laying hens have an average wingspan of 32 inches and since most are of the battery cage type, they are forced to live their lives in a cage that doesn't allow them to move, let alone spread their wings. Instead of the 67 square inches required now in the battery cages, within eighteen years, cage-free operations will have to provide 128 square inches for each bird. That sounds like a great improvement, doesn't it? But although it's better than a battery cage, each cage-free bird will only be allotted 128 square inches, which should not be considered humane. It is a space 10 inches by 12 inches—the size of an average laptop computer screen. Ask yourself how humane it would be to make a hen live and lay eggs in that space continuously, even if it were without a cage—eating, drinking, and laying eggs—for fifty-two weeks.

The chicken industry is comprised of two major categories: those chickens that produce eggs and chickens raised for us to eat. And while many consumers in the United States are going in the wrong direction with following the cage-free movement for egg purchases (under the false belief that it is healthy and humane), the other half of the chicken industry is running full speed ahead largely uncontested—the "broilers" (chickens that we kill and eat). These are hybrid chickens with rapid growth rates, bred specifically for meat and kept in cramped quarters for coerced low levels of activity. They are debeaked at seven days after birth and slaughtered five weeks later.

We need to set the record straight on debeaking. Nociceptors, which respond to noxious stimulation, have been identified in many different parts of the body of the chicken, including the beak, mouth, nose, joint capsule, and scaly skin. Pain perception, as well as associated behavioral changes consistent with those seen in mammals, has been confirmed in chickens, and the reactions consistent with feeling acute pain have been identified following beak trimming in chicks (this doesn't seem to matter to the entire poultry industry, which continues to debeak more than 9 billion chickens each year).[394]

And then there are the breeder chickens that are not used for meat or eggs but for producing the 9 billion broiler chicks each year. These breeder chickens are also debeaked and kept in small cages, where they are unable to move and are without fresh air or sunlight for more than a year, while laying eggs that will hatch chickens to be grown and slaughtered and eaten as broilers.

Whether it is breeder chickens, egg layers (cage-free or caged), or broilers, over 90 percent of the 10 billion chickens found at any one point in time in the United States are living their life in confined, dark warehouses without fresh air, unable to move, many times with 30,000 to 80,000 or more other chickens. In general, chickens function fairly well in groups of less than ninety, so that each bird is able to find its spot in a pecking order. When crowded in groups of thousands, though, a social order is impossible to establish, so frustration, anxiety, and stress are common findings. Relentless pecking is common, with ensuing injury and death.

Chickens and turkeys generally are killed in three different ways, depending on the type of farm on which they were raised and the intentions of the farmer. The methods used by more than 90 percent of all poultry operations are those supervised by the USDA and are as follows:

Meat Chicken Farm Sequence (processing)

- Removed from transport cages
- Hung by the legs on a shackle, mounted on a conveyer chain
- Stunned using an electrically charged water bath
- Killed by cutting the blood vessels in the neck
- Bled so that most blood has left the carcass
- Scalded to soften the attachment of the feathers
- Plucked to remove the feathers
- Head removed
- Gutted or eviscerated to remove the internal organs
- Washed to remove blood and soiling from the carcass
- Hock cutting to remove the feet
- Chilled to prevent bacterial spoiling
- Drained to allow excess water to drip off the carcass
- Weighing
- Cut selection to divide the carcass into desired portion (breast, drumsticks, etc.)
- Packed (for example, in plastic bags) to protect carcasses or cuts
- Chilled or frozen for preservation[395]

Processing and rendering plants continue, with additional operations such as cutting, deboning, and mixing of unused tissue with other animal parts.

Now go back and add to the beginning of this list:

- Growing and harvesting of crops to feed poultry
- Watering crops daily
- Expending electricity and fuel to maintain and clean the facilities

- Administering antibiotics and other pharmaceuticals or chemicals to treat the birds and reduce pathogens
- Capturing and transporting
- Cleaning all facilities, workers, machines, and vehicles

Now add to the end of the list:
- Continued refrigeration or freezing of the product
- Washing of the product after unwrapping
- Meticulous washing of your hands, utensils, and all surfaces touched
- Cooking and continued refrigeration of leftovers to reduce development of further pathogens

Please read this list over again in its entirety, and take a moment to grasp the amount of fuel, time, energy, and other resources reflected in those steps.

Then, read the following steps needed to produce and raise a plant-based substitute for chicken, such as broccoli or beans:
1. Growing and harvesting
2. Transporting (although many plant foods can be grown in your own garden or very close to home, which would reduce this step)
3. Washing

Nothing was slaughtered. Nothing was wasted.

The second type of killing that occurs with chickens and turkeys is found on smaller farms not associated with USDA slaughterhouses; it is the type found in more "local" pastured, grass-fed, and "organic" settings, such as that seen at Polyface Farms (the family-owned farming operation in Virginia, discussed in chapter 2, that heavily promotes itself as "sustainable") and described in Michael Pollan's book *The Omnivore's Dilemma*. Since a chicken is smaller than a pig or a cow and has been considered outside of the USDA Humane Slaughter Act, chickens and other poultry frequently are killed in a gruesome manner and then receive a "humane certification."

The American Humane Certified Welfare 2012 Standards Checklist for laying hens-aviary reads as follow:

"The farm performs one of the following approved methods of on farm euthanasia:

1. "Cervical dislocation; to be used in an emergency or for a small number of adult layer hens. Cervical dislocation involves stretching the neck to sever the spinal cord and cause extensive damage to the major blood vessels. Equipment that crushes the neck rather than dislocates the spine, such as pliers are not acceptable.

2. "Carbon dioxide, or a mixture of carbon dioxide and argon delivered in an appropriate container at acceptable concentrations.

3. "Electrical stunning immediately followed by neck cutting"

And, regarding what is referred to as "farm disposal" (getting rid of the chickens when they are no longer of use by the owner), we find the following protocol stipulated by the American Certified Humane organization:

"Routine on farm disposal of flocks at the end of production cycle shall be accomplished with minimum stress using an approved method of killing documented in Standard Operating Procedures or as above."

For "Depopulation and transport: no more than 3 birds carried in one hand …"[396]

"Depopulation" means gathering up, removing in a routinely rough manner, all of the thousands of cage-free birds to then be slaughtered, in order to start the whole process over again.

The third means of killing chickens is more of a "backyard method": catching one and then either slicing its head off at the neck or using a neck-crunching apparatus that breaks its neck as the poor chicken is fighting for its life. This method gives light to the phrase "Running around with like a chicken with its head cut off." These methods are not well known by the general public, because the egg industry obscures them to appear as if they care about the welfare of the hens that are being abused.

In summary, the production of every animal *product*, such as cheese, ice cream yogurt, or eggs, requires an inefficient use of resources and loss of lives. Eating animal products is no different from eating animals directly—it's just easier for the industry to hide the problems, and it's easier for you to not have to think about it. After all, it's just an egg on your plate and yogurt in your bowl. No animals were harmed, right?

Over 98 percent of all livestock raised in the United States is done so in a factory farm or confined animal feeding operations (CAFO) manner. Regardless of how "humanely" or "sustainably" the other 2 percent were raised—grass-fed, local, real food, organic—they join those 10 billion other animals each year that are transported and slaughtered, all in a similar manner. The rate of killing in modern slaughterhouses has reached 13,200 chickens per hour, over 1,000 pigs per hour, and 250 cattle per hour—in every one of the nearly 1,000 slaughterhouses across the country. Given those numbers, it is a logical assumption that many animals slaughtered will be alive and aware of being killed as it happens. USDA reports confirm that in many plants, up to 8 percent of pigs, 20 percent of cattle, and 47 percent of sheep were not stunned properly prior to being slaughtered.[397]

Chickens are stunned in slaughterhouses by placing their heads in electrified pool of water and then slitting their necks. The 300 million layer hens killed per year are usually not stunned, because they typically suffer from osteoporosis and their bones would break if electrocuted, so they are conscious while their throats are slit, in the same manner as accomplished on small "sustainable" and "humane" farms such as Polyface.

All animals deemed "kosher" or "halal" are slaughtered in this manner as well—cows, turkeys, chickens—are hung upside down and necks slit with a knife while they are fully awake and bleeding to death (stunning is not allowed). Cattle and pigs that are not kosher are typically stunned by a pneumatic bolt that is shot into their foreheads, although numerous investigative organizations attest to the fact that many are still alive and conscious as they proceed down the production line to be dismembered and their necks slit to bleed.

In an attempt to save money ($95 million over three years to the U.S. government, and $256 million annually to the poultry industry), in 2012 the Obama administration planned to fire USDA inspectors and let the poultry industry take over inspections of its own slaughterhouse lines, while at the same time speeding up the numbers killed by 25 percent. This adversely affects consumer health and the health of workers, and increases abuse of the birds. Abuse and atrocities of farm animals, while being raised and in slaughterhouses, have been well documented by Mercy for Animals, a nonprofit organization dedicated to preventing cruelty to animals through investigations, education, outreach, and legal advocacy. Their wonderful work, generating compassion and respect of animals, is to be commended.

Because we generally would rather not know the atrocities and persecution that accompany the animals found on our dinner table, changes in the way we manage livestock in the U.S. are slow to occur—but they are under way. In 2004, PETA (People for the Ethical Treatment of Animals) finally made progress with its release of an undercover video of a West Virginia slaughterhouse (part of the Pilgrim's Pride and Yum! Brands/Kentucky Fried Chicken enterprise) that recorded not just the barbaric manner in which chickens (and other animals) are killed but also management's utter disrespect and wanton cruelty of the animals prior to death—workers throwing live chickens into walls, "stomping on live chickens," tearing heads off of chickens to write graffiti with their blood, strangling and squeezing the birds until they "exploded," and "hundreds" of other acts of cruelty. Unlike the indifference historically seen with much other hidden camera footage, the corporate reaction to this was quick, with the firing of employees, reprimands, and signing new contracts incorporating the promise of humane animal management. PETA urged Congress to change the Humane Slaughter Act to include poultry. Ingrid Newkirk, founder of PETA, was quoted as saying, "I've stood on slaughter floors for chickens, horses in Texas, and for dogs in Taiwan. They are all asking, 'Why is this happening to me?' What we are asking is that [slaughterhouses] render [the animals] senseless first. Is that such a challenging idea?" No doubt, Ms. Newkirk has a long list of incredible accomplishments with PETA, but her statement in this situation may provide us with a clue as to why progress is so slow. As a society, we first do not respect other living beings, and when faced with the unacceptable actions of individuals or organizations, we ask for and find ways to modify those actions in order to justify the perpetuation of the original malice. Instead of rendering the animals senseless, I think it's time we focus on halting the slaughtering of animals altogether. From an environmental, human health, and ethics standpoint, rendering them senseless first doesn't get us there.[398]

The Humane Slaughter Act does not extend to poultry, rabbits, or fish. So the real effect of this cage-free effort, I feel, is that there has been increased awareness of our food choices, with regard to the lives to which egg-laying hens have been subjected. Becoming aware is the mandatory foundation from which all good things can be derived. But we need to recognize what's really happening behind the cage-free label. It is a matter of how something is defined. My definition of cage-free and humane is vastly different from that of the egg industry—this is similar to the grass-fed beef and sustainable seafood movements. Whatever animal or animal product you have on your plate brings with it global depletion and the very subjective topic and act of killing.

For much more on this subject, please familiarize yourself with Karen Davis, PhD, and her amazing work with United Poultry Concerns (UPC), a nonprofit organization she founded in 1990. Through her tireless and uncompromising educational efforts and advocacy, the harsh realities of the poultry industry are finally being exposed.

How do these atrocities regarding management of livestock relate to small family, "local" farms, where everything appears to be humane? Whether the animals raised are sent off to smaller-scale slaughterhouses or killed on the farm itself, there is still the blatant murdering of another life, violence, depletion of resources, and the perpetuation of producing an unhealthy food.

Let's go back to the typical, small local farm that "humanely" raises animals for food. Take a look around the back of the chicken coop. Sure, the chickens are "organically" produced, allowed to roam somewhat freely without being fed antibiotics, but soon they will struggle to get away as they are grabbed and taken to the back of the shed to the "neck cruncher." This is an odd, metal vise-like apparatus with a handle that can be turned quickly to engage the two pinchers around a screeching chicken's neck as it is being crushed. Why is this "neck cruncher" found at the back of the shed? If this process is so "humane," why hide it?

There is always another small building, usually tucked away from the other barns, that is used for hanging the newly slaughtered pig, cow, or chicken while it is bled and for processing the carcass prior to storage and eating it. By slaughter, I mean that the animal either is shot in the head or has its throat slit. It's interesting that this shed is always away from the farmer's house. Although fruits and vegetables are cleaned and prepared in the kitchen sink, the process by which animals are killed and blood drained is not likely to be seen anywhere near the dinner table.

Many local, organic, small family farms that raise animals for themselves and their communities (in a cooperative format, farm-to-table, or local markets) skirt USDA slaughterhouses for large or small livestock, because the meat does not cross state lines, which exempts it, in some instances, from the Federal Meat Inspection Act. Everything is sold locally, even right off the farm.

According to the Food Safety Inspection Service, a mobile slaughter service is allowed, "based on need," and pertains to cows, pigs, and goats, although there are "many more poultry exemptions" without inspection. All of the small farms that operate in this manner that I have visited—in the U.S. and other countries—kill their livestock by shooting them and then slicing their throats to bleed. Some have mobile slaughtering units (serving as a very small version of a USDA slaughterhouse) on site that they have purchased, ranging from $250,000 to over $1 million, but because of the high cost, most resort to accomplishing the task themselves or contract the services of a local butcher who engages them in farm calls.[399]

At one of many small farms I visited, the farmer/owner of a meat cooperative in Washington explained to me the cost effectiveness of having a mobile butcher come to his farm, park in the field where we were standing, next to the group of fifteen cattle that were herded up and placed into a 50-foot diameter grassy area and contained by a wire fence. The farmer then explained the butcher's routine: he takes out his shotgun and begins shooting the cows, one at a time, in the head ("Sometimes it takes an extra shot in the head"). But, he continued, "the butcher is pretty quick, so as to not have the cows panic too much, seeing what's happening." They are then processed right on the spot, and the farmer then hangs the carcasses in a refrigerated room for sale to those in the co-op, who paid for them in advance, months earlier, as "futures." I saw this same process, with minimal variation, occurring on small farms elsewhere in our country and in others.

Cages usually conspicuously line one side of the barn on a small family farm to constrain smaller animals, such as rabbits, and make it easier to catch and kill them. Small stalls and chutes are always present within the barn area, to prod and poke pigs and cows against their will to move to a more confined area to be killed.

How do I know these things? Aside from more than thirty-five years of research regarding this crucial topic and visiting hundreds of farms, I happen to live on a farm that originally was established as one of these local, small-animal farms more than 130 years ago. My wife and I established the property as an animal rescue and sanctuary in 1980 and have lived there and operated it since then, working with thousands of farm animals as well as wild animals. Also, many of my non-immediate family members were and are small farmers who include livestock in their operations.

It is interesting how very disparate my views are to those of small, local farmers who produce animals for food and their supporters who believe these operations are sustainable. They see green; I see red. For them, these farms represent the way animals should be raised and used for our food. So strong are their feelings that this is the best and most natural way for our food to be grown that their operations have been called "very sustainable" by author Michael Pollan, and small farmers have even been called "heroes" by such authors as Jonathan Safran Foer. Referring to small, local farms, Foer states, "Under these circumstances I could eat meat," in his book *Eating Animals*. For me, these very same small farms represent inefficiency, inappropriate use of our resources, apathy, violence, and massive and repetitive slaughtering. Additionally, they are just another poignant example of our cultural influences and misdirection, which has created a skewing of reality and state of being comfortably unaware. Are the people who operate this type of farm really "heroes," as many call them? I feel with the proper education, proper awareness, and transitioning of these farms to entirely plant-based foods, these farmers could, indeed, be heroes. As they currently stand—no, they are very far removed from being "heroes."

The cage-free movement has been extended to pigs. In 2012, restaurant chain Burger King announced that by 2017 "all eggs and pork [we use] will be of the cage-free type." And other major corporations, such as Subway, Unilever, Walmart, and Costco, have committed to transition, eventually, to 100 percent cage-free. Unfortunately, this effectively will create an enhanced corporate public image for these businesses, while at the same time diverting attention away from the much larger issues of:

1. continued animal abuse and slaughter of cage-free chickens (it just happens to be under a different theme)
2. rampant animal abuse and slaughter with all other livestock operations and fish
3. perpetuation of global depletion due to our food choice involving all animals

Burger King has made the decision to phase in all cage-free eggs and pork as part of the company's social responsibility policy, with McDonald's and Wendy's stating that they have "asked pork suppliers to outline plans for eliminating gestation crates they use to confine sows, without setting a timetable." With Smithfield Farms and Hormel, the largest pig producers in the United States, committing to ending the use of gestation crates by the year 2017, things seem to be moving in the right direction.

Or are they? An editorial in the pork industry's trade magazine concluded, "On the issue of gestation-sow stalls, at least, it's increasingly apparent that you will lose the battle." But there shouldn't be a battle over gestation crates, or battery cages, or factory farms, or trawling methods— the "battle" shouldn't be a battle at all, because the global depletion will continue, and the slaughtering of trillions of animals each year will become just that much more easily accepted. Instead, it should be a strong and swift movement of awareness and then action to no longer eat animals.[400]

I think there are two driving factors why we, as a society, generally lack compassion and respect for animals. The primary reason is that most of our population has had no experience with real animals (other than the fortunate species, like dogs and cats, that we somehow designate as pets), especially the ones we eat. For instance, how many of us have ever softly scratched a pig behind her torn but exquisitely sensitive ear (torn from the ear tag originally punched into it from the farmer who was planning to eat her) while she leaned her head into your leg, recognizing you, and looking up with her sensitive brown eyes? She might encourage you to continue scratching there or perhaps ask you, in a number of ways, to switch it up and rub her chest under her front leg, while she flops to the ground on her side, closes her eyes, and drifts off into a comfortable snooze—arm still held up, expecting you to keep up your end of the bargain.

Most of us will never have the opportunity to share our blueberries with a cow who had his ears tagged, horns burned off, and castrated without anesthesia, all at an early age, right after being separated from his mother, who called for him all day and all night for a week straight? Cows love blueberries. And this inquisitive guy prefers to use his stretched-out tongue to gently lift berries out of your hand, rather than use the gobble approach. Actually, he can get pretty slobbery with his tongue in pursuit of blueberries.

Have any of us experienced a curious hen who decided to jump up on your shoulder and sat there for a half hour or more while you were reading, just because she liked your company? And let's not forget the turkey, who was born into a genetic nightmare of clubbed feet and unnatural predisposition to rapid disproportionate growth of her body relative to her heart and other organs. Yet despite having life-threatening tachycardia and respiratory insufficiencies, her beak cut off, and unable to easily move or deal with stress, this turkey follows you, stumbling down a significantly large hill with great effort, just to go on a walk with you, not wanting to be left behind. There's never food involved or coaxing; she merely wants to be with you. She loves you.

If we have no idea that all farm animals are sentient, cognitive beings that display emotion, why should we have compassion for them or think they deserve respect? Perhaps the answer lies in the sad fact that we lack the ability to project outside of ourselves. Thirty thousand years ago, there may have been reason to defend ourselves in life-or-death battles with wild animals and then eat them. Today, there really is no excuse.

The second reason we do not have respect for animals is that we've actually relegated them to mindless, amoeba-like food-source status, and this is reinforced by our families, our social circles, our culture, our religion, and the media. When there is so much support of the notion that animals were placed here on earth for us to do whatever we want with them, including abusing and eating them, compassion and respect have no place. Compassion and respect require some degree of awareness and the ability to project outside of oneself and even education and reinforcement.

Consider the following example (one of countless examples) of how the media portrays animals as things we can selfishly manipulate and eventually consume. Someone asked me to watch an episode of *Bizarre Foods*, the wildly popular program hosted by Andrew Zimmern, whose professed creed is "If it looks good, eat it." The following is what I observed from that episode:

Andrew walks into a crowded, noisy restaurant in Japan and sits down between two people on a stool at a counter, behind which the cooking is accomplished for all to see. Zimmern tells us he loves restaurants in Japan because of "their noise and also freshness of seafood." The camera then captures the chef pulling a live octopus from a pan on the floor, as the octopus gracefully and purposefully moved the tips of its eight legs gently up and down the chef's hands and arms, trying to assimilate textures, colors, and temperatures, attempting to make sense out of its new surroundings. An octopus is an intelligent being, with a large cognitive brain and complex sensory-input mechanisms. Researchers have recently discovered that octopuses are able to problem solve. They can gather information, process it, and then implement well-thought-out functions. Female octopuses are very sensitive, with a strong maternal instinct—so strong that they mandatorily give up their life in the process of having offspring and protecting them after birth.

The person sitting on the stool next to Zimmern put her hand on his bald head and said, "The octopus has a head like yours." A good laugh ensued while the chef pushed the octopus down into a pot of boiling oil over a red-hot burner, in order to kill and cook the poor unsuspecting octopus. The camera didn't show the octopus's reaction to being held in oil as it was boiled to death—portions then served for Zimmern to eat.

Imagine for just a moment what that octopus must have experienced as it went using the thousands of sensory receptors on its legs to carefully feel, see, interpret, and adapt to the chef's hands, sending those inputs to an intelligent and quickly processing brain, to the next moment, being forcefully held in boiling oil and scalded to death.

Although we are still learning about octopuses (even as we kill 2.5 million tons of them and other cephalopods, such as squid, each year), it is has been quite well established that they are sentient beings that feel and think in ways we do not understand. It also can be said that, like all animals, octopuses only eat what they need to in order to survive. They kill *only* because they *need* to and without knowing that they are inflicting pain or suffering on any other living thing—quite unlike Andrew Zimmern and 98 percent of all other humans on this planet who kill because they *want* to kill, and then eat whatever it was that they just killed—all this for no nutritional reason.

More about the octopus

The common octopus (*Octopus vulgaris*) is found in many oceans worldwide. Numerous sushi restaurants in the United States and elsewhere in the world serve octopus, although it would be rare to know exactly which species you are eating.

All octopus species are suffering from overfishing, especially in the fisheries of Mauritania, Vietnam, and Japan. Researchers agree that octopus is a poorly understood species of dwindling numbers, with no fishery management. While large numbers of octopuses are caught as bykill—unintentionally caught in fishing gear—the majority of octopuses are caught by bottom-trawling techniques. In addition to loss of octopus species, bottom trawling further damages seabeds, other species, and interdependent ecosystems, having a detrimental impact on delicate and sensitive seafloor habitats.

From a nutritional standpoint, the octopus as "food" is vastly inferior to plants that we could eat. The highly respected Monterey Bay Aquarium Seafood Watch (MBASW) places a "Good Alternative" recommendation for octopus, especially if they are captured from Hawaii or the Gulf of California, despite admitting in their summary that octopus *"suffer from a lack of solid information and little or no fishery management."* This statement presents a frustrating dichotomy by such a guiding institution as MBASW.

It would be great to hear something along these lines from MBASW: *As with all sea life and consistent with other researchers, we at Monterey Bay Aquarium Seafood Watch admit to knowing very little about the octopus or what the effects of our attempts at capturing them have on all the ecosystems and habitats involved. Therefore, it is our humble opinion that we should stop all harvesting activities of octopus and any methods of fishing that affect them or their habitat, such as trawling and long-line operations that find them as bykill. Of course, these fishing activities in pursuit of octopus are propelled by and begin with our demand to eat them, so it is our strong recommendation that the ordering and consumption of octopus should end.*

Yes, that would be great. And appropriate.

More about Andrew Zimmern

If I seem harsh toward Andrew Zimmern, it's because he and his show are manifestations of our generalized lack of awareness—and greater lack of compassion.

Zimmern is an award-winning monthly columnist for magazines, a journalist with numerous national and international publications, spokesperson for large corporations, an acclaimed author of many books, and now is producer, writer, and host of a highly popular television program.

Zimmern's pilot show on November 1, 2006, was a solid indicator of what was to come. That first show highlighted Zimmern eating what he and the indigenous people of Japan, Malaysia, and Thailand consider "food." He proceeded to eat fish bladder, turtle, frog ovary, and even the beating heart of a frog, called *sashimi* (fresh). Zimmern revealed all of this in a positive, enthusiastically supportive manner. In the next two episodes, Zimmern showed his audience how acceptable and enjoyable it was to eat lamb tongue and eye, soup made from a bull's rectum and testicles, a pie made of pigeons, a calf's brain and a cow's heart, stuffed pig pancreas, more frog, and even balut—a duck embryo (pre-hatched chick) that was boiled alive in its shell. Somewhere buried in each of these segments, he threw in a brief comment about a unique fruit. For instance, in the first three episodes, he briefly introduced the calamondin (a citrus fruit native to the Philippines) and durian (known in Asia as "the king of fruit").

I feel Zimmern's show sensationalizes the gruesome, barbaric act of torturing, slaughtering, and eating creatures that certainly would run, fly, or swim away from this predator, if they had a choice. But it is not Zimmern who is at fault here; it is us. We are more interested in seeing the "bizarre," as it relates to killing and eating animals or body parts of animals, than we are in learning about bizarre or unusual plants—plants that are not only unique but also are healthy to our planet and for us. We should be interested in hearing about plants such as the sacha inchi seed or acai berry, which can be grown in the rainforests sustainably and which provide some of the most powerful phytonutrients and healthy micronutrients found in the world. We should be interested in learning how teff, an ancient grain from the highlands of Ethiopia, might be grown to help reduce world hunger and poverty in that region and elsewhere. We should be interested in the unique plants that can be eaten to cure diseases. Sadly, such an educational program most likely would not interest the populace. Zimmern apparently knows what the audience wants to watch, and that's why he is successful—at least from an economic and popularity standpoint. I mean no offense to Andrew Zimmern himself, but how can we—as an intelligent, compassionate society with a conscience; a society deeply concerned about all living things with which we share this planet—accept and applaud a show such as *Bizarre Foods*?

Eating wild animals: bush meat; cats, whales

It's not only our raising and eating animals for food that is causing global depletion. We also are killing and extracting wild animals, many to extinction—some that have been on earth longer than we have. Fish, of course, are in this category, but other wild animals also are under siege because of our desire to eat them. Zimmern and the octopus provide one example, but there are many others.

In addition to the 70 billion conventional farm animals raised and slaughtered each year and 1 to 3 trillion wild-caught fish, countless other wild animals are slaughtered. One example is the growing trend of bushmeat (the meat of wild terrestrial animals, including some that are endangered). Even if this is accomplished to help feed local or starving people, there still should be initiatives to divert this to plant-based alternatives. Bushmeat, however, typically ends up in expensive restaurants and city markets throughout equatorial Africa, international markets worldwide, and even in the United States.[401]

Gorilla hands (considered delicacies) and body parts of other wild animals can be found on dinner tables globally—it's often considered a sign of wealth to serve such food. In 2012, researchers found over 270 tons of bushmeat passing through Paris alone. The illegal bushmeat trade has increased, becoming more commercially viable, only since the early 2000s, when roads were built by logging companies to access remote forest areas. These roads not only fragmented families of animals but also made it easier for poachers to kill the animals. The result has been devastating to many animals, including the rare lowland gorillas, African forest elephants, and chimpanzees. Each year, illegal poaching extracts 1 million tons of bushmeat from African jungle forests and is responsible for the extinction of at least one primate species, as well as affecting numerous other endangered species. One hundred years ago, there were an estimated 2 million chimpanzees in the forests of Africa, whereas now there are 170,000, with an accelerated rate of decline due to the bushmeat trade. Overhunting of antelope and prey animals has greatly affected predators, such as lion, leopard, tiger, panther, and other large cats; birds of prey; and large snakes. One group addressing this serious problem is the Jane Goodall Institute. Dr. Goodall and her team are at the forefront of conservation, education, developing outreach programs, and supporting sanctuaries and policy change to help the habitat, animals, and people in Africa.

The October 28, 2011, edition of *USA Today* ran the headline "Extinct in 20 years?" The article, written by Dan Vergano, exposed the disturbing fact that many of our more iconic animal populations are nearing extinction. Mr. Vergano focused his article on the plight of our big cats—lions, tigers, leopards, and cheetahs—although numerous other plants, animals, and insects, in alarming numbers, face extinction as well. Vergano stated that many ecological problems occur when the predator-to-prey ratios change and the rapid diminishing of big cats in the world is due to human activities. Prey numbers explode and habitat becomes negatively impacted—essentially, nature becomes imbalanced.

The missing factor in this important article, however—one that I find omitted repeatedly in media coverage and in our society—is the food choice factor.

What we decide to eat, regionally or as a global society, has everything to do with the near-extinct status of big cats—it's similar to the effect our choice of food has on the loss of 10,000 or more other species each year. Vergano's article never mentioned the effect our food choices have on the issue of extinction; instead, it focused on the effects of the growing number of people in the world.

Overpopulation and expansion by way of living space *is* an issue, but it is not nearly as much of a problem as expansion by way of increased land use by livestock (what we are generally doing to our planet). Nearly all concerned researchers agree that the rapid loss in biodiversity on earth today is due to pastured or grazing livestock on land and by unsustainable fishing practices in our oceans.

Let's take a closer look at the information in Vergano's article, which was viewed by 3.2 million readers. As with thousands of other species of living things on our planet, the populations of lions, tigers, leopards, and jaguars has been decimated over the past fifty years. Lions have been reduced to 20,000 in the African wild, from 450,000 in 1960. They are now extinct in twenty-six countries where they used to flourish. Only seven countries have more than one thousand lions remaining. The principal reasons for this are the raising of livestock, which destroys the lions' natural habitat; killing lions for sport (as a trophy and/or eating them); and overhunting of their prey—all food-choice related.

In the period between 1998 and 2008, 64 percent of the nearly six thousand wild lions trophy-hunted in Africa were exported back to the U.S. hunters who killed them, adding to the decline seen from livestock and habitat encroachment, according to Jeff Flocken of the International Fund for Animal Welfare.

The dominant male lion is the one typically killed by trophy hunters. Aside from the needless act of slaughtering this poor individual, it has a tremendous impact on other lions, triggering unnatural battles for dominance in the pride, killing of offspring of the former rival, and general confusion and loss of direction in the family. Every hunter should fully realize that when he/she slaughters one male lion, that hunter is effectively "signing a death warrant for twenty to thirty other lions in a pride," as stated by researcher and *National Geographic* filmmaker Beverly Joubert. And so it is with every single animal killed by every single hunter or fisherman. There is an appalling lack of understanding or appreciation of the effect that one act will have on the family of that individual animal or on the other ecosystems and biodiversity impacted by its life.

In Africa and elsewhere in the world, land that was home to big cats has been destroyed and converted to pasture land to support cattle and other livestock. But lions face challenges other than simply the loss of their habitat—they are killed by poachers and poisoned because they interfere with livestock operations. Lions are also killed and eaten as substitutes for tiger bone wine and tiger soup bone used in Asian medicines. According to Panthera, a leading organization in wild cat preservation, there are only three main threats to Africa's lions:

1. Retaliatory persecution by livestock farmers and herders who see lions as a threat to their income. Although these individuals have cleared land, reduced prey, and forced their livestock on the lions' natural habitat, they now view lions as a nuisance and interference to their imposed, unnatural grazing of livestock on land that had been the lions' natural domain for thousands of years. Because of this, farmers and herders feel perfectly justified in killing lions by spearing, shooting, or even poisoning them. In Kenya alone, the Maasai kill more than one hundred of its two thousand wild lions each year.

2. Dramatic loss and fragmentation of habitat, due to the ever-expanding agricultural industry. Lions now are confined to isolated islands of habitat, which drastically increases the risk and rate of extinction.

3. Scarcity of wild prey because of overhunting by humans. When lions lose their natural prey, they are forced to feed on the livestock that was placed in front of them. Panthera states that this establishes "a vicious cycle in which lions are forced to prey on livestock, driving further conflict with humans, in which the lion ultimately loses."

Leopard populations are down to 50,000 from around 750,000, and cheetahs have been reduced to 12,000 from their stabilized numbers of 45,000 just fifty to seventy-five years ago. Reasons for their decreasing numbers are similar to those found with lions—loss of habitat due to the growth of livestock, the ensuing loss of animals on which they prey, and humans killing them.

Tigers in the wild number around only 3,000, with fewer than 1,200 breeding wild females left. Over 100,000 tigers roamed a number of Asian habitats just fifty to sixty years ago.

According to the Environmental Investigation Agency and the World Wildlife Fund, the Chinese government has allowed the sale of tiger skins and products, despite an international ban on this activity. Tigers are one of the world's most quickly vanishing endangered species and yet they continue to be killed and sold in a number of mostly Asian countries. Many conservation organizations report a thriving illegal commerce in tiger skins, bones, organs, and other parts that are loosely regulated by Chinese authorities. Many wealthy Chinese individuals eat tiger meat and organs in exclusive restaurants, and the use of all tiger parts has escalated since 2002, as more of China's population gain affluence and the ability to purchase products made from tigers.

With some estimates by the Wildlife Trust of India (WTI) of only 1,500 tigers in the wild, the Bengal tiger is predicted to become extinct in just ten years, following in the footsteps of the now extinct Bali tiger (1937), Javan tiger (1979), and the Caspian tiger (1968). The six remaining subspecies all live in Asia and are suffering rapid loss by poaching and habitat loss, with India's Bengal tiger perhaps the most vulnerable. A spokesperson for the WTI states, "A villager can poison and skin a tiger in one night and make more money selling it than he would make in five years of farming."

It was encouraging to see *USA Today* comment on the possible extinction of these great cats, but we have reached a point in our society where information from our media must be complete and accurate, and it must afford us full awareness. This is the only way we can make proper decisions about the choices we make and the only way we can understand the impact those choices have on our planet and, ultimately, ourselves.

Simply put, we are losing these large cats in the wild due to our increasing demand to eat meat. Even though population expansion and trophy hunting are factors, if we stop eating livestock, these cats and their habitat will be on a course toward survival, not extinction.

All species of animals in and around our oceans are affected, either directly or indirectly, by our demand to eat fish, but two oceanic species exemplify our inhumanity and disrespect: sea turtles and whales. We should afford these animals a degree of reverence, as we should with any animal, but I believe whales and sea turtles deserve an added degree. They have been on earth since the dinosaurs and now are nearing extinction—in our lifetime, because of our actions. Whales and sea turtles are killed and eaten for food and also are innocent victims of bykill. Vast numbers of them routinely are caught and drown in fishing nets that extract fish from our oceans. These animal species have survived cataclysmic events in the history of the world that caused mass extinction of other species; they evolved through major tectonic plate movements and rearrangements of continents, yet now find themselves in peril. Although whales and sea turtles have survived the effect of all species living on earth for the past 2 million years, they are struggling to adapt and survive the abuses imposed on them in the past 150 years by humans. Most large whale populations are endangered, as are six out of seven types of sea turtles. Pacific Leatherback turtle numbers have fallen by 95 percent since the 1980s, largely due to long-line fishing.

Over 300,000 whales, dolphins, and porpoises die from entanglement in fishing nets each year.

Over 250,000 endangered sea turtles are caught each year in fishing lines.

Our negative impact on whales and sea turtles falls into five categories:

1. Hunting and killing them for us to eat
2. Killing them as innocent bystanders (bykill) in our quest to catch and kill other fish and sea life
3. Killing them as innocent bystanders on migration routes when ships and tankers collide into them
4. Indiscriminately reducing their food supply
5. Climate change

Four of the five categories are related to our desire to eat animals.

In December 2010, officials from twenty-seven nations gathered in Shimonoseki, Japan, a traditional whaling hub, to discuss lifting a decades-old ban on whale hunting. Many countries who are involved in whaling wished to remain anonymous but were in attendance. Europe was represented by Norway and Iceland, who join Japan as historically significant whaling countries, despite the ban. Island countries in the Caribbean also were in attendance, because numerous whales reside in the waters surrounding their islands. In the twentieth century, over 1.5 million whales were slaughtered. Although a moratorium was placed in 1982 by the International Whaling Commission (IWC), at least 35,000 whales are killed each year by countries such as Japan, Russia, Norway, and Iceland that oppose the moratorium and set their own quotas—ignoring the fact that whales are endangered, many critically. The Institute of Cetacean Research, a Tokyo-based nonprofit organization, has for many years been the orchestrator of annual meetings aimed at furthering support of whale hunting, but this particular meeting, held in 2010, was hosted by the Japanese government. There is great contradiction in Japan's killing thousands of whales each year under the guise of "research" and orchestrating a pro-whaling conference, while at the same time, it holds the presidency of the Convention of Biological Diversity.

Traditional whaling countries like Norway, Iceland, and Japan continue to harpoon whales, slaughtering them and selling their meat in markets and to restaurants. These countries now pay millions of dollars to small island countries for the use of their surrounding waters. This allows Japan and others to carry out commercial whale slaughters in the last refuges of these great animals. For example, Japan has paid to use the ocean water surrounding Dominica and St. Lucia in order to hunt sperm whales, shooting them with harpoons that explode inside of them.[402]

Whale numbers have dropped primarily because we are killing them to eat, but the few remaining whales now are affected simply by our demand to eat seafood. This affects whales in two major ways: whales are caught and drown as bykill in fishing nets designated for other species, as well as being hit by fishing boats and larger tankers; and through overfishing of nearly all sea life (whether targeted or as bykill), whales now are faced with a dwindling food supply. A perfect example of this is krill, a significant food source for many types of whales. One adult blue whale may eat over 2,000 pounds of krill in one day. Krill, a 6-centimeter–long invertebrate, is the most abundant animal species on earth. It feeds on phytoplankton and is a very important part of the oceanic food cycle. Krill numbers have dropped substantially, in turn affecting the decline of certain penguin species. According to the International Union for Conservation of Nature, of the seventeen penguin species (on earth for over 70 million years), at least five are nearing extinction, largely because we're extracting their food sources from our oceans. The "quota" (the designated international cumulative limit) for killing krill has been placed at 1.5 million tons per year. But krill also are eaten by baleen whales, such as the blue, right, and fin, which are desperately trying to make a comeback from near extinction. Since there are hundreds of thousands fewer of these great whales due to our slaughtering them over the past two hundred years, the fishing industry feels there should be more krill for us to take now.[403]

Worldwide, sea turtles and their eggs are used for food. Large numbers of sea turtles also are victims of bykill, which only exists because of our demand to eat fish. There are seven types of sea turtles, and all face extinction. Three sea turtle types are critically endangered and may be gone in our lifetime. Six are found in U.S. waters, and all of them are endangered. The green sea turtle, for instance, is on the International Union for Conservation of Nature critically endangered list, but they still are widely killed for their meat and harvesting of their eggs. The most significant loss, however, is due to being caught in the nets and longlines of fishing vessels. An estimated 100,000 are killed in the Indo-Australian archipelago each year. Green sea turtles graze on sea grass beds, which are some of the most prolific ecosystems on our planet. With loss of these turtles, sea grass beds will become imbalanced, leading to loss of the ecosystem and other sea life.

The longest migration of any animal species on the planet is the loggerhead turtle, which spends the first twenty years of its life maturing and migrating through the Atlantic, to the waters of Iceland, Africa, and the Caribbean, before finding its way back to the very same beach where it was born, on the eastern shore of Florida. Loggerhead turtles are an integral part of many ecosystems. Up to one hundred different species of plants and animals have been recorded as living on one single loggerhead turtle.

All fishing vessels everywhere in the world are implicated in killing turtles and other sea life, but some of the most damaging has been found in the Gulf of Mexico. In 2009, it was estimated that commercial shrimping alone killed over 5,300 sea turtles—4,200 of them were the critically endangered Kemp's ridley sea turtle, which reproduces exclusively in the Gulf area. Another 860 were killed as bykill in the southeast Atlantic during the same time (National Marine Fisheries Service summary; Sea Turtle Restoration Project). Populations of Kemp's ridley sea turtles numbered at more than 40,000 nesting females in the 1940s, when first scientific recordings were made. They plummeted to a low of about five hundred nesting females in 1985. Certain fishing vessels are required to use turtle-excluder devices (TEDs) on their trawling nets, but many are exempt and most are not regulated or monitored.

All types of sea turtles play a critical role in the oceanic web of life. They are amazing beings that should be protected and respected—not eaten or killed—because they are innocent bystanders of our choice to eat fish. Although you may not eat turtle meat or their eggs directly, with every shrimp or other wild-caught seafood on your plate, you undoubtedly contribute to the loss of massive numbers of animals living in and around our oceans—the nearly extinct sea turtles and the ecosystems they impact are just some of them.

Disconnects with animals in the wild and biodiversity
Today, with massive loss of land, pollution, and climate change, thousands of species (plants, animals, insects) are going extinct each year because of the actions of just one—ours. There have been six known mass extinctions on earth. The first five were caused by uncontrolled natural disasters. The Triassic-Jurassic event, 200 million years ago, thought to have been caused by volcanic eruptions or an astronomical impact, ended life for more than half of all species on earth. The Permian-Triassic, roughly 250 million years ago, was the largest extinction; 95 percent of all species were killed. The late Devonian extinctions at about 360 million years ago were two sharp pulses of loss of species occurring 100,000 years apart caused by surface temperature drops by 20 degrees or more, thought to have been triggered by large volcanic

eruptions or astronomical collision and is the ensuing atmospheric ash. The first mass extinction, Ordovician-Silurian extinctions occurred around 444 million years ago due to falling sea levels. The fifth and most recent mass extinction that killed the dinosaurs and half of all species on the planet was the Cretaceous-Paleogene event, which occurred approximately 65 million years ago and thought to have been caused by impact of a comet or asteroid. The sixth mass extinction is occurring today, and we are the cause. Urban sprawl due to overpopulation is a precipitating factor, but it pales in comparison to the combined impact of pollution, climate change, and agricultural land-use inefficiencies—all resulting from our choice to raise and eat animals. Some of this effect is by direct hunting, which includes fishing (a commercial form of hunting) and generating livestock.

Biodiversity applies to various types of life-forms on earth, as well as ecosystems and a vast web by which they are connected. Biodiversity can be found everywhere, because it occurs on land on our highest mountain elevations, and in water, in the deepest ocean trenches; and it includes all organisms—microscopic bacteria, and complex animals and plants; all living things.

Biodiversity and food choice: a clarification

I'm reminded of the comments by medical researcher Jonas Salk: "If all insects on Earth disappeared, within fifty years all life on Earth would end. If all human beings disappeared from Earth, within fifty years all forms of life would flourish." We are, indeed, losing other species on the planet at an unprecedented rate.

Some researchers have placed the extinction number at 30,000 per year, which refers to the total loss of species of animals, plants, insects—not simply animals (the "animal" kingdom technically includes insects). This figure was first brought to light by Harvard naturalist and emeritus professor of biology Edward Wilson (*The Diversity of Life*, Harvard University Press, 1992) and supported by Niles Eldridge (*Life in the Balance*, Princeton University Press, 1998). Others, such as Georgina Mace, professor of

Conservation Science at Imperial College London, and Paul Ehrlich, biologist and Stanford University professor, have extinction estimates as high as 70,000 to 130,000 species per year (7,000 to 13,000 times the background rate—which is the pre-human rate or the more natural rate of extinction seen for the previous thousands of years).

After interviewing numerous researchers with the Species Survival Commission of the World Conservation Union and the Convention on Biological Diversity, I now feel there are many uncertainties surrounding attempts at quantifying the exact number of species becoming extinct per year. For this reason, it is more meaningful to view our planet's current loss of species and the impact of our food choices in the following manner:

1. We are losing species of life as well as ecosystems on earth at an unprecedented and alarming rate, estimated to be anywhere between 1,000 and 10,000 times the "background rate." Therefore, it is this massive *rate* of extinction, rather than number of loss, that becomes a more meaningful metric and cause for concern.

2. It is difficult, if not impossible, to accurately predict the number of species loss per year because of a number of factors. One of the largest unknowns is the exact number of species that we have on earth, which is a needed component when attempting to determine total numbers of species loss when using an extinction prediction equation. This is one of the reasons the Species Area Curve Relationship method of extinction calculation has led to speculation and wide ranges of numbers of extinct species. Most researchers today feel that although we have identified approximately 1.8 million species on our planet, most likely between 10 and 30 million exist.

3. Regardless of the exact number of species becoming extinct per year, it is alarming and can be most attributed to loss of habitat— and the predicted future escalation will be due to habitat loss combined with climate change.

4. With estimates of 45 percent of all the land mass on earth used by animal agriculture and 1 to 2 trillion fish extracted from our oceans each year (by fishing methods such as trawling, purse

seine, longlines, explosives and other techniques that are damaging ecosystems)—eating animals (fishing and livestock production) is the largest contributing factor in habitat loss and constitutes the second largest sector implicated in anthropogenic greenhouse gas emissions, which leads to climate change.

As of August 2012, the 2004 Global Species Assessment was the most recent empirical data on global extinction rates, based on birds, mammals, and amphibians. According to Simon Stuart, PhD, chair of the International Union for Conservation of Nature Species Survival Commission, "Most experts believe that the available data [contained in that 2004 assessment] indicate that the current extinction rate is at least 1,000 times higher than the background rate and getting worse." Many experts believe this is a very conservative estimate.

In the past, most extinctions of species could be attributed primarily to hunting, with a clear path following that of humans. The North American continent saw a number of animal extinctions when humans crossed over from Asia—most notably, the mammoth and other slow-moving, large herbivores. This set into motion loss of other dependent species, such as the long-nosed bear and giant vulture. Another wave of extinctions occurred when the Polynesians colonized the Pacific Islands. There, humans were the predators against many flightless and defenseless birds, such as the moa, which rapidly became extinct. On most of these islands, evidence suggests that more than 50 percent of all bird species were hunted to extinction.

Many animals, such as the thylacine (Tasmanian tiger) and Javan tiger, had four reasons for their demise—all related to our food choices:

1. They were hunted and eaten for food.
2. We hunted and ate their prey, leaving them with no food.
3. We took away their habitat and replaced it with pasture and livestock.
4. We shot the remaining animals because they interfered with our livestock operations.

The last single thylacine known to be alive was a female, and it was shot and killed by a farmer in order to keep it away from his henhouse. This followed a massive ten-year hunting campaign by their government, because these tigers were seen as threats to the growing livestock operations.

This situation is the common cause of extinction of nearly all predators on land, and it continues today with those that are endangered. The jaguar is nearing extinction because of habitat loss, and those few that remain are being shot because they try to eat the cattle that we have dangled in front of them, following our destroying their forests and prey.

The red wolf was declared extinct in the early 1980s, gone because of our hunting them, then habitat loss because of our clearing of land for livestock, and then our hunting and killing the last red wolves known to exist so they wouldn't hurt the cattle.

Let's summarize the loss of all predators and most other animals: we first take their land and other species away from them by clearing forests; then we dangle livestock in front of them; then we ultimately shoot them. That's pretty much the pattern of extinction on land.

Humans have a long and embarrassing track record of hunting animals to extinction, and we can find the same occurring today, whether in our oceans or with livestock on land. The process of extracting wild sea life and furthering loss of terrestrial and salt and freshwater habitat by way of our food choices now, however, is greatly accelerated.

These are a few of the many methods of direct cause of extinction, as it is occurring in our oceans, with the extraction of trillions of fish per year. The more insidious impact, however, is by indirect causes, such as habitat loss and pollution, where we simply take away the natural home of plants and animals, mostly because of raising livestock or fishing methods. Koalas, for instance, have been on earth for more than 50 million years, thriving in Australia until European settlers hunted them to near extinction and the few koalas remaining began seeing the effects of a quickly growing cattle population. Koala numbers have dropped precipitously since 1990 (more than 40 percent in areas such as Queensland) because of deforestation, loss of eucalyptus vegetation, and the introduction of chlamydia—all due to cattle. In early 2012, the Australian government finally listed the koala as "threatened," placing them on the national list of vulnerable species. An Australian senate report listed the reasons for loss of koala numbers, including "urban development, drought bushfires and climate change, disease, predation by dogs, and motor vehicles." Even though those were factors, nowhere in the report was the most significant factor discussed candidly, which is food choice to raise livestock. Australia has one of the fastest rates of deforestation in the world, and this deforestation is due to their increased livestock operations—they now rank as the third largest exporter of beef. While it is certainly good news for the koala to be listed as threatened, the primary "threat" needs to be properly addressed. Those researchers and kind caretakers who are close to the situation feel that even with these measures, the species may become extinct in the next twenty years.

There has been widespread thought that marine species are more resilient to extinction and our further exploitation. However, there is finally a growing amount of evidence that fish and wildlife in our oceans are as vulnerable to extinction (or more so) than many terrestrial and freshwater species. Despite continued massive harvesting of sea life from our oceans, researchers not affiliated with sustainable certifying organizations generally agree that the amount and distribution of threatened marine species is, at best, poorly known. Our demand to eat fish cannot be taken out of the equation when discussing our abuse of natural resources, eventual loss of species, and climate change.

Habitat loss is far and away the most pervasive threat to terrestrial animal species, impacting 86 percent of all mammals, 88 percent of amphibians, and 86 percent of all birds. One in every eight birds, one in every three amphibians, and one in every four mammals is facing an extremely high risk of extinction in the near future. Overexploitation of animals for consumption remains a second major factor for extinction, such as can be seen in bushmeat trade in Africa and Southeast Asia and all hunting endeavors on land, globally. The Alliance for Global Conservation estimates 36 percent of all species on our planet are in danger of extinction.

When put into context with habitat loss, endangered and extinct species becomes easy to explain: African countries average 68 percent habitat loss (with Gambia suffering 91 percent loss), Asian countries range from 34 percent to 96 percent habitat loss, Mexico has 66 percent habitat loss, and 45 percent of all the land on earth is used by or for livestock. Using land to raise livestock and the crops to feed them is a terribly inefficient use of resources that perpetuates climate change, which accelerates further loss of biodiversity—there simply isn't much room for anything else to live.

Scientists have divided our planet into 825 terrestrial "ecoregions" (as well as 450 freshwater and a number of oceanic ecoregions), each defined by its own distinct set of animal and plant species, as well as climate. Of all these land ecoregions, almost half are reported to have livestock as a current threat. The World Conservation Union reported in 2010 that "most of the world's endangered or threatened species" on their Red List (which lists the species that are most endangered) are suffering habitat loss due to livestock—not due to agriculture but to livestock.

A Convention on Biological Diversity was held in Nagoya, Japan, in October 2010, as a follow-up to the one held in 2002. Recognizing the importance of biodiversity and that the world is losing it rapidly, the United Nations gathered 193 countries, with policy makers, scientists, and stakeholders, to address the issue.

They agreed that none of their goals from 2002 for lessening the rate of biodiversity loss were met. The attendees confirmed that the main pressures for the rapid loss of species—habitat change, overexploitation, pollution, invasive species, and climate change—were all increasing in intensity. The nations in attendance then reworked their "targets" and subsequent strategies to meet them. Ultimately, they adopted a number of new goals and protocols intended to slow the rate of species extinction and increase the amount of land and sea areas that would be set aside for conservation but also ensure a fair distribution of the profits of scientific research. The areas focusing on conservation were termed the Aichi Biodiversity Targets, which attempt to reduce the rate of species extinction by 50 percent by the year 2020. In doing so, the conferees agreed to protect *17 percent of the land area of the world that remains,* an increase from 12.5

percent of the land area of the world, agreed upon in 2002 ("land" meaning terrestrial and inland water). Remember that livestock already are using 45 percent of the entire land mass on earth, so the thought at Nagoya was to protect 17 percent of *what's left over* for all the other millions of species of living things. There was also agreement to protect *10 percent of all our oceans (marine and coastal areas) by the year 2020* (an increase from 1 percent ocean protection of the 2002 convention). The other two Aichi targets established at Nagoya were to "restore at least 14 percent of degraded areas through conservation and restoration" and to "make special efforts to reduce the pressures faced by coral reefs." These two goals are illogical when millions of acres of land are converted to pasture for grazing livestock, and destructive fishing practices are rampant in our oceans. They simply will not be able to accomplish their less than ambitious objectives while such high rates of degradation due to food choice continue.

An international body of leaders and stakeholders assembled— and the above was the only protection they could provide. There were no political or economic motives established. Nations are to police themselves with a "flexible framework." That will not work. Nagoya identified the pressures affecting the loss of biodiversity (habitat change, overexploitation, pollution, invasive species, and climate change) and acknowledged that these pressures are increasing in intensity, but they did not connect this to how we raise food.

There has been no improvement since the last global conference; in fact, species loss has escalated, because we are failing to address the primary issue. The resolution from Nagoya, adopted by nearly two hundred countries, does not address our choice of food with regard to how it involves animals. If we hope to curb today's rapid loss of biodiversity, the leaders of the world will have to advocate the complete cessation of raising livestock and commercial fishing—and that begins with frank discussions at formal settings such as Nagoya.[404]

Current biodiversity assessments (as presented by Millennium Ecosystem Assessment, the IUCN Red List, and the Global Environmental and Biodiversity Outlook) now generally agree that land use change, modification of river flow, freshwater pollution, and exploitation of marine environments are the most significant drivers of biodiversity change and loss of species. Eventually, ocean acidification and climate change will become increasingly important. With overharvesting sea life in our oceans and raising livestock on land (grazing or Confined Animal Feeding Operations), our demand to eat animals and animal products remains the largest contributing anthropogenic factor to those accepted drivers of loss of species on earth.[405,406,407]

Bushmeat, endangered large cats, and whales are just a few examples of how we affect wild animals because of our desire to eat meat. The far more pervasive concern, however, is how we produce food and use animals in the process. The commercial raising of livestock and fish on land, as well as harvesting fish out of our oceans, has caused great damage to biodiversity by way of loss of habitat and species. As more of us become aware of what happens behind the scenes at factory farms and realize that over 95 percent of all the meat eaten in the United States is produced from factory farm settings, it is natural to seek alternatives. It's understandable that people will follow any food movement that seems to offer the same animals and animal products that we're used to eating but from a more "sustainable" system, especially if it purports to be "humane." With many of us aware of the negative impact that beef, or "red meat," has on our health, we are turning to eating pigs, chickens, turkeys, and fish and seeking "humane" certification. These are not the alternatives that we should seek. It is my hope that this chapter will have raised the level of awareness regarding what is really happening to the animals we are eating, what the new food movements are not telling you, and why eating pigs, chickens, turkeys, fish, eggs, and dairy, as well as cows—or any animal, wild or domesticated—is not only unsustainable but not at all humane. The alternative we should seek is plant-based foods. And contrary to what NY *Times* best-selling authors may be promoting (with highly successful books such as Pollan's *Cooked* or Bittman's *VB6*), in the end it really doesn't matter how a particular food item is cooked—or *if* it is cooked. Or what time of day it is eaten. Of much greater importance is what that particular food item is—what it represents—where it came from, what resources were required to produce it, and what lives were abused or extinguished to get it to our plate. This is the fundamental message of concern we all need to hear from those who influence us.

Please consider inviting your conscience to dinner the next time you're at the table and find fish, chicken, and any other animal or animal product on your plate. Every meal should be a celebration of life—a spiritual connection to the food that will sustain you—but produced from our planet, which needs to be sustained itself. The spiritual connection we make at every meal should be one of life, not death.

This chapter was co-written by the spirit of all those lives unnecessarily sacrificed in the past, and for all the animals, wild or raised, with voices that need to be heard—those voices that are unable to speak for themselves.

Closing Thoughts

SERIOUS ISSUES CAN be found when we, at any level of self-perceived sophistication, deem our actions of killing members of another living species as "sustainable." When regarding choices of food, I find this more a selfish act of fulfilling our desire to perpetuate culturally induced myths—a proclamation of sorts—that the earth and all its resources are here for us to use. This proclamation is now neatly tucked under the guise of sustainability, with some false sense that we (or others we rely on) have an understanding of all impacts when "harvesting" animals for us to eat—whether wild or domesticated. This simply displays our clear naiveté. Although more readily visible and measurable when witnessed on land, the effects of our miscalculations are perhaps more devastating on our oceans when we continue to consume fish taken from them. It thus forms perhaps our ultimate disconnect—an alienation from the very ecosystems that support us.

It doesn't have to be this way. There is an easy way to reduce global depletion, mitigate climate change, minimize world hunger and poverty, and use our land, water, and other resources more efficiently and peacefully—

with no slaughtering. The answer to achieving the highest level of relative sustainability can be found on our plates.

Endnotes

Chapter 1

1   Met Office, Peter Stott. http://www.ncdc.noaa.gov/bams-state-of-the-climate/2011.php, accessed October 2012.

2   http://www.climatewatch.noaa.gov/article/2012/state-of-the-climate-in-2011-highlights/2, accessed December 2012.

3   http://www.noaanews.noaa.gov/stories2012/20120710_stateoftheclimatereport.html, accessed August 2012.

4   http://news.yahoo.com/iea-time-running-limit-earths-warming-100049408.html, accessed December 2012.

5   EPA (2007). "Recent Climate Change: Atmosphere Changes," *Climate Change Science Program*, United States Environmental Protection Agency. Retrieved 21 April 2009.

6   Spahni, Renato, et al. (November 2005). "Atmospheric Methane and Nitrous Oxide of the Late Pleistocene from Antarctic Ice Cores." *Science* 310 (5752): 1317–1321.

7   Siegenthaler, Urs, et al. (November 2005). "Stable Carbon Cycle–Climate Relationship During the Late Pleistocene" (PDF). *Science* 310 (5752): 1313–1317.

8   Petit, J. R., et al. (3 June 1999). "Climate and atmospheric history
         of the past 420,000 years from the Vostok ice core, Antarctica"
         (PDF). *Nature* 399 (6735): 429–436.

9   Lüthi, D., M. Le Floch, B. Bereiter, T. Blunier, J. M. Barnola, U.
         Siegenthaler, D. Raynaud, J. Jouzel, et al. (2008). "High-resolution
         carbon dioxide concentration record 650,000–800,000 years
         before present." *Nature* 453 (7193): 379–382.

10   Pearson, P. N., M.R. Palmer (2000). "Atmospheric carbon
         dioxide concentrations over the past 60 million years." *Nature* 406
         (6797): 695–699.

11   IPCC, Summary for Policymakers, "Concentrations of
         atmospheric greenhouse gases," p. 7, *IPCC Third Assessment
         Report*, Working Group 1, 2001.

12   Le Treut et al., Chap. 1, "Historical Overview of Climate Change
         Science," Section 1.3.1.2: Intensities, in *IPCC Fourth Assessment
         Report*, Working Group 3, 2007.

13   NRC (2008). "Understanding and Responding to Climate
         Change." Board on Atmospheric Sciences and Climate, U.S.
         National Academy of Sciences. p. 2, accessed November 2012.

14   World Bank, (2010). *World Development Report 2010:
         Development and Climate Change.* The International Bank for
         Reconstruction and Development, World Bank.

15   "Managing the Risks of Extreme Events and Disasters to Advance
         Climate Change Adaptation," IPCC 2012, Special Report, 582
         pages, http://www.ipcc-wg2.gov/SREX/images/uploads/SREX-
         All_FINAL.pdf, accessed January 2013.

16   http://www.ers.usda.gov/Publications/OCE121/OCE121e.pdf,
         accessed January 2013.

17   FAO, 2006, "World Agriculture: Towards 2030–2050," Rome,
         Special Report.

18   Annual consumption of meat: http://www.beefusa.
         org/CMDocs/BeefUSA/Resources/Statistics/
         annualpercapitaconsumption-meat-retail.pdf, accessed October
         2012.

19   http://www.eea.europa.eu/highlights/european-demand-for-goods-and-1, accessed August 2012.

20   http://www.epa.gov/climatechange/Downloads/ghgemissions/US-GHG-Inventory-2012-Chapter-2-Trends.pdf, accessed January 2013.

21   Shindell, Drew T., et al. (2005). "An emissions-based view of climate forcing by methane and tropospheric ozone." *Geophysical Research Letters* 32 (4).

22   "Methane's Impacts on Climate Change May Be Twice Previous Estimates." Nasa.gov. 2007-11-30, accessed October 2010.

23   Audsley, E., M. Brander, J. Chatterton, D. Murphy-Bokern, C. Webster, and A. Williams (2009). *How low can we go? An assessment of greenhouse gas emissions from the UK food system and the scope to reduce them by 2050.* FCRN-WWF-UK.

24   Garnett, T. (2008). *Cooking up a storm. Food, greenhouse gas emissions and our changing climate.* The Food and Climate Research Network.

25   National Emission Inventory of Greenhouse Gas: 2010.

26   Harper, L. A., et al. "Direct measurements of methane emissions from grazing and feedlot cattle." *Journal of Animal Science* 1999, 77:1392-1401.

27   Report of the Ocean Acidification and Oxygen Working Group, International Council for Science's Scientific Committee on Ocean Research (SCOR) Biological Observatories Workshop. 2009.

28   Morley, Robert J. *Origin and Evolution of Tropical Rain Forests.* New York: Wiley, 2000.

29   Burnham, Robyn J., and Kirk R. Johnson (2004). "South American palaeobotany and the origins of neotropical rainforests." *Philosophical Transactions of the Royal Society* 359 (1450): 1595–1610.

30   Lewinsohn, Thomas M., and Paulo Inácio Prado (2005). "How Many Species Are There in Brazil?" *Conservation Biology* 19 (3): 619–624.

31   *Amazon Cattle Footprint: Mato Grosso: State of Destruction* (PDF).

32   http://news.mongabay.com/2009/0129-brazil.html, accessed July 2012.

33   Mongabay.com: Beef consumption fuels rainforest destruction (02/16/2009); Beef drives 80% of Amazon deforestation (01/29/2009), accessed August 2012.

34   http://rainforests.mongabay.com/0801.htm, accessed December 2011.

35   http://www.bbc.co.uk/news/world-latin-america-13449792, accessed January 2013.

36   http://www.huffingtonpost.com/2012/05/25/brazil-forest-code veto_n_1546803.html3, accessed January 2013.

37   "The forest code and new deforestation figures for the Amazon," http://www.bbc.co.uk/news/science-environment-13544000, accessed February 2013.

38   http://news.mongabay.com/2011/0614-moukaddem_brazil_ forest_code.html#ixzz1hlzwWj3K, accessed January 2013.

Chapter 2

39   http://mahider.ilri.org/bitstream/handle/10568/10601/ IssueBrief3.pdf, accessed February 2013.

40   http://www.fao.org/docrep/x5303e/x5303e05.htm, accessed March 2013.

41   http://www.contextnet.com/120420%20Global%20Crop%20 Production%20Systems.pdf, accessed February 2013.

42   FAO Corporate Document Repository, "World Agriculture Toward 2015/2030."

43   LEAD/FAO 2006 Livestock's long shadow, ftp://ftp.fao.org/ docrep/fao/010/a0701e/a0701e00.pdf, accessed November 2012.

44   FAO Global Market Analysis, June 2011, Grain Market Report, IGC, November 24, 2011.

45   International Center for Soil Fertility. Technical Bulletin citing Henao and Baanante, Agricultural Production and Soil Nutrient Mining in Africa, 2006.

46   http://edis.ifas.ufl.edu/fa145, National Chicken Council, accessed June 21, 2012.

47   http://www.brangusworld.com/documents/cattleon%20grass. pdf, accessed December 2012.

48   Michigan State University Extension, discussions August 2012.

49   Åsgård and Austreng (1995, 1998), notes from "Use of Fishmeal and Fish Oil in Aquafeeds," Corporate Document Repository, fao. org/, accessed November 2012.

50   https://www.msu.edu/~hilker/outlook.htm, accessed December 2012.

51   Feed grain, hay projections: http://usda01.library.cornell.edu/ usda/current/FDS/FDS-05-14-2012.pdf, accessed December 2012.

52   http://www.usda.gov/oce/commodity/wasde/latest.pdf, accessed January 2013.

53   Extrapolations from Wirsenius's thesis and International Livestock Research Institute Issue Brief, November 2011.

54   http://www.fas.usda.gov/psdonline/circulars/livestock_poultry. pdf, accessed February 2013.

55   http://www.guardian.co.uk/commentisfree/cifamerica/2012/ may/24/president-rousseff-forest-code-brazil, accessed January 2013.

56   Earth Policy Institute, earth-policy.org, accessed December 2012.

57   USDA-ERS, July 2012. http://www.earth-policy.org/plan_b_ updates/2012/update102, accessed February 2013.

58   http://www.hort.purdue.edu/newcrop/afcm/buckwheat.html, accessed November 2012.

59   http://www.ers.usda.gov/Publications/LDP/2012/04Apr/ LDPM214.pdf, accessed January 2013.

60   FAO, 1994. Global Environment Facility (GEF), 2003. Thegef.
        org/, accessed December 2012.
61   http://www.africa.ufl.edu/asq/v6/v6i1a10.htm#_edn9, accessed
        January 2013.
62   http://www.rodale.com/factory-farm-map, accessed March 2013.
63   FAO, Livestock and the Environment, Corporate Document
        Repository.
64   Johnson, Jane M. F., Alan J. Franzluebbers, Sharon Lachnicht
        Weyers, and Donald C. Reicosky. Environmental Pollution
        150 (2007) 107–124, Agricultural opportunities to mitigate
        greenhouse gas emissions, June 10, 2007.
65   Lotter, et al. 2003. Organic Agriculture. J Sustain Agric 21(4).
66   Lotter, et al. 2002; Pimentel, et al., 2005; Badgley, et al., 2007.
67   Proctor P. and Cole G. *Grasp the Nettle: Making Biodynamic
        Farming Work*. New Zealand: Random House Publishing, 2002.
68   Wu, L., et al. "Ecosystem Carbon and Nitrogen Accumulation
        after Grazing Exclusion." *Journal of Environmental Quality* 37
        (2008); Qiu, L. et al., Plosone.org January 2013, accessed
        February 2013.
69   "Edible and Medicinal Desert Plants," Arizona, Boyce Thompson
        Arboretum, University of Arizona, arboretum.ag.arizona.edu,
        accessed January 2013.
70   Glew, R. H., et al. (1997). Article no. FC970539, "Amino acid
        and mineral composition of 24 indigenous plants." *Journal of Food
        Composition and Analysis* 10: 205–217.
71   Barnes, D. L., and R. P. Denny (1991). "A comparison of
        continuous and rotational grazing on veld at two stocking rates."
        Journal of Society of South African Grassland 8:168–173.
72   Joseph, J., F. Molinar, et. al. (2002). "Short duration grazing
        research in Africa. An extensive review of the Charter Grazing
        Trials." *Rangelands* (24): 4 August 2002.
73   Hart, R. H., S. Clapp, and P. S. Test (1993). "Grazing strategies,
        stocking rates, and frequency and intensity of grazing on western
        wheatgrass and blue grama." *J. Range Manage.* 46:122–126.

74   Skovlin, J. *Rangelands* (94) August 4, 1987.

75   Briske, D.D., J. D. Derner, J. R. Brown, S. D. Fuhlendorf, W. R. Teague, K. M. Havstad, R. L. Gillen, A. J. Ash, et al. (2008). "Rotational Grazing on Rangelands: Reconciliation of Perception and Experimental Evidence." *Rangeland Ecology and Management* 61:3–17.

76   Norton 1998, 2003; Tainton et al. 1999; Teague et al. 2004; Heady 1961, 1970.

77   FAO http://www.fao.org/docrep/016/i3010e/i3010e00.htm, accessed February 2013.

78   Savory, C. A. R. (1969). "Crisis in Rhodesia." *Oryx* 10:25.

79   Lawton, R. M., and M. Gough. 1970. "Elephants or Fire—Which to Blame?" *Oryx* 10 (4): 244.

80   U.S.D.A. (2010). "Dietary Guidelines for Americans."

81   Raloff, J. "AAAS: Climate Friendly Dining ... Meats. The Carbon Footprints of Raising Livestock for Food." *Science News*. February 15, 2009.

82   United Nations Report, November 29, 2006.

83   U.S.D.A./NASS. "Livestock Slaughter Summary," 2009.

84   Interviews with USDA directors Drs. Holterman, Schultz, et. al, 2011, 2012, and Tracy Schohr, California Cattlemen's Association, July 2011 through October 2012.

85   U.S.D.A. Economic Research Service Data Sets, ers.usda.gov/, accessed December 2012.

86   Ibid.

87   Pimental, D. (2003), *The American Journal of Clinical Nutrition*, September Supplement 78.

88   Earthrise Spirulina, interview 2011; earthrise.com, accessed June 2012.

89   Jimenez, C., et. al. (2003). "The feasibility of industrial production of Spirulina." *Aquaculture* 217; 179-190.

90   U.S.D.A. (2009), National Agricultural Statistics Service, nass. usda.gov/, accessed January 2013.

91 http://usda01.library.cornell.edu/usda/current/CropProdSu/ CropProdSu-01-12-2012.pdf, accessed January 2013.

92 http://nwrec.hort.oregonstate.edu/collards.html, accessed January 2013.

93 http://pods.dasnr.okstate.edu/docushare/dsweb/Get/ Document-1372/HLA-6031web.pdf, accessed November 2012.

94 http://www.nass.usda.gov/Statistics_by_State/California/ Publications/Fruits_and_Nuts/201203frtrv.pdf, accessed January 2013.

95 FAO.org, accessed December 2012.

96 ERS.USDA.gov/, accessed December 2012.

97 Australian Lot Feeders Association, feedlots.com.au/, accessed April 2012.

98 U.S. Meat Export Federation, usmef.org/, accessed January 2012.

99 http://www.anra.gov.au/topics/land/landuse/index.html, accessed December 2012.

100 https://netfiles.uiuc.edu/mragheb/www/NPRE%20402%20 ME%20405%20Nuclear%20Power%20Engineering/Fresh%20 Water%20Augmentation.pdf, accessed March 2013.

101 siwi.org/statistics, accessed January 2013.

102 United Nations Commission on Sustainable Development (CSD), Summary 1997; United Nations/World Water Assessment Program Development Report 2003. Sustainabledevelopment.un.org/csd, accessed March 2013; unesco.org/water/wwap, accessed March 2013.

103 http://www.worldwater.org/data20082009/ch01.pdf, accessed January 2013.

104 Climate Change, Water and Risk. Natural Resources Defense Council, July 2010, http://www.nrdc.org/globalwarming/ watersustainability/files/WaterRisk.pdf, accessed November 2012.

105 Discussions with California Dept. of Water Resources and USGS, 2012.

106   United Nations Environment Programme, Annual Report 2007.
       Unep.org, accessed January 2013.

107   http://www.waterfootprint.org/Reports/Mekonnen-Hoekstra-
       2012-WaterFootprintFarmAnimalProducts.pdf, accessed March
       2013.

108   visityuma.com/agri, accessed July 2012.

109   FAO's Aquastat/World Database.

110   Water Footprint Network, waterfootprint.org/, accessed January
       2013.

111   California Farm Water Coalition, cfwc.com/, accessed February
       2013.

112   cspinet.org/eatinggreen/pdf/arguments4.pdf, accessed
       December 2012.

113   http://www.waterfootprint.org/?page=files/home, accessed
       February 2013.

114   ctwa.us/reports/water_facts, accessed December 2012.

115   California Farm Water Coalition and their Department of
       Agriculture and discussions with UC Davis 2011 through
       October 2012.

116   Hay and Forage Grower Report, thehoytreport.com, accessed
       January 2013.

117   http://www.sanjacintoriverauthority.com/facts/land-subsidence.
       html, accessed December 2012.

118   M. V. Guru and J. E. Horne (2000). *The Ogallala Aquifer*; and J.
       Opie (2000), *Ogallala: Water for a Dry Land.*

119   http://peakwater.org/tag/water-crisis/, accessed December
       2012.

120   http://pubs.usgs.gov/circ/circ1182/pdf/06SanJoaquinValley.pdf,
       accessed December 2012.

121   FAO, 2006, fao.org, accessed December 2012.

122   Stockholm Resilience Center, articles by Falkenmark and
       Rockström, 2004, 2006, 2009. Stockholmresilience.org, accessed
       December 2012. http://www.eqb.state.mn.us/documents/
       Falkenamark_20493345.pdf, accessed November 2012.

123   http://extension.unh.edu/resources/files/Resource000005_
        Rep4.pdf, accessed November 2012.

124   Hoekstra, A. Y., et al. (2011). *The Water Footprint Assessment
        Manual: Setting the Global Standard*, Earthscan, London, UK.
        Waterfootprint.org/publications, accessed January 2013.

125   FAO.org, accessed February 2013.

126   Environmental Working Group, ewg.org/, accessed February
        2013.

127   Organization for Economic Co-operation and Development
        (OECD) and FAO-Meat, OECD and FAO Agricultural Outlook
        2011-2020 (Rome: June 2011), oecd.org, accessed January 2013.

128   FAOSTAT.fao.org/, accessed December 2011.

129   http://www.kau.edu.sa/Files/320/Researches/57102_27371.
        PDF, accessed March 2013.

130   USDA, ERS 2012 annual summaries. Ers.usda.gov/, accessed
        January 2013.

131   http://www.fao.org/nr/water/aquastat/countries/pakistan/
        index.stm, accessed December 2012.

132   http://tribune.com.pk/story/387029/mixed-trends-in-
        agricultural-sector-livestock-grows-4/, accessed March 2013.

133   http://www.ecorazzi.com/2012/03/22/world-water-day-10-
        places-most-in-need-of-clean-water/, accessed March 2013.

134   Pokhrel, Y., et al. *Nature Geosci* 2012. Nature.com/news/source-
        found-for-missing-in-sea-level-rise, accessed January 2013.

Chapter 3

135   Diaz, R., et al. (2008). "Spreading Dead Zones and Consequences
        for Marine Ecosystems." *Science* 321, 926.

136   Scripps Institution of Oceanography (April 1, 2012). "New
        comparison of ocean temperatures reveals rise over the last
        century." *ScienceDaily*.

137   National Research Council (NRC), 2008, nationalacademies.org/
       nrc, accessed December 2012.

138   Intergovernmental Panel on Climate Change (IPCC), 2007. Ipcc.
       ch, accessed December 2012.

139   British Antarctic Survey, Statement of Findings, August 6, 2012.

140   Huxley, Thomas (1883). Inaugural Address Fisheries Exhibition,
       London, Scientific Memoirs.

141   FAO.org, accessed February 2013.

142   FAO.org, accessed December 2012.

143   Goode, G. B. and J. W. Collins (1887). "The fresh-halibut fishery."
       The fisheries and fishery industry of the United States. Section V.
       History and methods of the fisheries, Vol. I, Part I. Government
       Printing Office, Washington, D.C. p. 3–89.

144   Redclift, M. (2005). "Sustainable Development (1987–2005):
       An Oxymoron Comes of Age." *Sustainable Development* 13(4):
       212–227.

145   Fisheries and Aquaculture in Our Changing Climate Policy brief
       of the FAO for the UNFCCC COP-15 in Copenhagen, December
       2009.

146   Worm, et al. (2006). "Impacts of biodiversity loss on ocean
       ecosystem services." *Science*, 314 (5800), p. 787.

147   Frank, K. T., et al. (2005). "Trophic cascades in a formerly cod
       dominated ecosystem." *Science* 308, 1621–1623.

148   Heithous, M. R., et al. (2008). "Predicting ecological
       consequences of marine top predator declines." *Trends in
       Ecological Evolution* 23:202–210.

149   Pauly, D., et al. (1998). "Fishing down marine food webs." *Science*
       279:860–863.

150   Mora, C., et al. (2009). "Management effectiveness of the world's
       marine fisheries." *PLoS Biology*, 7(6).

151   http://icesjms.oxfordjournals.org/content/64/4/851.full,
       accessed December 2012.

152   NOAA, Coral Reef Conservation Program, coralreef.noaa.gov/, accessed December 2012.

153   Ibid.

154   http://worldwildlife.org/industries/wild-caught-seafood, accessed January 2013.

155   Marine Conservation Institute, http://www.marine-conservation. org/what-we-do/program-areas/how-we-fish/destructive- fishing/, accessed December 2012.

156   Fisheries and Aquaculture Department, FAO, http://www.fao. org/fishery/topic/16038/en, accessed December 2012.

157   Sea Shepherd Conservation Society, http://www.seashepherd. org/sharks/longlining.html, accessed November 2012.

158   World Resources Institute, http://www.wri.org/publication/ reefs-at-risk/cyanide-fishing, accessed December 2012.

159   Sea Shepherd Conservation Society, http://www.seashepherd. org/sharks/shark-finning.html, accessed November 2012.

160   Shark Life: A Conservation Group, http://www.sharklife. co.za/index.php/threats-facing-sharks/329-bycatch, accessed December 2012.

161   Scripps Institution of Oceanography, sio.ucsd.edu/, accessed November 2012.

162   http://www.sciencedaily.com/releases/2012/03/120319095043. htm, accessed January 2013.

163   Casselman, Anne (May 5, 2011). "Upstream Battle: What Is Killing Off the Fraser River's Sockeye Salmon?" *Scientific American*. Retrieved December 5, 2011.

164   "Missing salmon stocks to be probed: PM." *Fish Info & Services*. Agence France-Presse. Archived from the original on November 23, 2009. Retrieved December 5, 2011.

165   Canadian Press (August 13, 2011). "Up to 4 million sockeye expected in run." *CBC News*. Canadian Press (Toronto). Retrieved December 5, 2011.

166   Steering Committee (December 6, 2010). "Fraser Sockeye
       2010: Findings of a Scientist's Think Tank." Fraser Sockeye 2010.
       Speaking for the Salmon Program at Simon Fraser University.
       Retrieved December 5, 2011.

167   Holland, Richard (February 11, 2011). "Objection: Denmark
       North Sea Plaice Trawl Fishery." *Memo to MSC*. Marine
       Stewardship Council. Retrieved December 5, 2011.

168   "A reappraisal of the total biomass and annual production of
       Antarctic krill," conducted by the British Antarctic Survey, Sea
       Fisheries Institute, Dept. of Earth and Ocean Sciences, and Moss
       Landing Marine Laboratories. http://nora.nerc.ac.uk/10186/,
       accessed July 2012.

169   Oceana.org, "Despite Overfishing and Crashing...," accessed
       October 2012.

170   International Commission for the Conservation of Atlantic
       Tunas, http://www.iccat.int/en, accessed September 2012.

171   World Wildlife Fund, wwf.panda.org/, "Unsustainable Fishing,"
       accessed September 2012.

172   Greenpeace, http://www.greenpeace.org/new-zealand/Global/
       new-zealand/P3/publications/oceans/2010/Hoki%20_
       novaezelandiae.pdf, accessed October 2012.

173   International Union for Conservation of Nature, http://www.
       iucn.org, accessed December 2012.

174   Fenaughty, J. M., J. T. Eastman, and B. D. Sidell (2008).
       "Biological implications of low condition factor 'axe handle'
       specimens of the Antarctic toothfish, Dissostichus mawsoni, from
       the Ross Sea." *Antarctic Science*, 20:537–551.

175   http://www.asoc.org/issues-and-advocacy/antarctic-wildlife-
       conservation/southern-ocean-fisheries/marine-stewardship-
       council, accessed January 2013.

176   Chesapeake Bay Ecological Foundation Inc.

177   National Oceanic and Atmospheric Administration, noaa.gov/,
       accessed September 2012.

178   http://www.pewenvironment.org/news, accessed March 2013.

179   Oceana.org, accessed January 2013.

180   http://www.iucnredlist.org/details/21860/0, accessed January
       2013.

181   Business Insider, http://www.businessinsider.com/, accessed
       December 2012.

182   National Oceanic and Atmosphere Administration, http://
       wwwlnmfs.noaa.gov/, accessed December 2012.

183   Interview with Ted Danson, Climate One 2011. Climate-one.org.

184   USDA 2011, usda.gov/, accessed September 2012.

185   NOAA 2011, noaa.gov/, accessed July 2012.

186   http://www.ers.usda.gov/Publications/LDP/2012/04Apr/
       LDPM214.pdf, accessed February 2013.

187   Pure Salmon Campaign.

188   Food and Agriculture Organization of the United Nations,
       (FAO), fao.org/, accessed November 2012.

189   WWF.org/, accessed December 2012.

190   Food and Agriculture Organization of the United Nations, fao.
       org/, accessed December 2012.

191   Ecosystem Approach to Aquaculture, (FAO), fao.org/, accessed
       December 2012.

192   Volpe, J. P., et al. (2010). "Comparative analysis of the marine
       impact of the finfish sector" and "Global aquaculture performance
       index." University of Victoria, Victoria, B.C., Canada.

193   Life Cycle Analysis, Develop high-quality protein and lipid
       sources from plants and microorganisms. *Blue Frontiers: Managing
       the Environmental Costs of Aquaculture Report*, 2008.

194   The International Fishmeal and Fish Oil Organization (IFFO),
       iffo.net/, accessed December 2012. Fao.org, accessed December
       2012.

195   University of Florida, IFAS Extension 2011.Publication #FA122.
       http://edis.ifas.ufl.edu/fa122 , accessed February 2013.

196   IFFO, 2010, iffo.net/, accessed November 2012.

197   Institute of Food and Agricultural Sciences, University of Florida
        (IFAS), ifas.ufl.edu/, accessed December 2011.

198   Australis, TheBetterFish.com, accessed November 2012.

199   Food and Agriculture Organization of the United Nations (FAO),
        fao.org/, accessed November 2012.

200   National Cancer Institute, cancer.gov/, accessed December 2012.

201   Office of Environmental Health Hazard Assessment, http://www.
        oehha.ca.gov/, accessed January 2013.

202   USDA Publications, 2010 Dietary Guidelines for Americans.

203   Fishcount.org/uk, accessed July 2012.

204   Conversations with Stefania Vannuccini, Fishery Statistician
        (Commodities), United Nations FAO FIPS, 2012.

205   Fisheries and Aquaculture Statistics and Information Service,
        FAOstat.fao.org/, accessed November 2012.

206   FAO.org/, accessed December 2011.

207   NOAA, www.nmfs.noaa.gov/, accessed December 2012.

208   USDA.gov/, accessed 2011.

209   National Oceanic and Atmosphere Administration, http://www.
        nmfs.noaa.gov, accessed December 2012.

210   http://www.iisd.org/pdf/2011/greening_china_fish_en.pdf,
        accessed December 2012.

211   Oceana.org, accessed November 2012.

212   http://www.un.org/News/Press/docs/2012/sgsm14457.doc.
        htm, accessed January 2013.

213   http://www.mainstreamcanada.ca/about/index.php, accessed
        January 2013.

214   http://www.seashepherd.org/commentary-and-
        editorials/2008/08/28/aqua-cats-are-eating-the-oceans-207,
        accessed January 2013.

215   Assessment of the Marine Stewardship Council Fisheries
        Certification Programme, Greenpeace, June 2009, greenpeace.
        org/, accessed November 2012.

216   http://www.guardian.co.uk/environment/2011/jan/06/fish-
        marine-stewardship-council, accessed January 2013.
217   "This assessment is contentious." Greenpeace International
        Seafood Red list. Greenpeace.org/, accessed December 2012.
218   World Wildlife Fund, wwf.org/, accessed December 2012.

Chapter 4
219   http://ezinearticles.com/?World-Wide-Populations-of-
        Vegetarians&id=3515891, accessed January 2013.
220   McDonald's Annual Shareholders Report, 2012.
221   McDonald's Annual Shareholders Report, 2012.
222   Unilever.com/, accessed November 2012.
223   FAO.org/, accessed December 2012.
224   Science Council.cgiar.org http://www.omafra.gov.on.ca/english/
        engineer/facts/07-023.htm#7, accessed February 2013.
225   http://www.omafra.gov.on.ca/english/engineer/facts/07-023.
        htm#7, accessed February 2013.
226   FAO.org/, accessed January 2013.
227   http://www.ifpri.org/sites/default/files/publications/esspdp05.
        pdf, accessed March 2013.
228   http://faostat.fao.org/site/569/default.aspx#ancor, accessed
        February 2013.
229   World Bank, http://web.worldbank.org/, accessed December
        2012.
230   Central Intelligence Agency, https://www.cia.gov/, accessed
        January 2013.
231   FAO.org, accessed January 2013.
232   Ibid.
233   International Food Policy Research Institute, http://www.ifpri.
        org/sites/default/files/publications/esspwp26.pdf, accessed
        January 2013.

234   http://www.fas.usda.gov/pecad2/highlights/2002/10/ethiopia/
       baseline/eth_annual_rainfall.htm, accessed December 2012.

235   USDA.gov, accessed December 2012.

236   *The State of Food Insecurity in the World*, 2011 FAO, fao.org,
       accessed January 2013.

237   National Center for Charitable Statistics (NCCS), http://
       careerservices.colorado.edu/CommonFiles/PDFs/students/
       fastIntlHumanitarianAidRelief.pdf, accessed December 2012.

238   C. Weber and H. S. Matthews, "Carnegie Mellon University Food:
       Miles and the Relative Climate Impacts of Food Choices in the
       U.S. Environ." *Sci. Technol.* 2008, 42, 3508–3513. http://pubs.acs.
       org/doi/abs/10.1021/es702969f, accessed January 2013.

239   Food miles/locavore/local: http://news.mongabay.
       com/2008/0602-ucsc_liaw_food_miles.html, accessed January
       2013.

240   RealFoodChallenge.org, accessed July 2012.

241   http://www.universityofcalifornia.edu/sustainability/policy.
       html, accessed July 2012.

242   http://www.universityofcalifornia.edu/sustainability/policy.
       html, accessed July 2012.

243   Annual progress reports to the Regents: www.
       universityofcalifornia.edu/sustainability/reports.html, accessed
       July 2012.

244   USDA World Markets and Trade, November 2011.

245   http://www.fas.usda.gov/livestock_arc.asp., accessed November
       2012.

246   http://www.usmef.org (U.S. Meat Export Federation, 2012),
       accessed November 2012.

247   http://www.uncsd2012.org/objectiveandthemes.html, accessed
       December 2012.

248   http://unilever.com/sustainable-living/news/news/
       unileversrio20manifestoworkingtogetherforabetterworld.aspx,
       accessed January 2013.

249   Rio+20 Summit observations of proceedings, multiple sources, and the new metric of business success.

250   http://www.greenreportcard.org/report-card-2011/categories/food-recycling, accessed January 2013.

Chapter 5

251   Campbell, T. C. The China Study, http://www.tcolincampbell.org/, accessed January 2013.

252   The Physicians Committee for Responsible Medicine (PCRM), pcrm.org/, accessed January 2013.

253   American Dietetic Association, eatright.org, Position of the ADA and Dieticians of Canada: Vegetarian Diets, 2003, 2009, accessed January 2013.

254   NutritionFacts.org/, "Uprooting the Leading Causes of Death," accessed January 2013.

255   Campbell, T. C., The China Study, http://www.tcolincampbell.org/, accessed March 2013.

256   PCRM.org, "Meat Consumption and Cancer Risk," accessed February 2013.

257   NutritionFacts.org, "Animal Protein," accessed February 2013.

258   http://www.pcrm.org/health/reports/analysis-of-health-problems-associated-with-high, accessed February 2013.

259   National Institutes of Health, nih.gov/, accessed December 2012.

260   Hu, F., et al. (2012). Red meat consumption and mortality. *Arch of Intern Med* 172(7):555–63.

261   Vogel, R. A., M. C. Corretti, and G. D. Plotnick. "Effect of a single high-fat meal on endothelial function in healthy subjects." *American Journal of Cardiology* (1997) 79:350–354.

262   Spence, J. D., D. J. Jenkins, and J. Davignon. "Egg yolk consumption and carotid plaque." *Atherosclerosis* (2012 October) 224(2):469-73.

263   World Health Organization's International Agency for Research

on Cancer.

264   U.S. Dept. of Health and Human Services.

265   http://www.alz.org/alzheimers_disease_facts_and_figures.asp, accessed January 2013.

266   http://www.alz.org/alzheimers_disease_facts_and_figures.asp, accessed January 2013.

267   National Institutes of Health, nih.gov, accessed January 2013.

268   Gottfries, C. G., et al. "Early diagnosis of cognitive impairment in the elderly with the focus on Alzheimer's disease." *J Neural Transm* (1998), 105:8–9, 773–86.

269   USDA National Nutrient Database for Standard Reference.

270   BrightFocus.org, accessed February 2013.

271   http://www.sciencedaily.com/releases/2012/03/120306131845. htm, accessed January 2013.

272   alz.org, accessed January 2013.

273   (2010 and 2011 data) http://report.nih.gov/categorical_ spending.aspx, accessed December 2012.

274   http://www.deloitte.com/view/en_US/us/ Industries/US-federal-government/center-for- health-solutions/health-care-consumerism/ efcc19ce7f3ce210VgnVCM1000001a56f00aRCRD.html, accessed December 2012.

275   http://www.pcrm.org/search/?cid=2836, accessed January 2013.

276   http://www.news.cornell.edu/stories/April12/ObesityCosts. html, accessed January 2013.

277   http://www.reuters.com/article/2012/04/30/us-obesity- idUSBRE83T0C820120430, accessed January 2013.

278   Produce for Better Health Foundation's *State of the Plate: 2010 Study*.

279   http://www.oecd.org/health/healthpoliciesanddata/ BriefingNoteUSA2012.pdf, accessed January 2013.

280   *Journal of Occupational and Environmental Medicine*, news release, April 3, 2012.

281   Lawes, C. M., S. Vander Hoorn, and A. Rodgers. "Global burden of blood-pressure related disease," 2001. *Lancet* (2008) 371:1513–1518. Abstract.

282   Gaziano, T. A., A. Bitton, S. Anand, and M. C. Weinstein. "The global cost of nonoptimal blood pressure." *J Hypertens* (2009) 27:1472–1477. Abstract.

283   U.S. Treasury, 2012, http://www.treasurydirect.gov/NP/BPDLogin?application=np, accessed January 2013.

284   http://www.foxnews.com/politics/2012/09/04/who-do-owe-most-that-16-trillion-to-hint-it-isnt-china/#ixzz26CeYw73Y, accessed December 2012.

285   World Health Organization, http://www.who.int, accessed December 2013.

286   Wang, Y., M. A. Beydon. *Int J Obes* (June 2009) 33(6): 621–628.

287   American Diabetes Association, http://www.diabetes.org, accessed January 2013.

288   Barnard, N. D., *Dr. Neal Barnard's Program for Reversing Diabetes.* New York. Rodale, 2007.

289   http://www.pmri.org/dean_ornish.html, accessed January 2013.

290   Esselstyn, C. B. *Prevent and Reverse Heart Disease,* Avery Trade, 2008.

291   Halvorsen, B. L., et al. "Content of redox-active compounds in foods consumed in the United States. *AM J Clin Nutr* (2006) 84(1):95–135.

292   Phtyochemicals.info, accessed December 2012.

293   http://www.vrg.org/blog/2011/12/05/how-many-adults-are-vegan-in-the-u-s, accessed December 2012.

294   Center for Disease Control and Prevention, http://www.cdc.gov/, "Estimates of Foodborne Illness in the United States," accessed January 2013.

295   http://www.cdc.gov/foodborneburden/2011-foodborne-estimates.html, accessed December 2012.

296   http://www.agriview.com/news/, "Dairy meat antibiotic violations," accessed January 2013.

297   USDA Deputy Secretary, Kathleen Merrigan, in a Dec. 15, 2011, article in Agriview.

298   USDA Deputy Secretary, Kathleen Merrigan, in a Dec. 15th, 2011 article in Agriview.

299   http://www.huffingtonpost.com/david-katz-md/e-coli-vegetables-blame-meat_b_872055.html, accessed December 2012.

300   Dept. of Animal Science, College of Ag. and Life Sciences, Texas A&M University, "Beef Cattle Browsing," May 2011.

301   Center for Disease Control, http://www.cdc.gov/, accessed January 2013.

302   Consumers Union, January 2007; FSIS, 1998.

303   http://www.vegetariantimes.com/article/vegetarianism-in-america/, accessed January 2013.

304   http://www.beef.org/, accessed August 2012.

305   http://www.americangrassfed.org/about-us/, accessed August 2012.

306   http://www.agweb.com/blog/The_Farm_CPA_243/?Year=2012&Month=3, accessed September 2012.

307   http://www.hort.purdue.edu/newcrop/afcm/amaranth.html, accessed August 2012.

308   http://corn.agronomy.wisc.edu/Crops/Buckwheat.aspx, accessed August 2012.

309   http://www.hort.purdue.edu/newcrop/afcm/buckwheat.html, accessed August 2012.

310   http://www.agriculture.gov.sk.ca/Default.aspx?DN=cdc9fbf5-bc29-4981-9278-ba7232db7b52, accessed September 2012.

311   http://www.kamut.com/en/history.html, accessed August 2012.

312   http://www.agmrc.org/commodities__products/grains__oilseeds/spelt/, accessed August 2012.

313   http://www.blm.gov/wo/st/en/prog/grazing.html, accessed
        August 2012.

Chapter 6

314   *Forbes* magazine, forbes.com/, "Is Lipitor the New Aspirin?",
        accessed January 2013.

315   Mayo Clinic, mayoclinic.com/, "Statins: Are these cholesterol
        lowering drugs right for you?", accessed December 2012.

316   National Heart, Lung, and Blood Institute, http://www.nhlbi.nih.
        gov/, accessed January 2013.

317   Jenkins, J. A., et al. "Effects of a Dietary Portfolio of Cholesterol-
        Lowering Foods." *JAMA* (2003) 2904:502–510).

318   The Angiogenesis Foundation, angio.org/, accessed December
        2012.

319   CancerBattleField.com, Starve Cancer with Food 2012.

320   http://iom.edu/Reports/2012/Best-Care-at-Lower-Cost-The-
        Path-to-Continuously-Learning-Health-Care-in-America.aspx,
        accessed January 2013.

321   http://www.imshealth.com/ims/Global/Content/Insights/
        IMS percent20Institute percent20for percent20Healthcare
        percent20Informatics/IHII_Medicines_in_U.S_Report_2011.
        pdf, accessed December 2012.

322   http://www.sampler.isr.umich.edu/2012/research/decline-in-
        teen-smoking-resumes-in-2011/, accessed November 2012.

323   http://www.gallup.com/poll/156833/one-five-adults-smoke-
        tied-time-low.aspx, accessed December 2012. Initial Simplistic
        Eco and Health Care Tax calculations: At a 320 percent tax,
        buying idle calorie food would yield $7 trillion in five years.
        Adding only beef (which is ¼ of all meat eaten per person in
        terms of pounds), taxing at 320 percent would add $272 billion
        per year ($85 billion spent on beef according to the 2009
        Cattleman's Weekly Report and USDA per year x 320 percent)

totaling almost $2 trillion per year in revenues or almost $10 trillion in 5 years. With a surcharge/ health risk tax 320 percent = 30 percent avg. health risk factor x 9 (4 chronic diseases + 5 cancers) + 50 percent relative factor for contribution to GHG emissions. Studies have been conducted to project a 10 percent empty calorie tax but 10 percent will not work; this is too lenient and it excludes an important eco tax covering global depletion. At 50 percent it would yield $1 trillion in five years if just taxing idle calorie food or $7 trillion in five years.

Chapter 7

324 http://www.nffc.net/Learn/Fact%20Sheets/NFFC_Film%20Response.pdf, accessed December 2012.

325 http://necsi.edu/research/social/foodcrises.html, accessed December 2012.

326 FAO.org and unep.org/, accessed December 2012.

327 World Watch 2009, http://www.worldwatch.org/files/pdf/Livestock%20and%20Climate%20Change.pdf, accessed December 2012.

328 USDA, Economic Research Service, ers.usda.gov/, accessed January 2013.

329 USDA Long-term Projections, usda.gov/, accessed February 2012.

330 Livestock and Poultry World Market Trade 2013, fas.usda.gov/, accessed December 2012.

331 Humane Society International, his.org/, accessed December 2012.

332 USDA, usda.gov/, accessed December 2012.

333 FAO.org/, accessed November 2012.

334 Economic Research Service, ers.usda.gov/, accessed January 2013.

335   http://www.ers.usda.gov/topics/animal-products/cattle-beef/
      statistics-information.aspx.

336   Economic Research Service, ers.usda.gov/, accessed January
      2013.

337   USDA Agriculture Projections to 2020, ers.usda.gov/, accessed
      January 2013.

338   Wisconsin Milk Marketing Board, wmmb.com/, accessed
      December 2012.

339   http://www.ibisworld.com/industry/default.aspx?indid=49,
      accessed December 2012.

340   Global Industry Analysts, Inc., Fish and Seafood Industry: Market
      Research Reports. Reportlinker.com/, accessed January 2013.

341   http://www.uspoultry.org/economic_data/, accessed December
      2012.

342   nass.usda.gov/, accessed December 2012.

343   ERS, ers.usda.gov/, accessed January 2013.

344   http://www.ers.usda.gov/amber-waves/2012-march/data-
      feature-how-is-land-used.aspx, accessed January 2013.

345   Center for Rural Affairs, cfra.org/, accessed November 2012.

346   USDA Economic Research Service, ers.usda.gov/, accessed
      December 2011.

347   USDA, National Institute of Food and Agriculture, csrees.usda.
      gov/, accessed December 2012.

348   ERS, ers.usda.gov/, accessed January 2013.

349   Ibid.

350   Economics of organics:http://www.neon.cornell.edu/training/
      ppts/OrganicFarmYieldandProfitability.pdf, accessed January
      2013.

351   U.S. House Committee on Agriculture, agriculture.house.gov/,
      accessed January 2013.

352   Discussions with Andrew Stouts, interview on site, Washington
      State 2011.

353   FAO.org/, accessed January 2013.

354   Ibid.
355   Agriculture Reform, Food, and Jobs Act, U.S. Senate Committee on Agriculture, Nutrition, and Forestry. www. Ag.Senate.Gov/, accessed January 2013.
356   Ibid.
357   National Sustainable Agriculture Coalition, sustainableagriculture.net/, accessed February 2013.
358   International Monetary Fund (2011) Republic of Mozambique: Poverty Reduction Strategy Paper. IMF Country Report No. 11/132.
359   African Economic Outlook: Mozambique, African Development Bank. Africaneconomicoutlook.org and afdb.org/, accessed January 2013.
360   Bloomer, Phil (2012). The Great African Land Grab.
361   Land O' Lakes, Inc. International Development. http://www.idd.landolakes.com/, accessed January 2013.
362   BierraCorridor.com, accessed December 2012.
363   World Bank, United Nations. Worldbank.org/, accessed December 2012.
364   African Economic Outlook. http://www.africaneconomicoutlook.org/, accessed January 2013.
365   Millennium Challenge Corporation, Development Goals/ Mozambique Project. Mcc.gov/, accessed January 2013.
366   International Human Development Index, hdr.undp.org/, accessed December 2012.
367   Ibid.
368   MontereyBayAquarium.org/, accessed December 2012.
369   FAO.org/, accessed January 2013, extrapolated.
370   FAO.org/, accessed December 2013.
371   PetFoodIndustry.com/, accessed November 2012.
372   Vale, Robert, Linda Vale. *Time to Eat the Dog: The Real Guide to Sustainable Living*. London: Thames and Hudson, 2009.

373   http://www.fao.org/docrep/007/y5019e/y5019e0g.htm,
        accessed November 2012.

374   http://www.naturalcanines.com/gpage8.html, accessed
        December 2012.

375   Ceresfairfood.org, accessed December 2012.

Chapter 8

376   Humane Certifiers, Humanitarian.org, accessed January 2013.

377   Animal Welfare and Humane Slaughter (2004), Grandin.com,
        accessed July 2012.

378   The Temple Grandin video collection, 2012.

379   Humane Farm Animal Care Standards (HFAC), www.
        certifiedhumane.org/, accessed December 2012.

380   USDA.gov/, accessed January 2013.

381   Humane Farm Animal Care. Animal Care Standards,
        CertifiedHumane.org, accessed July 2012.

382   "Animals Fear Details that People Do Not Notice:
        Hyperspecificity of Perception," Grandin.com, accessed July 2012.

383   Grandin, T. (2011). DVD Collection. "Cattle Handling in Meat
        Plants." Directions for laying out curved cattle handling facilities
        for ranches, feedlots, and properties.

384   Sneddon, L., et al. (2003). "Do fishes have nociceptors?" *Proc. R.
        Soc. Lond. B* 270, 1115–1121.

385   http://news.uns.purdue.edu/x/2009a/090429GarnerPain.html,
        accessed August 2012.

386   http://dels-old.nas.edu/ilar_n/ilarjournal/33_1_2/
        V33_1_2Question.shtml, accessed September 2012.

387   http://www.oupcanada.com/catalog/9780199551200.html,
        accessed December 2012.

388   Physicians Committee for Responsible Medicine, pcrm.org/,
        accessed January 2013.

389   USDA, Nutrient Data Bank.

390   US Poultry & Egg Association, egg-cite.com/, accessed October
        2012.

391   An HSUS Report: *The Welfare of Animals in the Egg Industry*,
        humanesociety.org, accessed November 2012.

392   U.S. Food and Drug Administration, fda.gov/, accessed January
        2013.

393   United Egg Producers (2012). Statement of United Egg
        Producers Regarding Decision by Burger King. Unitedegg.org/,
        accessed December 2012.

394   Gentle, M. J. (2011). "Pain issues in poultry." *Applied Animal
        Behaviour Science*, 135 (special issue): 252–258.

395   Poultry Hub. 20 August 2010, poultryhub.org/, accessed
        December 2012.

396   H16, H17 The American Humane Certified Welfare 2012
        Standards Checklist for laying hens-aviary.

397   USDA, ERS and discussions with the American Meat Institute
        Directors, July through October 2012.

398   http://www.nytimes.com/2004/07/25/weekinreview/the-
        nation-gaining-ground-at-last-a-company-takes-peta-seriously.
        html?pagewanted=2&src=pm, accessed December 2012.

399   FSIS 2012, conversations with Dr. Kevin Gillespie, Dr. James
        Holterman, Dr. Curt Schulz.

400   http://www.humanefacts.org/labels.htm, accessed December
        2012.

401   Discussions with Jane Goodall Institute, 2011, 2012, 2013.

402   "Harpoons & Hookers: 27 Nations Gather at Japan's Pro-Whaling
        Conference," Globalanimal.org, accessed December 2012.

403   Greenpeace.org, accessed December 2012.

404   http://www.cbd.int/sp/targets/, accessed January 2013.

405   http://www-formal.stanford.edu/jmc/progress/biodiversity.
        html, accessed October 2012.

406   http://www.amnh.org/science/biodiversity/, accessed
        November 2012.

407   Extinction rates according to the following sources:

Wilson, Edward O. *The Diversity of Life*. Cambridge: Belknap Press of Harvard University Press, 1992).

Baskin, Yvonne. *The Work of Nature*. Washington, D.C.: Island Press, 1998.

Eldredge, Niles. *Life in the Balance: Humanity and the Biodiversity Crisis*. Princeton: Princeton University Press, 1998.

Lawton, John H., and Robert M. May, editors. *Extinction Rates*. New York: Oxford University Press, 1995.

Index